NIETZSCHE IN RUSSIA

edited by
Bernice Glatzer Rosenthal

NIETZSCHE
IN RUSSIA

PRINCETON UNIVERSITY PRESS

Copyright © 1986 by Princeton University Press
Published by Princeton University Press,
41 William Street, Princeton, New Jersey 08540
In the United Kingdom:
Princeton University Press, Guildford, Surrey

Library of Congress Cataloging in Publication Data
will be found on the last printed page of this book

ISBN 0-691-06695-7 (cloth)
0-691-10209-0 (pbk.)

Publication of this book has been aided by
a grant from The Andrew W. Mellon Foundation

This book has been composed in Linotron Electra

Clothbound editions of Princeton University Press
books are printed on acid-free paper, and binding materials
are chosen for strength and durability. Paperbacks,
although satisfactory for personal collections,
are not usually suitable for library rebinding

Printed in the United States of America
by Princeton University Press
Princeton, New Jersey

CONTENTS

PART I: NIETZSCHE'S INFLUENCE ON RUSSIAN RELIGIOUS THOUGHT

PART II: NIETZSCHE'S INFLUENCE ON RUSSIAN SYMBOLISTS AND THEIR CIRCLES

PREFACE

THIS BOOK is the product of a research conference on Nietzsche's influence in Russia which was held at Fordham University on 17 and 18 June 1983. Grateful acknowledgment is made to the Research Division of the National Endowment for the Humanities and to Fordham University for support of the conference. Acknowledgment is also made to Betty Forman for assistance in the early stages of planning the conference, the first round of editing, and participation in the conference, to Heinrich Stammler, for his participation in the conference, to Edith Finton Rieber for her piano recital, Paul Schmidt for his poetry reading, Aline Isdebsky-Pritchard for her slide presentation, and to Marvin Perry and Susan Ray for their comments on the Introduction. A very special debt of gratitude is owed to George L. Kline for his comments on the Introduction, the Zakydalsky and Mihajlov chapters, and for his encouragement, support, and advice throughout.

Edith W. Clowes's paper on Nietzsche and Russian censorship is not included in this volume because it was already committed to *Germano-Slavica*. The chapters by Mihajlo Mihajlov, Mary Louise Loe, and Taras D. Zakydalsky were added after the conference.

B.G.R.
New York, New York
November 1985

LIST OF ABBREVIATIONS

Nietzsche's works are cited parenthetically in the text. Unless otherwise specified, the following English editions are used:

A   *The Antichrist*, trans. R. J. Hollingdale (Harmondsworth and Baltimore, 1969)

BGE   *Beyond Good and Evil*, trans. W. Kaufmann (New York, 1966)

BT   *The Birth of Tragedy*, trans. W. Kaufmann (New York, 1967)

CW   *The Case of Wagner*, trans. W. Kaufmann (New York, 1967)

EH   *Ecce Homo*, trans. W. Kaufmann (New York, 1967)

GM   *Genealogy of Morals*, trans. W. Kaufmann (New York, 1967)

GS   *The Gay Science*, trans. W. Kaufmann (New York, 1974)

HH   *Human, All Too Human*, trans. Marion Faber and Stephen Lehmann (Lincoln, Neb., 1984)

TI   *Twilight of the Idols*, trans. R. J. Hollingdale (Harmondsworth and Baltimore, 1969)

WP   *The Will to Power*, trans. W. Kaufmann and R. J. Hollingdale (New York, 1968)

Z   *Thus Spoke Zarathustra*, trans. R. J. Hollingdale (Harmondsworth, 1961)

NOTE ON TRANSLITERATION

Transliteration follows the Library of Congress system, except that *y* has been substituted for *ii* in the endings of names, that is, Dostoevsky rather than Dostoevskii, Valery rather than Valerii.

Foreword

George L. Kline

FOR MOST RUSSIAN INTELLECTUALS their encounter in the early 1890s with the incandescent writings of Friedrich Nietzsche seems to have been a case of fascination at first sight. It was not total love, or pure love, for it was strongly mixed with shock and aversion. When Nicholas F. Fedorov referred to Nietzsche as "a *Russian* among the West Europeans"[1] he had in mind a cluster of national characteristics: passion, eloquence, powerful commitment to a cause, and "maximalism" or "extremism" in cultural and intellectual matters. Like many other Russians, Fedorov took Nietzsche to be an *odnodum*, a thinker with an obsessive *idée fixe*.

By the early 1890s not ony the Hegelianism of the 1840s and the anti-Hegelian positivism and materialism of the 1860s, but also the subjectivistic Populism of the 1870s, had lost their intellectual glitter. And although the "back to Kant" movement was flourishing in Germany, in Russia it reached only a relatively small, mainly academic audience. There was thus an intellectual and ideological vacuum, which Marxism was only beginning, one-sidedly, to fill. Furthermore, in Russia during the 1890s and early 1900s, more than in most other times and places, the linkage between belles-lettres and speculative thought was strong and close. Poets such as Afanasy Fet, Alexander Blok, and Andrei Bely, and novelists such as Leo Tolstoi and Bely, were deeply involved in both cultural criticism and philosophical speculation. On the other hand, speculative thinkers and cultural critics wrote novels (Konstantin Leontiev), poetry (Vladimir Soloviev), or brilliant aphoristic works in a partly philosophical, partly literary mode (Vasily Rozanov).

Thus it was quite natural that Russians would tend to see a kindred spirit in the "philosopher with a hammer" who addressed the grand themes

---

[1] N. F. Fedorov, *Filosofiia obshchego dela* [The Philosophy of the Common Task], 2 vols. 1906, 1913; reprint, Farnborough, 1970), 2:119; italics mine.

of speculative thought in a style that was brilliant, pyrotechnic, sometimes deliberately provocative, and whose literary versatility extended to the prose poem, the short lyric, and the pregnant aphorism.

Many of the targets of Nietzsche's irony and outrage were familiar objects of criticism and refutation by a variety of Russian thinkers. Utilitarian ethics, along with "rational egoism" and scientism, had been attacked by thinkers as different as Dostoevsky, Leontiev, Alexander Herzen, and Peter Lavrov. When Nietzsche went on to dismiss all such doctrines as shallow inventions of shallow English minds (pointing to John Stuart Mill, Herbert Spencer, and their epigoni)—though conveniently forgetting that these doctrines had intellectual roots in the *philosophes* of his beloved France—many Russians were ready to concur, with enthusiasm.

The social and cultural counterpart of utilitarianism and rational egoism was something for which the Russians had a word, or rather, two words: *meshchanstvo* ('philistinism' or 'shopkeeper mentality') and *poshlost'* ('vulgarity', 'lack of taste and imagination'). Nietzsche's ferocious onslaught upon the shallow pseudo-values of mass culture—timidity, mediocrity, conformity, complacency, philistinism—found an immediate echo in Russian minds, which had been prepared by the brilliant critiques put forward in the 1850s and 1860s by Herzen and again in the 1870s and 1880s by Leontiev.

Less familiar, though almost equally congenial, was Nietzsche's celebrated method of "unmasking," which probed to the alleged nontheoretical, precognitive roots of theories and cognitive claims, revealing their psychological and even physiological motivations. Thus Nietzsche claimed that the geometrical method used by Spinoza in his *Ethics* was just a kind of protective armor plate, the "mail and mask" of a timid, sick, and vulnerable recluse (*BGE*, 13). Or again—in one of Nietzsche's most notorious and shocking efforts at unmasking—that the roots of the Judeo-Christian virtue of agape ('love of one's neighbor') lie buried deep in the smoldering resentment and hatred of slaves for their lordly masters (*GM*, 33–39). Like the positivism and scientism of the 1860s, this approach provided a seductively easy and effective way of ridding oneself of difficult and unwelcome doctrines: once a position has been unmasked (as, previously, once it had been shown to be "unscientific") one is relieved of the need to study it, understand it, or subject it to rational or theoretical criticism.

Russians were fascinated—both attracted and repelled—by those passages in *Thus Spoke Zarathustra* (understandably, the work that was translated into Russian first and most often) in which Nietzsche explicitly and harshly repudiated "love of one's neighbor" (*Nächstenliebe*), declaring: "that which is falling should also be pushed [down]" (Z, 226). The virtue that Nietzsche punningly (but with entire seriousness) substitutes is *Fernsten-Liebe*, 'love of the farthest,' i.e., the most distant future generations (Z, 86–88).[2] Nietzsche's repudiation of good Samaritanism does not, of course, imply an advocacy of sadism, of cruelty for its own sake, although some of his admirers, including certain Russian "Nietzscheans," so interpeted him.[3] What Nietzsche preaches is "instrumental" cruelty, ruthlessness toward the weak, uncreative, and conformist masses, which has the aim of economizing and hence maximizing the limited energies available to the creative few.

But for *what* were these energies to be husbanded?

The answer seems to me clear enough, although not all of Nietzsche's Russian admirers had fully grasped it by the end of the 1890s. From his earliest works, such as *The Birth of Tragedy*, to the posthumously published *Will to Power*, it is the high culture of the remote world-historical future that Nietzsche identifies as the end for which the present should serve as a means. He complains bitterly that in the perverse conditions of the nineteenth century, as a result of institutionalized (and secularized) good Samaritanism, the present is living "at the expense of the future," and he emphatically urges a reversal of this situation (GM, 20; Z, 229–30).

The centrality, for Nietzsche, of cultural creativity was widely understood in *fin de siècle* Russia. But even Nietzsche's critique of Christianity found much approval; many secular intellectuals agreed that Christianity is indeed "Platonism for the people" (BGE, 3). But Russian thinkers who were moving toward, rather than away from, religious commitment—as, for example, Lev Shestov was in 1901 and 1903 when he first commented on Nietzsche[4]—could admire Nietzsche's seriousness about

---

[2]Cf. GS, 255: "[N]ot to perish when one inflicts great suffering . . .—that . . . belongs to greatness."

[3]Sadistic cruelty—*la cruauté pour la cruauté*—was explicitly repudiated by Nietzsche, e.g., in the scathing remarks which he directed at people who "enjoy" the spectacle of a bullfight—or a crucifixion (Z, 235)!

[4]In his two books, *The Good in the Teaching of Tolstoy and Nietzsche: Philosophy and Preaching* (1900) and *Dostoevsky and Nietzsche: The Philosophy of Tragedy* (1903). Both books are available in English translations by Bernard Martin and Spencer Roberts, respectively, in Lev Shestov, *Dostoevsky, Tolstoy, and Nietzsche* (Athens, Ohio, 1969).

religious questions and welcome his assertion that "the religious instinct is indeed in the process of growing powerfully," if not his further claim that this instinct is refusing "the theistic satisfaction" (*BGE*, 66). Many Russian intellectuals were impressed by Nietzsche's seriousness about the "ultimate religious question": what is it, in a world in which "God is dead," that serves as the ground and guaranty of the permanence of achieved values? Nietzsche's answer, of course, is the dark and problematic doctrine of "eternal recurrence." In the belief that all things become and recur eternally Nietzsche found a source of "consolation" (*Trost*) (*WP*, 548).

But Nietzsche's critique of philistinism had as a corollary a sustained attack upon social, political, and economic egalitarianism, upon that ideal of social justice which was shared by all Russian radicals and most Russian liberals. For Nietzsche the egalitarian ideal was no more than a secularization of the despised Judeo-Christian "slave morality." How could Russian intellectuals come to terms with this aspect of Nietzsche's social and political philosophy?

Curiously enough, certain of the Marxist socialists among them were able to deflect Nietzsche's criticism, insisting that, although fully applicable to the bourgeois society of the present, it would *not* be applicable to the socialist society of the future.[5] In direct opposition to Nietzsche, they asserted that social and political leveling does not have to be a leveling *down*, that in the socialist society of the future it will be a leveling *up*—bringing all men to the highest pitch of cultural creativity. That group of early Russian Marxists whom I have called "Nietzschean" were particularly impressed by two Nietzschean emphases: 1) the stress on the free creation of values and ideals by Free Spirits and, ultimately, "overmen";[6] and 2) the related stress on a powerful, almost voracious "will to the future."[7]

[5] Only in Russia, it seems, was there a sociopolitical and ideological *movement* that combined the ideas and insights of Nietzsche and Marx. In other East European countries there were only occasional, isolated theorists who did this, such as the Pole Stanislaw Brzozowski (1878–1911), who was at least partially influenced by Russian Nietzschean Marxism, having met Lunacharsky and Gorky in Italy in 1907.

[6] The writings of the Nietzschean Marxists stand in sharp contrast to those of other Russian Marxists (and for that matter non-Marxists) of the period in their copious use of such typically Nietzschean terms as 'value' (*tsennost'*), 'valuation' (*otsenka*), 'revaluation' (*pereotsenka*), 'ideal' (*ideal*), and 'goal' (*tsel'*), to say nothing of such expressions as 'fulness of life' (*polnota zhizni*) and 'love of the far-off' (*liubov' k dal'nemu*).

[7] Nietzsche did not, so far as I know, use this expression—in German, *Wille zur Zukunft*—in any of his published works, although the idea of a will to the future and images

When Anatoly Lunacharsky in 1909 thrilled to the anticipated "miracles of [human] culture of the year 3,000,"[8] he was expressing a thoroughly Nietzschean view in thoroughly Nietzschean language. After all, Nietzsche had summoned his contemporaries to undertake cultural projects "that would require thousands of years[9] for their completion" (GS, 303). But one can find examples of an equally extravagant future-orientation in the Russian tradition, for example, in the writings of Pisarev, who was much admired by Russian Marxists of all persuasions. Pisarev had asserted that the "realist" ideal which he championed would require "hundreds of generations" for its realization,[10] where even *two hundred* generations, on a conservative estimate, would stretch over at least *six thousand* years!

In any case, many Russian admirers of Nietzsche, and not just the Nietzschean Marxists, felt entirely at home with his rhetorical claim to be (in the person of Zarathustra) one of the "children of the future," one who prefers to live "in future centuries" (GS, 338, 339).

In the case of several other characteristic Nietzschean doctrines, it is at least possible that Russian intellectuals were absorbing, through Nietzsche, themes from their own intellectual history. The idea that slavery is a condition for high culture, that contemporary man is a bridge to the humanity of the future, that, as Nietzsche put it, "a people is a detour of nature to get six or seven great men" (BGE, 87), can be found in two of Herzen's writings of the 1850s. One of these, *My Past and Thoughts*, was, we know, familiar to Nietzsche in the German translation of his friend and correspondent Malwida von Meysenbug, who was also an intimate of the Herzen family in England and foster mother of Herzen's daughter Olga. Malwida von Meysenbug also urged Nietzsche in a letter of August 1872 to read Herzen's *From the Other Shore*, which had been published in a French translation in 1870. Although Nietzsche does not mention Herzen in any of his published works, the evidence of influ-

---

of such a will (e.g., the tautly drawn bow) are pervasive in his writings of the 1880s. However, the expression does occur among the posthumously published notes and drafts dating from the period 1882–1885, when Nietzsche was composing *Thus Spoke Zarathustra*. (Cf *Sämtliche Werke in zwölf Bänden*, ed. Alfred Baeumler [Stuttgart, 1965], 11:446.)

[8] A. V. Lunacharsky, "Eshcho o teatre i sotsializme" [Once More on the Theater and Socialism], in *Vershiny* (St. Petersburg, 1909), p. 212.

[9] In German, *Jahrtausende*, on the model of *Jahrhunderte* ('centuries') and *Jahrzehnte* ('decades'). The precise Russian counterparts are *tysiacheletiia*, *stolettiia*, and *desiatiletiia* (all plural).

[10] Dmitry Pisarev, "Realisty" [1864], sec. 20; in *Sochineniia* (Moscow, 1956), 3:84.

ence is strong. It is also true that in the same two books Herzen expressed other and quite contrasting ideas, which Nietzsche obviously did *not* take up, in particular (in *From the Other Shore*) that present living individuals should *not* be sacrificed for the sake of the future, should *not* be converted into "caryatids supporting a floor for others some day to dance on."[11]

In 1893, when the first serious philosophical discussion of Nietzsche's work appeared in a Russian journal, his name and his ideas were new and strange. But within a dozen years Chekhov in *Cherry Orchard* (1904) was able to treat both Nietzsche's name and at least one of his ideas as household words. Consider the following brief dialogue between the scatterbrained and insolvent landowner Pishchik and the "progressive" university student Trofimov:

> PISHCHIK: Nietzsche . . . , a very great, very famous philosopher . . . , a man of enormous intellect, says in his writings that one may counterfeit money.
>
> TROFIMOV: Oh, so you've read Nietzsche?
>
> PISHCHIK: Well . . . , Dashenka [his daughter] told me. And I'm in such a tight spot right now that I could use some counterfeit money.[12]

Pishchik's Nietzscheanism is naive and comical, but not grotesque or absurd. Chekhov's caricature, in other words, is effective because its object is readily recognizable despite the distorted form in which it is presented. Nietzsche's impassioned summons to create new and higher values and ideals "beyond [bourgeois-Christian] good and evil" has merely been trivialized and vulgarized into an endorsement of banal violations of criminal law. Such is the fate of household words!

Nietzsche's impact upon Russian literature and thought in the late nineteenth and early twentieth centuries is a topic of major importance in the intellectual and cultural history of modern Europe. The collection of thoughtful, perceptive, and judicious studies of this topic presented in this volume is as valuable as it is timely.

[11] Alexander Herzen, *From the Other Shore*, ed. Isaiah Berlin (New York, 1956), p. 36.

[12] Anton Chekhov, *Cherry Orchard*, Act 3, in, e.g., A. P. Chekhov, *Izbrannye proizvedeniia* (Leningrad, 1974), p. 674.

NIETZSCHE IN RUSSIA

Introduction

Bernice Glatzer Rosenthal

NIETZSCHE'S INFLUENCE IN RUSSIA was profound, widespread, and enduring. A philosopher for rebels, his impact proved greatest during what in retrospect can be seen as a transition period in Russian history, a period of the breakdown of old institutions and values. Mingling with Russian premonitions of the end of the old order and Russian visions of a new future of freedom, beauty, creativity, and love, Nietzsche invigorated the search for new values. His philosophy justified the secession of artists and writers from Populism; inspired experiments in painting, literature, and music; and challenged thinkers to develop a new life-affirming morality and to offer new interpretations of Christianity. His Prometheanism revitalized the image of the positive hero and engendered new antiauthoritarian interpretations of Marxism. In some circles, Nietzsche meant individualism, while in others he meant loss of self in a cultic community, collective creativity, or even self-sacrifice for the sake of the future. The nihilistic aspects of his philosophy were simplified and vulgarized for mass consumption. Rightly or wrongly, Nietzsche was often perceived as advocating promiscuity, hedonism, amorality, selfishness, contempt for the weak. Ironically, the positive aspects of his philosophy were subsumed into other isms, while the negative were labeled Nietzscheanism and condemned. After 1912, Nietzsche's influence becomes more difficult to trace. Writers avoided open acknowledgment of their debt to him. But his ideas were in the air and continued to influence Russian and even Soviet culture.

Nietzsche's philosophy was not simply a wave that crested, broke, and receded, leaving no trace on the land. On the contrary, his ideas had a lasting impact on the course of Russian history and culture. His injunction to "smash the old tables of values" (Z, 51–52) was a powerful ingredient in the revolutionary mix, sweeping away the old and clearing a path for the new. It justified the rebellion against tradition that was already underway and, in conjunction with other ideologies, stimulated alternative visions of a new order and a new man. Nietzsche's ideas imbued Bolshevism with a powerful Promethean thrust, a "will to power," while his belief in man's ability to create his own culture was a prominent feature of early Soviet thought and inspired various experiments in theater and cinema. Nietzsche indirectly influenced the Lenin cult and Stalin's cult of personality; Stalin himself became the all-knowing, all-powerful superman, the new god. In subterranean fashion, Nietzschean emphasis on the will permeated the grandiose economic projects of the Stalin era and the voluntarism of the first Five-Year Plans. In terms of culture, Nietzsche's legacy is not only the great works of art and literature produced by the artists he inspired, but, less directly, the Promethean projects of Magnitogorsk and the Dnepestroi Dam; his heirs are not only artists and writers, but engineers who conquer nature, bend it to their will.

Indeed, it is possible that a new chapter in the history of Nietzsche in Russia may be written, for many, though not all Silver Age (ca. 1890–1917) artists, writers, and philosophers have been rehabilitated. Their works circulate in official and *samizdat* editions (religious works are particularly popular) and there is widespread interest in Nietzsche among Soviet intellectuals today.

Despite all of this, Nietzsche's towering presence in Russian culture has remained in the shadows. The very fact of his enormous influence was ignored, understated, or underemphasized for both historical and political reasons. This is true of both the Soviet Union and (until recently) the West. In the Soviet Union, consideration of Nietzsche has been actively suppressed since the 1920s. His books were proscribed; many were removed from libraries or put on closed reserve, and some were actually burned by decree in 1923–1924.[1] During World War II, as in the West, Nietzsche was closely associated with National Socialism, erroneously called an ideologist of fascism because of the Nazi practice of quoting Nietzsche out of context so as to make him appear a supporter or even a prophet of Nazi racism and aggression. For these reasons, Soviet scholars have not been free to explore the full extent of Nietzsche's influence. His impact is now admitted for particular movements such as symbolism, and for particular writers such as Leonid Andreev, whom the Soviets regard as decadent. But, for the most part, Nietzsche is still not recognized as a creative influence on such Marxists as Gorky, Bogdanov,

[1] On early Soviet censorship see Bertram Wolfe, "Krupskaya Purges the People's Libraries," *Survey*, no. 72 (Summer 1969), pp. 141–55.

and Lunacharsky, nor on poets such as Maiakovsky. Indeed, Lunachar-sky's admiration for Nietzsche tends to be dismissed as a youthful aber-ration whereas some Soviet scholars deny that Bogdanov was a Marxist at all.

In the West, until quite recently, intellectual historians have focused on the explicitly political rather than the equally important cultural movements, thereby undervaluing philosophy, art, and religion—the areas in which Nietzsche's influence was concentrated. Western literary studies often emphasized structural issues to the exclusion of ideas, and thus have limited value insofar as analysis of the issue of Nietzsche's influence on Russian culture is concerned. Finally, Western writers and critics, though working from a different ideological perspective, frequently take their cues from Soviet writers, the best example being the Western schol-ars who ignore or deny Nietzsche's influence on Gorky. This seems to derive from work done by Soviet scholars unwilling or unable to examine all the sources of Russian Marxism in the 1890s, although this may be changing.

This book grows out of a research conference whose aims were to estab-lish the range and importance of Nietzsche's influence between 1890 and (roughly) 1930, to document the major facets of his appeal and his im-pact, and to lay the groundwork for further research. Several sets of in-terrelated issues emerged. The first set relates to the nature and timing of his reception. What was the nature of his appeal, to whom, why, and when? Was his influence felt all at once, or did it come in waves, and did interpretations of Nietzsche's works vary over time? A second set of issues stems from the fact that each writer had his or her own Nietzsche. How did particular writers interpret Nietzsche? Which elements did they stress? Which did they ignore or explicitly reject? What were the personal or social concerns that affected their selection? Related to the last ques-tion is the issue of the Russian intellectual heritage, the degree to which Nietzsche was perceived from one or more of the following perspectives: the treatment of moral, religious, and existential issues by Dostoevsky, Tolstoi, and Soloviev; the individual's acceptance or rejection of the in-telligentsia's duty to the people or of the self-denying ascetic morality preached by Russian Orthodox Christianity. And, finally, what was the reason for the retreat from Nietzsche, beginning about 1908 or even be-fore? Why did formerly enthusiastic Nietzscheans come to deny his influence, even while retaining key Nietzschean concepts or values? What, if any, was the enduring impact of these concepts or values on Russian/Soviet culture?

There were also methodological considerations. The first was the problem of documenting Nietzsche's influence. His impact on certain writers such as Merezhkovsky or Bely is obvious, for they themselves acknowledge it, quote Nietzsche directly, and discuss key Nietzschean tenets which they identify as such. But for other writers, such as Rozanov, Nietzsche's influence must be inferred from parallel texts, by the use of Nietzschean themes or images, and by occasional allusions to the German philosopher. In some cases influence was inferred from the fact that a given author moved in circles where Nietzsche was discussed, or read books and journals that treated his ideas; such an author's treatment bears the stamp of Nietzschean ideas in the air. The degree of Nietzsche's influence also varied. For some authors, such as Simon Frank (according to his own testimony), Nietzsche changed the future course of their intellectual development, while for others, such as the painter Michael Vrubel, Nietzsche served to confirm and reinforce convictions and attitudes already held. There is also the issue of positive or negative influence. Some Russians advocated Nietzsche's ideas and tried to realize them, while others reacted against them and developed their own ideologies to counter them. Not infrequently, people accepted some of Nietzsche's ideas but rejected others. A common pattern was enthusiasm for Nietzsche in one's youth but rejection or claims of rejection later on. Separating Nietzsche's influence from that of Schopenhauer, Stirner, or Wagner on the one hand and of Russian precursors such as Dostoevsky or Leontiev on the other cannot be accomplished with precision because certain of their ideas tended to merge with and reinforce one another. Finally, the way Russian intellectuals read Nietzsche was strongly influenced by Russian interpreters of Nietzsche such as Viacheslav Ivanov, Merezhkovsky, Shestov, Mikhailovsky, and Preobrazhensky. On the popular level, novels, short stories, and plays peopled by "Nietzschean" characters, usually in exaggerated or vulgarized form, shaped the common perception of his views.

How does one define vulgarization? How does one distinguish between the real Nietzsche and cheap imitations? Which writers really understood Nietzsche and his philosophy? Clearly, one's own subjective understanding of Nietzsche is involved here. No attempt has been made in this volume to enforce a particular interpretation. It was decided, however, that all the contributors would use the same English translation of his works for the sake of those who cannot read Nietzsche in the original German. The reader is reminded, however, that Russian intellectuals such as Ivanov, Merezhkovsky, and Bakhtin read Nietzsche in the original German, while others read him in French or in Russian translations, which varied in accuracy and completeness. Using an English translation, therefore, has the unavoidable consequence of working at one or even two removes from the original intellectual interchange and its emotional subleties. Some terminology has been standardized also, for example, 'revaluation of values' rather than 'reevaluation' or 'transvaluation' and 'eternal recurrence' rather than 'eternal return.' The choice of 'superman' or 'overman' for the German *Übermensch*, however, has been left to the contributors. The late Walter Kaufmann, a leading American interpreter of Nietzsche and still the leading translator, insisted on 'overman' because 'superman' was associated with the comic-strip hero and also because allusions to the Aryan superman were stock features of Nazi propaganda and American counterpropaganda. Hoping to rectify a popular misconception of Nietzsche's thought, Kaufmann emphasized its esthetic, psychological, and "existential" aspects, arguably going too far in his estheticization of Nietzsche. He ignored the undeniable ruthlessness of statements such as "You should love peace as a means to new wars. And the short peace more than the long" (Z,74), "That which is falling should also be pushed" (Z,226), and "And him you do not teach to fly, teach—to fall faster" (ibid.). Interestingly, Nietzsche's Russian admirers also stressed the esthetic/psychological/"existential" aspects, but were definitely aware of the dangerous ambiguities inherent in the concept of the 'will to power.' The Russian word *sverkhchelovek*, the usual translation, is almost a calque of the German *Übermensch*. But *sverkhchelovek* was subject to vulgarization and tended to be used as a pejorative, especially as in *sverkhbosiak* (supertramp), *sverkhpatriot* (superpatriot) or even *sverkhsobaka* (superdog.)[2]

There is an important distinction to be made between Nietzsche's thought as such and Nietzscheanism (Nitsheanstvo). 'Nietzscheanism' connotes a surrogate religion, a guide to life, which mandated a very specific set of values and attitudes, many of which were explicitly hostile to Christianity, as well as to Populism and Marxism. These values included individualism, self-affirmation, self-expression, sensuality, liberation of the in-

[2] Edith W. Clowes, "A Philosophy 'For All and None': The Early Reception of Friedrich Nietzsche's Thought in Russian Literature" (Ph.D. diss., Yale University 1981), p. 249.

stincts, pride, heroism, courage, struggle, affirmation of life, defiance of death, iconoclasm, antinomianism, and contempt for the mob, for bourgeois society, for tradition, and for custom. 'Nietzscheanism' was also used to accuse someone else of sanctioning, advocating, or practicing selfishness, hedonism, immorality, promiscuity, ruthlessness, oppression of the weak, and lust for power. The latter use of the word became especially common after 1905 as former admirers began to repudiate aspects of Nietzsche's thought, especially his individualism.

NIETZSCHE'S APPEAL AND INFLUENCE

Nietzsche's philosophy was extremely attractive to rebels; it served as a lightning rod for those dissatisfied with traditional Russian culture for many different reasons. His call for a 'revaluation of all values' (*Umwertung aller Werte*) inspired visions of a new order. Indeed, translated into Russian as *pereotsenka vsekh tsennostei*, the phrase was absorbed into the cultural baggage of the time, and used without quotation marks by writers, many of whom may not even have known that they were quoting Nietzsche. Nietzsche's detractors regarded him as a demonic figure, an apostle of immorality, a symptom of degeneration—as was argued by Max Nordau in his 1892 book *Degeneration* (*Entartung*), translated into Russian in 1893. To many Christians, Nietzsche was a tool of the devil, or even the Antichrist himself.

Different writers, and even the same writer at different times, selected those elements which they found most congenial from the vast and often contradictory corpus of Nietzsche's own works. Thus Nietzsche's impact varied from one writer to another. Moreover, his influence tended to shift over time, from esthetic, moral, and psychological issues in the 1890s, to religious, philosophical, and existential issues around 1900, to political and social issues around 1905. Related to the 1905 period was a widespread quest among Russian intellectuals for a new theater, modeled after the Dionysian theater of ancient Greece. But it must be emphasized that these phases were not sharply divided; different interpretations and emphases coexisted at all points in time. Writers such as Briusov and Bal-'mont, for example, never really abandoned their esthetic emphasis, while Shestov's primary concern was always ethical and philosophical, and Lunacharsky's mainly cultural and sociopolitical.

Nietzsche's initial impact in the 1890s must be understood in the context of the crisis of Populism. Russian intellectuals had traditionally lived for an idea that gave meaning and purpose to their lives. But Populism, the prevailing ideology since the late 1860s, was losing its ability to inspire faith. Decades of peaceful propaganda in the countryside had failed to produce results, and the assassination of Tsar Alexander II in 1881 had inspired horror rather than the expected mass revolt. In the repression that followed, radicals were arrested or fled abroad; their newspapers and journals were suppressed. Moreover, industrialization and urbanization were undermining the agrarian base of the Populist ideal. As the intelligentsia began to doubt itself, to lose faith in long-held values and ideals, some began to seek a new mission. Symbolism and Marxism arose out of this quest; both challenged the Populist idealization of the peasant, but for different reasons. Symbolists (a school of writers and artists who regarded art as a means to transcend everyday life and reach a higher reality), fortified by Nietzsche, refused to preach to the vulgar herd. They wanted to express themselves, to experiment with new forms and language, to be erudite and esoteric, incomprehensible to all but an elite, if they so chose. Marxists looked to the proletariat as the new force destined to transform Russia. In the proletariat of the future (it was minuscule in the present), they saw the new man, and he had Nietzschean traits: heroism, pride, activism, beauty, and strength.

Nietzsche seemed to offer a way out of the malaise that had affected Russian culture since the 1880s. Dostoevsky was dead and Tolstoi had passed his prime as a writer. Chekhov was at his peak in the 1890s, but his works seemed to exude pessimism, a sense of futility. Civic literature and poetry (works that preached a social message e.g., by Nekrasov [1832–1877] or Nadson [1862–1887]) had not produced any great works. In the universities the very discipline of philosophy was suspect and the repressive atmosphere stifled any expression of independent thought. For example, in the early 1880s, a student circle devoted to study of Molière was disbanded, its members arrested and interrogated.[3] These were the days of the "classic bondage," emphasis on learning Greek and Latin, which allegedly disciplined the mind and built character. Positivism still had many adherents among university students and was often coupled, as in the 1860s, with a utilitarianism that left little room for art, imagination, intuition, feelings. Students with a more metaphysical bent read Schopenhauer; sharing his pessimism, some tried to avoid suffering by deadening the will or by escaping into contemplation of art or nature.

[3]D. S. Merezhkovsky, "Avtobiograficheskaia zamet'ka," in *Russkaia literatura xx veka, 1890–1910*, ed. S. A. Vengerov, 3 vols. in 1 (1914–1916; reprint, Munich, 1972), 1:290.

The dissemination of Schopenhauer's esthetics and epistemology served to prepare Russians for Nietzsche, while the "classic bondage" familiarized them with the subject matter of *The Birth of Tragedy*, often the first Nietzsche book read by Russians. Nietzsche's philosophy appeared to them as a revitalizing force, the opposite of pessimism, passivity, resignation.

Russian intellectuals began to learn about Nietzsche around 1890. His works, not yet published in Russian translation, were summarized and their key tenets explained by Nietzsche's first Russian admirers—a cultural elite of artists and writers who read German or French and traveled extensively. The symbolist writers Merezhkovsky, Briusov, and Ivanov learned of Nietzsche while in Paris, where his works were already creating a sensation. Nietzschean motifs began to appear in their poetry and prose of the early 1890s. To them, Nietzsche was the prophet of a new culture of art and beauty. The Apollonian/Dionysian duality of *The Birth of Tragedy* gave them a conceptual framework for esthetic and psychological reflection and fueled their opposition to positivism and utilitarianism, sanctioning their demand that the needs of the inner man (the soul or the psyche) be heard. The Dionysian became a symbol for interrelated esthetic, psychological and religious impulses. Symbolists associated the spirit of music with Dionysus, but were unaware that Nietzsche himself had repudiated *The Birth of Tragedy* as too metaphysical in 1886 and that he had substituted a new duality, Hellenism versus Pessimism.[4]

Thus Spoke Zarathustra also appealed to symbolist artists and writers, as much for its poetic language and aphoristic style as for its philosophic content. They interpreted the latter as individualism, contempt for the herd, withdrawal from society. Proclaiming the artist as superman, they embraced an esthetic individualism, as distinct from the economic individualism of the West. Militantly apolitical and asocial, they scorned materialism, opposed rationalism and positivism, and contrasted Nietzsche's affirmation of life, including its suffering, with what they considered the shallow optimism of the West. The artist's duty, they insisted, was to himself, to express his own feelings and his own vision.

Russians also learned of Nietzsche from the 'thick journals,' especially *Problems of Philosophy and Psychology* (*Voprosy filosofii i psikhologii*, founded 1889, henceforth VFP) and Nicholas Mikhailovsky's *Russian Wealth* (*Russkoe Bogatstvo*). Since all publications had to be passed by two censors, a political and a religious one, considerations of censorship

---

[4]M. S. Silk and J. P. Stern, *Nietzsche on Tragedy* (Cambridge, Mass., 1981), pp. 118–19, 125.

may account for the editorial disclaimers of any sympathy for Nietzsche's ideas that preceded many journal articles about him. Often these were accompanied by allusions to Nietzsche's madness as a fitting end for a blasphemer and heretic. Nietzsche was good press. The January 1893 issue of *VFP*, which featured critical reactions to Preobrazhensky's sympathetic article "Friedrich Nietzsche: A Critique of the Morality of Altruism," which had appeared in the November 1892 issue, reached a new circulation high of 2,000. Nicholas Grot's article "The Moral Ideals of Our Time: F. Nietzsche and Count L. Tolstoi" was written with an ulterior motive; by upholding Tolstoi as an exemplar of the highest Christian values, Grot hoped to prevent the Holy Synod from excommunicating Tolstoi for heresy. (Nevertheless, Tolstoi was excommunicated in 1901.) In the mid-1890s, novelists and short-story writers such as Peter Boborykin began to popularize a stereotyped view of Nietzsche as an advocate of ruthlessness, cruelty, oppression, exploitation, and unbridled sensuality. Fostering this view was the tendency of the censor to pass only works critical of Nietzsche, for example, Max Nordau's *Degeneration*, which attacked Nietzsche's philosophy as sadistic hedonism and described the superman as a beast of prey.

Limited editions of Russian translations of Nietzsche's works began with the translation of *Zarathustra* in 1898, but the censors forced severe excisions, especially on the subjects of priests, the slave morality, and the Church.[5] Translations of other works soon followed, with excisions that varied with the caprice of the censor. By 1911 almost all of Nietzsche's works were available in Russian, but the translations varied widely in quality and some contained outright distortions. To remedy this, in 1909 a full academic edition of his collected works was planned; the philosopher Simon Frank was one of the editors. Four volumes were published between 1909 and 1912, but the war forced discontinuation of the series, for good, as it turned out. (See Richard Davies's chapter for a checklist of Russian translations, in chronological order.)

The organization of *The World of Art* in 1898 turned out to be a milestone in Russian cultural history. Some scholars even date the Silver Age from its inception, for it facilitated the coalescence of the various forces that had been germinating separately into a broad movement for a new Russian culture devoted to art and beauty. Its leading figures, Diaghilev and Benois, were devotees of Nietzsche and Wagner. They learned about

[5] Ann M. Lane, "Nietzsche in Russian Thought, 1890–1917" (Ph.D. diss., University of Wisconsin, 1976), p. 591.

Nietzsche (and Wagner, whom they regarded as the living embodiment of Nietzsche's 'spirit of music') in the early 1890s from Charles Birle, the cultural attaché to the French embassy in St. Petersburg. *The World of Art* grew out of their Nietzsche/Wagner-inspired desire to create a new culture in which art and esthetic sensibility would be central. They were not academic philosophers and the nuances of some of Nietzsche's concepts escaped many of them. 'Eternal recurrence,' for example, was used to mean, variously, historical cycles, cosmic cycles, reincarnation, endlessness; it was taken as the antonym of the enlightenment ideal of linear progress. The journal's logo, an eagle on a snowy peak surrounded by stars, is a Nietzschean image. It conveys Benois's belief that the world of art is above all earthly things, above the stars, reigning there proud, mysterious, and lonely, like an eagle. Featured were excerpts, in Russian translation, of works by Nietzsche and Wagner, Western works on these writers, and interpretations of their thought by Soloviev, Shestov, Minsky, Merezhkovsky, and other prominent Russians.

The World of Art actually comprised two groups: esthetes and symbolists. Esthetes such as Diaghilev expounded an art for art's sake position, while symbolists such as Merezhkovsky viewed art as a theurgy, a path to religious truths. The conflict between them was a factor in wrecking the journal, which ceased publication in 1904. But by then the movement for a new culture had other vehicles. Successor journals, *The Scales* (*Vesy*), *New Path* (*Novyi put'*), *Problems of Life* (*Voprosy zhizni*), *Golden Fleece* (*Zolotoe runo*), and others carried its banners, each journal, of course, contributing its own emphasis.

The 1890s were a period of ferment on the left as well. Political activists, disillusioned with Populism but unwilling to abandon their struggle for liberation, sought new sources of inspiration and vitality. Nietzsche was one of these sources. Radicals attracted by his doctrines grafted his Prometheanism, his elemental protest against bourgeois society, and his ideal of the heroic individual onto a traditional paradigm of social duty in which the strong leader saves the masses.

Nicholas Mikhailovsky set the precedent for the reinterpretation of Nietzsche's superman as the positive hero long sought by the left. As a Populist, Mikhailovsky believed in the supreme importance of the individual. Appreciating this aspect of Nietzsche, he hailed him as "the most noble and brave thinker, a kind of dreamer, an idealist,"[6] and denied that Nietzsche was an egoist in the vulgar sense of the word, or a preacher

---

[6]N. Mikhailovsky, "Literatura i zhizn'," *Russkoe Bogatstvo*, no. 12 (1894), p. 94.

of immorality. "Might, power of mind, of character, the strength of soul and body—this is the point beyond good and evil from which Nietzsche criticized and wanted to change contemporary morality. He did not preach 'debauchery' at all and . . . the shameless decadents, praising or practicing 'vices' have no right at all to quote him."[7] But Mikhailovsky was disturbed by Nietzsche's attack on equality, his contempt for the poor, and his division of humanity into master and slave, attributing these uncongenial aspects of Nietzsche's philosophy to the influence, on Nietzsche, of Darwin's concept of the struggle for survival.[8] Still, the idea of the superman as positive hero was picked up by other radicals, including Marxists.

Russian Marxism in the 1890s was very much in a state of formation, a state of flux, and was not at all monolithic. Philosophically inclined Marxists felt no compunction in comparing Marx to other philosophers or even in supplementing him with Kant or Nietzsche, where necessary, to fill in what they considered gaps or defects in his views. Using Nietzsche selectively, they could rationalize away his contempt for the mob as contempt for it in its present state, as distinct from the people as they will be under socialism. Nietzsche's conviction that there are no eternal truths, no absolute values, was definitely compatible with Marxist moral relativism. Both Marxists and Nietzscheans desired change and considered themselves brave fighters for a new order.

To the young Maxim Gorky, Nietzsche meant faith in the individual, while Marx meant the social revolution that would liberate the individual. Gorky had not yet opted for one or the other. Marxism, he said in 1898, "belittles man," yet the "meaning of life is in man." Citing Zarathustra's statement, "Man is something that must be overcome" (Z,65, 83), Gorky added, "I believe, I do believe, that he will be overcome."[9] He was particularly impressed by the section "Of War and Warriors in *Thus Spoke Zarathustra* and by Nietzsche's doctrine of *amor fati* (love of fate). "Song of the Falcon" ("Pesnia o sokole," 1895) is his paean to heroic individualism; it celebrates a gravely wounded falcon who opts for a mad last flight rather than mere survival. Scorning the latter, the falcon proclaims: "He who is born to crawl cannot fly."[10] The strong, solitary

---

[7] Ibid., no. 2 (1900), p. 163.

[8] Lane, "Nietzsche in Russian Thought," pp. 492–93.

[9] As quoted by Mary Louise Loe in chapter 11 in this volume.

[10] Clowes, "Philosophy," p. 118. On "Song of the Falcon" also see Betty Yetta Forman, "Nietzsche and Gorky in the 1890s: The Case for an Early Influence," in *Western Philosophical Systems in Russian Literature*, ed. Anthony M. Mlikotin (Los Angeles, 1979), pp. 158–60.

man who accomplishes great feats appealed to Gorky, who also had a strange attraction to the antidemocratic aspects of Nietzsche's philosophy. The tramp, a stock Gorky character, has contempt for society. He also has other Nietzschean traits: unabashed amoralism, egoism, and a belief that no truth exists. Indeed, in general, all Gorky's pre-1905 heroes have Nietzschean traits: rebelliousness, exuberance, and pride; they make themselves into the men they wish to be. Foma Gordeev, hero of Gorky's first novel (1899), exemplifies political *amor fati*, doing what is right, despite danger. Foma is the son of a merchant and himself a merchant who is destroyed in his valiant, but hopeless and therefore mad attempt to help the people. Gorky tended to contrast Dionysian madness with Apollonian rationality. By the turn of the century, many of Gorky's contemporaries considered him a Nietzschean; some of them viewed this favorably while others used it to attack him.

Virtually all Marxists shared Nietzsche's contempt for bourgeois society. Leon Trotsky, for example, affirmed that Nietzsche's superman grows out of "normal bourgeois morality" and is "opposed to it only as excess is opposed to the norm. . . . The immoral superman is to the virtuous middle class as the medieval robber is to the feudal lord. Nietzsche's ideal was the rapacious bourgeois, freed from inhibition and stripped of pretenses." Still, said Trotsky, the socialist "could not but admire the brilliant originality with which Nietzsche has shown how brittle were the normal workaday ethics of the middle classes."[11] These statements were made in Trotsky's first literary essay, significantly, a critical obituary of Nietzsche.

Nietzsche's vitalism and activism were correctives to the rather dry interpretation of Marxism offered by George Plekhanov (1857–1918), generally considered the father of Russian Marxism, and founder, together with Paul Axelrod, of the very first Russian Marxist organization, in 1883, in Western Europe. His Marxism deferred to the operation of historical laws, denied that there are heroes in history, and almost obliterated the human voluntarist element. Nietzsche helped restore the heroic dimension to radicalism and imbued Russian Marxism with a powerful Promethean thrust, which counterbalanced the emotional flatness of Plekhanov's position. Nietzsche particularly appealed to Marxists such as Anatoly Lunacharsky, who wished to reconcile cravings for personal development with the demand for social justice. Fascinated by the

---

[11] As quoted by Isaac Deutscher, *The Prophet Armed* (New York, 1955), p. 50.

avant-garde of Paris and St. Petersburg, he argued the importance of art in the social struggle and advocated a *Kulturkampf* against bourgeois dominance of art. "We differ with Nietzsche in much," he said, "but consider him a great joyful liberator."[12] Lunacharsky's many references to "joyful struggle" and "fullness of life" stem from Nietzsche. Like Gorky, he gave Nietzsche's concept of the warrior a political slant: the willingness to face danger, to take risks, even to die, for the sake of the revolution. Their superman was the political activist battling on behalf of the still uncomprehending masses. No weak and wavering Hamlet, the superman of the left is a reincarnation of Chernyshevsky's positive hero, but with new qualities added: beauty, exuberance, spontaneity.

Trotsky's 1901 essay "On Optimism and Pessimism, On the Twentieth Century and on Many Other Things," also bears a Nietzschean imprint: the refusal to succumb to pessimism. The pessimist says:

> —Death to Utopia! Death to faith! Death to love! Death to hope! thunders the twentieth century in salvoes of fire and in the rumbling of guns.
> —Surrender, you pathetic dreamer. Here I am, your long awaited twentieth century, your 'future.'
> —No, replies the unhumbled optimist: you—You are only the present.[13]

As a romantic revolutionary in 1904, Trotsky cursed Marxists who "want to bring dryness and hardness into all the relations of life."[14] Later on, however, as commissar of the Red Army, he may have recalled a different aspect of Nietzsche—*Become hard!* (Z,231); "*Do not spare your neighbor!*" (Z,216); "All creators, however, are hard" (Z,114)—which, fortifying Marxist-Leninist ruthlessness, created the iron will needed to win the Civil War.

Nietzsche's injunction to hardness was probably also an influence on the "legal Marxists' " (so-called because they published in the legal press) attack on Populism as sentimental and romantic. Berdiaev, Bulgakov, and Struve insisted on being scientific and objective, called for ruthless adherence to reality, and ridiculed the Populist idealization of the peasant. Their merciless attitude toward the peasant recalls Nietzsche's con-

---

[12] Anatoly Lunacharsky, "Russkii Faust" in *Etiudy kriticheskie i polemicheskoe* (Moscow, 1905), p. 188.

[13] As quoted by Deutscher, *Prophet*, pp. 54–55.

[14] Ibid., p. 97.

tempt for pity and his statement "That which is falling should also be pushed!" (Z, 226), though their interest in Kant is more well known.

As Russian Marxist theory developed, Nietzsche's influence tended to recede. Nevertheless, certain Nietzschean concepts, values, and attitudes had formed and continued to form a powerful subterranean current that fed into Russian Marxism, especially Bolshevism, endowing the latter with a strong Promethean thrust, a 'will to power' defined in exclusively political terms, as distinct from the original Nietzschean concept that glorified primarily, though not exclusively, artistic or esthetic power.

Indeed, is there a better example than Lenin of the 'will to power' applied to politics? Definitely aware of Nietzsche, Lenin attacked him, castigating his admirers as "literary supermen" in his 1905 essay "Party Organization and Party Literature." Lenin was quite correct in viewing Nietzschean freedom and creativity as a threat to the disciplined Party, conscious of its goals, strategy, and tactics, that he desired. But Lenin's own superhuman will, his self-discipline and single-mindedness constitute an example, intentional or not, of the Nietzschean concept of self-overcoming, while Lenin's conviction that the workers can never achieve true liberation on their own, but rather require the guidance of a disciplined elite, may indicate a certain affinity for Nietzsche's contempt for the herd. Moreover, Lenin's opposition to the "economists" in the Party who advocated agitation on bread and butter issues recalls Nietzsche's contempt for well-being and comfort, as well as Nietzsche's indifference to ordinary people.

The Russian Social Democratic Workers Party was formed in 1898, the same year as the organization of *The World of Art* and the first Russian translation of *Zarathustra*. In this decade, Nietzsche was discussed in study circles (*kruzhki*), which used informal translations of his works by intellectuals who knew German and which were roughly comparable to American counterculture seminars in the 1960s. Activists of all schools saw themselves as supermen, creators of new values and a new culture that would ultimately liberate and ennoble the people. By 1900, a contemporary reported, educated people were familiar with Nietzsche's basic ideas, even if only by hearsay, and "even in the illiterate countryside," Nietzsche's name was known.[15] The literary critic S. V. Vengerov, author of *Russian Literature in the Twentieth Century, 1890–1910* (*Russkaia literatura xx veka*), considered Marx and Nietzsche the dominant

---

[15] I. I. Satrapinsky, "Filosofia Nitche v ee otnoshenii k khristianstvu," *Pravoslavnyi sobesednik* 1 (1916), p. 29.

intellectual influences of this period and called volume I of his study *The Revaluation of All Values*, subtitled *Decadence and Marxism*.[16]

Nietzsche's rapid assimilation and appropriation was facilitated by the Russians' receptivity to new formulations of the familiar 'eternal questions.' Militant atheism, for example, had characterized the intelligentsia since the 1860s and even before, while defiance of the authority of Church and state, scorn for social custom, convention, and philistinism, and advocacy of free love were central tenets of the intelligentsia ethos. The Russian anarchist Bakunin's dictums "if God exists man is a slave" and "the passion for destruction is also a creative passion" may have predisposed Russian radicals to hail similar statements by Nietzsche. The 'new man' or positive hero sought by the intelligentsia was, perhaps, in his own way, a kind of superman. From Pushkin and Lermontov to Tolstoi and Dostoevsky, the central question of Russian literature had been the meaning and purpose of life, closely linked, in the cases of Tolstoi and Dostoevsky, with religious issues. Some Russians found precursors to Nietzsche in Dostoevsky's characters Kirillov and Raskolnikov. Others pointed to Lermontov's superfluous man and his demonic individualism, while still others called Constantine Leontiev (1831–1891) the "Russian Nietzsche" because of his estheticism, his elitism and contempt for democracy, and his ethical views, which were widely, though perhaps erroneously, perceived as amoralism. Nietzsche was frequently contrasted with Tolstoi or Tolstoianism (Tolstovstvo) because his views struck many Russians as epitomizing the Christian values of asceticism, altruism, self-denial, nonviolence, and love—which Nietzsche denied. Finally, the apocalyptic elements in Nietzsche's philosophy appeared to echo the eschatological predictions of Dostoevsky and Soloviev, while his stress on Western decadence might have appealed to the secret Slavophilism in some Russian souls.

Around the turn of the century, a new intellectual current affected the Russian assimilation of Nietzsche. This was the "new religious consciousness." D. S. Merezhkovsky, its formulator and chief proselytizer, preached an apocalyptic interpretation of Christianity and a forthcoming Third Revelation or Third Testament. Having been influenced by Nietzsche's critique of traditional Christianity, he desired a new form of

[16]Vengerov, *Russian literatura*, p. x.

Christianity that would foster esthetic and cultural creativity, self-expression, individuality, and also sanctify sex. The last was particularly emphasized by V. V. Rozanov, who criticized Christianity as a religion of death and preached a biological mysticism centered on procreation and childbirth. In 1901, Merezhkovsky, his wife Zinaida Gippius, and their associate Dmitri Filosofov founded the Religious Philosophical Society of St. Petersburg (first meeting November 1901). Featuring the novelty of debates between clergymen and intellectuals, it became a center of St. Petersburg intellectual life. Through its debates and discussions, Nietzsche's critique of Christianity and his call for a revaluation of all values gained wider circulation, especially since the minutes of the meetings were printed, in censored form, in the Merezhkovsky's journal *New Path*. In April 1903, however, Pobedonostsev, chief procurator of the Holy Synod, realized that he had permitted a forum for heresy and forbade further meetings, thereby inadvertently politicizing the hitherto apolitical symbolists, who reluctantly acknowledged that their religious search for new truths required the bourgeois civil liberties that some of them had formerly disdained.

Philosophic idealism was another major current of the religious renaissance. Its proponents included the former "legal Marxists," Berdiaev, Bulgakov, Struve, and Frank who were attempting to supplement Marx with Kant. The philosophy they later developed was, perhaps, more indebted to Dostoevsky than to Nietzsche, but the German was a major catalyst in their search for new moral values and the channel it assumed—their development of new interpretations of Christianity. In the symposium *Problems of Idealism* (*Problemy idealizma*, 1902) Frank and Berdiaev treated Nietzsche at length and Askol'dov, Bulgakov, and Zhukovsky treated him briefly. Indeed, S. N. Trubetskoi was so dismayed at the outburst of Nietzscheanism that he regretted his participation. Frank found Nietzsche a corrective to the abstract rationalism of Kant and was particularly influenced by the psychological aspects of Nietzsche's thought, especially the way in which Nietzsche demonstrated the existence of irrational elements in the human personality and the importance, the living reality, of ideals. Nietzsche's concept of "love for the most distant" (Z,88), which he contrasted to the Christian precept of love of neighbor, stimulated Frank to develop a future-oriented philosophy that stressed giving of oneself; he denied that Nietzsche was an egotist.

Berdiaev regarded Nietzsche as a mystic and a prophet, but even though he shared Nietzsche's contempt for bourgeois society, he considered him naive as a social theorist. During his Marxist phase in the late 1890s, Berdiaev condemned Nietzsche's individualism, but later on came to appreciate it. The individual person, personal freedom, and creativity remained central tenets of his world view. He saw Nietzsche as the proponent of a new, free (that is, not externally imposed) morality, which would replace what he considered the bourgeois elements of Kant's practical morality. Berdiaev was an elitist, whose belief in a spiritual or cultural aristocracy stemmed, partly, from Nietzsche, as did his lifelong apotheosis of the creative act. After the Revolution of 1905, Berdiaev's search for new moral values led him to return to Christianity; he developed a personalist Christianity that emphasized autonomy, authenticity, creativity, and freedom. He looked to a religious Dionysianism as the wellspring of freedom. He also credited Nietzsche with exposing the fallacy of secular humanism.

Lev Shestov, another leading figure of the religious renaissance, was also deeply influenced by Nietzsche, not his doctrine of the superman, but his trenchant critique of reason and logic. In *The Good in the Teaching of Tolstoi and Nietzsche* (1900), Shestov attacked philosophical idealism and the rationalism he believed it implied and expressed his admiration for Nietzsche's passionate and honest search for truth and his refusal to submit to traditional verities. Critical of Tolstoi's moralism, Shestov rejected his implicit substitution of goodness for God, arguing that Nietzsche had demonstrated the futility of such a substitution, and showed that tragedy, evil, and suffering are unavoidable and that they defy rational explanation. In his book *Dostoevsky and Nietzsche: The Philosophy of Tragedy* (1903) Shestov argued that the two writers are linked by their attack on rationalism and contrasted them both with Tolstoi, to the latter's disadvantage. In subsequent books and articles, Shestov maintained that no eternal verities exist, that both good and evil are inherent in the human condition, and that philosophy's task is not to comfort man but to stir him to struggle for the impossible. He has been compared to Kierkegaard (whom he discovered much later, in the late 1920s) because of his insistence on the irrationality of life, and on faith rather than reason. Nietzsche's continuing influence on Shestov has yet to be examined in depth.

Also contributing to the religious renaissance was a second wave of symbolists who emerged after 1900. Its outstanding figures were Viacheslav Ivanov, who maintained in *The Hellenic Religion of the Suffering God* (1904–1905) that Dionysus was a precursor of Christ, Andrei Bely;

and Alexander Blok. In different ways, all three combined Nietzsche and Soloviev and used Christian and Christological symbols and images including a Nietzscheanized Christ, a Christ/Dionysus archetype, in their poetry and prose. Bely stated that *Zarathustra* was his "manual." He saw in Nietzsche the "new man" the "practice of culture," "the rejection of the old way of life," and "an artist of genius whose rhythms would penetrate all artistic culture."[17] A lover of music, Bely knew that Nietzsche had tried his hand at composing, and hoped that through the spirit of music an all-embracing new culture could be formed that would incorporate the truths of art, science, religion, and philosophy. Various isms and influences combined in Bely's thought, so that Nietzsche's influence blended with that of Soloviev, Merezhkovsky, the Book of the Apocalypse, and various occult philosophies, first theosophy and then anthroposophy. Bely viewed music as a sacrament and linked it to the Nietzschean concept of the 'eternal recurrence,' which he linked in turn to the Apocalypse, and, at times, to occult doctrines of reincarnation. Blok knew of Nietzsche from Bely, Merezhkovsky, and others in his circle and shared Bely's hopes for a new musical culture, but he did not read *The Birth of Tragedy* (the first and only work of Nietzsche that he is known to have read) until 1906. Like Ivanov, Blok and Bely yearned for a new Russian culture that would be characterized by freedom, beauty, and love.

Viacheslav Ivanov's interpretation of Nietzsche (and Wagner) was particularly influential among Russian intellectuals. A major symbolist poet and theorist, he and his wife, Lydia Zinovieva-Annibal hosted a salon at their St. Petersburg apartment, "The Tower," that was a seedbed for ideas between 1904 and 1912. Idealists and realists, Symbolists and Marxists, Socialist Revolutionaries and Constitutional Democrats were frequent visitors. After the Bolshevik Revolution, Ivanov served as a member of TEO, the theatrical section of the Commissariat of Enlightenment. Thus, Ivanov's reinterpretation of Nietzsche's *The Birth of Tragedy* and his revision of the Nietzsche/Wagner model of the theater had far-reaching implications.

Ivanov maintained that Nietzsche had erred in regarding the Dionysian rituals as a purely esthetic phenomenon. Nietzsche had ignored the fact that the ancient Greeks worshiped Dionysus as a god. The rituals devoted to him, Ivanov emphasized, were religious rituals; they formed the basis of a cultic commune, which in turn formed the embryo of future

---

[17] Andrei Bely, *Na rubezhe dvukh stoletii* (Moscow, 1930), p. 466.

Greek culture. Stressing the communal or collectivist aspects of Nietzsche's thought, Ivanov hoped that reviving the Dionysian theater would inspire a culture-creating process in Russia. Thus he enjoined his fellow symbolists to emerge from their seclusion, to go forth to meet the folk soul, and to create new myths that would reconcile the intelligentsia and the people. "Individualism is dead," Ivanov proclaimed, for "individualism is aristocratism [and] aristocratism is obsolete." Alluding to Zarathustra, he charged that individualism "has killed the old gods and idolized the superman" and the superman has in turn killed individualism. "Individualism presumed the self-satisfied fullness of the human person, but we fell in love with the superman. The taste for the superhuman has killed in us the taste for the sovereign affirmation of the human in ourselves."

Arguing that the concept of the superman ignores an entire spectrum of human emotional needs, Ivanov advanced a new concept, "the suprahuman [*sverkhchelovecheskoe*]," asserting that the "suprahuman is a universal, even a religious concept, of which all humanity will soon be aware." Already, he said, "religious messianists, social messianists, messianists who struggle with God, all alike are living by the choral spirit and collective [*sobornyi*] hopes." The "age of the epic is gone," he declared, and presumably the supermen who were its heroes; "may that of the choral dithyramb begin. . . . He who does not want to sing the choral song may withdraw from the circle, covering his face with his hands. He may die, but to live in isolation is impossible."[18] Despite Ivanov's rejection of Nietzsche's individualism, he was still influenced by *The Birth of Tragedy*, offering a new interpretation that virtually ignored the Apollonian principle and apotheosized the Dionysian principle, which was, in Ivanov's eyes, self-transcendence in a cultic commune. His ultimate hope was the creation of a society based on the Russian ideal of *sobornost'*, originally an ecclesiastical principle that connoted the unity of all believers in the mystic body of Christ. Secularized, it meant an organic and harmonious community in which the members retain their individuality.[19]

[18] Viacheslav Ivanov, "Krizis individualizm," in *Po zvezdam* (St. Petersburg, 1909), pp. 86–102. Quotes are on pp. 98, 95–96, 99–100, respectively. English translation by Marian Schwartz is in A *Revolution of the Spirit: Crisis of Values in Russia, 1890–1918,* ed. B. G. Rosenthal and M. B. Chomiak (Newtonville, Mass., 1982).

[19] Incidentally, the Pernerstorfer circle in Vienna, which was strongly influenced by Nietzsche and Wagner, also hoped to realize their ideal of a cultural community, and stressed audience participation. William J. McGrath, *Dionysian Art and Populist Politics* (New Haven, 1974), esp. chap. 2, "Nietzsche as Educator." Ivanov does not seem to have known about this circle.

Ivanov celebrated the tragic chorus as the living embodiment of *sobornost'*. Following the Nietzsche/Wagner tenet that the disintegration of the Greek theater into separate art forms presaged the decline of the unified consciousness necessary for personal and social well-being, Ivanov hoped to restore this union by reviving the Dionysian theater. But he criticized Wagner for the passivity that his operas induced in his audiences and also for omitting human speech. "The crowd must dance and sing," Ivanov said, "praise the god with words."[20] He proposed a new theater that would feature choruses, audience participation, and the collective creation of new myths. He hoped that the mythopoetic unity evoked by the chorus, which created the myth as it chanted, would provide the new truths around which the intelligentsia and the people could unite, thereby achieving the ideal of *sobornost'*. To enhance the feeling of unity, he advocated the elimination of the stage; the spectators would also be actors. Hoping to transcend divisions based on rank or class by focusing on the inner experience shared by all people, he emphasized the erotic, orgiastic elements of the Dionysian rites as a means of self-transcendence and communion. He believed that myths link the individual to a timeless metaphysical reality, the World Soul, a concept drawn, via Vladimir Soloviev, from Schelling and ultimately from Plato.

As revolutionary turmoil increased, hitherto apolitical artists and writers were forced to recognize that they could not continue to insulate themselves from social and political problems. Some, affected by apocalyptic visions that had been circulating in Russia since 1900, regarded the Revolution of 1905 as the apocalypse and were receptive to radical visions of social transformation. Bely tried to reconcile symbolism and Marxism. Blok carried a red flag in a revolutionary procession, suddenly aware of the people's hunger and suffering. Merezhkovsky began to advocate a "religious revolution." Benois repudiated individualism, turned somewhat conservative, and urged the artist to contribute to the organic development of a new Russian culture. Berdiaev advocated Christian anarchism, while Bulgakov espoused Christian socialism and tried to form a Christian political party. Ivanov supported George Chulkov's "mystical anarchism," a political doctrine, apocalyptic in nature, which purported to reconcile individual freedom and social harmony. Rejecting all external constraints on individual self-affirmation, especially government, law, morality, and social custom, mystical anarchists distinguished between

[20]Viacheslav Ivanov, "Vagner i dionisogo deistvo," *Vesy*, no. 2 (1905), p. 14.

the "empirical person" who is egoistic, self-seeking, and aggressive and the "mystical person" who expresses himself through love, creativity, and sacrifice. Basing their theory on the latter, they hoped to achieve their ideal of a society without compulsion, a society whose ties are internal and voluntary.[21] Mystical anarchism was actually a variant of a host of similar doctrines such as Gofman's "collective individualism" (*sobornyi individualizm*) or Merezhkovsky's "religious sociality," all of which were influenced by Nietzsche. As a group, they formed a particular genre of sociopolitical thought, a politicized Dionysianism that hailed art, love, and mysticism (religious or secular) as the means to social unity.

Ivanov's and Chulkov's mystical anarchism was the most prominent of these doctrines. Elements of Nietzschean individualism lingered on in it despite paeans to social unity. Mystical anarchism's insistence on self-affirmation, self-determination, and the autonomy of human values stems from Nietzsche, as did its Dionysian attack on traditional morality. Chulkov sought new experiences 'beyond good and evil.' Ivanov proclaimed that mystical anarchism is "outside 'Yes' or 'No,' " outside norms and boundaries. He asserted that the "morality of conduct has become the morality of the passionate aspirations of the spirit" and refused to limit the "flowing energies of the infinitely self-liberating soul" by external norms or "static forms" of any kind. He considered the Ten Commandments a negative morality ("Thou shalt not") and advocated a positive morality, a "blinding Yes to the world."[22]

Sensitized by Nietzsche to the lure of power for its own sake, he and Chulkov repudiated the "lust for power and dominion" and deified a new ideal—"powerlessness"—the inverse of Nietzsche's will to power. They wanted all human beings, not just the strong, to be free to develop their individuality. Their call for energy, activity, daring, and struggle was Nietzschean in tone, while Ivanov's proclamation of "supraindividualism [*sverkhindividualizma*]" recalls Nietzsche's emphasis on self-overcoming as well as Soloviev's views of the God-man and *sobornost'*. "Supraindividualism" is virtually undefinable. Ivanov defined it "broadly" as "individualism that recognizes itself through mysticism" and "narrowly" as "emanating from the new tendencies in thought and artistic creativity."[23]

---

[21] For details on mystical anarchism see B. G. Rosenthal, "The Transmutation of the Symbolist Ethos: Mystical Anarchism and the Revolution of 1905," *Slavic Review* 36 (December 1977), pp. 608–27.

[22] Ivanov, *Po zvezdam*, pp. 119–22.

[23] Ibid., pp. 118, 121–22.

Like many symbolists, and like Soloviev, he considered art a kind of theurgy. Their epistemology, especially Ivanov's, stressed the irrational aspects of experience and existence. It was similar, though not identical, to Nietzsche's, for Ivanov believed that there was a higher truth hidden beyond the Dionysian flux. Nietzsche had advocated breaking the old tables of values and had referred to the state as the "coldest of all cold monsters" (Z,75). From him, reinforced by the eschatological expectations of Soloviev, Merezhkovsky, the early Bakunin, and Ibsen, stems mystical anarchism's stress on creative destruction. Chulkov stated:

> We can be *politicals*, but only in the reverse sense; that is, we may participate in political life only to the degree that it is dynamic and revolutionary, only to the degree that it *destroys* state norms; and we may participate in the social struggle only to the degree that it destroys that social order which economically enslaves the individual person. But all political and social construction is inadmissable from our point of view; our constructions are accomplished apart from mechanical relations.[24]

By "mechanical relations" Chulkov meant any relationship that is external to the individual, that is not based on the needs of the 'inner man,' such as contractual or legal relationships. Mystical anarchists rejected the liberal/rational world view of the West and disdained the newly instituted parliament (the Duma), for they believed that the chorus, rather than a parliament, was the "genuine referendum of the people's true will."[25] Actually, Ivanov's primary concern was inner freedom, but the nuances of his rather involved and abstract theory were less prominent than his invocations to Eros and ecstasy, and his refusal to "accept the world," by which he meant empirical reality and the laws of nature. His doctrines were attacked as nihilistic and amoral by symbolists such as Bely, Merezhkovsky, and Filosofov. The latter two wanted new values that were specifically Christian, while Bely, objecting to the emphasis on the Dionysian for personal and political reasons, expected new forms, new structures, to emerge from the Dionysian flux. He was unwilling to abandon rationalism entirely.

Just as the Revolution of 1905 led many symbolists to repudiate some of their previous values, especially their individualism, so it led many

---

[24]Georgy Chulkov, *O mysticheskom anarkhisme* (1906: reprint, Letchworth, Herts., 1971), p. 54.
[25]Ivanov, *Po zvezdam*, p. 219.

Marxists to a greater appreciation of the role of religion, myth, and the irrational in human behavior. Even before the revolution, as already indicated, certain Marxists had stressed the importance of art for the social struggle. Gorky had been changing his emphasis from self-overcoming to the regeneration of all humanity; he now believed that the social revolution would ennoble all men, not just a select few. The artist should not hold himself aloof from the people, but try to change them, inspire them to overcome their faults, to protest, to strive for great ideals. But his attempt to incorporate Nietzschean ideals into a socialist framework was criticized from all sides. He had hoped that his short story "Man" ("Chelovek," 1904) would form the basis of a socialist esthetic, but Marxist critics recognized and objected to the hero-creator archetype and accused him of scorning ordinary people, while symbolist critics charged him with vulgarizing Nietzsche. As the revolution erupted, Gorky moved closer to the Marxists, followed Lenin's lead in castigating "literary supermen," and repudiated Nietzsche in an essay "Notes on *Meshchanstvo*" ("Zamet'ki o meshchanstve," 1905). *Meshchanstvo* can be translated as 'middle class' (equivalent to 'petty bourgeois') or as 'philistinism'; like most Russian intellectuals Gorky equated the two. He attacked individualism as a middle-class ideology that could only harm the workers and extolled the heroic, creative, and rebellious proletariat. But privately, he still read, discussed, and praised Nietzsche. [26]

Nietzsche's influence is obvious in the religion of God-building (*Bogoistroitel'stvo*), the ideology formulated around 1905 by Gorky, Lunacharsky, Bogdanov, Bazarov, and Volsky. [27] God-building aimed to make man the master of his own fate. A kind of secular religion, or religion of socialism, it preached the strength and potential of man, his ability to set himself great tasks and to achieve them. There was to be no worship of anything nonhuman, no promises about vanquishing death, suffering, or evil. A self-overcoming humanity would replace God. *Amor fati* on a mass scale would inspire people to sacrifice themselves for the sake of the future, take on Promethean projects such as transforming human nature and culture and the physical universe. The God-builders emphasized the anti-individualist side of Nietzsche, the Dionysian principle of self-transcendence. They argued that creativity was a collective process, and fo-

---

[26] Clowes, "Philosophy," p. 157.

[27] George F. Kline, *Religious and Anti-Religious Thought in Russia* (Chicago, 1968), pp. 103–26 (chap. 4, "The God-builders"). See also Raimund Sesterhenn, *Das Bogoistroitelstvo bei Gorky und Lunacharsky biz 1909*, Slavische Beitrage, vol. 158 (Berlin, 1982).

cused on the future-oriented aspects of Nietzsche's philosophy, as expressed in statements such as "I love him who wants to create beyond himself and thus perishes" (Z,90–91), "man is a bridge and not a goal" (Z,215), and "we children of the future [prefer] to live in past and future generations" and "to undertake [cultural] projects that will take thousands of years to complete."[28] A purely humanity-based religion, such as the Greeks had (they immortalized man in their gods and thus worshipped that which was human elevated to 'divine' intensity) need not necessarily be anti-individualist, but the God-builders wanted to discourage egoism and hedonism and to motivate people to forgo personal interests or desires for the sake of the revolution. God-building was an intrinsic aspect of these Marxists' plans for a new proletarian culture that would liberate the people psychologically and emotionally, not just economically. A kind of secular eschatology, God-building promised a collective immortality, for one of its purposes was to counter the inroads which God-seeking (*Bogo-iskatel'stvo*) and the religious revival were making among intellectuals. Other sources of God-building were Ludwig Feuerbach's substitution of anthropology for theology, Joseph Dietzgen's view of socialism as religion, and Georges Sorel's *Reflections on Violence*, which was translated into Russian in 1906. Indeed, Lenin's vehement opposition to God-building was based, not only on his objection to religion of any kind, but on his fear of syndicalism, which was gaining adherents in Russia.[29] Lenin, of course, prevailed. Bogdanov was expelled from the Party in 1909 for factionalism and Gorky and Lunacharsky disowned God-building. But the idea of creating a new proletarian culture surfaced in 1917 in the *prolet-kult* movement.

Nietzsche, combined with Wagner, especially Wagner's *Art and Revolution* (1849), which was translated into Russian in 1906, influenced Bolsheviks and politicized symbolists, as activists of all schools sought new means to reach the people, to transform consciousness, and create a new culture. Ivanov's views on Wagner and the theater have already been noted, Lunacharsky, a frequent visitor to Ivanov's "Tower," considered Wagner's idea of a democratic theater a model for the Bolsheviks, even though he admitted that Wagner did not fulfill his youthful ideal and later even betrayed it. Blok maintained that the theater is a powerful

---

[28] George L. Kline, "The Nietzschean Marxism of S.Volsky," in *Western Philosophical Systems*, ed. Mlikotin, p. 178.

[29] For details on syndicalism see Robert C. Williams, "Collective Immortality: The Syndicalist Origins of Proletarian Culture," *Slavic Review* 39 (September 1980), pp. 389–402.

educational force that can "educate the will."[30] Symbolist theatrical ventures, most notably the Theater of Kommissarzhevskaia, experimented with changing consciousness. In an ongoing dialogue, symbolists and Marxists agreed that the theater of the future would appeal to all classes, not just the bourgeoisie, and that it would play a key role in the new society. Lunacharsky's article "Socialism and Art," read at a 1908 symbolist symposium on the new theater, denied symbolist charges that materialism stifles creativity and insisted that only under socialism will art be free. He wanted the new theater to be a "barbarian theater . . . with all the sounds and the smells, even if they affront the sensitive noses of the cultured public."[31] Shortly afterward, however, he repudiated the article, criticized symbolist "fog" and ceased calling the people "barbarians." Ivanov, too, referred to the people as "barbarians," seeing them as the "new barbarians" destined to revitalize a decadent Russian culture.[32] In 1909 the Marxist critics published their own symposium, *The Crisis of the Theater* (*Krizis teatra*) in which they advocated a democratic "People's Theater", their concept of which, however, was also shaped in part by Nietzsche and Wagner.

As the revolutionary wave receded, Nietzsche's influence waned. Some of his former admirers turned against him. For example, Ivanov proclaimed in 1908, "Dionysus in Russia is dangerous," and condemned critical culture (the opposite of an organic or integrated culture) as the "culture of the scions of Cain."[33] From then on he coupled individualism with adjectives such as 'demonic' or 'Luciferan' and began to preach a kind of Christian existentialism. Chulkov quoted Nietzsche's statement, "man is a bridge and not a goal," denied that he had ever sanctioned orgies, erotic communes, and demonic cults, and asserted that "every truly religious act is an overcoming of individualism."[34] Moving closer to the Marxists, he argued that a new consciousness cannot develop without a change in the socioeconomic system. Merezhkovsky referred to Nietzscheanism as a "childhood sickness" that could be fatal to adults; Rozanov did the same. Berdiaev scathingly referred to "whole crowds of Nietz-

---

[30] Aleksandr Blok, *Sobranie sochinenii*, 8 vols. (Moscow and Leningrad, 1960–63), 6:273. Henceforth cited as SS.

[31] Anatoly Lunacharsky, "Sotsializm i iskusstvo," in *Teatr, Kniga o novom teatre*, ed. G. Chulkov (St. Petersburg, 1908), pp. 7–40; quote is on p. 40.

[32] Ivanov, *Po zvezdam*, pp. 233–35, 240.

[33] Ibid., pp. 360, 325.

[34] G. Chulkov, "Pokryvalo izidy," in *Sochineniia*, 5 vols. (St. Petersburg, 1912), 5:125, 127.

scheans . . . suddenly everybody wanted to be a superman."[35] The term 'Nietzscheanism' was used almost exclusively as a pejorative, a club with which to beat one's opponents, a synonym for 'nihilism,' 'immorality,' or 'lust for power.' The pejorative use of the term 'Nietzscheanism' was not in itself new. Detractors of his philosophy had always so used it. But by 1908 Nietzsche had almost no defenders and few gave him credit for the new artistic, religious, and philosophical movements his ideas had stimulated.

Why this retreat? There are two main reasons. First, of course, there was the disappointing results of the Revolution of 1905. Nietzsche's call for a new culture, for revolt, daring, heroism, fed the eschatological expectations (both religious and secular) that had been growing among Russian society since 1900. But the revolution had come and gone and no new order was in sight. Neither Marxists nor symbolists considered the institution of the Duma a victory; quite the contrary, it was the epitome of the bourgeois society they despised. Exhausted and in despair, Nietzsche's former admirers succumbed to pessimism, as distinct from a tragic sense of life. Heroism lost its appeal; Prometheanism seemed hollow.

Secondly, there was the state of Russian society after the revolution. Relaxation of the censorship laws had unleashed a flood of pornography, which was blamed on Nietzsche. Characters in popular novels had traits that were rightly or wrongly associated with Nietzsche—promiscuity, hedonism, cruelty, contempt for the weak—which were defended with simplified or distorted renditions of Nietzsche's ideas. Sanin, for example, the hero of M. Artsybashev's (1878–1927) notorious novel *Sanin* (1907), is a blond beast to whom all is permitted; he preaches sexual license, exploits the weak, and, although he has read *Zarathustra*, he scorns philosophy. "Let him who likes worry about it; as for me, I intend to live." Manya, another example of a 'Nietzschean' character, is the heroine of Anastasia Verbitskaia's (1861–1928) best-selling series, *The Keys to Happiness* (*Kliuchi schastiia*, 5 volumes, 1910–1913). A kind of superwoman, Manya has been introduced to Nietzscheanism, the "keys to happiness," by her first lover and she follows his advice to "obey your desires" for the next five volumes, until, her desires sated at last, she commits suicide. Quotes from Nietzsche serve as epigraphs for the first two volumes.[36] Nietzsche was blamed for the unabashed hedonism of the young, for their amoral pursuit of self-interest in the narrowest sense of

[35] Nikolai Berdiaev, *Dukhovnyi krizis intelligentsii* (St. Petersburg, 1910), p. 77.
[36] Lane, "Nietzsche in Russian Thought," pp. 70–71.

the term. This was of particular concern to the left, for its ranks were thinning as young people defected from the cause, taking advantage of the new employment opportunities of industrialization. Suicide cults too were traced to Nietzsche, because of his concept of a free death. In short, instead of a 'revaluation of all values' on a high theoretical plane, and instead of the creation of an exalted new culture, Russians were witnessing the vulgarization of Nietzsche, the work of the 'terrible simplifiers' of whom his friend Jacob Burckhardt, in a different context, had warned. Smerdiakov, a character in Dostoevsky's novel *The Brothers Karamazov*, takes his brother Ivan's dictum, "If there is no God, everything is permitted," literally and kills his father. Nietzsche, of course, had said, "nothing is true, everything is permitted" (Z,285). Despite noble intentions, Nietzsche's philosophy, or so it seemed at the time, had served to sanction immorality, selfishness, nihilism, rampant violence, destruction for destruction's sake. As his former admirers came to recognize the difficulty of explaining Nietzsche's complex, nuanced, and often contradictory thought to ordinary people without vulgarizing or distorting it, they began to seek new, more applicable, more easily simplified dogmas, and to battle nihilism and 'decadence,' defining the latter, incidentally, in Nietzschean terms, as a falling away from the whole, an "anarchy of atoms," an absence of coherence, or cohesion (CW,170).

Elements of Nietzsche's philosophy still exerted influence, but in less obvious ways and subsumed into other frameworks. Ivanov still sought to reintegrate Russian society, still dreamed of a new culture, but now saw a Russian Idea as the integrating force and specified that this was a Christian idea. Berdiaev and Bulgakov returned to the Orthodox Church and attempted to define a new, explicitly Christian morality. Struve advocated transcending social and political conflict by creating a Great Russia with expanded borders. Blok, obsessed by Nietzsche's concept of culture as the spirit of music, associated culture with the Dionysian principle, the elemental folk, which he compared to a volcanic eruption breaking through the "encrusted lava" of bourgeois civilization. Blok considered bourgeois society Apollonian, the "dream of an ant" rebuilding its shattered anthill, but unable to control the forces that shattered it.[37] He predicted the triumph of Dionysus, the end of the intelligentsia.

After 1909 new artistic isms developed, all of which were indebted to Nietzsche in one way or another. The journal *Apollon* was founded, in

[37] Aleksandr Blok, "Stikhiia i kul'tura" (1908), SS, 5:353–54.

1909, by writers who objected to the recent emphasis on Dionysus; the acmeist writers who published in it—Osip Mandel'stam, Nicholas Gumilev, and Anna Akhmatova—emphasized form rather than flux, clarity rather than mystification, the concrete rather than the elusive: in other words, the Apollonian principle of form, clarity, and discreteness. Futurists (a group that wished to discard the past and create a new art consonant with the spirit of the machine age) and their successors hailed the artist as superman and championed iconoclasm, 'creative destruction,' and contempt for the bourgeoisie, epitomized in the title of their manifesto "A Slap in the Face of Public Taste" ("Poshchechina obshchestvennomy vkusu," 1912). Vehemently anti-intellectual, they sought to develop a transrational, or metalogical language (*zaum*) (literally beyond the mind, thus from the word to direct knowledge) and glorified violence, struggle, even war. Rebelling against symbolism, both acmeists and futurists were familiar with its ideology and definitely aware of the major tenets of Nietzsche's thought, even though they tended not to mention him by name. But by then his ideas were so much in the air that it was scarcely necessary.

Until around 1908, Wagner's reception paralleled Nietzsche's, but at that point they began to diverge. In contrast to widespread renunciation of Nietzsche, Wagner was admired by radicals and conservatives alike. Radicals appreciated his revolutionary activities in 1848–1849, especially his having fought alongside Bakunin on the barricades at Dresden. They interpreted the *Ring* as a revolutionary drama, the *Götterdämmerung* of bourgeois society. The loss of self celebrated in his operas was more compatible with the search for community (left or right), more easily assimilated to either socialist or Christian visions of a new society than was Nietzsche's individualism and iconoclasm. Socialists in Vienna, too, used Wagner's theatrical insights for political propaganda, deliberately couching socialist content in religious form.[38] Christians, moreover, considered Wagner's apotheosis of chastity and virginity highly moral. *Parsifal* was routinely called a mystery play; the prominent churchly aspects to which Nietzsche had objected were the very aspects that appealed to Russians. Its first Russian production was in 1913, the year the copyright that restricted it to Bayreuth expired, but many Russians had already seen it abroad or knew about it. By 1913 Wagner's operas so dominated the repertory of the Imperial Theaters that certain Russian nationalists de-

[38] McGrath, *Dionysian Art*, pp. 231–32.

manded an explanation. Performances were attended by high officials of the Imperial bureacracy, including Tsar Nicholas himself. Alexandra, his wife, was an ardent Wagnerophile. The Great War, however, resulted in the removal of Wagner's operas from the repertory. The war led to a suspicion of all things German, and Nietzsche was considered the ideologist of German militarism.

The influence of Nietzsche (and Wagner) revived around 1916, paralleling and reinforcing the revival of revolutionary sentiment and eschatological expectations. Bely perceived the Bolshevik Revolution as the first stage of a far greater cultural and spiritual revolution yet to come and expected the birth of a new artistic culture and a new man, a kind of worker-artist who combined Nietzschean and Christian ideals. Extolling Nietzsche and Wagner, rather than Marx and Engels, as the true revolutionaries, he condemned materialism as bourgeois. Using the Nietzschean concepts of Apollonian form and Dionysian flux to describe the revolution, Bely interpreted the current destructive stage as the breakdown of old forms, but fully expected new forms to develop. He frequently invoked the 'spirit of music' to communicate his vision of liberation. To him, music was the mathematics of the soul, a harmonious combination of Apollo and Dionysus, of structure and process.[39] Blok, too, associated the revolution with the 'spirit of music,' the old world crashing down, the birth of a new culture, a different combination of Nietzsche and Christ. Hailing the "Collapse of Humanism,"[40] the end of the rational individualistic civilization that had dominated the West since the Renaissance, he looked forward to a world of perpetual flux, a permanent revolution of the spirit, and the birth of a new man—an artist—who can live without structure, though Blok did not explain how. Blok distinguished between "calendar time" and "musical time," equating the latter with the "eternal rhythms of life," by which he meant Dionysian or cyclical time, as distinct from the linear goal-directed bourgeois civilization.[41] To him "musical time" also suggested the end of history, the timelessness prophesied in the Apocalypse.

In contrast, Gorky was dismayed at the end of humanism, the wanton destruction of culture. In a series of articles published in 1917 and 1918

[39] Andrei Bely, *Revoliutsiia i kul'tura* (1917; reprint, Letchworth, Herts., 1971). English translation by Marian Schwartz is in *A Revolution of the Spirit*, ed. Rosenthal and Chomiak.

[40] Aleksandr Blok, "Krushenie gumanizma" (1919), SS, 6:93–115, esp. pp. 113–115.

[41] Ibid., 7:360 (Diary entry 31 March 1919); 6:101–102.

in his newspaper *New Life* (*Novaia zhizn'*), in a column titled "Untimely Thoughts" ("Nesvoevremennye mysli"), and published in book form as *Untimely Thoughts* in 1918 after the Bolsheviks suppressed his newspaper, Gorky attacked Bolshevik encouragement of the anarchistic instincts of the masses. The title itself alludes to Nietzsche's work *Unzeitgemässe Betrachtungen* (1873–1876) and Nietzschean influence is suggested by Gorky's contempt for the rabble and his insistence on the importance of culture. Critical of both Bolsheviks and Cadets, Gorky urged the intelligentsia to cast aside its differences and unite in the common cause of enlightening the masses.[42] Bogdanov, Lunacharsky, and other Marxists influenced by Nietzsche, hoping to develop a distinctly proletarian culture, formed *proletkult* after the February Revolution.

Nietzsche's influence was not directly political, but it was a major factor in creating the cultural climate in which political action takes place. Would there have been a Russian Revolution without Nietzsche? Undoubtedly yes, for the conditions that led to the revolution were not of his making. But would it have had the same intensity, the same eschatological fervor, the same bold visions? Perhaps not, for Nietzsche's ideas eroded the very foundations of the old order, accelerated and justified the repudiation of old values and beliefs, thereby undermining existing institutions especially the Church and, by extension, the political and social order it sanctioned. Nietzsche provided powerful psychological motivation and philosophical ammunition to those, including political revolutionaries, who desired total change and who were convinced that it was imminent. Converging with and reinforcing the activist voluntarist element in Marxism, its faith in man's ability to shape his own world, Nietzsche's challenge to the status quo was radical in the most basic sense of the word, for it went beyond political and economic change to demand psychological, spiritual, and cultural transformation—the creation of a new man.

Elements of Nietzsche's thought compatible with the Promethean thrust of Bolshevism were absorbed into early Soviet culture, influencing concepts of proletarian culture, ideologies of leadership of the masses, and experiments in theater and cinema. Nietzsche's attack on Christianity reinforced the traditional atheism of the Russian intelligentsia and fed into the antireligious campaigns of the early 1920s. Gorky's "Song of the

---

[42] Maxim Gorky, *Untimely Thoughts*, trans. Herman Ermolaev (New York, 1968).

Falcon" and "Man" were frequently read at Party rallies. Red Army soldiers carried into battle banners with the slogan, from Gorky ("Song of the Falcon"), "To the madness of the brave we sing our song" (*Bezumstvu khrabykh poem my pesniu*).[43] *Proletkult* attracted thousands of members. It remained a separate entity until 1919, when Lenin, fearing it as a threat to Party unity, subordinated it to the Commissariat of Enlightenment, headed by Lunacharsky, and accused its leaders (especially Bogdanov) of separatism, factionalism, and nihilism. TEO, the theatrical section of the Commissariat of Enlightenment, was the prime locus of Nietzsche's (and Wagner's) influence. TEO included symbolists, futurists, and proletkultists, influenced in various ways by the ideal of a theater temple. Ivanov was an active member of TEO; his theories of collective creativity, audience participation, and myth-creation were broadly accepted and adapted to Soviet experiments in political theater, which he deplored. Vsevolod Meierhold, the celebrated Soviet theater director, was familiar with Nietzsche and Wagner through his association with symbolists such as A. Remizov in the 1890s (Remizov translated *Thus Spoke Zarathustra* into Russian around 1895, but it was not accepted for publication) and with Ivanov and the Theater of Kommissarzhevskaia after the 1905 Revolution. In 1909 he produced a stylized and controversial *Tristan und Isolde* at the Mariinsky Theater. Always something of an iconoclast, after the October Revolution Meierhold rejected opera and ballet as obsolete forms and advocated a theatrical October (revolution in the theater). His Soviet productions featured circus clowns, radio bulletins, newspaper clippings, gymnasts, and bourgeois villains wearing grotesque masks, in an updated and politicized version of the *Gesamtkunstwerk*. Futurists and proletkultists alike cooperated on theatrical festivals modeled on the national festivals of the French Revolution. Commemorating important events such as the "Storming of the Winter Palace," they were, in their own way, a kind of myth-creation and featured a 'cast' of thousands. Taking the Nietzsche/Wagner/Ivanov model a step further to the left, the *proletkult* theorist Paul Kerzhentsev (1881–1940) advocated a theater staffed by proletarians, rather than professional actors or directors. Such a theater, based on neighborhood communes, would become an intrinsic part of the life of the workers. Ordinary workers would write the script, design and build the sets, and serve as performers. He

[43] Clowes, "Philosophy," p. 163.

believed that the experience of creating, planning, and directing the entire production would foster a new collective consciousness: activist, self-confident, freed from the thrall of the past.

In the first years of the Bolshevik Revolution, culture was relatively unfettered. Preoccupied with economic collapse and Civil War, the Bolsheviks deferred formulation of a cultural policy and worked with intellectuals who were willing to work with them. Although certain intellectuals were harassed, and Gumilev, the acmeist poet, was executed for treason in 1921, those not deemed counterrevolutionary were tolerated for the most part. Moreover, most Bolsheviks, including Lenin, respected culture and regarded the great works of the past as the rightful legacy of the proletariat. But spokesmen for various artistic isms often claimed that theirs was the sole authentic voice of the revolution, pronounced anathema upon the others, and turned to the Party to enforce their claim. Cultural issues thus became political issues.

The politicization of culture was intensified by the struggle for succession triggered by Lenin's poor health from mid-1921 on and by his two strokes in May and December 1922. At first the Party skirted issues of culture, confining itself to vague resolutions that directed writers and artists to depict revolutionary themes and proletarian (or peasant) characters. But the issue could not be avoided indefinitely. Signs of tightening Party control began to appear around 1923–1924. "Bourgeois intellectuals" such as Ivanov, Frank, Berdiaev, and Bulgakov emigrated or were forcibly expelled, thereby removing carriers of Nietzsche's ideas from the scene. Others, such as Merezhkovsky, had emigrated earlier. Nietzsche's works were removed from libraries in factories and trade union halls and even from some university libraries and placed on closed reserve (*zakryti fond*) in the major research libraries, along with other works deemed counterrevolutionary. *Proletkult* was transferred from the Commissariat of Enlightenment to the trade unions in 1925. Formalism, a school of literary criticism and theory that had emerged during the Great War, which rejected metaphysical and sociological approaches to literature and stressed techniques and devices, came under attack. Its adherents were partially indebted to Nietzsche. Michael Bakhtin was just about the last figure to discuss Nietzsche openly.

Still, from time to time, traces of Nietzsche's influence surfaced. An outstanding example is Trotsky's prediction of a Communist superman in *Literature and Revolution* (1924).

Man will make it his purpose to master his own feelings, to raise his instincts to the heights of consciousness, to make them transparent, to extend the wires of his will into hidden recesses, and thereby to raise himself to a new plane, to create a higher social biologic type, or, if you please, a superman. . . .

[Man will develop] all the vital elements of contemporary art to the highest point. Man will become immeasurably stronger, wiser, and subtler; his body will become more harmonized, his movements more rhythmic, his voice more musical. The forms of life will become especially dynamic. The average human type will rise to the heights of an Aristotle, a Goethe, or a Marx. And above this ridge, new peaks will rise.[44]

With Stalin's victory, the process of cultural consolidation intensified and accelerated. Formalism was suppressed in 1930, despite some of its adherents' attempts to compromise with the demands of Marxist literary criticism. *Proletkult* was abolished in 1932. Socialist realism became the prescribed norm for all the arts. Of the former God-builders, Volsky and Bazarov had ceased to be Bolsheviks. Volsky had written an extremely anti-Bolshevik book describing the terror and the famine of 1917–1919 (*Dans le voyaume de la famine et de la haine: La Russie bolchéviste*, Paris, 1920), for this he was arrested, but then, surprisingly, released on condition he cease writing about current events. He died in the mid-1930s in Stalin's Gulag. Bazarov had become a Menshevik in 1917; he was arrested in 1930 and died in a camp in 1939. Bogdanov, as already indicated, was expelled from the Party in 1909. In the 1920s he devoted himself to scientific and organization theory and died, in 1928, as the result of an unsuccessful experiment in blood transfusion performed upon himself.

Lunacharsky was removed as commissar of enlightenment in 1929 and transferred to the Foreign Service. Both he and Gorky (who had left Russia in 1921, but returned to stay in 1931) were under pressure to conform to the new order. This involved attacks on Nietzsche, still, apparently, deemed threatening. In 1930, Lunacharsky referred to Nietzsche's psychopathology and explained that the mentally ill express, more profoundly than the healthy, the illness of a given social environment. In 1933 he termed Nietzsche an ideologist of fascism and imperialism. Still,

[44]L. Trotsky, *Literature and Revolution* (Ann Arbor, 1960), pp. 255–56.

he never lost his admiration for Nietzsche's vitalism. As late as 1933, shortly before his death, he protested the omission of *Zarathustra* from a planned series of translations of foreign works. Gorky was writing against Nietzsche even before his return to the Soviet Union. In a 1928 article "On Little People and Their Great Work" he reversed himself, repudiating his admiration for the strong and celebrated the incremental accomplishments of ordinary people.[45] In 1930 he denied that he had ever followed the "social philosophy" of Nietzsche, which he now interpreted as the fascist idea of master and slave, and espoused a third way, "support the man who rebels."[46] His novel *Klim Samgin* (1925–1936) contains over twenty references to Nietzsche, all of them negative. In general, Gorky assigned 'good' Nietzschean traits to his heroes—strength of will, heroism, rebelliousness, self-overcoming, defiance of society and convention—and 'bad' Nietzschean traits to his villains—cruelty, ruthlessness, hedonism, exploitativeness. In effect, he divided humanity into heroic (master) and unheroic (slave). He sincerely admired Lenin as a strong man, a man of will, determined to transform Russia. He idealized Soviet man as "more uncompromising and rebellious than all the Don Quixotes and Fausts in history" and lauded Promethean projects to transform nature such as the Baltic–White Sea Canal, going so far as to eulogize slave labor as a "socialist experience." The laborers on the canal, he said, felt themselves "the possessors of the immeasureable forces and treasures of the whole earth. To feel this way means to grow taller and bigger than all the heroes of all nations and ages." His slogan, "if the enemy does not surrender, he is to be destroyed," was used to justify the purges.[47] Such statements suggest Gorky's abiding attraction to Nietzsche's injunction to hardness, his division of humanity into master and slave—the very features Gorky condemned in fascism. There are some indications, however, that he did protest against some of Stalin's actions, for his last years were spent under virtual house arrest. He died (or was murdered) on 18 June, 1936.

Stalin rarely, if ever, mentioned Nietzsche, indeed may never have read him, but there are indications that ideas and attitudes associated with or derived from Nietzsche impressed him, as if by osmosis. Does not his famous description of the writer as "engineer of the human soul" testify, in a backhanded sort of way, to Nietzsche's emphasis, as mediated

[45] Katerina Clark, *The Soviet Novel: History as Ritual* (Chicago, 1981), p. 154.
[46] Lane, "Nietzsche in Russian Thought," p. 577.
[47] Ermolaev, in *Untimely Thoughts* by Gorky, p. xv.

by his various Russian interpreters, especially the God-builders, on the importance of art. Theirs was one of the influences that led Stalin to create the Lenin cult as a kind of socialist religion. Is it not possible then, that the influence of God-builders and proletkultists (whose ideas were advanced during the debates on cultural policy in the 1920s, which Stalin, as a contender for power, followed) extended beyond his decision to create the Lenin Cult? Could not Stalin have appropriated and distorted their views on culture, as he did Preobrazhensky's and Trotsky's on economics? The timing of the cultural revolution of 1928–1931 to coincide with collectivization and full-speed industrialization suggests his acceptance of the *proletkult* tenet that economic transformation alone will not create, automatically, the new consciousness Bolsheviks desired.

The extreme voluntarism of the First Five Year Plan may also derive, partly, from Nietzsche. Just as Lenin refused to defer to the laws of history, which would have delayed the proletarian revolution indefinitely, Stalin dismissed as "bourgeois" the economists and statisticians who noted realistic impediments to the plan's fulfillment such as inadequate transportation, shortages of materials and personnel, and potential bottlenecks. Refusing to modify his goals, Stalin proclaimed, "there are no fortresses Bolsheviks cannot storm." Nietzsche's warrior ideal may have been one of the factors (another was the Civil War model) that led Stalin to conduct the First Five Year Plan as if it were a military campaign.

Katerina Clark maintains that God-building was the "subtext of high Stalinist culture," for the "iconic attribute of all official heroes was 'daring' . . . [especially daring to defy tradition] a central concept in Nietzsche" and shows that one of the most popular slogans of the 1930s, "ever onwards, ever upwards" derives from Gorky's "Man." Noting that the allusions to "*re*making and *re*doing" so prominent in the imagery of the period may also derive, partly, from Nietzsche, she also perceives a "heavy dose of Nietzscheanism in that decade's political culture. Even the purges could be regarded as an exercise in Nietzschean praxis."[48] Whether she is alluding to Stalin's ruthlessness, his 'will to power' or his desire to create a new Soviet man is unclear.

Stalinist-style Prometheanism revived after the war, in various grandiose schemes to change the Russian terrain and climate (Fedorov was an influence here as well). Nietzsche, however, was more *persona non grata* than ever, because of the Nazi misappropriation of his ideas. During the

[48] Clark, *Soviet Novel*, pp. 152–53.

war itself, incidentally, Soviet aces who shot down many Nazi planes were rewarded with the title "Stalin's Falcons," an allusion to Gorky's Nietzsche-inspired story.

A DISTINCTIVELY RUSSIAN NIETZSCHE

To compare Nietzsche's impact on Russia with his impact on other nations would require a separate study, which is not yet possible, for much of the groundwork, in fields other than literature, has yet to be done.[49] Still, some brief remarks are perhaps in order. Russia was typical in that, as in the rest of Europe (and also in the United States), Nietzsche's first admirers were writers and artists rather than professional philosophers. Everywhere his appeal was greatest to rebels, whether avant-garde artists or political radicals. The English socialists H. G. Wells and George Bernard Shaw, the Irish visionary and poet William Butler Yeats, the Austrian socialist Victor Adler and the Austrian composer Gustav Mahler, represent only a few of many possible examples. As in Russia, Western Europeans and Americans perceived Nietzsche through the prism of their respective national cultures, finding precedents for him in their own legacies. In England, for example, Nietzsche was frequently compared to William Blake.[50] National variations affected which elements of Nietzsche's thought were emphasized, ignored, or consciously rejected. Thus the distinct variations in the Russian and Western receptions of Nietzsche.

In Russia, Nietzsche was perceived as a mystic and a prophet. His thought was a major stimulus to the religious renaissance. Russian intellectuals discovered him at a time, the 1890s, when they were seeking a new vision of man and of the world. The obsolescence of Populism (due to industrialization) left a spiritual vacuum that secular liberalism and one-dimensional positivism could not fill. Nietzsche spoke to the 'eternal questions' that had long occupied the Russian intelligentsia. He appealed to people who were disoriented and confused but also liberated and en-

---

[49]For Nietzsche in other European nations see David S. Thatcher, *Nietzsche in England: The Growth of a Reputation, 1890–1914* (Toronto, 1970); Patrick Bridgewater, *Nietzsche in Anglosaxony* (Leicester, 1972); Geneviève Bianquis, *Nietzsche en France* (Paris, 1929); Bruno Hillebrand, *Nietzsche und die deutsche Literatur*, 2 vols. (Munich, 1978); R. Hinton Thomas, *Nietzsche in German Politics and Society* (Manchester, 1983); Herbert W. Reichert, *Friedrich Nietzsche's Impact on Modern German Literature* (Chapel Hill, N.C., 1975); Gonzalo Sobejano, *Nietzsche en España* (Madrid, 1967); Manuela Angela Stefani, *Nietzsche en Italia; rassegna bibliografica, 1893–1970* (Rome, 1975).

[50]Thatcher, *Nietzsche in England*, pp. 130–31, 139–41, 157, 234, 244, 255.

ergized by the accelerating forces of change, people seeking, consciously or unconsciously, a new faith by which to live. His philosophy provided the rationale, so essential to the intelligentsia mentality, for hitherto forbidden personal development and enjoyment of life. It opened a new channel for both destructive and creative energies—smashing the old tables of values and then writing new ones—the foundation stones of a new culture.

Unlike the Catholic Church in France, the Russian Orthodox Church did not offer a haven to disillusioned intellectuals seeking the comfort of faith. Linked to an autocratic state, the Russian Church had neither the freedom nor the intellectual tradition to tackle the religious, moral, and ethical problems of the new era. This task was taken on by laymen: Dostoevsky, Soloviev, Tolstoi, and the philosophers of the religious renaissance. It was the philosophers who directly confronted Nietzsche's challenge to Christianity and attempted to develop a new Christian culture. Apocalyptic elements in Nietzsche merged in their minds with the eschatological premonitions of Dostoevsky and Soloviev and were confirmed by rising revolutionary turbulence, social disintegration, and cultural crisis.

Activists of all schools believed that in the imminent new order, their particular sociocultural ideal would be the one to take root and flourish. Nietzsche's idea of deliberate cultural creation took root in Russia, as nowhere else in Europe, not even Vienna. There is simply no Western counterpart to the eschatological intensity of Russian visions of a new culture. The Revolution of 1905, endowed by many Russians with apocalyptic significance, religious or secular, made these visions even more compelling. Symbolists, intent on overcoming individualism and class conflict, stressed art, love, and sacrifice as the key elements in the new communal consciousness they desired. By contrast, Marxists wished to heighten class conflict and to create a specifically proletarian sense of solidarity. Both camps recognized the importance of appealing to the unconscious and used symbol, myth, and religious imagery to forge the subliminal bonds their particular sociocultural ideal required. The concept of deliberate cultural creation came to the fore again during the Bolshevik Revolution and retained a powerful appeal all during the 1920s. Defining the nature of proletarian culture and determining the best means to develop it were persistent issues in Party debates until Stalin curtailed discussion and resolved the issue by instituting his own version of proletarian culture—socialist realism.

Russians were among the first to recognize the cultic and collectivist aspects of Nietzsche. Their own cultural heritage predisposed them to reach beyond individualism to some greater whole. Vestiges of the self-denying intelligentsia ethos, which was in turn a reflection of the Ortho-dox emphasis on humility and self-sacrifice, made them uncomfortable with a philosophy of pure hedonism and selfishness. Belongingness was so central a value in Russian culture (there is no word for privacy in Russian) that even the individualistic symbolists yearned to be part of a spiritual community. In the 1890s, when the interpretation of Nietzsche as a philosopher of individualism was strongest in Russia, his admirers realized the twofold nature of the Dionysian principle—liberation of the instincts and transcendence of self. They saw self-fulfillment as the cre-ation of great works or art or the performance of great deeds—activities that would ultimately benefit the people. The Dionysian principle en-abled intellectuals to argue that personal development was the precondi-tion for cultural renewal. Positing the existence of a primeval sense of oneness, they considered the modern sense of separateness artificial and harmful, and maintained that eliminating repression would release hith-erto suppressed wellsprings of creativity and love. In cultic unity, conflicts within man and between men would be reconciled, the lost wholeness restored. To some Russians, the Dionysian principle combined self-affir-mation and self-sacrifice, leadership and martyrdom; they saw the intel-ligentsia or the rebellious proletariat as the tragic hero. For Gorky and Mikhailovsky, the related concept of *amor fati* had a particular appeal. Indeed, as Gorky used the term it was a kind of *podvig*, a great deed with connotations of martyrdom.

The Revolution of 1905 inspired an explicitly sociopolitical interpre-tation of the Dionysian principle. Symbolists emphasized loss of self in communal ecstasy as the means to demolish artificial social barriers and foster the new sense of voluntary unity essential to a free society. Nietz-schean Marxists wanted to promote proletarian unity and militancy by means of ritual, theater, and myth. Claiming that bourgeois society re-presses individuality, they argued that socialism would make self-devel-opment possible for all. Adaptations of the Dionysian theater, stressing audience participation, appeals to the unconscious, and the creation of new ritual and new myth, were attempted by activists who wished to reach the people and create a new consciousness. The mass festivals, pageants, and people's theaters of the early Soviet period reflect the con-tinued influence of Dionysian models of cultural creation, as, in different ways, did the mass meetings and civic rituals of mature Soviet society.

There were other differences in the Russian and Western reception of Nietzsche as well. Conspicuously absent in Russia was Nietzsche's misogyny. Equality of women had been a key tenet of the Russian intelligentsia ethos since the 1860s. Soloviev, Idealist and symbolist dissenters from intelligentsia positivism, materialism, and atheism were even more radical than the left on the woman question for they moved beyond social and economic equality to a consideration of the tyranny of gender and asserted the existence of a female principle of creation or of feminine elements in the Godhead. Zinaida Gippius wrote in both masculine and feminine cases and signed her critical articles with a male pseudonym, Anton Krainyi (Anton the Extreme) or Comrade Herman. Some symbolists regarded the androgyne as the perfect human being. They and neo-Idealists (later neo-Christians) such as Bulgakov apotheosized the Divine Sophia, the Wisdom of God; some symbolists, however, metamorphosized Sophia into the apocalyptic image of the Woman Clothed in the Sun. Merezhkovsky accused Christians of hating women and was dismayed by Tolstoi's belief that a woman cannot be a friend. Russian avant-garde painters and writers included a surprisingly large number of women, whose male colleagues never questioned their creative ability. Nietzsche's contempt for women (or at least for the women of his time) was simply alien to the intelligentsia tradition. Gorky and the futurists, however, may be exceptions, for a corollary to their apotheosis of the 'masculine' qualities of daring and strength was a contempt for 'feminine' weakness. Another possible exception is Fedorov, who referred almost exclusively to the fathers, rather than to the mothers, or even to the parents, in his cosmic project of resurrecting humanity.

There was no counterpart in Russia to the racist or eugenic interpretation of Nietzsche so prominent elsewhere in Europe.[51] This was based on a literal interpretation of Nietzsche's concept of breeding the superman, fortified by Darwin or Social Darwinism, and by the ideas of various local racists. Russian symbolists and idealists, however, were hostile to Darwin per se, believing, as Nietzsche did, that Darwin demeaned man. Championing the ideal of *sobornost'*, they objected to the very idea of a struggle for survival. The Russian left reacted similarly. The anarchist Peter Kropotkin (1842–1921) wrote *Mutual Aid: A Factor in Evo-*

---

[51] In literature intended for a mass audience, however, such as Boborykin's or Verbitskaia's prose, Nietzsche was sometimes interpreted as an anti-Semite, but this is not the same as the emphasis on breeding in the eugenic sense, nor is it the same as the Western European sense of supremacy of the white race over the peoples of Asia and Africa.

lution (published as a series of articles in the 1890s and as a book in 1902) to prove that cooperation is necessary for survival. He condemned competition as a characteristically English idea. Marxists believed that equality would be achieved through social revolution, not genetic manipulation. Trotsky's allusion to a "higher social biologic type" and Bogdanov's experiments with blood transfusion, however, may constitute notable exceptions. Bogdanov, also influenced by Fedorov's ideas on the conquest of nature and on universal resurrection of the dead by scientific means, may have hoped to create, quite literally, in the laboratory, an immortal superman.

So far as can be determined, the traditional Russian right was not influenced by Nietzsche, for they found the subversive implications of the 'revaluation of values' too threatening. Many Russians regarded the 'will to power' as a German principle and rejected it as such, preferring to think of Russians as embodying the Christian principles of love, humility, and self-sacrifice. Many political radicals were motivated by the 'will to power' but would not admit it. Indeed, Lenin and Stalin testify to the accuracy of Nietzsche's prediction of a new psychological type, motivated by power rather than economic gain and intent on remolding humanity in his own image. On the other hand, as already noted, radicals such as the populist Mikhailovsky and the Marxist Gorky, especially Gorky, found Nietzsche's concepts of *amor fati*, self-overcoming, and self-perfection extremely appealing, appropriating them for a vitalized and joyous interpretation of the positive hero. Symbolists, generally speaking, found the concept of sublimation less appealing, for they emphasized liberation of the instincts. Merezhkovsky did mention "power over oneself" approvingly in *Julian the Apostate*, but did not dwell on it.

There is one other difference. Nietzsche's impact in Russia was concentrated in the years 1890–1910. After that, though his ideas persisted, his popularizers repudiated him and in the Soviet period he was proscribed altogether. In Western Europe, by contrast, his works remained readily available even though they fluctuated in public acceptance. Secondary and tertiary layers of his influence developed as great writers such as André Malraux, André Gide, Thomas Mann, and D. H. Lawrence popularized their interpretations of his ideas[52] and as noted philosophers such as Martin Heidegger, Karl Jaspers, Jean-Paul Sartre, Albert Camus, and, recently, Jacques Derrida, acknowledged Nietzsche's impact on their

[52] For details see John Burt Foster, *Heirs to Dionysos* (Princeton, 1981).

own thought. There is no counterpart to this continuity in Russia. It is possible, however, that Soviet writers now living in the West may formulate a new and uniquely Russian reinterpretation of Nietzsche.

THE PLAN OF THE BOOK

The subject of Nietzsche's influence in Russia is so vast, touches on so many disciplines, and requires so much specialized expertise, that a single scholar, working alone, could not hope to do it justice. The chapters that follow reflect the different perspectives of intellectual history, literature, philosophy, art history, and political science. Their focus varies. Some chapters trace the influence of Nietzsche's thought on the entire course of a writer's (or artist's) career; others treat intensively one period or one aspect of Nietzsche's effect on a writer's work. This volume is intended to serve as a starting point for studies of Nietzsche's influence in Russia, not as the last word.

The book is divided into four parts, corresponding to the major areas of Nietzsche's impact on Russia. Part I treats his influence on Russian religious thought. Ann Lane discusses early Russian reactions, including Soloviev's, to Nietzsche's challenge to traditional Christian morality. Bernice Glatzer Rosenthal follows Merezhkovsky's shifting view of Nietzsche, from enthusiastic acceptance, to an attempt to merge Nietzscheanism and Christianity, to condemnation and denial. Anna Lisa Crone explores the possible Nietzschean roots of Rozanov's critique of Christianity. Taras Zakydalsky explains Fedorov's condemnation of Nietzsche as a mere esthete. Mihajlo Mihajlov, playing the devil's advocate, minimizes Nietzsche as a creative influence on Berdiaev, Frank, and Shestov, arguing that his importance was limited to that of a catalyzer.

Part II treats Nietzsche's influence on the literature, painting, and music of the Russian symbolists and their circle. Evelyn Bristol describes Blok's vacillation between Soloviev's Divine Sophia and Nietzsche's Dionysian principle, between the ethereal and the elemental, a common phenomenon, incidentally, among the symbolists. Virginia Bennett analyzes Bely's integration of *The Birth of Tragedy* into his own esthetics. George Kalbouss finds echoes of Nietzsche in Sologub's emphasis on myth, his concept of the Dionysian, his critique of Christianity and bourgeois morality, and his own search for a new man, a kind of poet-priest. Ann Lane describes the reverberations of Nietzsche's idea of the artist as a superman in the work of the poet Bal'mont and the composer Skriabin.

Aline Isdebsky-Pritchard discusses Vrubel's receptivity to Nietzsche and limns Nietzsche's effect on Vrubel's painting and thought.

Part III treats Nietzsche's influence on Russian Marxism. Mary Louise Loe analyzes Nietzsche's appeal to the young Gorky, distinguishing Gorky's image of the ideal man from both Nietzsche's and the Russian Populists. A. L. Tait traces Lunacharsky's intellectual debt to Nietzsche as it evolved from youthful enthusiasm to later public condemnation, highlighting the Nietzschean ideas and ideals that were reflected in Lunacharsky's essays, dramas, and in his cultural policy as commissar of enlightenment. Zenovia Sochor explores the Nietzschean underpinnings of Bogdanov's theories on the cultural liberation of the proletariat, including Bogdanov's emphasis on values or norms.

Part IV treats other aspects of Nietzsche's influence. Edith Clowes outlines the vulgarization of Nietzsche's thought in popular literature, as exemplified by Andreev's spiritually lost rebels and Artsybashev's sexual hedonists. James Curtis examines the Nietzschean features of Bakhtin's literary criticism, and explains how Bakhtin's view of Nietzsche was affected by his contemporaries, especially his mentor, the classicist Tadeusz Zieliński, a rare academic admirer of Nietzsche. Richard Davies has compiled a chronological list of works about Nietzsche and by Nietzsche (in Russian translation) published in Russia between 1892 and 1919, which will prove to be an indispensable bibliographic tool for scholars. Finally, having discussed Nietzsche's impact on Russia and Russians, it was deemed suitable to explore Nietzsche's view of Russia and Russians; hence the afterword by Susan Ray.

A cautionary note: Because of the protean nature of Nietzsche's thought and the wide-ranging interests of the Russians treated, the four parts of this volume should not be thought of as hard-and-fast divisions. Merezhkovsky, for example, was both a religious thinker and a major symbolist writer, while the symbolist writers Bely and Blok were interested in religious questions, as were some Nietzschean Marxists, especially Lunacharsky.

FURTHER DIRECTIONS FOR STUDY

It is hoped that this volume will inspire and provide the groundwork for continued scholarship, because much remains to be done. Following are some suggestions for investigation.

A detailed study of Russian translations of Nietzsche's work, including the circumstances under which each translation was undertaken and actually published, and problems with the censorship, would shed important light on Nietzsche's reception and fate in Russia, especially if it compared variants of the same texts, including distortions and omissions, deliberate or not.

Still outstanding is an intensive analysis of Soloviev's critique of Nietzsche, which is important both because of Nietzsche's challenge to Soloviev and because of Soloviev's influence on the Silver Age. Another important subject requiring investigation is Lev Shestov, one of the most important interpreters of Nietzsche. James Curtis has already written on Shestov's use of Nietzsche;[53] Ann Lane devotes a chapter to Shestov in her dissertation, and Spencer Roberts and Bernard Martin have translated his essays on Tolstoi and Dostoevsky,[54] but an English-language study of Nietzsche's influence on Shestov's overall intellectual development is desperately needed. Nietzsche's influence on the neo-Idealists needs further study, for the problem of disentangling his influence from that of Dostoevsky (or Leontiev) is especially complex in their case, as can be seen in Mihajlo Mihajlov's view that much of what the neo-Idealists attributed to Nietzsche really stemmed from Dostoevsky. Ann Lane (in the chapters on Berdiaev and Frank in her dissertation) credits Nietzsche not only with stimulating their religious search, but also with shaping Berdiaev's views on individuality, self-development, creativity, and spiritual aristocratism, and with motivating Frank's ruminations on psychology and ethics. Bedevilling the issue is that certain neo-Idealists themselves at first acknowledged their debt to Nietzsche, but then, conforming to a common cultural pattern, slighted or disregarded his influence in their mature philosophical works, many of which were written as expatriates. Nietzsche may also have had an impact, possibly in combination with Dostoevsky's nationalism, on the neo-Idealists' political opinions, especially on Struve's advocacy of a "Great Russia." Study of the following would provide a fuller understanding of Nietzsche's impact on Russian religious thought: his role in the intellectual evolution of the theologian Paul Florensky and an analysis of the reaction to Nietzsche in the Orthodox press, seminaries, and theological academies.

Aspects of Nietzsche's influence on Viacheslav Ivanov have been treated

---

[53] James M. Curtis, "Shestov's Use of Nietzsche in His Interpretation of Tolstoy and Dostoevsky," *Texas Studies in Literature and Language* 27 (1975), pp. 289–302.

[54] Lev Shestov, *Dostoevsky, Tolstoi, and Nietzsche*, trans. and ed. Bernard Martin and Spencer E. Roberts (Columbus, Ohio, 1969).

elsewhere by Rosenthal, Lane, Stammler, West, Kleberg, and Averin-tsev,[55] but there is as yet no complete study of Nietzsche's impact on the entire course of Ivanov's intellectual and religious development. The same applies to Nietzsche's impact on Bal'mont, Bely, Blok, Briusov, and Rozanov, though aspects of it are treated in this volume. Not treated at all, however, is Remizov, perhaps the most understudied of the major symbolists, nor Annensky. Nietzsche's impact on acmeism, futurism, and other avant-garde literary and artistic movements that arose after 1909 is still uncharted; one hopes this volume will stimulate research in this important area. Scholars will have to grapple with distinguishing Nietzsche from Bergson or Marinetti, themselves influenced by him, and with the reluctance of acmeists or futurists, for different reasons, to identify their intellectual forebears. Katerina Clark states that Nietzsche influenced Eugene Zamiatin, Yuri Tynianov, and V. Kaverin in the 1920s;[56] this too warrants investigation, as does his influence on formalism in general.

Needed are more studies that investigate not only Nietzsche's influence on the fine arts in the general sense, that is, his inspiring painters, composers, and writers to seek new forms, new means of self-expression; but also on specific questions such as whether his ideas affected their choice of form, style, technique, and subject matter. This question, of course, requires the specialized expertise of art historians and musicologists, particularly since his influence in music is commingled with that of Wagner and of Russian composers.

Nietzsche's continuing influence on Gorky requires further study, and work is needed on two almost forgotten formulators of God-building, Bazarov and Volsky.[57] Other writers on the left who very likely were influenced by Nietzsche include Isaac Babel and Vladimir Maiakovsky.

[55] Rosenthal, "Mystical Anarchism," and "Theater as Church: The Vision of the Mystical Anarchists," in *Russian History* 4, no. 2 (1977), p. 122–41; *idem*, "Ivanov's Socio-Political World View," to be published in the proceedings of the second Vyacheslav Ivanov Symposium, ed. M. Colucci, held in Rome, Italy, June 1983; *idem*, "Wagner and Wagnerian Ideas in Russia," in *Wagnerism in European Culture and Politics*, ed. David Large and William Weber (Ithaca, N.Y., 1984); James West, *Russian Symbolism* (London, 1970); Heinrich Stammler, "Vyacheslav Ivanov and Nietzsche," in *Vyacheslav Ivanov, Poet, Critic and Philosopher*, ed. Robert L. Jackson (New Haven, in press); Lars Kleberg, " 'People's Theater' and the Revolution," in *Art, Society, Revolution, Russia 1917–1921*, ed. Nils Nilsson (Stockholm, 1979), pp. 179–95; S. S. Averintsev, "Poeziia Viacheslava Ivanova," in *Voprosy literatury* 8 (1975), pp. 145–92.

[56] Clark, *Soviet Novel*, p. 152.

[57] Kline's article on Volsky, "Nietzschean Marxism," breaks ground for further study. Lane touches on Bazarov, "Nietzsche in Russian Thought," pp. 553–560.

A study of Nietzsche's impact on Lenin, Trotsky, the realist critics, and *proletkult* would shed new light on the dynamics of the Russian Revolution. Plekhanov, incidentally, found nothing positive in Nietzsche, regarding his individualism as bourgeois fear of the working class, the expression of a decadent bourgeois sensitivity. It is quite likely that the Mensheviks reacted similarly and that there is a correlation between their distaste for Nietzsche and their preference for gradual historical processes over revolutionary leaps into the void. Finally, a chronological study of the entire question of Nietzsche's treatment by Soviet critics from 1917 to the present would add a new dimension to our knowledge of Soviet cultural policy and might also serve as a starting point for study of Nietzsche's impact on Soviet culture in the 1920s and on Stalinism. Any study of Nietzsche during the Soviet period, as well as any attempt to bring Davies's chronological checklist up to the present, will have to grapple with the problem of censorship and with new forms of Aesopian language. For example, "*re*making and *re*doing" may have had a Nietzschean resonance to contemporaries; the new Soviet man may have had a partly Nietzschean origin and the regime's determination to "break the writer's individualism!"[58] may indicate Nietzsche's abiding appeal in the period of the cultural revolution, 1928–1931.

A comprehensive treatment of Nietzsche's effect on Andreev, Artsybashev, and other neorealist dramatists and writers would enhance our understanding of their life and work. Other suggested subjects: Chekhov's view of Nietzsche, Tolstoi's view of Nietzsche, and Nietzsche and the occult—the latter because Nietzsche influenced Rudolph Steiner's anthroposophy, which in turn influenced many Russians, most notably Andrei Bely. Peter Uspensky, a disciple of the occult philosopher G. I. Gurdjieff, gave a lecture, "On the Superman," in 1913 in St. Petersburg, Several writers, including Mikhailovsky, Minsky, Merezhkovsky, and Fedorov attributed uncongenial aspects of Nietzsche to Darwin's influence on him; a systematic study of Darwin's reception in Russia would yield valuable insights on the process of mediation.

Finally, a very different subject: Nietzsche's influence on Russian Zionism. Micah J. Berdichevsky (1865–1921) who preached a revaluation of all values of the Jewish tradition, is the outstanding example of a Nietzschean Zionist. Russian Jews probably knew that Max Nordau, author of *Degeneration*, became a Zionist in 1896. For him, Zionism served

[58] Katerina Clark, "Little Heroes and Big Deeds," in *Cultural Revolution in Russia*, ed. Sheila Fitzpatrick (Bloomington, Ind., 1978), pp. 192, 196.

as a kind of revitalization movement. The 'new kind of Jew' he and other Zionists desired, was the inverse of the ghetto Jew and a direct counterpart to the 'new man' desired by symbolists and Marxists. Parallels can also be drawn between Zionist views of Orthodox Judaism and gentile views of historical Christianity. Russian Jews suffering from savage persecution and pogroms may have found appealing Nietzsche's call to activism, his *amor fati* instead of despair, as well as his scorn for passive acceptance of suffering. The Zionist 'new man' rejected the intellectuality of the Jewish tradition; he worked the land, returned to the very sources of life. In Russian Zionism, Nietzschean vitalism mingled with, indeed was overshadowed by, Tolstoi's preachments of the dignity of manual labor. Tolstoi's Jewish disciple, A. D. Gordon (1856–1922) believed that national redemption would result from reclamation of the land. There is even a strange parallel between the fate of Nietzsche and the fate of the Hebrew language in Russia; the latter was proscribed as the language of two bêtes noires of Bolshevism—Zionism and Orthodox Judaism.

To repeat, the above suggestions for further directions in research are not intended to be exhaustive. Indeed, further investigations will, in all likelihood, lead to further questions. But the effort will open up an important new dimension in the complex and nuanced fabric of Russian and Soviet culture.

PART I

NIETZSCHE'S INFLUENCE ON RUSSIAN RELIGIOUS THOUGHT

1.

Nietzsche Comes to Russia: Popularization and Protest in the 1890s

Ann M. Lane

DURING THE 1890S, the decade of his debut in the Russian cultural world, Nietzsche's ideas were popularized—and protested—in several important forums, including the "thick journals" and the discussion circles of early Russian modernists. This chapter will describe the early response to Nietzsche of the prominent literary figures and institutions: the debate in the journal *Problems of Philosophy and Psychology* and its reverberations, the interpretations of Nietzsche by the modernists Nicholas Minsky and Akim Volynsky, the populist Nicholas Mikhailovsky's reaction to Nietzsche, and the philosopher Vladimir Soloviev's protest against Nietzsche's critique of Christianity. As the 1890s drew to a close, not only was Nietzsche's thought fairly well known; it had garnered considerable acceptance, despite the initial denunciations, and was on the verge of manifesting itself thematically in the work of Russian writers, artists, and philosophers.

The controversy over Nietzsche began in 1892 with the sober and ordered presentation of Nietzsche's thought in the highly respected journal *Problems of Philosophy and Psychology* (*Voprosy filosofii i psikhologii*, 1889–1918).[1] V. P. Preobrazhensky's article "Friedrich Nietzsche: The Cri-

---

[1] The journal *Voprosy filosofii i psikhologii* was founded in the late 1880s by N. A. Grot, a professor of philosophy at the University of Moscow; it played a major role in the renaissance of philosophical thought in Russia. Preobrazhensky had previously read his article to the Psychological Society in Moscow in October 1892. The Psychological Society included most of the leading scholars, scientists, and thinkers; it published *Problems of Philosophy and Psychology*, (henceforth cited as VFP). The minutes of the meeting say that Preobrazhensky's paper "aroused a lively interest and exchange of opinions among the members."

tique of the Morality of Altruism" engendered a discussion in a subsequent issue, which soon spilled over into other journals and also inspired
the first Russian novel with a Nietzschean protagonist.

The young philosopher Preobrazhensky (1864–1900) felt a sense of
kinship with Nietzsche. His only trip outside Russia was planned with
the idea of visiting all the places in Germany, Italy, and Switzerland
where Nietzsche had ever lived and worked. Preobrazhensky's devotion
to Nietzsche was nourished by several factors. His close friend and colleague N. Kotliarevsky felt that Preobrazhensky's "unbelievably careful
mind" was more disposed to go along with a merciless critique of the
present than to permit himself to be carried away by optimistic dreams of
the future. When Preobrazhensky began to examine Russian society closely
he became so upset that he lost faith in the inevitability of progress;
moreover, socialism with its potential for regimentation frightened him.
There remained only one hope for Preobrazhensky: "To save at least the
faith in the solitary, unusual man in whom bravery, profundity of intellect, freedom of the feelings and strength of will were united into one
harmonious whole. . . . Nietzsche helped V. Preobrazhensky to strengthen
this hope." Preobrazhensky especially appreciated Nietzsche's "apotheosis
of the human will, which, as it seemed to him, now needed such a bold
reminder of its power and strength." Finally, he had an abiding interest
in literature; Nietzsche's literary skill strongly attracted him and he believed that Nietzsche was the greatest German writer since Heine.[2]

Preobrazhensky's defense of Nietzsche did not interfere with the clarity
of his presentation. The editors of the journal, however, were perturbed
by Nietzsche's "shocking" ideas, and may have been concerned about the
reaction of the government censor as well. In a note appended to the
beginning of Preobrazhensky's article, the journal's editors explained that
they had decided to print this exposition of Nietzsche's moral doctrine,
"scandalous in its final conclusions," in order to show "what strange and
sick phenomena" were being engendered by a "certain aspect of Western
European philosophical thought." Acknowledging that Nietzsche was a
talented writer and thinker, the editors stated that Nietzsche had been

---

See "Psikhologicheskoe Obshchestvo: XCIII zasedaniia 24 oktobria 1892 goda," VFP 16
(January 1893), p. 111.

[2] N. Kotliarevsky, "Vospominaniia o Vasilii Petroviche Preobrazhenskom," VFP 54 (September–October 1900), pp. 531–35. For more information on Preobrazhensky see V. I.
Ger'e, "Pamiati V. P. Preobrazhenskogo," VFP, (September–October 1900), pp. 731–40;
and Kn.S.N. Trubetskoi, "Pamiati Vasiliia Petrovicha Preobrazhenskogo," VFP (September–October 1900), pp. 481–500.

blinded by his hatred for religion, Christianity and "God Himself," and that Nietzsche condoned crime and the "most frightening debauchery." "What a great and instructive lesson serves the fate of this unfortunate proud man who fell into the power of the *idée fixe* that he was the Creator of the world," concluded the editors, saying that Nietzsche's insanity was the result of his "philosophical aberrations."[3]

Far from viewing Nietzsche as a symptom of Western decadence, Preobrazhensky described him as a moralist, comparing him to Pascal, La Rochefoucauld, Leopardi, and Schopenhauer. Praising Nietzsche's skill as a writer, he acknowledged that Nietzsche's *oeuvre* was full of seeming contradictions, but interpreted these as the product of "a life full of intense inner change." He compared Nietzsche to Alexander Herzen, whose life was also a "martyrdom of sincerity, spent in incessant analyses and merciless destruction of his dearest illusions," and concluded that Nietzsche was both a difficult and rewarding thinker precisely because he was an "artist-thinker."[4]

Preobrazhensky tried to show that Nietzsche's critique of altruism arose out of other truly admirable values. Nietzsche, he argued, felt that too often those who promulgated a system of morality as true and universal did not take into account the beliefs of other cultures or historical eras and, therefore, did not see that morality had a relativistic aspect. Moral philosophers should rise above their narrow perspectives to try to see the whole; different systems of morality can come into conflict with one another, and no one can assert the superiority of a particular one. This, Preobrazhensky maintained, is the meaning of Nietzsche's phrase "beyond good and evil,"[5] the concept used by Nietzsche, according to Preobrazhensky, to analyze the commonly accepted virtue of altruism. Nietzsche showed that altruism was given a moral value because it was "useful" to society, but then went on to claim that societally imposed morality leads to a "herd morality" that values the individual only insofar as he or she serves the group. People are valued only for their social virtues, especially obedience and respect for authority. The altruistic society fears individuality; society's fear of the individual becomes the very source of its "morality." Nietzsche despised the ideals of equality and altruism. He saw them as virtues generated out of fear that made man into a domestic

[3]V. F. Preobrazhensky, "Fridrikh Nitsshe: Kritika morali altruizma," VFP 15 (November 1892), pp. 115–16.

[4]Ibid., pp. 116–19.

[5]Ibid., pp. 120–32.

animal, "cheapened" him. "It [altruism] made man and society safe and calm, but it also made life insipid and sterile; it made the petty satisfactions of life more accessible for all; but it destroyed the strength and will for the risk and sufferings of life. . . . It made mediocrity the ideal of man," Preobrazhensky asserted.[6]

Explicitly taking Nietzsche's views as his own, Preobrazhensky then argued that individuals must freely establish their own duties, not have duties forced upon them. "We ourselves must answer for our lives—be the real pilots of our lives." It is better to be free and "evil" than a slave who is "good." Furthermore, Preobrazhensky emphasized, there are higher goals beyond freedom in Nietzsche's philosophy. In the elevation and strengthening of the human personality, *"it is possible to attain the high power and magnificence of the human type and of human culture."* At the root of Nietzsche's ideas is the view that life in its highest development must serve as the basis of morality, and not the reverse. Nietzsche objects to all the narrowness and pettiness of conventional morality because it hinders the creative impulses; this, Preobrazhensky asserted, is what Nietzsche means by the superman. Preobrazhensky concluded his article by stating that he tried to show the relationship of Nietzsche's positive moral ideals to his critique of the morality of altruism.[7]

Preobrazhensky's positive interpretation of Nietzsche's ideas evoked three responses in the next issue of the journal. The editor, L. M. Lopatin (1855–1926), noted that the article on Nietzsche had gained special attention among readers and made a "rather strong impression." Lopatin set out to dispel the favorable interpretation of Nietzsche made by Preobrazhensky, describing Nietzsche's ideas as "gloomy and merciless to everything that up to now has been most holy for mankind." Lopatin insisted that Nietzsche's work was rife with serious contradictions and that the main attraction of his work was the "sick sincerity of his rejections," a quality that fit in well with the cynicism and skepticism evidenced in recent European philosophical work. Nietzsche's attempt to construct a positive moral ideal was bound to fail, said Lopatin, for such an ideal could not be constructed upon the view expressed by Nietzsche that there is nothing absolute in the world.[8]

N. Ia. Grot (1852–1899), the respected founder of the journal, contrasted Nietzsche's anti-Christian individualism with Lev Tolstoi's Chris-

---

[6] Ibid., pp. 133–39, 141–42.
[7] Ibid., pp. 143–50, 157, 159.
[8] L. Lopatin, "Bol'naia iskrennost'," *VFP* 16 (January 1893), pp. 109–13.

tian altruism, finding Nietzsche to be a "representative of Western European decadence," a "materialist, atheist and evolutionist of a rather fantastic type."[9] P. E. Astafiev took the same negative view of Nietzsche in his article "The Genesis of the Moral Ideal of a Decadent."[10]

Influenced by the controversy in *Problems of Philosophy and Psychology*, V. Chuiko (1839–1899), in the Moscow journal *The Observer* (*Nabliudatel'*), made a serious attempt to analyze Nietzsche early in 1893, but found little to commend, linking him to the decay of the West.

> Schopenhauer preached rejection of earthly goods, peace in nonexistence, contemplation of human nothingness, compassion, self-denial. Nietzsche revealed to European society another ideal, much lower, but harmonizing better with the new instincts and demands. The cult of strength, the merciless condemnation of weaknesses . . . , the bowing before the rights of the strongest, the justification of low instincts, of any kind of force, of all egoism.[11]

The author raises all the stereotypes and caricatures of Nietzsche's ideas— for example, "Nietzsche thinks a people is created only so that five or six outstanding individuals should exist. These are the tigers and lions born to devour the sheep." He compared Nietzsche to the Russian Slavophiles but felt that he went much further in his rejection of Western ideas: "He lost faith in the very essence of European civilization." Still, he did take note of some of the more interesting aspects of Nietzsche's ideas, stating, for example, that Nietzsche's *Übermensch* was a "mystical ideal" that showed Nietzsche's faith in man's perfectibility. Noting the importance of estheticism in Nietzsche's value system, he ultimately conceded that Nietzsche was one of the most original thinkers of Germany in the last few decades.[12]

Others also had a mixed response to their first contact with Nietzsche. P. Skriba (Eugene Soloviev) (1866–1905), who later (around 1900) was to become a Nietzschean Marxist,[13] initially rejected Nietzsche on the

---

[9] N. Ia. Grot, "Nravstvennye idealy nashego vremeni: Fridrikh Nitsshe i Lev' Tolstoi," *VFP* 16 (January 1893), pp. 141, 143.

[10] P. E. Astafiev, "Genezis nravstvennogo ideala dekadenta," *VFP* 16 (January 1893), pp. 56–75.

[11] V. V. Chuiko, "Obshchestvennye idealy Fridrikha Nitsshe," *Nabliudatel'*, no. 2 (1893) p. 233.

[12] Ibid., pp. 231–47.

[13] See Chapter 10 in Ann M. Lane, "Nietzsche in Russian Thought 1890–1917" (Ph.D. diss., University of Wisconsin, 1976).

basis of what he had read in the articles in *Problems of Philosophy and Psychology*. He felt that the journal had treated Nietzsche too kindly. "What is new and talented here, I don't see." He thought that Nietzsche and the European decadents had much in common: "hypertrophy of the personality, deification of the self, a wild and unbridled egoism which sometimes is downright sick." He, like others, suggested that Nietzsche's thought was the product of mental illness.[14]

The controversy started by Preobrazhensky continued in popular fiction. The new largely forgotten chronicler of the fictional intelligentsia Peter Boborykin patterned his protagonist Kostritsyn, in the novel *Pereval* (*The Divide*, 1894), in part upon Preobrazhensky. This was the first novel with a Nietzschean hero to appear in Russia. Boborykin later wrote:

> Everybody has repeated that my Kostritsyn—a Moscow Nietzschean—was similar to Preobrazhensky. Many of my Moscow acquaintances made remarks about it, and sometimes they put the question in a more categorical form. The appearance of the first chapters of the novel, if I am not mistaken, almost corresponded with the printing of Preobrazhensky's *études* on Nietzsche. . . . In them for the first time a Russian writer with a philosophical education speaks with the feeling and understanding of the German thinker who created the teaching of Zarathustra. . . . Never before that had I read such a brave and objective discussion of these ethical ideas. . . . This especially attracted me to the intellectual makeup of [Preobrazhensky]. . . . And if his personality was similar to my character's, then the author of *The Divide* can only thank fate.[15]

Kostritsyn, the Nietzschean protagonist, converts Lyzhin, a former populist and revolutionary, to his views. Lyzhin is a man of the 1870s and

---

[14]P. Skriba, "Sovremennye literaturnye motivy (Simvolisty, dekadenty)," *Russkaia zhizn'* (St. Petersburg) no. 27 (1893), p. 2. Later a certain psychiatrist, V. F. Chizh, who was a fervent admirer of Nietzsche, gave a series of lectures on Nietzsche between 1901 and 1908 in Moscow, St. Petersburg, and in a number of provincial cities. In these lectures he took the opportunity to dismiss Nietzsche's thought as a symptom of mental illness, pointing out that many great men and thinkers have suffered from mental illness. See V. F. Chizh, "Nitsshe kak moralist," *VFP* 94 (September–October 1908), pp. 335–76, especially p. 340. As it did elsewhere, the issue of Nietzsche's insanity gained wide notoriety in Russia, some seeing it as the logical outcome of his megalomania (the philosopher Vladimir Soloviev), others seeing it as the origin of his thought in the first place (Lopatin), as the sign of prophecy (Bely and Merezhkovsky), or the sign of martyrdom (Shestov and Lunacharsky).

[15]P. Boborykin, "O nitssheianstve (Pamiati V. P. Preobrazhenskogo)," *VFP* 54 (September–October 1900), p. 540.

1880s seeking a change of ideals, for he no longer believes in populism, which he now considers "spiritual bankruptcy," comparing it to the "fanaticism of some kind of dirty fool-in-Christ [*iurodivyi*]." "Self-denial," he says, "is nothing but spiritual disorder."[16] Having sold his land, which he considers "an oppressive symbol of and link with the *narod*," he meets Kostritsyn, a "new man" of the nineties, who preaches a not very orderly conglomeration of Nietzschean views, apparently drawn on Preobrazhensky's article, other popularizations, and Nietzsche's own writings.[17] Kostritsyn preaches about the "superman" (using both the German *Übermensch* and the Russian *sverkhchelovek*) and, in one scene, retells the fourth part of *Thus Spoke Zarathustra* to win over Lyzhin and a group of students. In the conclusion when both men go off to fight the famine (1892–1893) that has devastated the peasants, Kostritsyn justifies this action not as populist altruism but as heroism.[18]

The characters in Boborykin's novel manifest a range of reactions to Nietzsche. Boborykin himself admired some of Nietzsche's ideas, writing:

Nobody before him understood so well all the personality of man, man's spiritual strength, and nobody has with such talent and inspiration dreamt about the possibility of the birth of the superman. The word soon became funny, but the idea is not at all funny and will shine eternally before mankind as a guiding star.[19]

Boborykin's interpretation of Nietzsche's ideas, displayed in the ending of the novel, foreshadowed a significant strain in Russian interpretations of Nietzsche: heroism and altruism ultimately merged in "God-building" (*Bogostroitel'stvo*). Boborykin used Kostitsyn's fate to show the probable course of Nietzsche's ideas in Russia. Incidentally, Boborykin, like many other readers, believed that Nietzsche was an anti-Semite, and this is also reflected in Kostritsyn's attitudes. Compared with several novels presenting Nietzschean protagonists written after 1900, however, *Pereval* cannot be classified as a sensationalist distortion of Nietzsche's ideas. Boborykin generally presented Nietzsche's ideas in a positive light. This is probably due in part to the relatively reasoned—albeit heated—discussions of Nietzsche, especially Preobrazhensky's, on which Boborykin drew as source material.

[16] *Pereval*, in P. D. Boborykin, *Sobranie romanov, povesti i rasskazov*, 12 vols. (St. Petersburg, 1897), 7:9–10.

[17] Ibid., pp. 219–21.

[18] Ibid., pp. 286–97; ibid., 8:87.

[19] Boborykin, "O nitssheanistve," pp. 543–44.

Meanwhile, another aspect of Nietzsche interpretation had been developing more calmly. Even before Boborykin's novel appeared, other Russian writers had begun to adopt Nietzsche's writings for their own ends. Tired of the populist tradition in literature, with its emphasis on social conscience, these writers started to explore themes focusing on the individual and his psyche. Because of his emphasis upon esthetic values and his crusade against altruism, Nietzsche was an ideal source of support and stimulus for these writers, who were seeking philosophical justification for their work. The first attempt to use Nietzsche's thought in this way occurred in 1890, and, in fact, accounts for Nietzsche's first, albeit disguised, appearance in Russia. That year N. M. Minsky (N. M. Vilenkin, 1855–1937) published a book called *In the Light of Conscience* (*Pri svete sovesti*), a shrill echo of Nietzsche's critique of altruism and his defense of individualism. The book drew on Minsky's exposure to Nietzsche's writings during his travels to Europe. Six years earlier Minsky published an article in the Kiev newspaper *Zaria* (*The Dawn*) attacking the populist conception of literature as social service and contending that art was valuable in itself, but this article had provoked little interest.[20] But now this book, published in St. Petersburg, attracted the attention of more people, including D. S. Merezhkovsky, who praised it.[21]

Until 1884 Minsky had marched under the populist banner, which valued "social consciousness" (*grazhdanstvo*) as the prime value of literature, an attitude Nekrasov had expressed in the lines:

One does not need to be a poet,
But one must be a citizen [*grazhdanin*].[22]

(One of Minsky's poems, about a revolutionary who proclaims his creed to the court upon receiving the death sentence, inspired Repin to do a painting on this theme.)[23] Minsky, however, was not a very talented poet; he wrote such lines as "Burning weakly with a tubercular flush, / The evening dawn slowly goes out" and "O my motherland! My motherland of sufferings!"[24] Despite his populist profession of faith he had begun to feel the futility of the populist dogmas:

[20] See N. Brodsky, ed., *Literaturnye manifesty* (Moscow, 1929), pp. 3–5.

[21] D. S. Merezhkovsky, *O prichinakh upadka i o novykh techeniiakh sovremennoi russkoi literatury* (St. Petersburg, 1893), pp. 90–91.

[22] "Poet i grazhdanin," in *Russkie poety: Antologiia*, 4 vols. (Moscow, 1966), 3:66.

[23] "Poslednaia ispoved'," in N. Minsky, *Polnoe sobranie stikhotvorenii*, 4 vols., 4th ed. (St. Petersburg, 1907), 1:46–55.

[24] Ibid., pp. 5, 45.

I am alone, a stranger to the crowd. But I love the crowd,
The blind, stupid crowd, with a hopeless anguish.
Only for the crowd do I pray, only for it do I grieve.
I am alone. But without it I labor in vain.[25]

Nietzsche's work enabled Minsky to extricate himself from his unhappy position. Minsky made frequent trips to Western Europe and prided himself on keeping abreast of the latest trends; his book reflects the recognition beginning to be accorded Nietzsche in Western Europe. Much of the book is a crude parroting of Nietzsche's thoughts and language, as, for example:

> The usual advice of the moralists—love your neighbor, live as do the simple people, fling yourself into real life—turns out to be useless. To love your neighbor, of course, is better than to hate him, but in what way can the supreme goal of my life be contained in love for a being just as aimless and pitiful as myself? After all, you are supposed to love your neighbor as yourself. Well, if you despise yourself, then what?

Minsky explained that he became disillusioned with the stupidity and ignorance of the "simple people" and realized that if there is a goal in life it is in "something deep, intimate, secret that must be found not outside one's self but within one's very self." Thus he turned away from love of neighbor to a "higher" love of self: "Infinite as the sky, immeasurable as eternity, strong as the gravity of the planets is the love of each person for himself." Moralists who teach "love of neighbor" waste their words and tears, for self-love is not a vice, nor a moral illness, but the soul's "supreme, most treasured principle." The "love for existence" and the craving for primacy are the "ruling principles" of the soul. "One moment of the bright, intense consciousness of life is more joyful and desired than many years of decaying stagnation. In love for existence and horror before nonexistence begin all our concepts of usefulness and harm, pleasures and sufferings, good and evil, beauty and ugliness." The dream of a general equality is just as unrealizable and alien to our nature as is the idea of disinterested love of neighbor, and Minsky attacked the "utilitarian idea of the most happiness for the most people that Russian populism wants." The "completely ecstatic bliss of existence" is attained

[25] Minsky, "Odinochestvo," ibid., pp. 197–98.

only "when before the bright light of my soul another soul willingly fades, admits my primacy."[26]

Having thus espoused individualism and the will-to-power, Minsky then turned to the idea of the eternal recurrence.

> If it is true that nothing can disappear, then, obviously, not one part of my consciousness will be lost, and good and evil will be equally infinite. . . . Thus, looking into the mirror of the future, I see my consciousness reflected in an infinite number of images, and each such image will possess eternal existence.[27]

Minsky proceeded to interpret Nietzsche's concept of *amor fati* (love of fate). In Nietzsche's view, expressed in *The Birth of Tragedy*, the ancient Greek was saved from fear of death and despair by the Dionysian and Apollonian principles—the ecstatic upsurge of primeval forces and their expression in art. Nietzsche believed that modern man, too, could save himself from despair through *amor fati*. A contorted version of this idea is the foundation of what Minsky ideology called "Meonism." "Meons" refer to the fundamental units of the universe; they are particles of anti-matter, the "opposite of all that exists" (apparently the correlation to the ancient Greek concept of nonexistence as discussed by Nietzsche). When a person realizes that life is based on nonexistence, "then he is like a mountain pine which has grown up over the abyss [Nietzsche's image]—thus the teaching about meons defends the soul from weak despair because this teaching itself has grown out of despair." The followers of Meonism, according to Minsky, do "not flatter themselves with the dangerous illusion that the goal of development is in the happiness it gives." They know that the "goal of learning, glory, and action is in their rejection, that life is a sacrifice consumed in the fire of ecstasy."[28] In other words, Meonism exalted the purposelessness of life.

The literary historian S. A. Vengerov, who knew and wrote about many of the literary figures of the turn of the century, thought that Minsky's ideas in *The Light of Conscience* laid the foundation for that "amoralism which was the essence of the first period of the new trends."[29] This is an exaggeration because the book was not widely noticed nor was

---

[26] N. M. Minsky, *Pri svete sovesti: Mysli i mechty o tseli zhizni* (St. Petersburg, 1890), pp. v–vii, 1, 6–8, 18–21.

[27] Ibid., pp. 127–28.

[28] Ibid., p. 254.

[29] S. A. Vengerov, "N. Minsky," *Russkaia literatura XX veka 1890–1910*, ed. S. A. Vengerov, 3 vols. (Moscow, 1914–1916), 1:359.

it the only source of new concepts of good and evil—Baudelaire's *Les Fleurs du mal* (1857), for example, had a much greater impact—but it is true that Minsky's book was one of the earliest expressions of antipopulist attitudes in literature. Minsky himself remained interested in the concept of "beyond good and evil." His play *Al'ma*, staged in 1900, is about a woman who lives according to the ideas expressed in *The Light of Conscience*. He used one of his poems as the epigraph to the play. It reads, in part:

There are not two ways of good and evil,
There are two ways of good.
Freedom led me
To a crossroads at one in the morning

And said: There are two paths,
Two truths, two goods—
Discord and torture for the crowd,
Play for the wise man.

What until now among people
Passed for sin and evil,
Is only the principle of two paths,
Their first turn. [30]

Minsky later disavowed Nietzsche, explaining only that the more he understood Nietzsche's philosophy the less he liked it. [31] Nevertheless he had been the first Russian intellectual to take up Nietzsche's ideas. In his attempt to pose as an original philosopher, however, he did not attach Nietzsche's name to these ideas, and the blame for the outlandish ideas accrued mostly to Minsky himself. [32]

Beyond Minsky's rather muddled efforts, Akim Volynsky-Flekser (1863–1926) carried on the effort to derive the philosophical underpinnings for literary modernism from Nietzsche in a more influential fashion. He was the editor (1891–1898) of the first journal of literary modernism, *Severnyi*

[30] N. Minsky, *Al'ma: Tragediia iz sovremennoi zhizni* (St. Petersburg, 1900). The play was discussed heatedly by the critics.

[31] N. Minsky, "Fridrikh Nittsshe," *Mir iskusstva*, no. 19–20 (1900), p. 140, literature section.

[32] Vladimir Solov'ev called Minsky's meonism "abracadabra." "Po povodu sochineniia N. M. Minskogo 'Pri svete sovesti'," in Vladimir Sergeevich Soloviev, *Sobranie sochinenii*, ed. S. M. Soloviev and E. L. Radlov, 10 vols., 2nd ed. (St. Petersburg, 1911–1914), 6:263–68.

vestnik (*Northern Messenger*, 1885–1898); here the Petersburg modernists—Minsky, Merezhkovsky, Gippius, and others—published during their "decadent" phase, ca. 1891–1898. Volynsky was already known for his daring (for that time) attacks on populist writers, insisting that literature had to be more than an expression of social conscience. Volynsky had religious inclinations and defended Idealistic philosophy, but scorned the moralistic outlook of the populists. He preached a kind of individualism that he called demonism. In one article in 1896 he advocated the rejection of politics.[33] Nietzsche could not fail to interest this homegrown decadent. He devoted a long article to Nietzsche at the end of 1896, focusing upon Nietzsche's *The Birth of Tragedy* and agreeing wholeheartedly with Nietzsche's explication of art. "No matter how the concept of Dionysus has changed, the inevitable link between metaphysics and art is explained and proven with great strength," he wrote of Nietzsche's first book.[34]

His reading of Nietzsche strengthened Volynsky's belief that art and philosophy were inextricably linked:

Being the expression of the mystical secret of life in abstract concepts, philosophy gives that light in which elements can be known in their most various relations and submitted to deep analysis. Seeing objects well, through, in depth, knowing the relative value of things, internally attaining the unconquerable law of dissolution and liberation, the artist with talent is at the same time an enormous intellectual source, and a convinced bearer of the elevated secrets of life, revealed in complete ecstasy. Nietzsche many times returned to this theme, constantly developing it in the same direction. The kingdom of Apollo, he writes, submits to the kingdom of Dionysus. This means that all that is individual submits to the universal, that the phenomena of life are in an unbreakable link with metaphysical forces, that each accidental event of whatever kind can receive a correct interpretation only with the help of critical analysis of the firm basis of philosophical idealism.[35]

[33] Cited in P. S. Kogan, "Literaturnye napravleniia i kritika 80 i 90-x godov," in *Istoriia russkoi literatury XIX veka*, ed. D. N. Ovsianiko-Kulikovsky, 5 vols. (Moscow, 1911), 5:96.

[34] A. Volynsky, "Literaturnye zametki. Apollon i Dionis," *Severnyi vestnik*, no. 11 (1896), p. 251.

[35] Ibid., p. 251. Volynsky noted correctly that Nietzsche's ideas in *The Birth of Tragedy* were drawn from Schopenhauer. Ibid., pp. 252–53.

Volynsky helped to canonize Nietzsche for the decadents. He took up the theme of the interconnection between art and philosophy that the decadents and later the Russian symbolist poets used to counter philosophical materialism and positivism. Russian modernism began to develop a central idea: the importance of art in bringing closer to consciousness the mysteries that lie beyond the corporeal world. Nietzsche's theories on esthetics, especially as expressed in *The Birth of Tragedy*, played an enormous role in the thinking of the Russian symbolists. They embraced his contention that this world can be justified only as an esthetic phenomenon.

Nietzsche's work also found a powerful, if unexpected, exponent in Nicholas Mikhailovsky (1842–1904), the leading theoretician of populism in the 1890s. Despite Nietzsche's polemics against social altruism, and despite the fact that Russian populism, as the "old" dogma, had the most to lose from the defection of a newly apolitical Nietzschean segment of intelligentsia, Mikhailovsky reacted favorably to Nietzsche. This is because Mikhailovsky himself had long defended the role of the critically thinking individual in history and insisted that all social change had to promote the value of the individual. In his earlier writings he had sought to temper the tendency of his fellow populists to idealize the commune. In the 1890s he directed his polemics against Marxist socialism with its emphasis upon the collective character of society. As an editor of one of the most prominant of the thick journals, *Russian Wealth* (*Russkoe bogatstvo*), he was well placed to disseminate his appreciative interpretation of Nietzsche.

Mikhailovsky read many of Nietzsche's works in the original, and did not accept the negative view of Max Nordau[36] or of the earlier articles in *Problems of Philosophy and Psychology*. His first substantial treatment of Nietzsche appeared in late 1894 in *Russian Wealth*. The review is perceptive and sympathetic; he especially liked Nietzsche's *On the Use and Abuse of History for Life*, and applauded Nietzsche's rejection of determinism in history. (Mikhailovsky's first important early work, *What Is Progress*, 1873, challenged the evolutionary theories of English writers with their emphasis upon fatalism.) He criticized Nordau's treatment of

[36] An Austrian critic, who lived permanently in Paris, whose *Entartung* (*Degeneration*) (1892) appeared in Russian translation (*Vyrozhdenie*) in 1893, 1896, and 1901; it was virulently critical of not only Nietzsche but the French symbolist poets as well. Some of the Russian critics of Nietzsche drew their arguments from this book.

Nietzsche, and, in comparing Nietzsche to Max Stirner, found him to be a far superior thinker to Stirner.[37] Mikhailovsky's enthusiasm for Nietzsche's brand of individualism was pronounced:

> We see in Nietzsche neither a rationalist—that is simply nonsense—nor the theoretician of egoism, nor the "immoralist" which Nietzsche is usually considered and which he considered himself to be. We see a most noble and a brave thinker, a kind of dreamer, an idealist, who posits his demands from the point of view of an extremely elevated concept of individualism. The human personality is for him the measure of all things; but he demands for it such a fullness of life and has such a hostility for any utilitarian considerations or conditions that belittle its dignity, that there can be no talk here of egoism in the vulgar sense or of any kind of immoralism.

Although ardent, Mikhailovsky's response to Nietzsche was not unqualified. In the same article he expressed uneasiness about Nietzsche's conception of society.[38] For all his interest in and respect for Nietzsche, Mikhailovsky could not completely reconcile Nietzsche's work with populist values. His article of 1900 on Nietzsche again strongly defended the "nobility" of Nietzsche's individualism, but suggested that Nietzsche's attitude toward society was too extreme. Noting that one of the central Nietzschean themes was the struggle between individual and society, a struggle that Mikhailovsky thought was always one of the main problems of history, he added:

> Perhaps this struggle will never end, perhaps even the end of the world will not witness the end of this struggle. But man, in whom thought, feeling, and will are active, cannot help but take part in this struggle, and one has to chose. The problem is not whether the intellect of the modern European should be united to the moral type of the primeval man, and not whether the "superman" should be made possible through the sacrifice of the life and dignity of millions of human beings. The problem is to find and bring into existence a form of social life that would not place chains upon the personality. I repeat, perhaps this goal is unrealizable even in the course of the

[37] The German exponent of "rational egoism" in *Der Einzige und sein Eigentum* (*The Ego and His Own*) (1844), who was popularized by Dimitri Pisarev; Stirner's work subsequently fell into eclipse, but Nietzsche's growing popularity in the 1890s stimulated a revival of interest.

[38] N. Mikhailovsky, "Literatura i zhizn'," *Russkoe bogatstvo*, no. 12 (1894), pp. 84–110.

hundreds of thousands or millions of years which still remain to mankind, but one cannot refuse to deal with it, one must participate in its resolution either actively or passively.[39]

While Mikhailovsky used Nietzsche's writings to explore the individual's struggle in society, Vladimir Soloviev (1853–1900), the most influential philosopher and religious thinker of the period, concentrated on Nietzsche's spiritual and religious themes. Ironically, many of the Russian symbolists who paid great reverence to Soloviev combined, in various ways, his mysticism and Nietzsche's estheticism, undeterred by Soloviev's hostility to Nietzsche's anti-Christian views.

Soloviev's complex outlook in simplified form was the following: history is a process through which mankind gradually approached divinity; through human action, especially artistic creativity, man himself would help to make divinity manifest in mankind and the world; at the end of history, the world, mankind, and God would become fully synthesized in "God-manhood," united by divine love. Soloviev saw Nietzsche's ideal as the corruption of this vision; that, instead of "God-manhood," Nietzsche's individualism and rejection of religion would produce a "man-godhood." In his first treatment of Nietzsche (the article "The Justification of the Good" ["Opravdanie dobra"], 1897), he critiqued Nietzsche's separation of beauty and power from a religious context; he insisted that only within a framework of religion could these values be fully realized. Moreover, only Christianity could free beauty from death.[40]

In his second article "The Idea of the Superman" ("Ideia sverkhchlov-eka," 1899), a year before his death, Soloviev identified three currents of thought that he believed dominated the 1890s—economic materialism, abstract moralism, and the "demonism of the 'superman' ":

Of these three ideas, linked with the three great names of Karl Marx, Lev Tolstoi, and Friedrich Nietzsche, the first is addressed to the present, the second to tomorrow, and the third to what will come

---

[39] N. Mikhailovsky, "Literatura i zhizn'," *Russkoe bogatstvo*, no. 2 (1900), p. 165. His other writings on Nietzsche are to be found in the same journal, no. 2 (1898), pp. 132–62; and in "O literaturnom obshchestve i nashikh literaturnykh nravakh: O sistemkh moral: O Makse Stirnere i Fridrikhe Nichshe"; "Optimisticheskii i pessimisticheskii ton: Maks Nordau o vyrozhdenii: Dekadenty, simvolisty, magi i proch"; "Eshche o Fridrikhe Nichshe," N. K. Mikhailovsky, *Literaturnye vospominaniia i sovremennaia smuta*, 2 vols. (St. Petersburg, 1900), 2:1–31, 378–404, 443–65.

[40] "Opravdanie dobra: Predislovie k pervomu izdaniiu," in SS, 8:12–14.

the day after tomorrow and further. I consider it the most interesting of the three.

There are obviously unacceptable elements in Nietzsche's doctrines, but the idea of the superman can be interpreted positively. "It is natural for man to want to be better and greater than he is in reality, it is *natural* for him to be attracted to the ideal of the superman."[41] But this desire for perfection must not be understood in a biological sense, for man is more than animal.

> History does not create or demand any new superhuman form of the organism, because the human form can perfect itself infinitely, both internally and externally, *while remaining the same thing*: it is capable in its essence of finding a place for and uniting in itself everything, of becoming the means and bearer of all that it can strive for—it is capable of being the form of perfected unity, or divinity.

Soloviev repeated his earlier contention that Nietzsche's ideals could only be realized under the aegis of Christianity. But, he concluded, Nietzsche served a useful function in reawakening many people to the possible meaning of "superman."[42]

Soloviev dismissed Nietzsche's views on religion, finding his polemics against Christianity "stunningly trite" and his pretensions to being Antichrist "funny to the highest degree if they had not ended so tragically."[43] Still, Soloviev, at heart a great reconciler, was the first Russian thinker to consider Nietzsche from the religious point of view.

Many others found a spiritual meaning in Nietzsche's writing. For example, the philosopher S. L. Frank reported Nietzsche's impact upon him as a young man:

> I was completely shaken by the depth and tension of the spiritual wrestling, by the incisiveness with which he [Nietzsche] all over again posited the problem of religion (earlier it had seemed to us that it had long ago been resolved—in a negative sense—by all enlightened people) and by the examination of the basic positions of moral life. Under the influence of Nietzsche, there took place in me a genuine spiritual upheaval, which in part was obviously prepared by both all my past intellectual development, and by my personal experiences:

[41] "Ideia sverkhcheloveka" (1899), ibid., 9:266.
[42] Ibid., pp. 266–74.
[43] Ibid., 8:13.

I can say that for the first time there was revealed to me the reality of a spiritual life. In my soul there began to take shape a certain "heroic" philosophy, defined by faith in the absolute value of the soul and in the necessity of struggle for it. [44]

Berdiaev, who developed a philosophy of religion that incorporated Nietzsche's apotheosis of creativity, believed that the influence of both Soloviev and Nietzsche was a fundamental factor in the development of the Russian religious renaissance of the early twentieth century. Bely agreed: "Without Nietzsche the preaching of neo-Christianity would not have arisen among us."[45]

Soon Nietzsche's name dominated the consciousness of the avant-garde. Eugene Soloviev in 1901 found that the Russian spellings of Nietzsche's name—Nitshe, Nichshe, Nitche, Nittsshe, Niche—were as various as the opinions about him.[46] Belyi wrote of these years: "Everywhere there appeared the symbolics of the mountain ascent [from Nietzsche]."[47] Nietzschean words and phrases such as "superman," "heroism," "on the heights," "the spirit of music," "tragedy," achieved a shorthand status among the cognoscenti. Bely wrote that he turned from Schopenhauer's "pessimism" to Nietzsche's "tragism." In 1900 the classicist George Rachinsky published a long article exclaiming: "Tragedy! That is Nietzsche's conception of culture. Around the new art there is growing up a new tragic culture."[48]

That same year, 1900, upon the occasion of Nietzsche's death, the influential journal of the new modernist generation, *Mir iskusstva* (*The World of Art*), extolled Nietzsche's importance. The first page of the issue is an elegantly printed death notice and portrait. The eulogy began, "He is especially close to us Russians," and continued: "Nietzsche, like Dostoevsky, believed in the future world destiny of Russia. Comparing it with the Roman Empire and contrasting it to Western Europe, he said that Russia alone was still young enough to expect something, that she had

[44] S. L. Frank, *Biografiia P. B. Struve* (New York, 1956), pp. 28–29.

[45] Nikolai Berdiaev, *Russkaia ideia (Osnovnye problemy russkoi mysli XIX veka i nachala* *veka)* (Paris, 1946), p. 230. Andrei Bely, "Nastoiaschchee i budushchee russkoi literatury," *Lug zelenyi: Kniga statei* (Moscow, 1910), p. 81.

[46] Andreevich (Evgeny Soloviev), "Ocherki tekushchei russkoi literatury: O Nitche," *Zhizn'* (April 1901), p. 286.

[47] Andrei Bely, "Krugovoe dvizhenie: Sorokh dve arabeski," *Trudy i dni*, no. 4–5 (July– October 1912), p. 60.

[48] G. A. Rachinsky, "Tragediia Nitsshe," *Voprosy filosofii i psikhologii* 55 (November– December 1900), p. 1003. The article was dedicated to Preobrazhensky.

an indestructible strength." The editors proclaimed their spiritual kinship to Nietzsche:

> For that circle of thoughts and actions which is close to *The World of Art*, and for all of future Russian and European culture, Nietzsche is not dead. Whether we are for or against him, we must be with him, close to him. . . . Nietzsche cannot be understood only with the heart, or only with the mind—he must be experienced with one's whole being.[49]

The positive response to Nietzsche among Russian intellectuals in the 1890s was due in large part to his protest against what they, too, felt was the excessive rationalism and positivism of the age. Nietzsche's provocative novelty presented a contrast to the cultural stagnation of the 1880s. They responded to Nietzsche's theme, "Spirit is the life that itself strikes into life: through its own torment, it increases its own knowledge." (Z, 127)

Those Russian intellectuals who reacted negatively to Nietzsche generally believed that his critique of religion was overwrought and might result in a serious undermining of social and personal ethics. But both proponents and opponents of Nietzsche reacted not only to what he said but to how he said it. Viacheslav Ivanov thought that Nietzsche possessed the gift of speaking like the gods. Many times in this decade of Nietzsche's debut into the Russian cultural world, Russian thinkers from various camps paid tribute to his literary power. Nietzsche's ability to poeticize philosophical argument attracted many Russians who were developing a new appreciation of the arts; indeed, Nietzsche's work itself accelerated the focus upon esthetics in these years. Acceptance and appreciation of Nietzsche's work decidedly outweighed fulminations and denunciations by the end of the 1890s. The stage was set for the next decade, when Russian writers, artists, and philosophers would draw upon, interpret, reinterpret, and transmute various aspects of Nietzsche's thought.

[49] *Mir iskusstva*, nos. 17–18 (1900).

2.

Stages of Nietzscheanism: Merezhkovsky's Intellectual Evolution

Bernice Glatzer Rosenthal

A SEMINAL FIGURE of the Silver Age, Dmitri S. Merezhkovsky (1865–1941) was one of the first Russians to popularize French symbolist poetry and the philosophy of Nietzsche. Also a major figure in the religious renaissance of the early twentieth century, Merezhkovsky is a prime exemplar of the catalytic effect of Nietzsche on Russian thought. For him, Nietzsche meant individualism, artistic and cultural creativity, worship of beauty, and rejection of the traditional Christian values of altruism, asceticism, and humility. Championing these views in the 1890s and in the early years of the twentieth century, he began to incorporate them into a new interpretation of Christianity. After 1905, Merezhkovsky distanced himself from Nietzsche, but Nietzschean elements remained a permanent feature in his world view. Nietzsche's challenge to Christian values, he said later, had forced Christians like himself to redefine them.[1]

Merezhkovsky first learned about Nietzsche in the late 1880s, a time when populism, hitherto the "faith" of the intelligentsia, was losing its vitality. Like other university students, Merezhkovsky read Schopenhauer and Spencer, but found ultimately unsatisfying secular philosophies that ignored metaphysical questions of the meaning of life and the problem of death. But Russian Orthodox Christianity also failed him, because it proscribed the intellect and the joys of this world. He was thus receptive to new ideas on contemporary problems. Nietzsche was already being discussed in his circle. Nietzsche, of course, was a favorite of the French

---

[1] Dmitri S. Merezhkovsky, *Polnoe sobranie sochinenii*, 24 vols. (Moscow, 1914), 13:25. Henceforth cited as *PSS*.

symbolists whose poetry Merezhkovsky admired, and by 1890 Nietzschean themes were evident in his own work. His drama *Sil'vio* (ca.
1890) deals with a would-be superman, a bored Renaissance prince, whose only
goal is to fly like an eagle (one of Zarathustra's animals) and whose greatest joy is battle. The unhappy prince is saved by a humble Christian
woman who teaches him to "love the people."[2] Merezhkovsky had not
broken with populism, even though he recognized that he himself did
not love the people and had no faith to offer them. At this point, however, he regarded Nietzsche's philosophy as a crass warrior's creed, un-
suited to sensitive souls.

A trip to Greece and Italy, in 1891, inspired a new interpretation of
Nietzsche, one that centered on the Nietzschean values of art, beauty,
and cultural creation. The art and architecture of ancient Greece had an
enormous impact on Merezhkovsky. To him the Parthenon was a revelation—beauty incarnate, "living eternal beauty," the ideal become real.[3]
So completely was the Parthenon in harmony with its natural setting that
it appeared to have grown from the soil in accord with divine laws. But
the fact that it was created by human beings testified to human powers
and demonstrated what daring men could achieve. He literally fell in
love with the "naked beauty" of the goddesses of Greece and with the
spirit they symbolized. Ancient Greece became Merezhkovsky's symbol
of harmony, a life-affirming culture that fused heart and mind, body and
soul, religion and life, into an integrated whole. Esthetic creativity became his prime value, and beauty became the means to make life meaningful, to give man the courage to go on living. The influence of
Nietzsche's *The Birth of Tragedy* is obvious. Nietzsche had stated that the
"existence of the world is *justified* only as an esthetic phenomenon," and
that art enables man to face the horrors of existence without becoming
"rigid with fear." (*BT*, 22, 104).

Accepting Nietzsche's glorification of the pagan virtues, Merezhkovsky
hailed his belief in a new way of life based on art. In "Acropolis" ("Akropol'," 1891) he called for a "new Parthenon," to be created by "godlike
men on earth."[4] Liberated from the slave morality, he implied, men,
need account to no one but themselves, to live "only for happiness . . .
for life."[5] Merezhkovsky used the words "Nietzscheanism" and "pagan-

[2] D. S. Merezhkovsky, *Sil'vio, Severnyi Vestnik,* 1890, no. 2 (pp. 69–90), no. 3 (pp. 68–
81), no. 4 (pp. 45–58), no. 5 (pp. 57–75).
[3] "Akropol'," *Vechnye sputniki, PSS,* 17:14.
[4] Ibid.
[5] "Volny," *PSS,* 23:157.

ism" interchangeably, for he regarded Nietzsche as a bard of paganism. Since Nietzsche's works were then banned in Russia, "paganism" might also have functioned as a code word for Nietzsche's philosophy, an example of the Aesopian language intellectuals had to use.

Still, Merezhkovsky was not yet a Nietzschean. He could not accept Nietzsche's statement "God is dead," nor could he believe that art was *only* an illusion. While desiring happiness on earth, he still feared death and desired eternal life. His wife Zinaida Gippius (1869–1945) was seriously ill at the time and his mother, to whom he was extremely attached, had died in 1889. Torn between love of beauty and desire to be reunited with her in heaven, he asked:

> Where then is the truth . . . in death, in heavenly love and
>   suffering?
> Or in the shadow of the gods, in your earthly beauty?
> They quarrel in the soul of man as in this divine temple,
> Eternal joy and life do battle with eternal mystery and death.[6]

Between 1891 and 1893 Merezhkovsky's Nietzscheanism coexisted with a romantic semi-religious mysticism that viewed art as a path to the World Soul. Attracted to the symbolist poetry he had discovered in France because of its mystical yearning for "other worlds than ours," he hoped that esthetic intuition and metaphysical idealism would lead to the new truths, the new faith, that he sought. During these years he conceived the idea for his historical trilogy *Christ and Antichrist*, as a means of depicting the eternal clash of world views.

Symbols (*Simvoly*, 1892) a collection of verse inspired by French symbolism, is a mixture of Christian and pagan themes that exalt both pagan and biblical heroes. Already, Merezhkovsky hoped for a new faith that would restore human greatness and unify the world. Rome was his symbol of world unity, first under pagan rule, then under the popes, then under yet unknown new faith.

> Faith died out in our hearts.
> Now in ancient ruins, we wander around full of grief.
>   O can it be that we will not find such a faith that would again
> Unite all tribes and peoples on earth?
>   Where are you, O Future Rome? Where are you,
>   O Unknown God?[7]

[6]"Panteon," *PSS*, 23:159–60.
[7]"Budushchii Rim," *PSS*, 23:160.

Merezhkovsky warned against a superficial classicism that emphasized Greek serenity and ignored the Greek consciousness of suffering and tragedy. Never advocating simple imitation of the ancients, he argued that mere forms cannot serve as a guide to life. Cultures must be studied in depth, their eternally valid principles separated from their obsolete forms.[8] An entirely new faith must be created. Merezhkovsky saw himself as its prophet, as one of the creators of a new Russian culture.

In his 1892 lecture "On the Causes of the Decline of and on the New Trends in Russian Literature" ("O prichinkah upadka i o novykh tech-eniiakh sovremennoi russkoi literatury"), Merezhkovsky attacked the utilitarian esthetics and the atheism of the populist intelligentsia.[9] Reason has failed man, he insisted; populism, materialism, and science cannot answer Russia's needs. A declaration of war against positivism, the lecture exalted symbolist art in particular as the vehicle that would lead to higher truths. Mystical, introspective, and imaginative, symbolism explores the human soul and the cosmos; it enables the artist to penetrate the veil of phenomena, to perceive the eternal forms that are inaccessible to ordinary men. The artist's intuition and imagination are divine gifts. As the artist provides the materials for a new idealistic culture, inspires spiritual transformation, the gulf between secular intelligentsia and religious peasants will narrow and disappear. Merezhkovsky still had not completely abandoned populism; indeed, he modeled himself partly on Vissarion Belinsky (1811–1848) and particularly admired Nicholas Mikhailovsky's (1842–1904) insistence on the importance of the individual.

The lecture combined romantic, symbolist, and Nietzschean themes: art as the highest form of human activity, imagination as the highest human faculty, and the artist as hero, daring explorer of the human soul, creator of a new culture. Its apotheosis of metaphysical idealism, however, is strikingly reminiscent of Vladimir Soloviev's (1853–1900) belief that art is a theurgy, a means to divine truth, the glimpse of eternity visible to man on earth.

But the epistemological and metaphysical premises of Nietzsche's philosophy, Merezhkovsky brushed aside. He did not even discuss them at length until 1915. In 1892–1893 he simply refused to accept Nietzsche's idea that the world is meaningless and ultimately incomprehensible. Nietzsche's conviction that higher truths do not exist (they are merely beautiful illusions) was still in the background of Merezhkovsky's con-

[8]"A. N. Maikov," *Vechnye sputniki*, PSS, 18:71.
[9]*PSS*, 18:175–275.

sciousness. The essential thrust of Nietzsche's philosophy, in particular its "affirmation of the earth," its concentration on life in this world, directly contradicted Merezhkovsky's desire to use art as a theurgy to reach other worlds. A common hope of ennobling man, a mutual love of beauty, and a common hatred of philistinism were the points at which the conflicting orientations intersected, but a true synthesis had not been achieved. One or the other element was bound to prevail.

In the space of a year or two, Merezhkovsky opted for Nietzsche. His earlier hopes that symbolist poetry would enable the artist to reach the people and create a new national culture were clearly not being fulfilled, since symbolist art was far too esoteric to serve as the basis for any new movement "to the people." Even the artists themselves had difficulty understanding one another's work. Nietzsche's philosophy provided a theoretical justification for Merezhkovsky's failure to reach "the people"; it permitted him to acknowledge his secession from Populism with finality, and to proclaim proudly the individualism and elitism that had formerly been a source of embarrassment and guilt. The poet was not only a prophet; he became a hero—a "hero of contemplation," while his creativity became the "highest form of action."[10] Opposed to materialism, indifferent to economic progress, Merezhkovsky insisted that the frenetic activity of economic man was trivial. It is the artist who destroys the old life and creates the new; a warrior for culture, his field of action is the human spirit.

The years 1894–1896 mark the highest point of Nietzsche's influence on Merezhkovsky. He exalted the Nietzschean values of courage, pride, and earthly beauty, and mocked Christian asceticism and humility. A creed of defiant asocial individualism, Merezhkovsky's Nietzscheanism enabled him to affirm his own importance and the centrality of art, to set himself off from the vulgar herd. Deliberately turning his back on those "other worlds" of symbolism that had not led him to a new faith, determined to forget the "mystery in all things," the "eternal darkness and horror," he set about overcoming the "fear of life" (and of death) that had enveloped him since childhood. He would strive for earthly joy instead.[11] "*Remain true to the earth*," Zarathustra had counseled. "Do not believe those who speak of superterrestial hopes! They are poisoners,

---

[10] "Pushkin," *Vechnye sputniki*, PSS, 18:137.

[11] *Smert bogov: Iulian Otstupnik*, PSS, 1:183–85. First published as *Otverzhenyi* in *Severnyi Vestnik*, 1895, no. 1 (pp. 71–112), no. 2 (pp. 73–125), no. 3 (pp. 1–52), no. 4 (pp. 1–46), no. 5 (pp. 1–35), no. 6 (pp. 41–88), henceforth cited as SV.

whether they know it or not. They are despisers of life, atrophying and self-poisoned men . . . so let them be gone. . . . To blaspheme the earth is now the most dreadful offense." (Z,42).

Soul became psyche as Merezhkovsky's search for higher truths assumed a secular form. Art and sensuality would make life bearable. Man would create himself, transcend his present human limitations. Beauty became Merezhkovsky's god and he based a new way of life on its worship. It featured defiance of established verities, smashing the old "tablets of values," adoration of the flesh, and exaltation of the artist as superman. The prime virtues became integrity to the artist's own goals and courage to defy convention and society; the prime sins, banality and ugliness. All other forms of morality were obsolete. "For the new beauty," Merezhkovsky proclaimed, "we will break all laws, trespass all limits."[12] No constraints, no inhibitions to esthetic expression would remain standing. For the artist, "all is permitted."

Death of the Gods: Julian the Apostate (Smert' Bogov: Iulian Otstupnik, 1895) is Merezhkovsky's most famous work of this period. In many respects a Nietzschean tract,[13] its central figure is based on the Roman emperor (ca. 331–363) who attempted to restore paganism. Originally the work was titled *The Outcast (Otverzhenii),* for Merezhkovsky refused to call Julian an apostate. For him, Julian was the prophet of a still unknown new faith.

Julian represented Merezhkovsky, or more exactly, the new man Merezhkovsky hoped to become. Julian's paganism resulted from his having fallen in love with a statue of Aphrodite while still a young man, an allusion to Merezhkovsky's experience in Greece. Hating the Christians who smashed such statues, Julian determined to destroy such iconoclasts. He referred to the Christians as the "crows of Galilee," and condemned them, their slave morality, and their obsession with death and suffering. Julian perceived their symbol, the cross, as an instrument of torture that did not merit the worship of free men. To their sickly religion, Julian counterposed his own—worship of the "living soul of beauty."[14] The bright happiness joyous love and self-exaltation brings men will eliminate all

---

[12] "Deti nochi," *Novye stikhotvoreniia, 1891–1895* (St. Petersburg, 1896), p. 5. *PSS,* 17:171 omits the last two lines. His views had changed by then and he himself deleted lines that he considered offensive.

[13] Compare Orest Holovaty, "Merezhkovsky's Christ and Antichrist" (Ph.D. diss., Vanderbilt University, 1977), pp. 35–36. Holovaty denies major Nietzschean influence and views Julian as a seeker of transcendence.

[14] *PSS,* 1:275–76.

shadows, all anxious questioning. Despondency,, fear, sacrifice, and prayer will all become superfluous. Man will decide his own destiny, create his own meaning. Esthetic gratification and the excitement of battle and struggle will bring man such ecstasy that he will cease to think of death. "Eternal Olympian laughter" will drive out the sound of weeping in a new world where men themselves are gods.

> Do not say: the gods *already* are no more, but rather, the gods *as yet* are not! They are not but they shall be, not in the heavens, but on earth. We shall all be as gods—only it is necessary to possess great daring such as no one on earth has had, not even the Hero of Macedon himself.[15]

Julian proudly proclaims: "Rejoice, tribes and peoples of the earth. I am the messenger of life, I am the liberator, I am the antichrist!"[16]

Epitomizing Nietzsche's ideal of a "free death" ("Die at the right time!" [Z,97–99]), Julian overcomes his fear of death. Meeting it courageously on the battlefield (the second best death according to Nietzsche), he proclaims: "Let the Galileans triumph, we shall conquer later on. The reign of godlike men, eternally laughing, like the sun, will exist on earth."[17] Laughter is Julian's leitmotif. A symbol of lightheartedness, it was considered the weapon of the devil by medieval Christians. The same theme is echoed by Charles Baudelaire.

Julian is a personification of the "will to power," who dares to be great, to go beyond good and evil. At times he exhibits a less attractive trait of Nietzscheanism: gratuitous cruelty. He rapes his still virginal unloved wife[18] and refuses a Christian couple's request that he restore land taken from them, telling them to practice the poverty their religion preaches. Nietzsche's contempt for the "herd" is seconded by Merezhkovsky's reference to them as "human refuse," and by the pagan priest's statement "God is not there where the rabble prays."[19] As the rampaging mob smashes the beautiful Greek statues, Merezhkovsky states: "is it not shameful to be human—the same flesh, the same filth as these?"[20]

Nietzsche's exaltation of sensuality ("sensual pleasure, innocent and

---

[15] *Otverzhennyi, SV*, no. 6, pp. 53–54 (omitted from *PSS*).

[16] *PSS*, 1:209.

[17] *PSS*, 1:335–36. For last lines, omitted from *PSS*, see *Otverzhennyi, SV*, no. 6, pp. 53–54.

[18] *PSS*, 1:163.

[19] *PSS*, 1:205, 280–81.

[20] *PSS*, 1:55–60.

free, to free hearts, the earth's garden joy" [Z, 207]), is muted in Julian,[21] but it is the theme of Merezhkovsky's introduction to his 1896 translation of Longus's *Daphnis and Chloe* (*Dafnis i Khloia*). Seconding Nietzsche, and possibly Soloviev, Merezhkovsky charged that Christian asceticism is directly responsible for man's misery, for it forces him to deny his most vital instincts. Physical love, he said, is not sinful; it is the "eternal return of the human essence to nature, to the bosom of unconscious life. Love and nature are one and the same; love is the passionate flight of the soul to primordial spontaneous health from that artificial cultivated sickness which we call culture."[22] The essay lauds the "guiltless and natural love" of beasts and gods, invokes Pan, and bewails the loss of the natural spontaneous life. Typically, Merezhkovsky concluded that old forms cannot be resurrected; instead, new forms that suit modern life must be created.

Man still does not know what these new forms are. But they cannot emerge until the old order has been destroyed; destruction, therefore, has priority. But destruction is a task for supermen. Only they are capable of authentic rebellion, of pushing forward into the void. Lesser men lack the strength to maintain their revolt and, devoid of staying power and of the courage to proclaim their own goals, they cannot bear the loneliness of long-term rebellion. Seeking social acceptance and security, they backslide to conventional behavior after a brief show of defiance.

New Verse (*Novye stikhotvoreniia*, 1896), exalts heroes who challenge tradition, who wrestle with God, in order to create a truly new culture. The poem "Michaelangelo" ("Mikel'Anzhelo") lauds the artist as a lonely superman, "a demon hideous and great,"[23] whose stubborn attempt to dethrone old values was unceasing and uncompromising. "Song of the Bacchanal" ("Pesnia vakkanok") glorifies the Bacchanalian orgies, the casting off of all restraints. The Dionysian (ceaseless flux, instinct) overpowers the Apollonian (structure, reason), thus liberating the inner man. Through ecstasy, he achieves oblivion and overcomes his fear of death.

> Do not be ashamed of nudity.
> Fear neither love nor death.
> Do not fear our beauty.
> . . . To you, O youth

---

[21] Holovaty, "Christ and Antichrist," p. 62, claims Merezhkovsky had an antisexual bias.

[22] *Dafnis i Khloia*, PSS, 19:220. Vladimir Soloviev's essay *Smysl' liubvi* (*The Meaning of Love*), published in 1893, also attacked asceticism, claiming that the physical expression of love could overcome individual isolation.

[23] PSS, 22:141.

Despondency is the greatest sin.
There is one exploit in life—joy.
There is one truth in life—laughter.
Our groans are just like laughter.
Approach, all-powerful Bacchus, dare
Break all limits and all laws
With innocent laughter.
We will drink the nectar of life.
To the dawn, like gods in the heavens.
With laughter we will conquer death.
With mad bacchanal in our hearts.[24]

The line, "Our groans are just like laughter," suggests that Nietzschean-ism had not enabled Merezhkovsky to overcome suffering. Arsinoe, a character in *Julian*, is the spokeswoman for Merezhkovsky's continuing reservations, although, having led Julian to the forbidden Greek statues, she was directly responsible for Julian's paganism. A self-confessed lover of power, she had accused him of lack of will, had urged him to "dare" to conquer, to become emperor. Her subsequent conversion to Christian-ity is, therefore, crucial. Paganism had failed to bring her happiness; it has not obviated her distaste for life. Life, she tells Julian, is "more ter-rible than death." Desiring to be reunited with her recently deceased sister, she has converted to Christianity. Happiness *after* death, at least, will be hers. She will attain belief by squelching her intellect. "Intelli-gence is more seductive than any passion," but through faith, life and death will become equal.[25] She will then be immune from life's vagaries (a Schopenhauerian rather than a Nietzschean stance). Arsinoe still seeks power, but over herself rather than over others. She tells Julian of a different Christ than that worshipped by the Galileans.

> Those who torment their flesh and spirit in the desert—they are far from the gentle son of Mary. He loved children and freedom and merry feasts and white lilies. He loved life, Julian! Only we have departed from him, have become confused and darkened in spirit. They all call you apostate. But they themselves are the real apostates.[26]

And:

[24]*PSS*, 22:45–46.
[25]*PSS*, 1:240–41. The reader is reminded of Merezhkovsky's mother's death a few years before.
[26]*PSS*, 1:324.

I know that you love Him. . . . When your lips are cursing the
Crucified, your heart is thirsting for Him. When you are struggling
against His name, you are closer to His spirit than those who repeat,
with dead lips, Lord! Lord! And it is they who are your enemies,
not He.[27]

Arsinoe's statements indicate that at the very height of Merezhkovsky's
rebellion, in a book celebrating an Antichrist, Merezhkovsky still yearned
for Christ. But Arsinoe fails to convince Julian. He is not the one to
reconcile what Merezhkovsky was already calling the "two truths," Titan
and Galilean, Olympus and Golgotha, God and the Devil.[28]

Yet Julian does embody certain elements of the desired reconciliation.
He is spiritually oriented, has an ascetic streak and detests the licentiousness of paganism. His Dionysus is a god of love, not lust. Even though
Julian restores the pagan temples, he rejects part of the pagan past, for
he wishes to free the slaves and close the circuses. But he is advised not
to do the latter, for "without blood there is no merriment. The smell of
Rome is the smell of blood."[29] Merezhkovsky now recognized the cruelty
and blood-lust of paganism, saw that it was not all joyousness and light.
A poem of the same period, "Children of the Night" ("Deti nochi") also
indicates Merezhkovsky's disillusion with Nietzscheanism as a guide to
life.

Children of grief, children of the night,
Wait, our prophets will approach.

With hope in our hearts,
Dying, we yearn
For worlds not yet created.
We have a presentiment of the future.

Our speech is daring,
But we have been condemned to death.
Too early forerunners
Of a too slow spring.

. . . .

We are hanging over an abyss,
Children of darkness, waiting for the sun.

[27] Ibid.
[28] *PSS*, 1:70, 72. See also p. 247.
[29] *PSS*, 1:252.

The sun will come, and like shadows,
We will die in its rays. [30]

Nietzsche had stated that the firstborn is always sacrificed by old idol-priests (Z,217). Presumably Merezhkovsky and his contemporaries would be the unfortunate casualties of a transition era; they would not live to see the new world.

Other aspects of Merezhkovsky's growing reservations on Nietzschean-ism, which led him to reject it as a self-contained creed, can be inferred from his literary criticism. In an essay on Gustave Flaubert, he attributed the latter's unhappiness, as revealed in his letters, to the psychologically distorting effects of living only for art. [31] He treated Henryk Ibsen as an examplar of the negative aspects of individualism, the destructive conse-quences of a stance of perennial revolt. [32] Dostoevsky's characters dem-onstrate the failure of secular philosophies as guides to life. [33] The poet Fedor Tiutchev (1803–1873) is discussed as the very symbol of esthetic individualism. Tiutchev's epistemology of an orderless universe (really Nietzsche's), Merezhkovsky implied in 1915, almost brought Merezhkov-sky to suicide in the 1890s. Unable to bear the idea of a cosmic void, a world without order or meaning, of constant struggle, where evil is indis-tinguishable from good, Tiutchev (really Merezhkovsky) "having recoiled in horror, grasped at Christianity like a drowning man at a straw." [34] Mer-ezhkovsky's attempt to create a life centered on art crumbled before the prospect of the abyss. Reluctantly, he realized that he was not a super-man, that he could not sustain a philosophy of self-exaltation in a cosmic void. Thus he began to seek a specifically Christian faith to provide ab-solute values and the certainty of eternal life.

His essay on Pushkin (1896) marks the beginning of his lifelong at-tempt to reconcile the "two truths," paganism and Christianity. Merezh-kovsky believed that Pushkin had done so unconsciously and set about trying to find his "secret." As Merezhkovsky used the terms "paganism" and "Christianity," they are not historical or philosophical categories but clusters of attitudes. Paganism contains the "truth of the earth"—art, beauty, sensuality, self-affirmation. Christianity contains the "truth of heaven"— eternal life, brotherly love. Neither is complete in itself, for paganism

---

[30] *PSS*, 22:171 (exact date of poem not given).
[31] *PSS*, 17:189–204.
[32] *PSS*, 17:240–42.
[33] *PSS*, 18:14.
[34] *Dve tainy russkoi poezii* (Petrograd, 1915), pp. 95–97.

denies the soul and Christianity denies the body. Beauty was not enough
for him, so Merezhkovsky sought to reconcile heaven and earth, spirit
and flesh, intellect and feeling.

His treatment of Greek culture shifted to an emphasis on its tragic
aspects. Its joy became almost inconsequential. Apparently, the emotional gratification he had sought in Nietzscheanism still eluded him; his
life (like Nietzsche's) remained basically ascetic. Even as his doubts about
pure paganism increased, he immersed himself in its art and in the translation of additional Greek tragedies. His version of Sophocles' *Oedipus
the King* appeared in 1894. He interpreted the tragedy as Oedipus' opposition to the entire world order, his attempt to make himself into a
god, and claimed that the ending epitomized an almost Christian tender-
ness because of Oedipus' love for his daughters, a love that immortalizes
human will and defeats blind fate. His translation of *Oedipus at Colonus*
appeared in 1896 and of *Antigone* in 1899; he considered the last a tragedy of wisdom and voluptuousness that prefigured the Christian theme
of sacrifice for an ideal. Finally, in 1899, he "turned to Christ."

Merezhkovsky did not abandon Nietzsche when he turned to Christ.
Indeed, only one year before, he had told Briusov, "when I read Nietzsche
I thrill from head to toe."[35] The "new religious consciousness" that he
preached after 1900 was his answer to Nietzsche's attack on Christianity.
Allowing Nietzsche's critique of Christianity as a critique of "historical
Christianity," Merezhkovsky maintained that the latter would soon be
superseded by a forthcoming Third Revelation or Third Testament. The
joys of this world would then be permitted to Christians, the joys of love
and personal immortality. Basing this interpretation on the Apocalypse of
St. John, he called his new religion "The Religion of the End."[36]

Merezhkovsky's trilogy of historical novels *Christ and Antichrist* (1896–
1905) and his study of Tolstoi and Dostoevsky (1901–1902) document
the initial stages of his search for a resolution of the "two truths." The
protagonists of the trilogy, Julian the Apostate, Leonardo da Vinci, and
Peter the Great, embody the changing nature of Merezhkovsky's hopes
for a superman who could end the conflict. Merezhkovsky's conception

[35] Valery Briusov, *Dnevniki* (Moscow, 1927), p. 53.

[36] For details, see Bernice Glatzer Rosenthal, *D. S. Merezhkovsky and the Silver Age*
(The Hague, 1975), pt. 2; *idem*, "Nietzsche in Russia: The Case of Merezhkovsky" *Slavic
Review* 33 (September 1974), pp. 429–52; C. H. Bedford, *The Seeker: D. S. Merezhkovsky*
(Lawrence, Kansas, 1975), chaps. 5 and 6; J. Scherrer, *Die Petersburger Religiös-Philoso-
phischen Vereinigungen* (Wiesbaden, 1973), *passim*.

of history wavered between a Dionysian concept of time as an endless cycle of conflicting values and an apocalyptic view, which sees progression toward a final resolution.[37] Ultimately the apocalyptic view prevailed.

He conceived the idea for the trilogy after being inspired by the twin visions of the Parthenon and the Hagia Sophia. As already noted, Julian was first published as *The Outcast*, and later retitled to fit into the scheme of the trilogy. Julian is the most Nietzschean of Merezhkovsky's protagonists; the portrayal of Christianity in the novel is the most negative and the concept of history the most cyclical.

Resurrection of the Gods: Leonardo da Vinci (*Voskresshenie bogi: Leonardo da Vinchi*) appeared in 1901. A new kind of superman, with marked Christian traits coexisting in harmony with pagan, Leonardo is kind. As a child he rescued a moth from sadistic schoolboys; he delights in freeing caged birds, does not eat meat, and feels an affinity with all living creatures. Unlike Julian, Leonardo does not exult in transgression and is not motivated by a will to power. He does not laugh, but observes everything with the same detached interest, and in his smile is a hint of resignation. (Later in life Merezhkovsky emphasized that Jesus never laughed; He only smiled.) Leonardo considers the sexual act not sinful, but gross, and avoids women. Disgusted by the mob, he advises his disciple that the artist's strength lies in solitude.[38]

Yet, Leonardo is not the reconciler Merezhkovsky seeks; he is but a forerunner. His mechanic, aptly named Zoroastro da Peretola, remains a lifelong cripple; having been injured in the crash of Leonardo's flying machine, he is a living reproach to Leonardo's premature attempt to provide man with wings. Shortly before his death, Leonardo begins a painting of Bacchus, but leaves it unfinished. Instead of the thyrsus of the Dionysian rites, Bacchus holds a cross made of a desert reed, a prototype of the cross of Golgotha, and he smiles with a smile that contains a hint of sadness and mockery.[39] Leonardo begins to paint John the Baptist. He has no wings as he would in a more conventional painting, and as the work on John progresses, John begins to resemble Bacchus, and

[37] For an interpretation of Merezhkovsky's conception of historical time, see Edith W. Clowes, "The Integration of Nietzsche's Ideas of History, Time, and 'Higher Nature' in the Early Historical Novels of Dmitry Merezhkovsky," *Germano-Slavica* 3 (Fall 1981), pp. 401–16.

[38] *PSS*, 2:192.

[39] *PSS*, 3:323–26.

also the Mona Lisa.[40] Leonardo becomes conscious of the secret he has been concealing, even from himself, that Dionysus and Christ, Christ and Antichrist, are one.[41]

Leonardo's disciple, Giovanni Beltraffio, records his conflicting feelings about Leonardo in his diary. He recognizes the Christian elements in Leonardo but also fears that Leonardo is being seduced by the "wise serpent," by Antichrist.[42] He also falls under the influence of Cassandra, a young witch. She tells Giovanni of Dionysus, hinting that Dionysus and Christ, or Antichrist and Christ, are one.[43]

> One god among the Olympian gods who was nearest of all to his subterranean brothers, a god radiant and dark, like the morning twilight; as merciless as death; who has come down to earth and bestowed to mortals a forgetfulness of death—a new flame from the flame of Prometheus—in his own blood, in the intoxicating juice of the grape of the vines. And who among the people, O my brother, who shall understand and proclaim to the universe, that the wisdom of the one crowned with clusters of grapes is like the wisdom of the one crowned with thorns—of Him who has said: 'I am the true grape of the vine'—and that He, even as the god Dionysus, doth intoxicate the world with his blood.[44]

Giovanni views her prophecy as comforting and they drink "to the Unknown whom we are both summoning—to the ultimate reconciler."[45] But subsequent passages to Giovanni's diary reveal his continued spiritual torment:

> The resemblance of Christ and Antichrist is a perfect resemblance. The face of Christ in the face of the Antichrist. Who shall distinguish them? Who shall resist their temptation? The ultimate mystery is the ultimate sorrow, whose like the world has never seen.
>
> In the Cathedral of Orvieto, in the picture of Luca Signorelli— are windblown folds in the garb of Antichrist falling into an abyss. And just such folds, resembling the wings of a gigantic bird, were at Leonardo's shoulders as he stood on the edge of the precipice.[46]

[40] *PSS*, 3:343–44, 347.
[41] *PSS*, 3:358.
[42] *PSS*, 2:164–205.
[43] *PSS*, 3:252.
[44] *PSS*, 3:253.
[45] *PSS*, 3:258.
[46] *PSS*, 3:288.

And on the last page of Giovanni's diary, in a very different handwriting:

> The White She-Demon is everywhere, always. May she be ac-
> cursed! The ultimate mystery: two are one. Christ and Antichrist are
> one. Heaven above and heaven below. Nay, may this never be—
> may this never be! Better death![47]

Cassandra has seduced him and he commits suicide. The internal conflict is too much for him.

Minor characters in *Leonardo* indicate Merezhkovsky's abiding attraction to certain "Nietzschean" views. Savanarola, for example, incarnates
"historical Christianity's" fanaticism as well as its injunction to shun the
beauties of this world. Fra Giorgio, outwardly the "meekest of men," but
actually a sadist who invents tortures for the Inquisition, personifies
Nietzsche's view of the link between asceticism and cruelty. Cesare Bor-
gia (also a favorite of Nietzsche's) is described admiringly as strong, fearless, amoral, a "man of will," and compared to a beast or a god because
he has progressed beyond good and evil. Merezhkovsky has Machiavelli
accuse Leonardo of lack of will, according to Merezhkovsky, Leonardo's
chief shortcoming. Machiavelli states:

> People should either accept or reject Christ. We have done neither
> one nor the other. We are neither Christians nor pagans. We have
> left one shore but have not reached the other. We lack sufficient
> strength to be righteous and fear to be evil. We are neither white
> nor black—merely grey; neither cold nor hot—merely tepid.[48]

Machiavelli realizes that Leonardo is a true Christian, even though the
latter's enemies call him a heretic and an Antichrist.[49] Merezhkovsky,
however, recognizing Leonardo's limitations (and the limitations of the
Renaissance), was already seeking entirely new solutions to the problems
he saw in "historical Christianity," and, in the process, to distance himself from Nietzsche. The apocalyptic visions of the Epilogue—the White
Cowl (or Hood) of the Russian Old Believer legend and the Woman
Clothed in the Sun—are described by a young Russian painter visiting
Italy and portend the future direction of Merezhkovsky's views.

Antichrist: *Peter and Alexis* (*Antikhrist: Petr i Aleksei*) was published in
1904–1905.[50] Only a few years before, in *Tolstoi and Dostoevsky*, Me-

[47] Ibid.
[48] *PSS*, 3:193. Compare a similar statement in *Julian* (by Arsinoe), 1:243.
[49] *PSS*, 3:194.
[50] Comprises vols. 4 and 5 of *PSS*.

rezhkovsky had viewed Peter positively as an exemplar of superhuman will, but in the novel, Peter is treated very critically. His drunken orgies and sadism are extensively depicted. Fond of pulling teeth, Peter also carries around a lancet in order to perform surgical operations, but he himself cannot endure pain. He demonstrates that creation and destruction, good and evil are two sides of the same coin. Whether Peter himself is a man-god, a man-beast, or Antichrist is not clear, for he is beyond good and evil. Convinced that if his son Alexis accedes to the throne, Russia will sink back into medieval darkness, he breaks the moral law and he kills his own son, assuming full responsibility for the deed and praying that God punish him, not Russia. Peter is last seen (in the novel) sailing through a sea made blood-red by the rays of the setting sun. The helmsman, noting that a storm is coming up, advises Peter to turn back, but Peter refuses, saying, "God is with us."

Merezhkovsky's evolving attitude toward Christianity can be seen in his compassionate rather than contemptuous attitude toward the pious but weak and confused Alexis. But the key to the future is held by neither Peter nor Alexis, but by a minor figure, Tikhon, a former government official. Having rejected the Christianity of the official Church and of the Old Believers, wandering in search of religious truth, he comes across a sect, "The White Death," which practices "Vigils of Joy." These include Dionysian chants and dances, sexual orgies, and flagellation. With them, Tikhon learns to laugh and to dance. But he flees the sect when h discovers that they practice ritual sacrifice, and saves the intended victim, a baby boy. The episode illustrates Merezhkovsky's rejection of Dionysianism (because of its cruelty and blood-lust), in favor of Christian love. Resuming his wanderings, Tikhon meets an old man, Ivanushka, diminuitive of John, who tells him of the approaching Apocalypse and the forthcoming Third Testament. Struck dumb by the magnitude of this revelation, Tikhon is unable to impart his new wisdom, but the radiance of his countenance testifies to its beauty. The book concludes with a prophecy of a great battle in which the forces of Christ defeat the forces of Antichrist. The "two truths" have separated and will be reconciled by the Second Coming of Christ.

Apocalyptic yearnings are prominent in Merezhkovsky's study of Tolstoi and Dostoevsky. Nietzsche, however, as Ann Lane rightly notes, is as prominent a presence as the two Russian giants.[51] who are compared

---

[51] Lane, "Nietzsche in Russian Thought," p. 235.

not only with one another, but with the German. Merezhkovsky considered Nietzsche one of the most sensitive people in the West and recalled how he had hailed the resurrection of the "two Olympian gods, Apollo and Dionysus" in the "youthful and so springlike book of Friedrich Nietzsche, *The Birth of Tragedy*."[52] He also recalled that he had hailed

> the union of the two opposing demons or gods in the even more unusual and mysterious phenomenon of Zarathustra. And we would not but recognize in him he who pursued and tormented Dostoevsky all his life, could not but recognize the man-god in the superman. And miraculous, almost unbelievable for us, was the coincidence of the newest, the most extreme of the Europeans, and the most Russian of the Russians [Nietzsche and Dostoevsky].
>
> From two different and opposing sides they reached the very same abyss. The superman is this final point, the sharpest summit of the great mountain range of European philosophy, with its centuries-long roots which engendered the secluded and isolated person. Farther one cannot go; the historical road has been trodden to the end; farther is the precipice and the abyss—fall or flight—the path of the suprahistorical—religion.[53]

And in the same vein: "Man-god and God-man—Christ and Antichrist— here are the two opposite shores, the two edges of the abyss"; only religion can give man the wings that will enable him to fly over it.[54]

Merezhkovsky considered Nietzsche particularly relevant to Russians.[55] As already indicated, he believed that Peter the Great provided the world with an exemplar of superhuman will. He interpreted Nietzsche's counterposing of Russia as a new incarnation of pagan Rome, Imperial Rome, to Western Europe decomposing under the influence of democratic Christianity to mean that Nietzsche expected Antichrist to emerge in Russia. Dostoevsky, of course, argued for the Christian nature of Russia with equal conviction. Therefore, Merezhkovsky concluded, the fate not only of Russia, but of all humanity, hinged on whether his generation of Russians opted for Nietzsche's superman or Dostoevsky's Christ, or, in Soloviev's words, became the "East of Xerxes" (worldly empire) or the "East

[52] *PSS*, 9:viii. Tolstoi and Dostoevsky comprise vols. 9–12 of *PSS*.
[53] *PSS*, 9:viii–ix.
[54] *PSS*, 9:x.
[55] *PSS*, 9:ix.

of Christ."[56] Elsewhere in his study of Tolstoi and Dostoevsky, Merezh-kovsky posited the fateful choice as between atheism and his own "Religion of the End." He distinguished between two forms of atheism: the "social tower of Babel," which leads to a "universal anthill" (socialism); and "decadence," which leads to the madness of [Dostoevsky's] Kirillov and Nietzsche."[57]

Merezhkovsky now superimposed a polarity *within* Christianity—the flesh and the spirit, symbolized by Tolstoi and Dostoevsky, respectively—onto the polarity of paganism and Christianity. Maintaining that "historical Christianity" has emphasized the spirit at the expense of the flesh, Merezhkovsky advocated "holy flesh," the sanctification of sex. He claimed that what Nietzsche said of Christianity "was not religiously, not mystically, but historically true"[58] and argued that if Christianity could return to the flesh, it would not be the Buddhist nihilism of which Nietzsche accused it of being.

Tolstoi, treated as Nietzsche's antipode, is a vehicle for Merezhkovsky's attack on "historical Christianity." He is accused of a "will to nothingness," the inverse of Nietzsche's "will to power" (a term that Merezhkovsky used quite loosely), and of preaching that "all is forbidden."[59] Critical of Tolstoi's preachments of asceticism, altruism, passivity, and of his "flight from culture," Merezhkovsky contrasted Nietzschean self-affirmation with Tolstoi's denial of the importance of the individual in history and his rejection of the Promethean elements in the human personality. From this, Merezhkovsky claimed, stemmed Tolstoi's failure to recognize the "tragic greatness" of Napoleon.[60] Merezhkovsky considered Napoleon a man-god, an Antichrist, whose actions inspired the revaluation of values that has been going on from Goethe's *Prometheus* to Nietzsche's *Antichrist*; he considered this process of major religious-moral significance.

Yet, Merezhkovsky concluded, despite the surface opposition, Tolstoi and Nietzsche reached the same conclusions about Christ, each interpreting His teaching as self-denial, asceticism, passivity, resignation. Indeed, Merezhkovsky claimed, Tolstoi is as much of a pagan as Nietzsche; for both emphasize the flesh and ignore the spirit. Tolstoi's writings evidence his obsession with the flesh, even though he condemned it, while

---

[56] *PSS*, 12:72–73. See also 10:124, 176.
[57] *PSS*, 10:160.
[58] *PSS*, 12:50.
[59] *PSS*, 11:101; 12:55.
[60] *PSS*, 11:86. See also pp. 44–118 *passim*.

Nietzsche celebrated the pleasures of the flesh but did not experience them. Merezhkovsky maintained that Nietzsche curses Christ, while Tolstoi blesses Him, but that Nietzsche was a secret disciple of Christ and an open opponent while Tolstoi was an open disciple and a secret opponent. (He considered Tolstoi's ethics and epistemology Buddhist, not Christian.) Nietzsche's denial of Christ led to his madness, while Tolstoi's religion led to a worse fate—common sense and mediocrity.[61] Merezhkovsky believed that Christ had two faces, the "dark face" of "historical Christianity" that Tolstoi and Nietzsche saw, and a second face, that of the apparent Antichrist, but actually the real Christ, which would be revealed in the future.[62] It was this second face of Christ, Merezhkovsky insisted, that Tolstoi and Nietzsche unconsciously sought, despite Nietzsche's blindness to the holy elements in paganism, his failure to recognize the link between Dionysus and Christ until the very end.[63] Seeking evidence in Tolstoi's works of flesh desiring to unite with spirit, to become "holy flesh", Merezhkovsky pointed to Uncle Eroshka (in *The Cossacks*) as a kind of Christian pagan, for he loves all God's creatures, sees the divine element in all that surrounds him. Merezhkovsky regarded Uncle Eroshka as an involuntary or unconscious ally of Zarathustra and of Antichrist.[64]

The parallels Merezhkovsky perceived between Nietzsche and Dostoevsky are even more important to his apocalyptic vision. He noted Nietzsche's allusion to Dostoevsky in *Götterdämmerung*, and counterposed quotations from Nietzsche to statements by various Dostoevsky characters, especially Kirillov (in *The Possessed*) to demonstrate the spiritual kinship of the two authors, the close relationship of Dostoevsky's man-god and Nietzsche's superman.[65] For example, Kirillov's statement, "If there is no God I am God,"[66] is akin to Nietzsche's "If God exists how can I endure not to be a God?" Nietzsche's concept of a free death is anticipated by Kirillov's committing suicide to affirm his freedom. Ivan Karamazov's statement, "If there is no God everything is permitted," parallels Zarathustra's statement, "Nothing is true, all is permitted." Zarathustra's command, "Remain true to the earth, my brothers," echoes Father Zo-

[61] *PSS*, 11:237–39.
[62] *PSS*, 11:94.
[63] *PSS*, 11:237.
[64] *PSS*, 9:9, 26.
[65] *PSS*, 12:165.
[66] *PSS*, 12:193.

sima's kissing of the earth and Dmitri Karamazov's references to "damp Mother Earth."[67] Nietzsche's statement that a people who believe in themselves will also have their own god is replicated by Shatov's nationalism, his belief that Russians are the God-bearing people.[68]

Merezhkovsky emphasized that Nietzsche and Dostoevsky both had visions of the approaching end and of a new man.[69] Shortly before his madness, Nietzsche called himself Antichrist and signed one letter, "the last student of the philosophy of Dionysus" and another letter, "The Crucified."[70] Shortly before his death, Dostoevsky warned of the Antichrist in his diary. Nietzsche complained of his "human, all too human" limitations and described man as "something that must be overcome." Kirillov stated that man cannot endure in his earthly form, that he will change physically: "Then the new man, then all will be new. Then history will be divided into two parts, from the gorilla to the death of god and from the death of god to the physical transformation of earth and man,"[71] in other words, the superman. Dostoevsky, a Christian, was anticipating both physical and spiritual changes in man, while Nietzsche expounded a secular philosophy. His superman, said Merezhkovsky, was a reaction to contemporary science, to Darwin and the idea of evolution. For Nietzsche, Merezhkovsky argued, man is not an end, not the final link, but only one of many links in the endless chain of cosmic development; his superman is an animal form, a "new creature,"[72] rather than a god.

Kirillov and Shatov, Ivan and the Devil, Raskolnikov and Svirdigailov (in *Crime and Punishment*, 1867) discuss the idea of endlessness, of the eternal present, a version of Nietzsche's eternal recurrence. But Raskolnikov is horrified by the very idea of the absence of goals, the lack of any final resolution.[73] Merezhkovsky interpreted Nietzsche's madness and Dostoevsky's epilepsy (the holy sickness) as part of the pain of birth, a great sickness that will lead to the ultimate liberation of the spirit, symbolized, to him, by sprouting wings.[74] More sympathetic to Dostoevsky's

---

[67] PSS, 12:46.
[68] PSS, 12:156.
[69] PSS, 12:187–88.
[70] PSS, 12:114.
[71] PSS, 10:119–20.
[72] Ibid.
[73] PSS, 12:187–88. See 10:151 for Merezhkovsky's view of "metaphysical delirium."
[74] PSS, 10:120.

apocalyptic Christianity, he now viewed Nietzsche's madness as "not only logically, but mystically just,"[75] testimony that man cannot live without God.

Challenged by Nietzsche to revalue his values, to predict what new values lay beyond good and evil, Merezhkovsky tried to posit a new Christian morality. Again contrasting Nietzsche and Dostoevsky, he opposed Nietzsche's anarchism ("the state, the coldest of monsters") to Dostoevsky's monarchism, rejecting both. Dostoevsky, Merezhkovsky charged, confuses Christian morality, which is internal, with external laws, penalties, and punishments.[76] Indeed, up to now, Merezhkovsky continued, Western culture has not followed Christ's law, but the laws of the Old Testament, Rome, and the categorical imperative. Christ's law is love and Christ Himself represents freedom. Nietzsche errs in considering Him the preacher of a slave morality, while Dostoevsky's refusal to recognize that Christ is freedom stems from the writer's own fear of freedom. Christ, said Merezhkovsky, is "not a moral but a religious supramoral phenomenon which transgresses all limits and barriers of the moral law, a phenomenon of the greatest freedom beyond good and evil."[77] Uniting in Himself the poles of the man-God and God-man, His teaching does not imply leveling, as Nietzsche wrongly charged, but the creation of new and deeper valleys, new and higher mountains.[78] Rather than self-abnegation, His doctrine of personal immortality is the greatest self-affirmation of all. To Merezhkovsky eternal life meant resurrection of the spirit *and* the body, as distinct from the obliteration of the individual in Buddhism or in the eternal recurrence of Nietzsche.

Taking upon himself the role of Christian prophet, Merezhkovsky called upon his fellow symbolists to follow him in his new Christianity. Russia, he said, is like a dry forest. The life-giving sap of faith is gone. The decadents are the highest branches of the trees. When the inevitable lightning strikes, it will hit them first. From them the entire forest will go up in flames. An answer to Zarathustra's secular apocalypticism ("And *soon* they shall stand before me like arid grass and steppe, and truly, weary of themselves—and longing for *fire* rather than for water! . . .One day they shall proclaim with tongues of flame: It is coming, it is near,

[75] PSS, 12:200.
[76] PSS, 11:155.
[77] PSS, 11:186.
[78] PSS, 12:201, 24.

the great noontide!" [Z, 192]), for Merezhkovsky, "the great noontide" was the Second Coming of Christ.[79] He insisted that the universe is not ceaseless flux; it has a definite meaning, a definite beginning, and a definite end: the Second Coming of Christ.[80]

But the nature of Merezhkovsky's Christ was still undefined. He was still ambiguous on whether Christ and Antichrist are one and the same, or different sides of the same coin, or eternal enemies destined to do battle. The ambiguity remained for several years.

The Revolution of 1905 caused Merezhkovsky to revise many of his views; as new priorities and goals (especially sociopolitical goals) came to the fore, Nietzsche moved to the background. Repudiating his former individualism and reversing his previous asocial stance, Merezhkovsky began to preach a "Religious Revolution" that would inaugurate the Kingdom of God on Earth. A new concept, "Religious Sociality," was a kind of Christian anarchism. Formulating these views in conscious opposition to Nietzsche, Merezhkovsky hoped to substitute the Christian principle of love for the Nietzschean principle of power. He now maintained that love is power, that where love is present, freedom is also. In Merezhkovsky's ideal society, men would not have power over other men and the only law would be Christ's law—love—indelibly engraved on every human heart.[81] Love would provide the means to reconcile what he now called "the truth of anarchism" (personal freedom) with "the truth of socialism" (belonging to a community). This new esteem for belongingness was also, in part, a reaction to Nietzsche.

But Merezhkovsky retained a Nietzschean hostility toward the mob with his contempt for the "slave morality" of Christianity, liberalism, and socialism. More sympathetic to anarchism than to socialism, Merezhkovsky charged that socialism denies individuality and that in a socialist society the mob would rule. As his apocalypticism took on a sociopolitical dimension, he praised Nietzsche, along with Max Stirner, Michael Bakunin, and Ibsen for seeing "the first days of the sun of the great universal revolution."[82] He included Nietzsche as one of the "nobility of culture" that withdrew from public affairs during the nineteenth century and com-

---

[79] *PSS*, 13:84.

[80] *PSS*, 12:272.

[81] For details see Rosenthal, *D. S. Merezhkovsky*, pt. 3; and "Eschatology and the Appeal of Revolution: Merezhkovsky, Bely, Blok," *California Slavic Studies* 11 (1980), pp. 105–40.

[82] *PSS*, 13:169.

pared such figures to artesian wells that require a "geological shift, an earthquake for the subterranean waters to burst forth and flood the plain, carrying away the anthills, overturning the old shops of bourgeois Europe."[83] Having long associated the bourgeoisie with spiritual philistinism (*meshchanstvo*), banality, and mediocrity, Merezhkovsky's championing of a Religious Revolution gave his distaste a more explicitly political cast. "When Nietzsche makes eyes not merely at Bismarck but at the Russian Autocracy as well, as the greatest manifestation of the 'will to power,' in the midst of the modern European impotence—then on the pale brow of the crucified Dionysus also appears some black spot of bourgeois contamination."[84] Despite his disapproval of Nietzsche's admiration of the autocrat, Merezhkovsky feared that the weakening of the Russian autocracy after the Revolution of 1905 might leave Russia open to infection by the bourgeois spirit of Western Europe—comfort, convenience, compromise, instead of the City of God.

Seeking new Christian values with ever greater urgency, he attacked those who, in his view, propagated Nietzschean amoralism.

> As we looked and listened more carefully, we found that just as the Russian Marxists were repeating Marx the German, the Russian tramps were also repeating Nietzsche the German. The tramp took one-half of Nietzsche—our decadent orgiasts took the other. 'Dancing Foot' had not yet had time to hide before the worshippers of the new Dionysus began to chant: 'Raise higher your dithyrambic legs!' One German cut in two suffices for two Russian 'new words'.[85]

Afraid that Russians would remain with no values at all, that they would become like beasts, Merezhkovsky regarded the utilitarian morality preached by the left as a mere transition stage. To Merezhkovsky, Gorky's openly amoral tramp revealed the face of the future. "At times," Merezhkovsky

---

[83] *PSS*, 14:22–23.

[84] *PSS*, 14:24.

[85] *PSS*, 14:35. The tramp is a key character type in Gorky's works. "Dancing Foot" is a reference to a Gorky story in which a tramp horsethief sees his companion lynched by peasants, then avenges his death by turning them in. The phrases "decadent orgiasts" and "worshippers of the New Dionysus" refer to the mystical anarchism of Vyacheslav Ivanov and George Chulkov. I am indebted to Betty Forman for the information on "Dancing Foot" ("Pliaschchii noga," in his collected works, 1898). For details on mystical anarchism see Bernice Glatzer Rosenthal, "The Transmutation of the Symbolist Ethos: Mystical Anarchism and the Revolution of 1905," *Slavic Review* vol. 36, no. 4 (December 1977), pp. 608–27.

remarked, "it appears that the tramp has read Nietzsche, but in a cheap semi-literate translation." Emphasizing the tramp's contempt for the Christian peasant, Merezhkovsky noted that the tramp hates the peasant more than he hates the aristocrat.[86] Merezhkovsky's objection to mystical anarchism stemmed from its promulgation of an eroticized Dionysian mysticism as the cement of social unity, while *he* desired a mysticism that was specifically Christian. Affirming that Nietzsche did not sanction evil, but sought new religious values on the other side of good and evil, Merezhkovsky now maintained that Nietzsche's error was in discovering America after Columbus. The superman Nietzsche sought had already appeared as the god-man, Jesus Christ.[87]

From 1908 on, Merezhkovsky viewed Nietzsche in primarily negative terms. In a 1908 article attacking Peter Struve's advocacy of a "Great Russia," Merezhkovsky accused him of a "will to power" and of other "items from the Nietzschean inventory" which others, like himself, had long since jettisoned. He described Nietzscheanism as a "childhood sickness" like measles or scarlet fever, which is dangerous to adults. He denied that he had ever been seduced by it, and condemned it as "eternal romanticism," "eternal demonism," and "resurrected paganism."[88] More frequently, however, he tended to refer to his Nietzscheanism of the 1890s as a period of "religious trial," and to maintain that in order to realize the truth about Jesus Christ he had had to pursue falsehood to the end. Admitting that he had been dangerously close to Antichrist, he stated that he now recognized that both truths (heaven and earth, spirit and flesh) are contained in the person of Jesus Christ and condemned the idea of the identity of Christ and Antichrist as dangerous blasphemy.[89]

Indeed, as he became more Christian, he referred less to Nietzsche. His essay *Lermontov: Poet of Superhumanity* (*Lermontov: Poet Sverkhchelovechestva*, 1909), amazingly, contains virtually no references to Nietzsche at all, though Nietzschean themes are present.[90] Lermontov's rebelliousness, now seen as Luciferan, is contrasted with the God-man ideal of Soloviev and Dostoevsky. *Two Secrets of Russian Poetry: Tiutchev and Nekrasov* (*Dve tainy russkoi poezii*, 1915) attributes the loneliness and despair of Russian decadents in the 1890s not to Nietzsche, but to Tiutchev,

[86] *PSS*, 14:78, 80.
[87] *PSS*, 13:69–71.
[88] *PSS*, 16:54.
[89] *PSS*, 13:82–84; 1:vi–vii.
[90] *M. Iu. Lermontov: Poet Sverkhcheloveshestva* (St. Petersburg, 1909).

especially to Tiutchev's poem "Silentium," which conveyed the idea that true communication between people is impossible, and also to Tiutchev's epistemology (as discussed above).[91]

During the Great War, Nietzsche was widely associated (and not only in Russia) with the "will to power" as embodied in German militarism. General reluctance to admit Nietzsche's influence in Russia was reinforced by a neo-Slavophile tendency to focus on Russian sources. Merezhkovsky was affected by these tendencies. But even without the war, aspects of Nietzsche's philosophy had been so absorbed into Merezhkovsky's new interpretation of Christianity that it ceased to exist as a separate entity. A catalyst that inspired Merezhkovsky's revaluation of Christian values, it disappeared within them.

[91] *Dve tainy russkoi poezii: Nekrasov i Tiutchev* (Petrograd, 1915).

3.

Nietzschean, All Too Nietzschean? Rozanov's Anti-Christian Critique

Anna Lisa Crone

VASILY VASILIEVICH ROZANOV (1856–1919) has been called "the Russian Nietzsche" by several critics in Russia and the West. The reasons for this are two: his virulent attacks on the Christian religion and his provocative, aphoristic prose style. Nietzsche's *Ecce Homo* bears remarkable similarity to Rozanov's late "confessional" works, which it may well have in part inspired.[1] Yet the issue of Nietzsche's influence on Rozanov has not been investigated so far. This chapter is an attempt to address the question by calling attention to the similarities in Rozanov's and Nietzsche's attacks on Christianity and by assessing the influence on Rozanov of two Russian writers who held certain views in common with Nietzsche: Konstantin Leontiev and Feodor Dostoevsky.

Vasily Rozanov was one of the leading philosophers and literary critics of Russia's Silver Age and is considered by many among the greatest Russian writers of the twentieth century.[2] His early philosophical works dealt with problems in epistemology and the philosophy of history.[3] From

---

[1] The stylistic similarities include the use of hyperbole, self-contradiction, a provocative attitude toward the reader, excessive braggadocio, and expressive punctuation as well as a preference for aphoristic formulations. Nietzsche in *Ecce Homo* and elsewhere strikes a tone of intimacy with the reader that is similar to Rozanov's.

[2] For a detailed introduction to Vasily Rozanov, see E. Gollerbakh, V. V. *Rozanov: Zhizn' i tvorchestvo* (Petrograd, 1922); Renato Poggioli, *Rozanov* (London, 1957). There are two doctoral dissertations devoted to an overview of his work: Zoreslava Kaulbach, "The Life and Works of V. V. Rozanov" (Ph.D. diss., Cornell University, 1973), and Janet S. Romanoff, "V. V. Rozanov: The Jurodivyj of Russian Literature" (Ph.D. diss., Stanford University, 1974).

[3] These works include *O ponimanii* (1886), and the articles collected in *Religiia i kul'tura*

the late 1880s well into the 1890s, Rozanov was under the tutelage of Slavophile historian Nicholas N. Strakhov and was for a while a disciple and interpreter of the arch-conservative philosopher, critic, and belletrist, Constantine N. Leontiev.[4] Rozanov first received general recognition as a critic in 1891 when his book on *The Brothers Karamzaov, The Legend of the Grand Inquisitor* (*Legenda o velikom inkvizitore*) began to appear serially in *The Russian Messenger* (*Russkii vestnik*).[5] From the late 1890s until his death in 1919 Rozanov published voluminously on the relationship of marriage, sex, and the family to Russian Orthodoxy and Christianity in general. He was one of the leading participants in the Religious-Philosophical Society meetings, organized by Dmitri Merezhkovsky and Zinaida Gippius with the aim of bringing about a rapprochement between the Russian intelligentsia and the Orthodox Church.

Rozanov's biological mysticism, sometimes called his "religion of sex," generated controversy as a result of his discussions at those meetings. Especially shocking was his suggestion that Christianity be reinfused with the sexual attitudes and practices of pagan fertility cults. Among existing religions, Rozanov felt Judaism accorded sex and procreation a more honored and sacred place than Christianity, and he exhorted the Church to learn about family life from the Jewish example.[6]

By 1906–1907 Rozanov apparently lost hope that Christianity would change its monastic attitudes and he embarked on a series of more detailed investigations of the religion, probing deeper into its nature and the reasons why sensual vitality and joy were so incompatible with Christian tenets. In *Around the Church Walls* (*Okolo tserkovnykh sten*, 1906) he set forth with great power and single-mindedness the idea that Russian Orthodoxy was first and foremost a "religion of death."[7] In two subsequent studies, *The Dark Face: The Metaphysics of Christianity* (*Temny lik: Metafizika khristianstva*, 1909) and *People of the Moonlight: The Me-*

(1901), *Priroda i istoriia* (1903), *V mire neiasnogo i nereshennogo* (1901), and *Sumerki prosveshcheniia: Sbornik statei* (1899).

[4] Nicholas N. Strakhov (1828–1896) was a leading Russian critic and philosopher of the late nineteenth century. Constantine N. Leontiev (1831–1891) is difficult to classify. He was a historiographer, philosopher, literary critic, and fiction writer who corresponded with Rozanov during the last six months of his life (1890–1891).

[5] Rozanov, *Russkii vestnik*, no. 1 (1891), 223–74; no. 2 (1891) 226–84; no. 3 (1891), 215–53; no. 4 (1891), 251–75.

[6] See "Zapiski Petersburgskogo Religiozno-filosofskogo Obshchestva: 1901–1902," serialized in *Novyi put'* (1903–1904); also B. G. Rosenthal, *D. S. Merezhkovsky and the Silver Age* (The Hague, 1975), pp. 80–151.

[7] Rozanov, *Okolo tserkovnykh sten* (St. Petersburg, 1906).

taphysics of Christianity (Liudi lunnogo sveta: Metafizika khristianstva, 1911) he further developed his critique of Christianity.[8] *The Dark Face* contains the essay, "Sweetest Jesus and the Bitter Fruits of the World," one of Rozanov's best known anti-Christian articles. In these two collections Rozanov provided the sharpest anti-Christian critique ever expressed in the Russian language.

Rozanov's reputation as a great stylist and innovator rests on three late works: *Solitaria (Uedinennoe,* 1913) and *Fallen Leaves: Basketful One and Basketful Two (Opavshie list'ia: Korob pervyi, Korob vtoroi,* 1913 and 1915). These are a kind of extended writer's notebook, full of aphorisms, sayings, short essays, conversations, random ideas, polyphonically orchestrated. (A Bakhtinian concept, "polyphonically orchestrated" means presented through a series of distinct literary masks or voices, each of which is in dialogue with the others on an equal footing. There is no dominating voice, no omniscient author.) Close to them in style and manner is Rozanov's last work, *The Apocalypse of Our Time (Apokalipsis nashego vremeni,* 1918–1919), his profoundly prophetic commentary on the Bolshevik Revolution, which he wrote and published serially at his own expense during the last two years of his life.[9]

Any treatment of the possible influence of Friedrich Nietzsche on Rozanov must be prefaced by a discussion of the peculiar problems besetting such an analysis. Rozanov consciously promulgated the myth or "fiction" of his own unbounded originality and specifically disavowed the influence of Nietzsche and Leontiev:

> Articles about me . . . I read them and don't understand a thing. "It's just not about me." The impression is so *alien* that it's weird to see my name on the page. . . . I have no similarity to Nietzsche: And no personal resemblance to Leontiev. I merely love the man.

---

[8] Rozanov, *Temnyi lik: Metafizika khristianstva* [Dark Face: Metaphysics of Christianity] (Wurzburg, 1975). All quotations from "Sweetest Jesus" and "Christ and 'the Rich Youth' " are to this edition, my translation. An English translation of "Sweetest Jesus" is available in Martha Bohachevsky-Chomiak and Bernice Glatzer Rosenthal, eds., *A Revolution of the Spirit: Crisis of Values in Russia* (Newtonville, Mass., 1982). References to *Liudi lunnogo sveta: Metafizika khristianstva* [People of the Moonlight: Metaphysics of Christianity] (St. Petersburg, 1913) are translated by me. Henceforth cited parenthetically in the text under the English title, *Dark Face* or *People of the Moonlight*.

[9] All quotations from *Solitaria, Fallen Leaves, Basketful One* and *Two,* and *The Apocalypse of Our Time* are from W. Rosanow, *Ausgewahlte Shriften* (Münich, 1970) and are given in my translation. Henceforth cited parenthetically in the text under shortened English titles.

> But similarities and fondness are different things. . . . Yes, things
> have occurred to me that never occurred to *anyone* before me, in-
> cluding Nietzsche and Leontiev. In the complexity and quantity of
> original ideas, I place myself first. (*Fallen Leaves: Basketful Two*,
> p. 258)

Although Rozanov often takes a very intimate tone and seems to be "con-
fessing" secrets about himself to his reader, he is in fact often creating
"fictions" about Rozanov, in effect *lying*. Rozanov is the first to admit
this and call the reader's attention to it, in his usual self-contradictory
way:

> It's amazing how comfortable I felt lying. Falsehood never tor-
> mented me and for a strange reason: "What business is it of yours
> *precisely what I think?*" . . . If, nevertheless, I wrote . . . sincerely
> for the most part, it was not out of love for the truth, which I never
> felt and "couldn't even imagine," but out of carelessness. (*Solitaria*,
> p. 54)

One of these "fictions" was Rozanov's claim that he had never read certain seminal thinkers such as Hegel and Schopenhauer. These lies, often
so boldfaced as to be humorous, were repeated frequently enough that
some Rozanov scholars have come away with the idea that he was less
well-informed than his contemporaries. Yet, if one excepts people of truly
prodigious erudition such as Viacheslav Ivanov, Rozanov's myriad articles and reviews on the most diverse topics, which appeared in the most
prominent journals of his day, reveal him to be at least as well-read as
his peers and better informed than they on certain subjects.[10] The critic
faces in Rozanov a person who deliberately obscures the origin of certain
derivative or partially derived ideas in his works. If Rozanov agrees with
an idea, he often presents it as his own original insight.

While Rozanov explicitly denies the influence of Nietzsche, the German thinker's *The Antichrist* and *The Twilight of the Idols* (prepared for
publication in 1888) appear to have made a particularly strong impression
on Rozanov. In Rozanov's anti-Christian critique, as in Nietzsche's, there
is a striking coincidence in ideas and in the phrasing, metaphors, and
even choice of words used to express those ideas. It is important to ob-
serve textual parallels because there has been no attempt heretofore to
pinpoint what ideas and stylistic traits led to Rozanov's being nicknamed
"the Russian Nietzsche." I cite these parallels in the authors' own words

---

[10] These subjects include Greek mythology and philosophy, Judaism and occult religion.

because they constitute strong evidence for direct influence, as well as for a more diffuse general influence.

In generality and importance the main set of parallel texts involves Nietzsche's well-known declaration of "the death of God":

> The greatest recent event—that God is dead, that the belief in the Christian God has ceased to be believable—is even now beginning to cast its shadow over Europe. . . . In the main, however, this may be said: the event itself is too great, too far from the comprehension of the many, even for the tidings of it to be thought of as having *arrived* yet, not to speak of the notion that many people know of what has happened here and what must collapse now that this belief has been undermined—all that was built upon it, leaned upon it, grew upon it; for example, our whole European morality. (G5,279)

Rozanov wrote more than thirty years after Nietzsche:

> The "Apocalypse of Our Time" is a title that should not require explanation given events that have a definitively apocalyptic character [specifically, the Bolshevik Revolution]. . . . There is no doubt that the deep foundation of all that is now taking place lies in the fact that among Europeans (including us Russians) there have formed colossal voids left over from the Christianity of the past; and into these hollow spaces everything is falling . . . thrones, classes, estates, wealth. All this is shaken utterly. (*Apocalypse*, p. 444)

Both these excerpts contain three salient points within a few lines: the death of God, the fact that people do not recognize or comprehend what has happened and, finally, that this will result in the collapse of all social and cultural values based on Christianity.

A second similarity in these authors' critique of Christianity lies in the idea that religion saps the life forces out of those people who profess it. Nietzsche in this connection speaks of the very sexual vibrancy and sensual joy that is a constant theme in Rozanov:

> . . . In Christianity . . . the highest things are considered unachievable . . . the hole-and-corner, the dark chamber is Christian. Here the body is despised, hygiene is repudiated as sensuality. . . . Mortal hostility against the masters of the earth, against the "noble"—and at the same time, a covert, secret competition . . . that also is Christian. Hatred of *mind*, of pride, courage, freedom, *lib*-

ertinage of mind is Christian; hatred of the *senses* of the joy of the senses, of joy in general is Christian. (A,131).

And in *Dawn*:

Christianity has succeeded in turning Eros and Aphrodite into hellish goblins—In themselves the sexual feelings . . . are such that one human being thereby gives pleasure to another . . . through his delight; one does not encounter such beneficent arrangements too often in nature. And to slander just such a one and to corrupt it through bad conscience! To associate the procreation of man with bad conscience![11]

This is Rozanov's most frequent and well-known theme:

There is no laughter and no falling in love in the Gospels and a drop of one or the other singes the pages of the book. ("Sweetest Jesus,", p. 255)

'Immaculate conception," conception without semen . . . just what is this anyway? This is the "+0" of sex; or the "±0" of sex . . . the minute you give sex a *positive value*, be it a *whole number* or a *fraction* . . . you have rejected and overthrown the Gospels and Christianity. For its very essence is the zero meaning of sex. This is not one aspect of Christianity: this is *its essence*. The Church so insists on this that nothing can offend it more . . . than the assertion, the hint, or supposition that in Christ or the Blessed Virgin there was something *genuinely sexual*. . . . "No! No!" says the Church, "the Mother of God was a *nun*, in her essence a *nun*, though without a habit, *and she could be nothing else*, because *otherwise there would be no Christianity as something completely new appearing in the world!*" . . . Thus, conception without semen indeed is preached in the gospels, and the one so conceived was Himself *without semen* [*bessemennyi*]. . . . And as soon as you bring the sexual element into Christ, you destroy, break apart, and ruin His image. (*People of the Moonlight*, pp. 58–59)

Consonant with this attitude, both Nietzsche and Rozanov find monasticism repugnant. From Nietzsche comes: "Christ . . . the *anti-natural* castration of a God" (A,126); "The divinity of decadence, pruned [Kauf-

[11] Nietzsche, *Dawn*, in *The Portable Nietzsche*, trans. Walter Kaufmann (New York, 1968), p. 79.

mann translation: 'gelded"] of all its manliest drives . . . " (A,127); "The saint in whom God takes pleasure is the ideal castrate. Life is at an end where the 'kingdom of God' begins" *(TI,45)*. Whereas Nietzsche speaks of "castration" in Christianity mainly as a figurative concept *(TI,42* and in *GM* in the section on the "ascetic ideal," pp. 97ff.), Rozanov dwells on figurative as well as actual castration in the rites of the Russian sectarian *skoptsy*.[12] On "moral" monasticism Rozanov says:

> A monk can sin with a young woman: he can beget a child, but the child must be drowned. The minute the monk clings to the child and says:"I won't give him up" and as soon as he grabs hold of the woman and cries out:"I love her and I won't stop," Christianity has been done away with. When the family becomes serious, Christianity turns into a joke.   ("Sweetest Jesus,". pp. 258–59)

Comparison of Christ with the ancient Greek models of powerful, virile, and efficacious gods is a favorite method of attacking Christ for both authors:

Nietzsche:
The Christian conception of God—as God of the sick . . . is one of the most corrupt conceptions of the divine arrived at on earth: perhaps it even represents the low-water mark in the descending development of the God type. (A, 128)

Rozanov:
. . . the image of Christ in the Gospels . . . shows nothing . . . but weakness and exhaustion. Try to crucify the sun [Apollo] and you will see what a real god is!!!

(*Apocalypse*, p. 508)

Both Rozanov and Nietzsche are repelled by the monotony of Christianity as opposed to the endless variety of pagan religions. For them Christianity lacks imagination and a rich esthetic sense. Nietzsche says:

> That the strong races of Northern Europe have not repudiated the Christian God certainly reflects no credit on their talent for religion—not to speak of their taste. . . . they have taken up sickness, old age, and contradiction into all their instincts—since then they

[12]The *skoptsy* were a Russian religious sect that practiced castration. Description of their castration rites and their meaning is found in the essay "An Incident in the Village" ("Sluchai v derevne") in *Temny lik*, pp. 74–97.

have failed to *create* a God! Almost two millennia and not a single
new God! . . . As if existing by right, like an ultimate and maxi-
mum of the God-creating force . . . in man, this pitiful God of
Christian *monotonotheism*! [Italics mine]. (A, 128–29)

One of Rozanov's constant ideas, too, is that a true Christian cannot
experience full esthetic enjoyment. In "Sweetest Jesus" he states this very
strongly, disagreeing with Merezhkovsky's "Gogol and Father Matvei"
where he claimed that the "historical Christianity" (personfied by Father
Matvei) was wrong, that the Gospels were indeed compatible with the
enjoyment of all great human art and culture. Rozanov takes as his example the Christian Nietzsche most detested, St. Paul, to refute Merezhkovsky:

Paul lived in the material world, but he distanced himself from matter profoundly, because he no longer [after his conversion—he had
known esthetic enjoyment while still a Jew] loved or admired anything earthly or material. He took those things . . . as utilitarian
only. He knew and needed only the prose of the flesh. . . . Christ
was the only flower [in his world] a *monoflower*. . . . Christianity
is a religion of diminishing returns, eternally striving and never quite
reaching the quantity: Christ +o. (p. 254)

Neither Rozanov or Nietzsche tires of noting the negative value of Christ
as a deity. Rozanov often describes him as a total negativity: "What paint-
brush can capture and show an observer . . . *this sum of missing defects?*" ("Christ and the 'Rich Youth,' " p. 70). Nietzsche and Rozanov
use the same example to show that great esthetic sense and great art are
incompatible with true Christianity.

Rozanov:
But who took his inspiration from Christianity? The artists of the
Renaissance who barely consulted the Gospels, or Calvin, Luther
. . . who considered this painting to be "Satan's sting," the devil's
seduction, totally analogous to the *skoptsy* [castrates of the Russian
sect] who were opposed to the "beauty of this world" . . . Luther is
right . . . Raphael and Correggio are totally wrong.

("Christ and the 'Rich Youth,' " p. 93)

Nietzsche:
Raphael said Yes [to life]. Raphael did Yes; consequently, Raphael
was not a Christian. (*TI*, 72)

Although Nietzsche was consistent in his view of Christianity as anti-esthetic, Rozanov's attitude was subject to regular and extreme vacillation. He believed, on the one hand, that a Christian's esthetic tastes were greatly weakened and that the true Christian would lose all desire to visit theaters or the Hermitage. On the other hand, the severe art of Byzantine Christianity, the dark weeping face of Christ, exerted an esthetic force of its own to which Rozanov was powerfully drawn.

The final area of similarity in the anti-Christian critiques of Rozanov and Nietzsche concerns their common analysis of the Church as the purveyor of a slave morality, as an institution inducing men to powerlessness. This is a major theme in *The Genealogy of Morals* as well as in *The Antichrist*:

> What is good? All that heightens the feeling of power in man, the will to power, power itself. . . . What is bad? All that proceeds from weakness. . . . What is more harmful than any vice? Active sympathy for all the ill-constituted and the weak—Christianity.
>
> (A, 115–16)

Here Nietzsche evaluates moral phenomena in terms of the will to power. Rozanov, in his late period, likewise places a very positive valuation on power. In the *Apocalypse* he deals with this problem in the context of the God–man relationship (which implies, at the least, man's becoming, in Rozanov's terms, "more than he has been," perhaps even "more like God"):

> The Apocalypse rejects the God–man connection as something useless and worn out. . . . But why? why?
>   Powerlessness.
> The end of the world and of Christianity will come to pass because the Gospels are books about being tired out, about exhaustion. Because there is power and there is nonpower, and Christ lived and died in the name of nonpower: that is why Christianity is powerless.   (*Apocalypse*, p. 456)

Both authors treat this will to nonpower as a will to nothingness. In the opening to the third essay of *The Genealogy of Morals* we read: ". . . the basic fact of the human will is its *horror vacui*. It needs a goal—and it will rather will *nothingness* than *not* will" (p. 97). Rozanov and Nietzsche both attack the anti-vitalism of desiring nothingness.

Nietzsche:

Anti-natural morality . . . turns . . . precisely *against* the instincts
of life. . . . By saying "God sees into the heart," it denies the deepest and highest desires of life and takes God for the *enemy of life.* . . .

If one has grasped the blasphemousness of such a rebellion against
life as has, in Christian morality, become virtually sacrosanct, one
has . . . grasped something else: . . . a condemnation of life by
the living. (*TI,* 45)

Rozanov:

No empires are necessary . . . no need for the world. NIHILISM
. . . The world without content—a pie without a filling. Is it tasty?
In truth, Christ threw the entire filling out of the pie and this is
called Christianity.   (*Apocalypse,* p. 477)

With the birth of Christ . . . all the fruits of the world grew sour.
. . . In Christ the world grew bitter. . . . Everyone, insofar as he
gazed upon the face of Christ, cast away whatever he was doing *and
died* to the world.   ("Sweetest Jesus," p. 265)

These textual parallels provide very strong evidence for a Nietzschean
influence on Rozanov. The case is strengthened by Rozanov's frequent
mention of the German philosopher in his works. Rozanov's close association with Merezhkovsky during the latter's most Nietzschean period
enables us to assume that Rozanov knew Nietzsche at least as well as the
other members of Merezhkovsky's circle. Moreover, Rozanov was a frequent contributor to N. Grot's *Problems of Philosophy and Psychology*
where Nietzsche and Nietszcheanism were often discussed.[13]

The problem in assessing and characterizing the influence of Nietzsche
on Rozanov lies in separating out with definity and finality Nietzschean
influence from native influences that might lead a thinker to similar ideas.
The two Russian thinkers who in addition to Rozanov are commonly
compared to Nietzsche are Dostoevsky and Leontiev.

Scholarship has established the influence of both Dostoevsky and
Leontiev on Rozanov. Lev Shestov's famous study *Dostoevsky and Nietzsche*
(1903), well known to Rozanov, outlines the many similarities of those

[13]Concerning Merezhkovsky's Nietzschean period, see Bernice G. Rosenthal's chapter in
this volume. In 1904 N. Grot's *Problems of Philosophy and Psychology* published Eugene
Trubetskoi's "Filosofiia Nitshe," a 200-page summary of the German philosopher's main
works.

two writers.[14] As concerns Leontiev, Rozanov himself was one of the first to point out that Leontiev was a Nietzsche *avant la lettre*. Most probably Dostoevsky and Leontiev sensitized Rozanov to certain problem areas in Christianity that were then reinforced and reconfirmed in his mind when he read Nietzsche in the 1890s and 1910s.

Constantine Leontiev dismissed as erroneous any treatment of Christianity as a life-affirming religion. For him both Tolstoi and Dostoevsky preached a "rosy Christianity" that bore no resemblance to the true religion. Leontiev's perception of Christianity as anti-vital may have led Rozanov to his vision of it as a "religion of death." In *The Dark Face*, Rozanov exposes the "rosy Christianity" of Father Zosima in terms that recall Leontiev:

> Zosima . . . expresses the pre-Christian, primordial naturalism, that worship of nature, that "reverence for everything" (pantheism) that Christianity condemned from the very start . . . the very thing John the Baptist came to uproot. There is no timbre of soul *more opposed to Christianity* than the spiritual tranquillity of Zosima, which excludes any real need for Christ in the first place. Why, after all, should Christ come if *everything* is happy and joyous on earth . . . without him, "on its own"? . . . No, in this point Dostoevsky was completely wrong: "he was in a pagan funk."   (*Dark Face*, p. xii)

Despite Christianity's anti-vitalism and its destruction of beauty in the world, which for Leontiev was the first requirement of life, the conservative philosopher embraced Christianity in the end. He was tonsured in 1891 and spent his last days in the monastery at Sergiev Posad. He made this concession to Orthodoxy out of fear of death and damnation and because he felt it was a weapon against the culture of the nineteenth-century bourgeois West.[15] During the last six months of his life Leontiev carried on a philosophical correspondence with Rozanov that centered on the problems of "estheticism" (the exalted beauty of classical antiquity) and "progress" (the democratized culture of post-1789 Europe, which Leontiev detested) and the role of Christianity in the future survival of the best of Russian and European culture. Leontiev maintained that

[14] Lev Shestov, *Filosofiia tragedii: Dostoevsky i Nitshse* (St. Petersburg, 1903).

[15] On Leontiev's life and philosophy, see Iuri Ivask, *Konstantin Leontiev: Zhizn' i tvorchestvo* (Bern, 1974); and N. Berdiaev, *Konstantin Leontiev—Ocherk iz istorii russkoi filosofskoi mysli* (Paris, 1926).

Christian teaching and European progress in joint effort aspire to kill the esthetics of life . . . that is, life itself. . . . What should we do? We must help Christianity to the detriment of our beloved estheticism . . . out of fear for the judgment beyond the grave, for the salvation . . . of our souls; but we must oppose progress wherever we are in the slightest able to do so, since it is equally detrimental to Christianity and estheticism.

(Letter to Rozanov, August 1981)[16]

When Leontiev died in 1891, it was Rozanov who most often "introduced" this still obscure figure and explicated Leontiev's views in a series of articles in the 1890s. In one of these, "The Unrecognized Phenomenon," Rozanov called Leontiev "the true Nietzsche" and said that the German was but a weak reflection of his Russian counterpart.[17] Rozanov's awareness of the similarities of Nietzsche and Leontiev, in particular their consistent application of an esthetic criterion to all spheres of life (including the moral) and their abhorrence of bourgeois culture, demonstrates that Rozanov was familiar with the basic tenets of Nietzsche's thought as early as 1892. It appears that Rozanov viewed Leontiev and Nietzsche as co-authors of a very important criticism of Christianity with which he often agreed: it opposed life and esthetic pleasure. This conflated view of Leontiev and Nietzsche later became an important element in Rozanov's anti-Christian critique.

Dostoevsky's influence on Rozanov was even more important and of longer standing than Leontiev's. Rozanov specifically acknowledged Dostoevsky as his mentor, inaugurated his critical career with his study of the "Legend of the Grand Inquisitor," constantly referred to Dostoevsky and his literary creations. He liked to cast himself in the role of certain Dostoevskian characters (Shatov, Ivan, Lebedev, Smerdiakov, the underground man). He even married Dostoevsky's former mistress, the "demonic" Apollinaria Suslova, to achieve a closer "spiritual" connection with his great predecessor.[18]

The aspect of Dostoevsky's *oeuvre* that appears in Rozanov's anti-Christian writings and may therefore seem "Nietzschean" derives from Dos-

[16] K. N. Leontiev, "Letter to V. V. Rozanov, August 14, 1891," *Ruskii vestnik* (June 1903), 420.

[17] Rozanov, "Neuznannyi fenomen," in K. Leontiev, *Analiz, stil', i veianie* (Providence, R.I., 1965).

[18] An excellent description of Rozanov's life is found in Zinaida Gippius, "Zadumchivyi strannik," in *Zhivye litsa* (Prague, 1925).

toevsky's post-Siberian decades of struggle with certain aspects of Christianity. It culminated in the "rebellion" of Ivan Karamazov, who rejects God's world as unjust and rife with suffering. Rozanov takes a Dostoevskian inquisitorial stance toward Christ in his *Apocalypse*:

> [to Christ]: . . . You are no friend to man. No, you're not. "A pact," "a testament," even this seems formal and dry. And how you oppressed them is frightening, to the extremes of slavery . . . even to death, to martyrdom. . . . Isn't it shocking to read:"Not one martyr was shown mercy" But you could have shown it? . . . Couldn't you?
> Oh . . .
> Of course, the one who raised Lazarus—*could*. That means, *you didn't want to*, doesn't it? . . .
> You could do *anything*, Lord Jesus. . . . And you didn't even rescue the children from heavenly or earthly torments. . . . And you don't understand why righteous Israel rose against you? It rose against you in confusion: "Something is not right in this."
>
> (*Apocalypse*, p. 476)

In such passages we hear Ivan Karamazov's doubts of God's goodness, as well as doubts of His omnipotence:

> The world is harmonious . . . wise, good and there is beauty which is divine. . . ." "But scavengers feed on herbivorous animals." An owl will devour a little hare—this is not from God, the God of harmony and good. What is this?—not even God knows about this or understands it. God himself is helpless to change this. . . . The world is in truth unjust.   (*Apocalypse*, pp. 459–60)

Despite his problems with God's world, Dostoevsky embraced Christianity at the end of his life, as Leontiev did. Dostoevsky accepted Christianity on moral grounds rather than esthetic ones: he believed man needed belief in the immortality of the soul to keep him from degenerating into a beast or a criminal. Without Christianity, Dostoevsky feared man would act as if "all were permitted" and neglect his moral and social duties.

Rozanov, who absorbed Ivan's revolt, which Dostoevsky had intended to expose as wrong and evil, was no moralist. In his essay on "The Legend of the Grand Inquisitor" Rozanov saw Ivan's "poem" as a Nietzschean "God is dead" vision: "The Legend" and the novel as a whole were "a great and powerful reflection of that peculiar post-Christian spirit."[19] Of course, Nietzsche himself discovered these similarities with Dostoevsky when he first read the Russian writer in Nice in 1886.[20] In *The Legend of the Grand Inquisitor* Rozanov deals with similarities between Dostoevsky and Nietzsche that could be attributed to the *Zeitgeist* of the post-Christian "God is dead" era, which both writers experienced independently in their own countries.

There is yet a final element in Rozanov's anti-Christian critique that goes beyond Ivan's rebellion and his Inquisitor and the estheticism of Leontiev. It is the irreverent manner of address, the unbridled use of language, a verbal bravado reminiscent of Nietzsche's, which produces a shocking effect. This daring irreverence, seen in some of the parallel texts above and in Rozanov's anti-Christian writings in general, provides evidence of direct Nietzschean influence. Of course, the freer language after 1907 may be in part the result of relaxed censorship. Whatever the reasons, Rozanov's tendency to broad statements "of Nietzschean flight," as he called them, increases markedly after that year. It may, indeed, be the most significant result of Rozanov's acquaintance with Nietzsche: he gives the Russian reader Nietzscheanlike ideas in Nietzscheanlike form. Late works of the German philosopher, such as *The Antichrist*, *The Twilight of the Idols*, and *Ecce Homo* may well have encouraged Rozanov to sharpen his assault on Christianity and on the person of Christ. The strident, self-contradictory, even visceral mode of Nietzsche's style in the late 1880s most probably did affect the extremes of metaphor and simile, the paradoxes and antinomies of Rozanov's mature style (1907–1919).

Just as scholars have overlooked Nietzsche's specific philosophical influence on Rozanov, they have eschewed concrete comparisons of his style with Nietzsche's. These comparisons weaken to some degree Rozanov's reputation for stylistic originality. Only two close stylistic studies of

[19] In M. Holquist, *Dostoevsky and the Novel* (Princeton, 1978), p. 31, we find this: "Rozanov's book is a *catalogue raisonné* of what have become clichés for the modern predicament. It is the age of alienation ("No common idea binds the nations together any longer, everyone in every particular nation works only at his particular job" [p. 188]); of pessimism (Rozanov wrote "Everything sad and gloomy attracts contemporary man, for there is no longer joy in the heart," [p. 189]), the death of God (Rozanov wrote, "For more than two centuries the people of Europe have been acting counter to the Saviour's great precept 'But seek ye first the Kingdom of God' " [p. 187])." "The Legend of the Grand Inquisitor, so far as history is concerned, can be regarded as a great and powerful reflection of *that peculiar post-Christian spirit*," p. 31, pp. 168–70.

[20] C. A. Miller, "Nietzsche's 'Discovery' of Dostoevsky," in *Nietzsche Studien* 2 (1973), 202–57.

Rozanov have been carried out to date and they are confined to *Solitaria* and *Fallen Leaves*, and, to a lesser extent, *The Apocalypse of Our Time*.[21] A detailed stylistic analysis of Rozanov's and Nietzsche's anti-Christian writings in particular would yield interesting material for a definitive solution of the Neitzsche–Rozanov problem. Yet even in the absence of such a major study, if one reads *Ecce Homo* or *The Antichrist* and then turns immediately to *Solitaria* of *Fallen Leaves*, one's impression of Rozanov's originality is sharply diminished. Rigorous stylistic analyses are needed for us to be able to assess Nietzsche's stylistic influence on Russian symbolist prose and poetry in general, as well as on the prose of Rozanov, but limited space prevents that here.

Returning to possible influence in the ideological sphere, we can conclude that there was a conflation of Leontiev and Nietzsche in Rozanov's mind as "two Nietzsches." There appears to be no confusion of Dostoevsky with Nietzsche and a clear rejection of the brand of Christianity preached by the vital Zosima, as well as by the weak Myshkin. After all, the abortive mission of Myshkin on earth may have served to convince Rozanov that Christianity was incompatible with a full life in the world, which was Rozanov's highest priority. Merezhkovsky, as we noted earlier, persisted in his hope that secular pleasures could be compatible with true Christianity. Rozanov, in "Sweetest Jesus," refuted this position incontrovertibly, conceding that the resexualization of Christianity that he advocated would de-Christianize the religion.

In his anti-Christian critique Rozanov often expressed the desire that Christ and Christianity be more powerful, more efficacious in solving man's earthly problems. In those criticisms, there emerges an exultation in power, particularly that of pagan gods and Jehovah, that may have been Nietzschean in origin.

Both Leontiev and Dostoevsky relinquished beauty and power and capitulated to Christianity for reactionary reasons: to maintain the social, moral, and cultural order. For Leontiev, Christianity might help stave off the leveling bourgeois culture that had already swept Europe. For Dostoevsky, it might protect against further breakdown of the moral fiber of society and thus prevent further social and cultural decadence. Nietzsche detested choices of the "lesser evil," seeing in them cowardly compromise. Henri Lubac emphasizes that what caused Nietzsche to repudiate Dostoevsky is Dostoevsky's retreat to reactionary religion and nationalist

---

[21] Victor Shklovsky, *Siuzhet kak iavlenie stilia* (Petrograd, 1921); and Anna L. Crone, *Rozanov and the End of Literature* (Wurzburg, 1978).

politics.[22] Rozanov also distrusted such decisions, particularly in the case of Leontiev, whose conversion he attributed to fear.

Rozanov, the great Russian "Antichrist," also returned to the Christian fold on his deathbed. Some of his detractors have attacked him for this as if it were no more than a Pascalian attempt to "insure" himself in case there really was a Christian afterlife. In so doing, they overlook factors that differentiate Rozanov's acceptance of Christianity from Leontiev's volte-face: Rozanov was always passionately attached to Christianity and the person of Christ; but he continued attacking Christ and Christianity right up until his death asking forgiveness from the Jews for offensive things he had written about them but refusing to repudiate his anti-Christian works, the strongest of which is his last, *The Apocalypse of Our Time.*

Rozanov's "rebellion" is at times a bewailing of the fact that the God and the Orthodoxy he so loves are flawed. Zinaida Gippius, in her brilliant character sketch of Rozanov, speaks of the amazing tolerance the Orthodox clergy showed for this "dangerous heretic." She implies there and in *Dmitry Merezhkovsky*[23] that the clergy tolerated Rozanov's dissent because they knew he loved Christ and Christianity and was passionately challenging the religion to improve itself before it was too late. Part of Rozanov's paradoxical attitude was his love for the Orthodox rituals, especially the funeral rites. It is difficult to imagine that he would have voluntarily denied himself the final sacraments. Rozanov did not admire self-denial and he had all along stressed that Orthodoxy was wonderful for the dying. It was its negative affect on the affairs of the living that he opposed.

Rozanov, then, for most of his literary career voiced anti-Christian ideas that in Western thought are commonly associated with Friedrich Nietzsche: 1) the lack of any objective need for Christianity and its imminent passing from the scene; 2) its inability to deal with everyday problems of the modern world; 3) its anti-vital, anti-esthetic character; 4) its hindrance to the full development of the individual personality. Rozanov proclaimed these ideas with the exuberance of Nietzsche. At other times, however, he would shrink from his own statements, like Nietzsche's "pale criminal," frightened by the power of his own words. Then he would lament in sadness and dismay the predicament of modern Christianity, its ineffectuality and its doom.

Both Nietzsche and Rozanov agreed that Christianity fettered man,

[22] Henri Lubac, *The Drama of Atheistic Humanism*, trans. Edith M. Riley (New York, 1969), pp. 168ff.

[23] Zinaida Gippius, *Dmitri Merezhkovsky* (Paris, 1951).

impeding his optimal self-realization, his *coming closer to God*, or *becoming more godlike*. For the mystic Rozanov, the divine element in man was bound up with his bodily nature as much as with his spiritual, intellectual aspect—the "spirit of the flesh" and the "flesh of the spirit." The sensual liberation that is part of man's self-realization for Nietzsche does not receive in his works the single-minded emphasis that Rozanov gives it. Nietzsche felt that Christianity enslaved man in many ways. Rozanov concentrated on how the religion deprived man of his proper relation to sexuality, and he preached a spiritualized sex that would transcend the ascetic attitudes of Russian Orthodoxy. While Nietzsche attacked the "ascetic ideal," the role of sex and sensuality in man's progressive self-realization is less spelled out in his *oeuvre*. Nietzsche hoped for a higher evolution of the human species. Rozanov had no such grandiose expectations for the human race and was quite satisfied with many aspects of existing human life, especially the creature comforts. He was often attacked for these bourgeois attitudes, which Nietzsche and Leontiev would have held in contempt, as did Trotsky, who dubbed Rozanov "the poet of the cozy corner."[24]

Nicholas Berdiaev has observed that the Russians read Nietzsche as a religious thinker and a prophet. This seems especially true of Rozanov, who did not ignore the most important anti-Christian critique in Western philosophy, and who himself became the foremost Russian prophet of the end of Christianity. In an important essay "Concerning the Russian Idea" ("Vozle russkoi idei," 1911), Rozanov writes of Nietzsche's unprecedented popularity in Russia:

> Russians have this characteristic: they give themselves up fully to foreign influences. . . . But the more completely they give themselves over, . . . the more powerfully do they exert a mysterious influence on that which they gave themselves over to . . . Did we ever become enthralled with any Russian thinker . . . did we ever devote so much strength and enthusiasm, so much reading and so many sleepless nights to a Russian as we have to Buckle and Spencer? Or to Nietzsche in recent years? Nietzsche's "Zarathustra" has been quoted here like our most favorite Russian verses, like a cherished . . . fairytale; Pushkin never knew a period of popularity comparable to our "Nietzschean period" at its height.[25]

---

[24] Leon Trotsky, *Literature and Revolution* (New York, 1957), p. 44.
[25] Rozanov, "Vozle russkoi idei," in *Sredi khudozhnikov* (St. Petersburg, 1914), pp. 371–72).

He goes on to say that Russians immerse themselves in those Western works because this allows them to affirm certain aspects of themselves, certain "Russian traits," Russian qualities of "soul":

> The main thing is that when Russians give themselves over to something foreign, in the very transfer they preserve their . . . ego [self-principle, "ia"] . . . they preserve their "souls," acquiring merely the body, the external forms of the foreign thing.[26]

Like most of Rozanov's generalizations, this is directly applicable to the writer himself and to what we have said here about Nietzsche's influence on him. Nietzsche's influence on Rozanov most likely encouraged him to develop and intensify certain anti-Christian attitudes and stylistic proclivities, certain Russian "tendencies" that were present in Leontiev, Dostoevsky, and in Rozanov himself prior to Nietzsche's vogue in Russia.

[26] Ibid., p. 372.

4.

Fedorov's Critique of Nietzsche, the "Eternal Tragedian"

Taras D. Zakydalsky

NICHOLAS FEDOROVICH FEDOROV (1828–1903) was one of the most original Russian thinkers of the nineteenth century. His philosophy, which he called "supramoralism" is not a speculative system or theory in the usual sense of the term, but an outline of the "common task," a vast project of universal salvation. According to Fedorov, by working together for many generations in developing science and technology, mankind can attain, eventually, sufficient control over nature to realize in this world the Christian ideal of the Kingdom of God. While in traditional Christianity perfect happiness is understood as a transcendent reward bestowed by God on the righteous only, for Fedorov it is a goal attainable by all men in this world through their own efforts. To achieve this goal all people must join together and devote their mental and physical energies to the "common task" of restoring life to the dead. The resurrection of the dead is the highest duty based on love. At the completion of the task of resurrection, mankind passes from the "moral" stage of its development to the "esthetic" stage, in which all the generations of immortal human beings settled throughout the universe will be united by love into one harmonious society—the psychocracy—and, possessing complete control over nature, all will freely create collective works of art on a cosmic scale.[1]

---

[1] *Filosofiia obshchago dela: Stat'i, mysli i pis'ma Nikolaia Fedorovicha Fedorova*, ed. V. A. Kozhevnikov and N. P. Peterson, 2 vols. (1906, 1913; reprint, Westmead, Farnborough, Hants, 1970), 1:116. Henceforth cited parenthetically in the text as *FOD*. A systematic and critical exposition of these ideas is given in chapter 2 of my dissertation, "N. F. Fyodorov's Philosophy of Physical Resurrection" (Ph.D. diss., Bryn Mawr College, 1976).

Being impatient for action, Fedorov devoted very little attention to the final stage of history, concentrating instead on justifying on moral grounds the task of resurrection and on outlining immediate measures that could be undertaken to unite men in the effort to master nature. For example, he advocated a book exchange between the French and Russian national libraries, organizing local libraries out of private book collections, educational reforms, weather modification experiments by the army, and a new peacemaking and scientific role for the tsar.

A good portion of Fedorov's writings consists of his critique of the major Western philosophers—Kant, Hegel, Schopenhauer, and Nietzsche—and the major Russian thinkers—Dostoevsky, Tolstoi, and Soloviev. Fedorov's criticisms are usually external; he regards other philosophers not as teachers, but as opponents against whom he can test his own ideas. The clash of ideas gave rise to further clarification of Fedorov's own thought.[2] Fedorov's tone is often hostile and sarcastic. Sometimes his criticisms are unfair. Yet, by approaching an important philosopher from the unique perspective of the "common task," Fedorov usually uncovers interesting new aspects of his opponents' thought. In the last few years of his life, Fedorov devoted more attention to Nietzsche than to any other philosopher.[3] In the incomplete collection of his works, Fedorov's comments on Nietzsche occupy more space (sixty-six pages) than his comments on any other thinker.

When and how Fedorov first came into contact with Nietzsche's ideas is unknown, but it is clear that he was keenly interested in them. According to Vladimir Kozhevnikov, one of Fedorov's closest friends, Nietzsche attracted Fedorov by his

> . . . indubitable power and originality, . . . his almost unparalleled openness bordering on cynicism and directness in the expression of his convictions and their application, for all their extremeness and crudeness, to the very end; . . . that success which in recent times replaced Nietzsche's initial failure in the West and in our country, and finally the complete antithesis between his philosophy and the teachings of Nikolai Fedorovich himself.[4]

Oddly enough, Kozhevnikov says nothing about the strong affinities between the two thinkers, not only in the style of their thought, but also in

[2] V. A. Kozhevnikov, "Nikolai Fedorovich Fedorov," *Russkii arkhiv*, no. 9 (1904), p. 116.

[3] Ibid., no. 10 (1904), p. 248.

[4] Ibid.

its content. Fedorov, I think, was more fascinated by Nietzsche than by any other major thinker.

The principal similarity between Nietzsche and Fedorov lies in their ambition as practical philosophers not merely to transform individual values and behavior but also to set a task for all mankind. Fedorov was, no doubt, aware of this when he pointed out that:

> Nietzsche is a philosopher of a new kind and a new generation, a philosopher of the unified "New Germany," completely different from the old philosophers who were merely thinkers. The task of this new philosophy is to set the goal of life, to direct life.
>
> (FOD, 2:101)

For both thinkers this means going "beyond good and evil," beyond traditional Christian morality, which for Fedorov is a morality of individual action incapable of gaining control over nature and conquering evil at its root. "Nietzsche's great contribution is to summon us to advance beyond good and evil" (FOD, 2:117), although the path indicated by Nietzsche leads only to the diminution of the pitiful good attained through the old morality and the expansion of the enormous evil that already overwhelms mankind (FOD, 2:131). While Fedorov identifies his own doctrine with "active Christianity" and associates Nietzsche with the Antichrist (FOD, 2:100), he admits that "even in this Antichrist not everything proves to be anti-Christian" (FOD, 2:119).

Both Nietzsche and Fedorov view man from a purely naturalistic standpoint: as a being cast up by evolution who must work out his salvation in this world. Divine intervention and transcendent life are ruled out.[5] Fedorov was impressed by Nietzsche's affirmation of life, and went so far as to claim that Nietzsche's declaration in The Dawn that "there are men healthy in body and spirit, they rejoice in life, they say 'yes!' to life and have the right to reproduce life, to make it eternal," implicitly contains the idea of resurrection, "only Nietzsche does not know how to express what he himself desires!" (FOD, 2:163). To give life meaning both thinkers demand self-transcendence from man—Nietzsche in the superman and Fedorov in superhumanity—and understand this task as a collective, long-term project. Hence, both are interested in power, and,

---

[5] Fedorov taught that if men failed to unite and to resurrect the dead, God would eventually intervene, destroy the world, and reward the righteous with transcendent life. This doctrine seems to be a concession to traditional Christian teachings as it is inconsistent with his basic principles.

more precisely, in man's capacity to create culture (religion, morality, art, and science). For Nietzsche this power is valuable for its own sake, while for Fedorov it is valuable as a means of controlling nature.

In spite of these affinities between him and Nietzsche, Fedorov repeatedly stressed that Nietzsche's philosophy is completely opposed to supramoralism (*FOD*, 1:429) or to "active Christianity" (*FOD*, 2:109, 133) and expressed his opposition to Nietzsche in vehement emotional language.[6] To account for Fedorov's total and violent rejection of Nietzsche it is not enough to point to his strong antipathy to this or that Nietzschean doctrine. One must find the basic idea that determines Fedorov's whole interpretation of Nietzsche.

Because of its unsystematic and unfinished character, Fedorov's thought demands ordering into a coherent whole. Our philosopher was blessed with a prodigious memory and a lively imagination, but lacked the intellectual discipline to construct a unified, logically organized system. Hence, his writings are unbalanced: relatively trivial matters receive more attention than fundamental questions; important problems are overlooked and key concepts are insufficiently defined; logical connections between doctrines are not made explicit, and contradictions, real and apparent, are unnoticed or ignored. Serge Bulgakov (1871–1944), one of the earliest investigators of Fedorov's philosophy, complained, "I have never encountered a writer who was more unliterary, arbitrary, outlandish, unsystematic."[7] Any consistent, unified interpretation of Fedorov has to be selective, and probably more than one interpretation is possible. These observations on Fedorov's thought as a whole apply, *mutatis mutandis*, to his comments on Nietzsche. Although Fedorov managed to bring together in a concise article many of his key objections to the German philosopher,[8] he never tried to work out a systematic critical interpretation of Nietzsche. In constructing such an interpretation from Fedorov's comments on Nietzsche, I have tried to bring into it Fedorov's most interesting insights. In addition, there are several criticisms of Nietzsche

---

[6] Fedorov calls Nietzsche the "philosopher of the Black Kingdom" (*FOD*, 2:100), the "Black Prophet" (*FOD*, 1:100, 102), the "Prophet of darkness" (*FOD*, 2:104), the "learned philistine" (*FOD*, 2:121, 140), and "the Antichrist Nietzsche" (*FOD*, 2:109), and refers to his philosophy as "mad ravings" (*FOD*, 2:102), "lackey aristocratism" (*FOD*, 2:119), "Nietzschean twaddle" (*FOD*, 2:136), and the "philosophy of stupefaction" (*FOD*, 2:148).

[7] Sergei Bulgakov, *Dva grada*, 2 vols. (Moscow, 1911), 2:261.

[8] This summary (*FOD*, 1:429–33) is a section of a larger article on supramoralism and does not contain many of the criticisms that appear in volume 2. The materials in that volume are Fedorov's rough notes, which were not intended for publication.

that are worthy of attention, although they are not logically connected with what I take to be Fedorov's main line of attack on Nietzsche.

Central to Fedorov's interpretation of Nietzsche is his assertion that, deep down, Nietzsche was neither a lawgiver nor actor, but a spectator addicted to the theater. Contrary to Nietzsche's own declarations, he enjoyed nothing so much as passively watching a play (*FOD*, 2:128). Here is the key which, Fedorov asserts, will unlock the secrets of Nietzsche's philosophy:

> Zarathustra, i.e., Nietzsche, desires without realizing it, of course, to remain forever immature, . . . for although he claims to be seeking not happiness but action, he is mistaken about himself and in fact seeks only happiness, which he locates in spectacles, performances, and plays, and for this reason in his soul he transformed the whole world into performances [*predstavleniia*] and craves to enjoy their endless repetition. . . . In this insatiable craving for theatrical plays, performances, we have the key to both Nietzsche's life and doctrine. From childhood he passionately loved music, then he became a Wagnerian and finally an anti-Wagnerian. But he remained always an esthete and was never an agent, never desired action. Unsatisfied with the German Bayreuth, in his imagination he transformed the whole world into a theater, into a play, and desired nothing but a play.   (*FOD*, 1:432–33)

This surprising conclusion about Nietzsche is not intended as a biographical or psychological statement, but rather as an interpretative key to Nietzsche's philosophy. By approaching Nietzsche as an esthete, Fedorov claims, one can readily understand why he proposed the values he did (*FOD*, 2:128 n. 1).

If Nietzsche's philosophy is an esthetic interpretation of existence, then clearly "*supramoralism*, or unification for the sake of resurrection, is completely *contradictory to the immoralism of Max Stirner and Nietzsche*" (*FOD*, 1:430). It is not a question of conflicting solutions to a number of philosophical problems, but of incompatible philosophical perspectives. Fedorov approaches all philosophical problems from an essentially moral point of view,[9] while Nietzsche approaches them from an esthetic

[9] Although Fedorov teaches that, with the completion of the resurrection, the moral stage is superseded by the esthetic stage, the duty of resurrection is the dominant theme of his philosophy. The logical difficulties in his claim that the task of resurrection is finite, and the inconsistency in giving morality primacy, but not permanence, in human life are discussed toward the end of chapter 2 of my dissertation.

viewpoint. To understand life as a play is to assume an external stance toward it, a stance that logically rules out action or solidarity with the participants in the play. A spectator who intervenes in a performance or mourns the fate of a dramatic character simply does not understand what a play is. Passivity is an essential element of the esthetic attitude, and according to Fedorov this is one of Nietzsche's cardinal faults (*FOD*, 2:143). Furthermore, if life is a spectacle, then all men, except the spectator himself, are members of the cast. There can be no bond of fellowship, no mutual recognition, between the spectator and the actors. The esthetic view of life entails a kind of solipsism that is expressed in Stirner's formula "I am unique and recognize nothing else." For Fedorov this form of egoism, which he attributes to Nietzsche, represents the culmination of the egoist tradition in Western thought, a tradition that originated with Socrates' imperative "know only thyself" (*FOD*, 1:429–30). The rejection of kinship brings the esthetic outlook into direct conflict with the moral one. Finally, the spectator's view of life is immature and childish in Fedorov's eyes (*FOD*, 1:432; 2:127, 128). The spectator cannot really dissociate himself from existence, except in his imagination. He remains subject to the same evils that afflict others and, whether he realizes this or not, his passivity does have an impact on the course of events.

From Nietzsche's esthetic point of view death and destruction appear in a very different light than from the moral point of view. For Fedorov death is the greatest evil and the destruction of the world, which scientists infer from the law of entropy, is a conditional, not a necessary, fact (*FOD*, 1:92, 209, 343). He claims that all forms of destruction are due to the blindness of nature, that is, to the absence of rational regulation in nature. By gaining control over nature mankind can arrest and even reverse entropy. The world will come to an end, according to Fedorov, only if men fail to unite and to bring nature under their control. The fate of the universe, then, depends on human action. Nietzsche, on the other hand, believed that universal destruction is inevitable (*FOD*, 1:430; 2:109). In spite of his declared love of life he accepted death without resistance. This apparent inconsistency disappears when life is viewed as a tragic play. Nietzsche accepted an inevitable end of the universe, because he was enraptured with tragic endings (*FOD*, 2:128–29 n. 1). "The eternal tragedian" (*FOD*, 2:128) wanted to turn history into a sublime tragedy and, therefore, "used every means at his command to make the apocalypse, that is the horrible news of cosmic destruction, fascinating and enthralling, to transform horror into grandeur and to give destruction itself in its artistic presentation a seductive aspect" (*FOD*, 2:133). In fact, Nietzsche became so captivated with destruction, according to Fedorov, that he wanted to witness the tragedy of universal annihilation not once, but again and again ad infinitum.

The doctrine of eternal recurrence can be understood only by reference to Nietzsche's basic outlook on life:

> By viewing life as a play and the world as a theatrical performance one can also understand that absurd nonsense, the desire "that everything recur *precisely the way it is* forever and ever" (no matter how bad it might be!), i.e., in its most imperfect form. Nietzsche not only reconciles himself with what has happened, but also shouts insatiably, "da capo!" or "bis!" demanding endless repetitions with not only himself but the whole cosmic comedy in mind.
>
> (*FOD*, 2:136)

The doctrine of eternal recurrence differs radically from Fedorov's idea of resurrection. To begin with the repetitions are "blind," that is, purposeless and outside human control. Secondly, not only does each individual return to life but also dies again and again. Hence, in the eternal recurrence mankind remains forever immature and powerless against death, while in the single resurrection envisioned by Fedorov, men attain full and perfect life for themselves. Thirdly, the eternal recurrence includes the repeated annihilation of the world, while the resurrection saves the world from destruction.

For Fedorov the idea of eternal recurrence is a mere superstition without practical consequences. If it were demonstrable that everything is recurring, then men would be obliged to counteract this tendency and to replace it with one universal resurrection (*FOD*, 2:103–104 n. 2). But, as Fedorov correctly points out, the doctrine of eternal recurrence is empirically meaningless, because there is no memory of previous occurrences:

> In accepting or assuming the passive recurrences, man, like any other entity or phenomenon, cannot but recur: but he returns (according to Nietzsche) without being conscious of his return. But if that is the case, then for conscious beings the recurrences absolutely do not exist. (*FOD*, 2:119–20)

He goes on to add that only by attempting to carry out the task of resurrection can we either prove or disprove the hypothesis of the eternal recurrence (*FOD*, 2:120). On this point Fedorov is only partly right. The two concepts are logically related in the following way: the occurrence of the universal resurrection rules out the eternal recurrence. But, contrary to Fedorov, the absence of the universal resurrection entails nothing about the eternal recurrence. Furthermore, Fedorov believes that, in principle, the universal resurrection can be completed and hence verified (*FOD*, 2:139). It can be easily shown that this is not the case and, therefore, that the eternal recurrence cannot be disproved.[10]

As an invention of Nietzsche, the "eternal tragedian," the idea of the superman does not contradict, but rather complements the concept of eternal recurrence. To be more than a horror story, a tragedy must have heroes. For Fedorov, Nietzsche's superman is essentially a tragic hero who, faced with universal destruction, strikes a beautiful pose (*FOD*, 2:127). This is the character who *"with tragic understanding goes out to meet his approaching doom"* and dies "in vain" but "fearlessly" (*FOD*, 1:430). In fact, the superman is required to face destruction not merely with equanimity but with rapture. Nietzsche's heroes are "tragic individuals who become intoxicated with the destruction of everyone, not excluding themselves" (*FOD*, 2:150).

Fedorov spoke about the idea of the superman more frequently than of any other Nietzschean doctrine. While welcoming it as a call to self-transcendence, he subjected it to severe criticism. A number of his telling objections to the concept of the superman deserve to be mentioned, although they are not logically linked with his basic interpretation of Nietzsche as the "eternal tragedian." The concept of the superman, according to Fedorov, is internally inconsistent and Nietzsche's proposed method for producing supermen is incoherent.

The superman is essentially a creator of cultural values. His superiority over other men lies in his exceptional intellectual or artistic ability. But, according to Fedorov, this difference is trivial in comparison to what the superman has in common with other men—his mortality. A superman who is mortal is too similar to other men to be above them, and turns into an absurd being. "A '*super*man *superior* to *beings like him*' is not only an immoral concept, but an obvious contradiction, absolute nonsense: either *they* are unlike him, or (if they are like him), he cannot be *superior* to them" (*FOD*, 2:111). Only an immortal superman would be

---

[10]It is the universality of the resurrection that makes it unverifiable. Even if at some future point all the dead happen to have been resurrected, it will be impossible to prove that no one has been omitted.

sufficiently different from other human beings to deserve the status of superman. It would be objectionable, however, to correct this logical flaw in the concept by redefining the superman as an immortal being, for privileged immortality, according to Fedorov, is immoral. Immortality would confer infinite superiority on a few individuals and this would be infinitely more immoral than the superiority envisioned by Nietzsche (*FOD*, 2:121). The only acceptable ideal of the superman, from both a logical and moral viewpoint, is the Christian, Fedorovian idea of a superman who attains immortality together with all other men through the resurrection of the dead (*FOD*, 2:110, 121).

Fedorov rejected Nietzsche's idea of creativity, but omitted to note what this entails for the concept of the superman. Every work produced by an individual is a reflection of the creator's mind and personality. But an individual is not his own creator: what he is is determined largely by the culture into which he is born. That culture is the product of many generations. Hence, what one creates, according to Fedorov, consists mostly of what one has borrowed from others—one's predecessors and contemporaries. What is truly original and one's own can be only a minute element of one's work. Thus, Nietzsche is gravely mistaken in attributing cultural achievements to individuals:

> . . . Nietzsche elevates arbitrariness from an abuse into a principle, into a competence, and substitutes an individual's arbitrariness for evolution. The rationalist formula for explaining the genesis of entities and phenomena, 'nascuntur' [they are born] which was put forth in opposition to supernatural creation, is here again replaced by the formula 'fiunt' [they are made]. However, this is not a collective genesis, but a subjective, individualistic one: thus, religions do not arise by themselves but are created, not by priests (as the freethinkers of the time of the English deists and Voltaire mistakenly claimed), however, but by a solitary genius; and language does not arise by itself nor is it created by the people but is invented and prescribed by the exceptional genius.   (*FOD*, 2:116)

To ascribe to an individual what has been created by many men could be merely an error of judgment or it could be a kind of theft. Compared to the ancient practice of attributing works to prominent authorities who did not produce them, "to claim a work for *oneself*, for a single individual, when it is obviously the result of many preceding works" (*FOD*, 1:351 n. 14) is far more reprehensible. According to Nietzsche's own

account, the superman is the end result of the labors of many generations. Hence, his works are not, strictly speaking, his own. What then
entitles the superman to a status above other men? Once again the superman turns out to be a "wholly unjustified form of self-exaltation above
others like oneself, more like oneself than one thinks" (*FOD*, 2:117).

Fedorov's moral objections to Nietzsche's doctrine of the superman are
not original, but the language in which he states them is colorful. Some
of the objections are related to Fedorov's interpretation of Nietzsche as a
tragedian. Implicit in the idea of the superman is the division of mankind
into "supermen and swine" (*FOD*, 2:120). Fedorov condemns the contempt for human beings that is inherent in this division and points out
that by treating ordinary human beings as swine, supermen do not raise
themselves above the human level but, on the contrary, sink to the sub-
human level—to the level of beasts of prey (*FOD*, 2:111). Furthermore,
the sharp division of mankind into two classes is immoral in itself and
immoral in its effects. Since "morality is neither mastery [*barstvo*], nor
slavery [*rabstvo*], but kinship [*rodstvo*]" (*FOD*, 2:127), it is wrong to divide men into masters (supermen) and slaves (the rest of mankind who
exist only for the sake of the supermen). Also, division leads to conflict
and discord (*FOD*, 1:431). Nietzsche's glorification of war brings out what
is implicit in his division of human beings. By advocating conflict Nietzsche
strengthens the power of blind nature over men and increases the evil it
inflicts upon men (*FOD*, 1:432; 2:127). His demand for cruelty and
pitilessness toward the weak is consistent with his desire for more suffering and death. Conflict, suffering, and death are evil from the moral
point of view, but are desirable from the esthetic viewpoint. To a tragedian they are the essential elements of his drama.

Nietzsche's false idea of the superman arose from his perverted notion
of power. According to Fedorov, Nietzsche was right to value strength
and power, but instead of defining power as power over nature he defined
it as power over human beings (*FOD*, 1:430; 2:100). This error clearly
reveals Nietzsche's class prejudices: as an intellectual belonging to the
"inactive class," he did not appreciate the importance of labor by which
men change the material world (*FOD*, 1:431), and as a descendant of
Polish aristocracy he preferred freedom undisciplined by a sense of responsibility (*liberum veto*), and domination over others to control over
nature (*FOD*, 2:117–18).

To produce supermen Nietzsche proposed something like a "common
task." For many generations all men are to sacrifice happiness and even

life to give rise by selective breeding and education to ever greater ge-
niuses from whom supermen will finally be born (FOD, 2:120–21, 149).
Fedorov's basic objection to this "task" is that it is accomplished not so
much by human action as by the blind forces of nature:

> But Nietzsche, as a learned philistine, is completely incapable of
> grasping the meaning and value of *action*: instead of restricting it to
> conscious and will-possessing beings, he attributes it to will-less and
> blind force. Under these conditions the superman is nothing but a
> felicitous contingency, the result of separate happy chances spring-
> ing from the most diverse localities and among the most diverse
> cultures.   (FOD, 2:121)

Some action involving purpose and knowledge is, of course, indispensable to Nietzsche's proposed method of producing supermen, but Fedorov is basically right in pointing out that the outcome is dependent mostly
on blind nature. First, according to modern genetic theory an advanta-
geous combination of genes, which is a precondition for the work of
selection and education, is a matter of chance. Secondly, the rich culture
that is necessary for the emergence of the superman is attained not through
planned, regulated work, but "blindly" through competition and conflict.
Restricted by these conditions, the role of human consciousness in the
evolution of the superman is confined to the narrow sphere of individual
effort. Thus, Nietzsche obviously fails to live up to his claim that creativity, that is, the activity of the mind, has the highest value (FOD, 1:311–
12). Fedorov's argument that Nietzsche understands the production of
supermen not as a project but as a blind process reinforces his basic
assertion about Nietzsche—that he is not a philosopher of action, but a
philosopher of esthetic enjoyment.

In Fedorov's mind Nietzsche was closely associated with Tolstoi. This
association may strike us as strange, but to Fedorov the two thinkers, who
enjoyed great popularity in Russia at the turn of the century, were the
chief proponents of passivity and the principal opponents of his own active Christianity (FOD, 2:133). There are important differences between
them to be sure: Tolstoi places morality above everything else including
life, while Nietzsche gives priority to esthetic values; Tolstoi rejects culture, while Nietzsche finds in it the justification for existence. Yet, when
one approaches them from the standpoint of Fedorov's philosophy of the
"common task," one can detect an important similarity. The world-views
articulated by Tolstoi and Nietzsche can be seen as profoundly personal

attempts by both thinkers to reconcile themselves to the necessity of suffering and death without renouncing reason for faith.[11] Unlike Fedorov, both thought of human action in individualistic terms and failed to envision the possibility of conquering suffering and death.

During his lifetime Fedorov published a few brief articles outlining some immediate steps for beginning his "common task," but none of them contained any references to Nietzsche. Hence, his criticisms of Nietzsche could have influenced only those of his contemporaries who knew him or his followers personally. Vladimir Soloviev (1853–1900) was acquainted with Fedorov since the early 1880s and could well have been familiar with his views on Nietzsche. Although Soloviev wrote very little about Nietzsche, what he did write bears a striking resemblance to Fedorov's criticisms. In the article "The Idea of the Superman" ("Ideia sverkhcheloveka," 1899)[12] and the public lecture on Lermontov[13] of the same year Soloviev admits that Nietzsche's idea of the superman contains an important truth—that man is perfectible, and goes on to argue that the true superman is a conqueror of death, an immortal man. In "Literature or Truth" ("Slovesnost' ili istina," 1897),[14] after comparing the Christian and Nietzschean ideas of the superman, Soloviev attributes the shortcomings of Nietzsche's teachings to the fact that Nietzsche was a scholar and a learned philologist. Not only the content but the sarcastic tone of the article is reminiscent of Fedorov. It is quite possible that Soloviev's views on Nietzsche were influenced by Fedorov, but there is no hard evidence for this. Relations between the two thinkers became strained toward the end of the 1880s and may have been broken off. Furthermore, since Soloviev's philosophy is in many important respects close to Fedorov's, his reaction to Nietzsche could have been similar without any prompting from Fedorov.

Apart from Soloviev I have not found any echoes of Fedorov's ideas on Nietzsche among Russian thinkers. It is doubtful that his criticisms had any influence in Russia, because Fedorov's ideas were practically unknown when interest in Nietzsche was at its height, and his most telling criticisms of Nietzsche are rooted in his own philosophical perspec-

---

[11] This theme was developed at length by L. Shestov in his *Dobro v uchenii gr. Tolstogo i Fr. Nitshe* (St. Petersburg, 1900), trans. by B. Martin as *Dostoevsky, Tolstoy, and Nietzsche* (Athens, 1969), pp. 1–140.

[12] *Sobranie sochinenii V. S. Solovieva*, eds. S. M. Soloviev and E. L. Radlov, 11 vols. 2nd ed. (1911; reprint, Brussels, 1966), 9:265–74.

[13] Ibid., 9:348–67.

[14] Ibid., 10:28–32.

tive. They are unintelligible to those who do not have a grasp of Fedorov's basic doctrines and are unconvincing to those who reject his doctrines.
Fedorov's criticisms of Nietzsche first appeared in print as part of Kozhevnikov's lengthy exposition of Fedorov's thought in *Russkii arkhiv*, 1903–
1906.[15] Few readers of this prestigious historical journal would have read
Kozhevnikov's lengthy articles, which consisted mostly of paraphrases of
Fedorov's writings. The first volume of Fedorov's collected works, containing a short summary of his criticisms of Nietzsche, appeared in 1906,
but only in 480 copies. The second volume, containing forty-five brief
articles on Nietzsche, appeared seven years later, probably in a similarly
limited edition. There was very little discussion of Fedorov's ideas in
scholarly periodicals when these volumes appeared. The symbolists showed
some interest in his ideas and even published two of Fedorov's articles in
The Scales (*Vesy*, 1904 and 1906), but they were too hostile to Fedorov's
"materialist" and "positivist" outlook to take his view of Nietzsche seriously. The same can be said of Nicholas Berdiaev and Serge Bulgakov,
who appreciated certain aspects of Fedorov's thought but rejected what is
essential in him. The "Nietzschean Marxists"[16] who would have been
more sympathetic to Fedorov's ideas seem not to have heard of him. The
few disciples whom Fedorov acquired after the First World War did not
show any interest in Nietzsche and did not discuss him in their writings.

While a number of Fedorov's criticisms directed at particular doctrines
such as the doctrine of the superman and the doctrine of the eternal
recurrence are quite perceptive and to the point, the main thrust of his
attack on Nietzsche as the "eternal tragedian" is extremely one-sided and
unfair. An interpretation that highlights passivity, solipsistic egoism, and
delight in destruction as the essential features of Nietzsche's philosophy
is not merely eccentric, it is gravely distorted. At most it raises some
interesting questions about the genesis of Nietzsche's doctrines and emphasizes the enormous differences between Fedorov's and Nietzsche's assessment of man's creative powers. Although Fedorov's critique of Nietzsche
had no significant impact on other thinkers, it is historically important as
one of the first and most vehement reactions to Nietzsche in Russia.
Fedorov's treatment of Nietzsche as his most dangerous philosophical
rival would have been appreciated by Nietzsche himself as the highest
compliment.

[15] Kozhevnikov, "Fedorov," *Russkii arkhiv*, no. 10 (1904), pp. 248–61.
[16] See G. L. Kline, " 'Nietzschean Marxism' in Russia," in *Demythologizing Marxism*,
ed. F. J. Adelmann (Chestnut Hill, Mass. and The Hague, 1969), pp. 166–83.

5.

The Great Catalyzer:
Nietzsche and Russian Neo-Idealism

Mihajlo Mihajlov

TRANSLATED BY ANDREW GRIFFIN

> The "Superman" is the path from man to God!
> —*Nicholas Berdiaev*

WHEN ONE UNDERTAKES the study of Nietzsche's influence on Russian Neo-Idealist philosophy, one quickly concludes that despite virtually across-the-board assurances of both Russian and Eastern scholars of the decisive influence of the German philosopher on a brilliant galaxy of Russian Neo-Idealist philosophers, the number of works on this topic is next to none and the affirmation of Nietzsche's crucial impact is virtually unsubstantiated and cannot be taken at face value.

Nevertheless, it is symptomatic that after having analyzed the numerous difficulties encountered by the researcher—the complete absence of scholarly secondary works, the polar opposition of the spiritual thrust of Friedrich Nietzsche's nihilism and of Russian philosophers' idealism—and having expressed the need for a more thorough study on this topic in the future, one scholar, Heinrich Stammler, is still firmly convinced that Nietzsche must be acknowledged as the "patron saint and founding father of the movement which we know as the renaissance of religious and moral philosophy in Russia."[1] Another American scholar, George Kline, in his extremely informative book, *Religious and Anti-Religious Thought in Russia*, says virtually the same thing: "The Western thinker

---

[1] Heinrich Stammler, "Nietzsche and Neo-Idealism" (Paper delivered at the Nietzsche in Russia conference, Fordham University, 17–18 June 1983), p. 4.

who most pervasively influenced this galaxy, in ways too complicated to summarize here, was Nietzsche. The impact of Nietzsche's thought was clearest in the religious existentialists Shestov and Berdiaev, and the Marxist 'God-builders' Gorky and Lunacharsky. But Leontiev and Rozanov were 'Russian Nietzscheans'—as Alexander Herzen had been to some extent—*avant la lettre.*"[2] Much more cannot be found in any other existing work on the history of Russian philosophy. The sole substantial scholarly work known to me that deals with this question is Ann M. Lane's doctoral dissertation, entitled "Nietzsche in Russian Thought, 1890–1917,"[3] a lengthy and informative study, unfortunately still unpublished, which devotes three chapters to an analysis of Nietzsche's impact on Berdiaev, Frank, and Shestov.

However, at a time when such Marxist God-builders as Gorky, Lunacharsky, Bogdanov, and Bazarov can easily be termed "Nietzscheans," the most important Neo-Idealists—Nicholas Berdiaev, Semen Frank, Nicholas Lossky, Serge Bulgakov, and Lev Shestov, cannot possibly, even in part, be characterized as such. (Strictly speaking, Shestov was not a Neo-Idealist, but shares their opposition to positivism and rationalism.) Vasily Rozanov was a "Nietzschean" before Nietzsche was, and relies in the spiritual sense on Leontiev.

All of the Russian religious thinkers are Christian (except Shestov, who does not make his views completely clear; sometimes it is as if he was closer to the God of the Old Testament. [Shestov, like Frank, was born to a Jewish family, but unlike Frank, he never became a Christian. He can be considered a 'non-Jewish Jew.'] Nietzsche is an antitheist and a fanatic anti-Christian. What can be more opposed to Nietzsche's declaration that "God is dead," than Frank's "God is with us" (the title of his last book), a no less confident assertation? What is there is common between Nietzsche's exhortation—"Be true to the earth, my brothers," and Berdiaev's anti-earthiness, his conviction that any "objectification" is an evil, that is, any realization of the spiritual in the physical world is evil. One of Nietzsche's most important ideas, for example, was the concept of *amor fati*: "My formula for greatness in a human being is *amor fati*, that one wants nothing to be different, not forward, not backward, not in all eternity. Not merely bear what is necessary, still less conceal it—all

[2]George L. Kline, *Religious and Anti-Religious Thought in Russia* (Chicago, 1968), p. 6.
[3]Ann M. Lane, "Nietzsche in Russian Thought" (Ph.D. diss., University of Wisconsin, 1976).

idealism is mendaciousness in the face of what is necessary—but *love* it" (*EH*, 258). The complete polar opposite is Shestov's basic idea that man can only hope that "God can make what has been, not to have been"? Is there really much in common between those who openly raise the banner of idealism in the struggle against positivism, and Nietzsche who espouses totally opposite and even hostile ideas: "We laugh at man's pretentious attempts to seek values which would surpass the values of the real world"?[4]

Yet, in spite of all this, according to the admissions of the Russian thinkers themselves, Nietzsche opened the door to religion for Berdiaev; he led the way to the realization of the spiritual world for Frank, and he obviously helped Shestov, who wrote more about Nietzsche than anybody, to believe in the possibility of "overcoming self-evident truths," even the most insurmountable "self-evident truth"—that which has already happened. Such was the influence of the thinker who proclaimed the "death of God," the illusoriness of the spiritual world, and "eternal recurrence," that is, perpetual self-evident truths.

So Nietzsche is the pathfinder to the spiritual world, God, and religion! Nietzsche leads the way to Christian mysticism! Nietzsche is the "creator of a whole grandiose moral system!"[5] The superman is a stepping stone to God!

There can be, however, no doubt. The Russian philosophers understood the German genius in precisely this manner. Shestov ended a work from his early period, *The Good in the Teaching of Count Tolstoi and F. Nietzsche* (1900) with these words: "Nietzsche discovered the way. We must seek what is higher than compassion, what is higher than good. We must seek God."[6] Frank, recalling what effect the reading of *Thus Spoke Zarathustra*" had on him, wrote:

> I was completely shaken by the depth and tension of the spiritual wrestling, by the incisiveness with which he all over again posited the problem of religion (earlier it had seemed to us that it had long ago been resolved—in a negative sense—by all enlightened people) and by his examination of the basic positions of moral life. Under

---

[4] Nietzsche, *Radostnaia nauka* [*The Gay Science*], as quoted by Shestov, *Dobro v uchenii gr. Tolstogo i F. Nitshe* (St. Petersburg, 1900), p. 189.

[5] S. Frank, "Fr. Nitshe i etika liubvi k dal'nemu," in *Problemy idealizma*, ed. P. I. Novgorodtsev (Moscow, 1902), p. 142. The essay is reprinted in S. Frank, *Sbornik statei, Filosofiia i zhizn'* (St. Petersburg, 1910), pp. 1–71.

[6] Shestov, *Dobro*, p. 209.

the influence of Nietzsche, there took place in me a genuine spiritual upheaval, which in part was obviously prepared by both all of my past intellectual development and my personal experiences: I can say that for the first time there was revealed to me the reality of a spiritual life. In my soul there began to take shape a certain "heroic" philosophy, defined by faith in the absolute value of the soul and in the necessity of struggle for it.[7]

One would think that such a peculiar interpretation of Nietzsche on the part of the Russian Neo-Idealist thinkers is one of the difficulties that accounts for the almost complete absence of scholarly works devoted to the impact of Nietzsche on Russian philosophy. James Scanlan summarizes Nietzsche's role in the history of Russian thought in the following words:

> The remarkable renaissance of Russian art, literature, religion, and philosophy in the first decade of the twentieth century owed much to a small group of religious rebels who drew their inspiration from neither of the two great reservoirs of earlier Russian culture—the radical intelligentsia and the Orthodox Church. Their secular guide was not Nicholas Chernyshevsky, but Friedrich Nietzsche, who showed them the sanctity of paganism and classical antiquity. . . . The earthly and the heavenly, long divorced in Russian cultural life, began to come together for these thinkers in a strange blend of paganism and Christianity. They read of the twice-born Dionysus, and were reminded of the resurrected Christ; they studied the Christian scriptures, and found a Dionysian, fleshly spectacle, the Apocalypse. The result was an intoxicating new vision of the world and its future—a "new religious consciousness" which not only made the body the equal of soul, but prophesied an imminent golden age, in which that equality would transfigure the earth.[8]

Actually, however, Nietzsche's impact was quite different. His teaching helped Russian philosophy find the way to the spiritual, religious, and mystical, certainly not the fleshly pagan. The originality of Russian philosophy rests in that it perceived Nietzsche in a manner not at all like that of the great majority of Nietzscheans, then as well as now.

[7] S. Frank, *Biografiia P. B. Struve* (New York, 1956), pp. 28–29.

[8] James P. Scanlan, "The New Religious Consciousness: Merezhkovskii and Berdiaev," *Canadian Slavic Studies* 4 (Spring 1970), p. 17.

In the works of Nietzsche, Russian philosophers heard the tragic cry of a human soul crucified in a world devoid of God. The intensity of this cry, audible even earlier in the works of Dostoevsky, helped them to become aware of the existence of the human soul. The very existence of a metaphysical reality—the soul—led directly to the discovery of the spiritual and religious. For this reason, Shestov, Frank and Berdiaev, while they were quite enthralled with Nietzsche, constantly reiterated his "blindness" to the fundamental basis of his ideas of which he was himself ironically unaware, and the tragedy of his failure to understand transcendency. Lev Shestov explains that Nietzsche's "eternal recurrence" is only an unconscious hope and belief in a "new heaven and a new earth." In short, Nietzsche, in the eyes of the Russian Neo-Idealist philosophers, is a tragic victim not only of the cosmic and social universe, but also of his own religious blindness. He is the victim of positivism and the spirit of his age—an age of faith in progress and socialism. Thus writes Serge Bulgakov in 1903: "It is not necessary to share consciously the ideas of an age in order to be a product of it nevertheless; sometimes complete denial indicates a much more passionate relationship with the teaching that has been rejected than does its indifferent acceptance. In this sense, we can say apropos of Nietzsche that in his hostility to socialism, he is fully a product of the socialist world outlook, a spiritual bastard son."[9]

Considering that almost all the great Neo-Idealist thinkers began with Marxism, and were even participants in the so-called "first Marxist wave" in Russia, the tragic voice of Nietzsche seemed to be the voice of their own soul. This is even more so since Nietzsche's voice resounded at just that time when the most talented, thoughtful people in Russia ceased to find in Marxism answers to questions that had begun to trouble them. Even if Nietzsche was a tragic victim, in their eyes, he certainly was not without a purpose. They set out on a path that went the exact opposite direction to the one that Nietzsche trod, and thus emerged one of the most original philosophical currents of the twentieth century, a current still relatively unknown both in the West and in Russia—for different reasons, of course.

MAJOR OBSTACLES

An analysis of the difficulties that the researcher encounters when he attempts to define the specific character and extent of the impact of

[9] Sergei Bulgakov, *Ot Marksizmu k idealizmu* (St. Petersburg, 1903), p. 108.

Nietzsche on Russian philosophers paradoxically leads him to an understanding of the impact itself. Besides the aforementioned fundamental difficulty—the polar opposition of the philosophies of the Russian Neo-Idealists and of Nietzsche, there exist four main problems for the researcher:

1. The absence, also already mentioned, of any substantial scholarly work devoted to Nietzsche and the Russian Neo-Idealists (except for Ann Lane's dissertation). While it is perfectly understandable why Nietzsche and, even more so, the Russian non-Marxist philosophers are a topic that is still virtually taboo in the Soviet Union, the absence of such scholarship in the West is explained by the fact that the most significant works of Shestov, Berdiaev, Frank, and Lossky were written between the World Wars, after their authors had emigrated, and printed in small editions, which were read by a very limited number of persons. These books, although translated in the West, did not demonstrate the extent of Nietzsche's influence, because by then, this influence was imperceptible. Nietzsche's influence was more obvious in the earlier writings, but it was the rare historian of Russian thought who studied articles and books by Russian philosophers from the first decade of the twentieth century. Only recently has interest in the Russian renaissance of religion and philosophy increased in both the Soviet Union and the West. The total elucidation of the relationship between Nietzsche and the Russian Neo-Idealists is an extremely complex task and one that demands a painstaking study of an enormous amount of material heretofore untouched.

2. The study of Nietzsche's influence on Russian philosophers is made much more difficult by the fact that long before Nietzsche, authentic "Nietzscheans" lived and wrote in Russia. Besides the man rightly known as the "Russian Nietzsche," Constantine Leontiev, Michael Bakunin expressed theomachistic ideas long before the German philosopher and in practically the same terms.

3. Dostoevsky's influence, on the one hand on Nietzsche, on the other on Russian philosophers, is even more significant. After the publication in 1970 of the second part of volume eight of Nietzsche's *Collected Works* (containing his notes and rough drafts written during the winter of 1886–1887), it became indisputable that the influence of the Russian novelist was absolutely crucial on Nietzsche's most important books. Nietzsche not only constantly mentions and refers to Dostoevsky, he even makes abstracts of several of his works. On the other hand, all the greatest philosophers of Russian Neo-Idealism made thoroughgoing studies of Dos-

toevsky and all wrote a great deal about him. An attempt to sort out what originates from Nietzsche and what from Dostoevsky would be difficult indeed.

4. The greatest problem of all is that the philosophy of the Russian Neo-Idealists is itself not completely understood. This is because, despite their common spiritual aim, each philosopher of the philosophical and religious renaissance was in his own way distinct from the others. Russian philosophy still awaits the thinker who will summarize it, the person who will elucidate the common foundation of the most important ideas and theories of Berdiaev, Lossky, Frank, and Shestov, the four most significant Russian thinkers of the first half of the twentieth century. The appearance of certain philosophical works in *samizdat* in recent years leads us to hope that the completion of a solid framework for Russian thought may not be so far off.

The basic difficulty in understanding Russian Neo-Idealism is that it is not at all the idealism of classical philosophy—Greek *or* German. It is no accident that Frank called his philosophical system "ideal-realism." Philosophical idealism from Plato to Hegel assumes the domination of the spiritual world, the realm of ideas, over the physical world and matter. Materialism, on the contrary, assumes the predominance of material existence, and defines the spiritual world, the world of ideas, and the ideal world as worlds that exist only in illusion, that is, in the consciousness of man and mankind. The originality of Russian philosophers consists in the fact that they (most clearly expressed, however, by Frank and Lossky) saw three, not two, levels of existence. One level is the world of objects, that is, the physical world. The second level is the spiritual world, the world of ideas, which opens itself up to the human mind and consciousness. And the third level is *unobservable* reality in which both worlds—material and spiritual—are united in some mysterious way. In the West only the German philosopher Nicolai Hartmann came close to this conception; however, it should be stressed that he began to write his own works after having studied philosophy with Frank at St. Petersburg University before World War I. It appears that this novelty in Russian thought is one of the most important reasons why it is yet to be understood. American scholars, for example, are uniformly convinced that they are merely contending with a new form of the classical idealism that began with Plato, in other words, a response to the call of "back to Kant." It must be stated at the outset that this is completely wrong, just as wrong as the aforementioned opinion that Nietzsche revealed to the Russian philosophers the pagan and fleshly essence of existence. Russian Neo-Idealist philosophy, by its discovery of the third unobservable level of the ontology that unites the physical world and the spiritual world, the world "for us" and the world "for the self," has completely overcome Kant, and overcome the break of the "two worlds." This is what has yet to be understood.

The very definition of Russian thought as a religious philosophy also prevents it from being understood. In the West there is theology and there is philosophy; Russian thought, however, is a third concept. Whereas theology is thought that is based on the initial presupposition of the existence of a Creator, Russian religious philosophy, just as Western philosophy, contains no such presupposition. However, Western philosophy is reflection about man and the world, as if there were no God at all, and leaves the question of the Creator to theology. Russian religious philosophy (that is, the philosophy known as Neo-Idealism), beginning without presuppositions, just as Western thought does, comes to conclusions that are expressly religious. Without faith in God, any philosophical discipline—logic, epistemology, ethics, esthetics—loses its basis.

Frank's intellectual journey is symbolic of his era: in his youth he was a Marxist; next he went through a transition (with Nietzsche's help) straight into classical idealism and attempted to "supplement" Kant with Nietzsche's ideas; he then came out with his first original book, *The Object of Knowledge* (*Predmet znania*) (it was this period during which Hartmann studied with Frank); later he published his full exposition of the third level of ontology in *The Unfathomable* (*Nepostizhimoe*); and finally produced the work *God Is with Us* (*S nami Bog*). Thus, he took the road from Marxism and classical philosophical epistemology to Neo-Idealism, or, more precisely, "ideal-realism," and finally to a full conviction in the existence of God. In a sense the Russian philosophers discussed here closed the circle of European thought. Western thought became detached from theology at the end of the middle ages and in the course of three or four centuries of development arrived at Marxism and existentialism; it developed logic and epistemology to an extreme and made them much more complex; it shook the world in a spiritual sense with such major phenomena as Kant, Hegel, and Nietzsche, and became bogged down for a long time in logical positivism, structuralism, and existential nihilism. The philosophers of the Russian religious and philosophical renaissance took up precisely at the place Western European thought ended its development, and, in possession of all the achievements and all of the tools of Western philosophy, they came around to the starting point of European thought for the new century: the unity of philosophy and theology, the realization that philosophy, like any thought, can exist only because God exists.

This truly revolutionary (in the spiritual sense) achievement of Russian philosophy is still completely unrealized, especially in professional circles, for many reasons, including those mentioned here. Until Neo-Idealist Russian philosophy is learned and mastered, it is vain to expect any serious works on the impact of Nietzsche on this philosophy to appear.

NIETZSCHEANS BEFORE NIETZSCHE

In 1892, when Vasily Rozanov first read an article about Nietzsche in a Moscow journal, he exclaimed, "That's Leontiev all right, without any changes."[10] Both Leontiev and Rozanov are known as "Russian Nietzsches"; Leontiev, however, wrote his "Nietzschean" works about ten years before Nietzsche was ever published, and died before Nietzsche's fame reached Russia. Just as Nietzsche did, Leontiev passionately hated the European petty bourgeoisie and the democratic leveling of the social life; he wrote: "The teachings of Christianity and European progress aspire in their collective efforts to kill the esthetics of life on earth, i.e., life itself."[11] Although Leontiev was an adherent of Byzantine Christianity, in which he saw the "live-giving forces of social inequality," his own brand of Christianity was virtually identical with Nietzsche's anti-Christian doctrine. (He was also, incidentally, an admirer of the East in general, having learned about it while Russian envoy to Constantinople.) Leontiev glorified the stormy periods of history, risk, strife, and even bloodshed, and contrasted their creativity to a boring vegetative life in the comfort and security of nineteenth-century European civilization. He attacked liberalism and socialism with particular fury, seeing in them death for the social organism. "Esthetic amoralism," "transcendental egoism," nostalgia for the Renaissance (just as Nietzsche later exalted the heroism, tragedy, and even demonism of the Renaissance)—all these traits make Leontiev a direct predecessor of Nietzsche. As George Kline correctly noted, Leontiev even came very close to the idea of a "superman."[12] In 1882, Leontiev expressed the following "Nietzschean" thoughts:

[10] Constantine Leontiev, *Pis'ma k Vasiliiu Rosanov* (London, 1981), p. 34.
[11] Ibid., p. 104.
[12] Kline, *Religious and Anti-Religious Thought*, p. 47.

Would it not be dreadful and offensive to think that Moses went up to Sinai, that the Greeks built their splendid Acropolises, the Romans waged their Punic Wars, the handsome genius Alexander, in a plumed helmet, crossed the Granicus and fought at Arbela, that the apostles preached, martyrs suffered, poets sang, painters painted, and knights shone in the tourneys, only in order that the French, German, or Russian bourgeois, in his ugly and comical clothing, should sit complacent . . . upon the ruins of all this past greatness?[13]

Rozanov saw in Leontiev's denial of a universal moral criterion that which later became known with Nietzsche and the Nietzscheans as "beyond good and evil."[14] Although Leontiev was little known in his own time in Russia, starting with the last decade of the nineteenth century his influence on the philosophers of Russian Neo-Idealism was unquestionable, thanks to Rozanov who was the first to realize Leontiev's significance and began to write about him. Berdiaev devoted an entire book to Leontiev (*Constantine Leontiev, An Essay in the History of Russian Religious Thought*, 1926). To determine exactly where Nietzsche or Leontiev's influence is felt and keep them apart is not an easy task.

If, speaking in general terms, one can call Leontiev's teaching "esthetic amoralism," and Nietzsche's "cultural amoralism," then the teaching of the second "Russian Nietzsche," Rozanov, is "existential amoralism." Rozanov is one generation younger than Leontiev, and felt his influence long before he became acquainted with Nietzsche. Of course, he disliked European "leveling" civilization as much as they did, and went even further than Nietzsche in his critique of Christianity by proclaiming it the "religion of death" and by stating that Christians worship "a God in the grave." All the same, the only thing one can be certain reveals Nietzsche's influence on Rozanov is the style of his writings. Rozanov, like Nietzsche, wrote mainly in aphorisms, and it appears that it became possible to write in such a manner in Russia only after Nietzsche.

While Leontiev revered Byzantine Christianity, and Rozanov the "sacred sexuality" of the Old Testament, long before Nietzsche one of the founders and theoreticians of anarchism, Bakunin, attacked religion and belief in God with the same force as Nietzsche and in practically the same terms. He wrote: "If God exists, then man is a slave; but man . . .

---

[13]"Pis'ma o vostochnykh delakh" ["Letters on Eastern Affairs"] (1882–1883), in *Sochineniia*, 9 vols. (Moscow, 1912–1914), 5:426.

[14]Leontiev, *Pis'ma k Vasiliiu Rosanovu*, p. 106.

is free; therefore God does not exist" and "if God is everything, then life and man are nothing."[15] Bakunin also anticipated Nietzsche in his criticism of priests, believing that even the most humane of them "still have something cruel and bloody at the bottom of their hearts."[16] It was he who wrote: "I am turning Voltaire's aphorism around and saying: If God exists then it is necessary to abolish him."[17]

When we read later in Nietzsche that "it is better to make do without a God at all, it is better to determine one's fate at one's own peril, it is better to be a fool, it is better for one to be God himself,"[18] how can we distinguish the influence of Nietzsche from that of Leontiev, Bakunin, Rozanov, or even Herzen, with his criticism of Western European civilization?

DOSTOEVSKY, NIETZSCHE, AND THE NEO-IDEALISTS

As I have already mentioned, in 1970 in Germany, the second part of the eighth volume of Nietzsche's works was published, in which the German philosopher's notebooks and rough drafts for several of his most significant works were made public for the first time. His constant references to Dostoevsky, the frequent excerpts, quotes, and abstracts from the Russian writer's books, have already caused a wave of commentary, even in the Soviet Union. Along with George Fridlender's chapter "Dostoevsky and F. Nietzsche," in his book *Dostoevsky and World Literature*, there is Iury Davydov's extremely interesting book, *The Ethics of Love and the Metaphysics of Self-Will*,[19] which analyzes the influence of Dostoevsky on Nietzsche.

Even before Nietzsche's notebooks were published, the following quotation was well known: "Dostoevsky was the only psychologist from whom I ever learned anything; I count my acquaintanceship with him as being among the greatest successes of my life."[20] In his notebooks Nietzsche

---

[15] Thomas G. Masaryk, *The Spirit of Russia*, trans. Eden and Cedar Paul, 2 vols. (London and New York, 1955), 1:447; M. Bakunin, *God and the State* (New York, ca. 1916), p. 25; see also Bakunin, "Fédéralisme," in *Oeuvres*, 6 vols. (Paris, 1913), 1:64, 63, respectively.

[16] Bakunin, *Oeuvres*, 1:115, 132, 66.

[17] Bakunin, *God and the State*, p. 28.

[18] *Tak govoril Zaratustra* [*Thus Spoke Zarathustra*], as quoted by Shestov, *Dobro*, p. 137.

[19] Iury Davydov, *Etika liubvi i metafizika svoevolia* (Moscow, 1982); G. Fridlender, *Dostoevsky i mirovaia literatura* (Moscow, 1985), pp. 251–89.

[20] As quoted by Lev Shestov, *Dostoevsky i Nitshe* (*Filosofiia tragedii*) (1903; reprint, Berlin, 1922), p. 19.

continues: "He belongs to greatest strokes of luck in my life, even to a greater degree than my discovery of Stendhal. . . . This most profound man who was a thousand times right when he despised shallow Germans, came to understand in a way completely different than he himself expected, those Siberian convicts, hardened criminals to the bone, among whom he lived a long time, and for whom there was no return to society, since he was convinced that it was as if they had been sculpted from the best, most durable, most valuable tree [wood] that ever grew on Russian soil."[21] This idea is repeated in *Twilight of the Idols*, 1889.

Nietzsche studied Dostoevsky especially intensely at the very last stage of his life while he was contemplating nihilism. Nietzsche even made an abstract of Dostoevsky's *The Possessed*, and Davydov convincingly shows that the German philosopher's *Diary of a Nihilist* is based on a simple interpretation of the letter Stavrogin wrote before his suicide.

Besides *The Possessed*, Nietzsche thoroughly analyzed and made comments upon *Notes from the House of the Dead* and *The Insulted and the Injured*. Of course the problem of crime fascinated the philosopher most of all; Nietzsche wrote in 1887: "To give an evil man back his clean conscience—isn't this my involuntary aspiration? . . . and only an evil man since it is he who is strong?" (at this point bringing up Dostoevsky's views on criminals who have been released from jail). Later he reaffirmed his view: "Dostoevsky was not wrong when he wrote about the prisoners of that Siberian jail, saying that they formed the strongest and most valuable constituent part of the Russian people."[22]

Notes from the House of the Dead was Nietzsche's reference while he was working on *Twilight of the Idols*, and *The Possessed* served as a source when he was preparing *The Antichrist*. The influence of Dostoevsky's *The Idiot* is also apparent in the background of the latter book. Nietzsche wrote: "What a pity that [Christ's] society did not have its own Dostoevsky: indeed the entire history [of the emergence of Christianity] suits a Russian novel better than anything, by its morbidity, pathos, its isolated streaks of sublime strangeness among the abysmal licentiousness and filthy vulgarity . . . (such as Mary Magdalene)."[23] And further:

> That strange and sick world into which the Gospel leads us, a world which seems to be out of a Russian novel, where it is as if a great

[21] *Nietzsches Werke: Taschen-Ausgabe*, 10 vols. (Leipzig, 1906), 10:333.

[22] *Nietzsche: Werke: Kritische Gesamtausgabe*, ed. Giorgio Colli and Mazzino Montinari, 15 vols. to date (Berlin, 1967–   ), vol 8, pt. 1, p. 291; pt. 2, p. 146.

[23] Ibid., pt. 2, p. 417.

rendezvous of the dregs of society, nervous ailments, and "childish" idiocy is taking place—in any case had to *coarsen* the type [Jesus]. . . . Prophet, Messiah, future judge, moralist, miracle worker, John the Baptist, all of these reasons in order to designate the type. . . . It is regrettable that a Dostoevsky was not around at the time of this most interesting decadent, that is, someone who could have perceived the entrancing charm of such a confusion of the lofty, the sick, and the childlike. [24]

And later in a passage entitled "Jesus: Dostoevsky," Nietzsche wrote that Dostoevsky was the only one who "figured out Christ." According to Nietzsche, Dostoevsky instinctively avoided "portraying the character with the vulgarity of Renan. . . . In Paris they believe that Renan suffers from too much refinement! But is it possible to make a more serious blunder than to make a genius out of Christ, who was an idiot?"[25] And again: "Jesus is the opposite of genius: he is an idiot."[26] But in the final text of *The Antichrist* the word "idiot" was replaced by three dots: "And 'genius' is such a misunderstood word! All of our notions, our cultural notions of 'intelligence' mean nothing in the world of Jesus. Precise psychological terminology compels us to say that in this case another word would be more appropriate . . ."[27]

Nietzschean "revaluation of all values," "beyond good and evil," his radical nihilism and theomachy, even the idea of a "superman," can all be easily found in Dostoevsky's novels, although, of course, all of the opposite ideas are there as well. One can say that Dostoevsky struggled all his life against his "Nietzschean" ideas.

Shestov, Berdiaev, Frank, Lossky, Bulgakov, and Rozanov all read and reread Dostoevsky before anyone began to read Nietzsche in Russia. Almost all of them wrote a major work about Dostoevsky, and they were intimate with Dostoevsky's "Nietzschean" ideas well before they became acquainted with Nietzsche himself. So why was Nietzsche nevertheless received with such enthusiasm among these philosophers? Why did Shestov write two books about Nietzsche: *The Good in the Teaching of Count Tolstoy and Friedrich Nietzsche* (1900) and *Dostoevsky and Nietzsche— The Philosophy of Tragedy* (1903)? Why did Berdiaev, in an extremely

[24] *Antikhrist* (St. Petersburg, 1907), pp. 65–66. See also *Nietzsche: Werke: Kritische Gesamtausgabe*, vol. 8, pt. 2, pp. 406, 407, 417; pt. 3, p. 203.
[25] *Kritische Gesamtausgabe*, vol. 8, pt. 3, p. 203.
[26] Ibid.
[27] *Antikhrist*, p. 62.

important collection of articles, *Problems of Idealism* (1902), publish a long article about none other than Nietzsche—"The Problem of Ethics in the Light of Philosophical Idealism," and why did Frank produce a lengthy article—"Friedrich Nietzsche and the Ethics of Love of the Distant and Remote"? Why was Bulgakov likewise unable to avoid the topic of Nietzsche in his well-known collection, *From Marxism to Idealism* (1903), and why did he write about him in the article "Ivan Karamazov as a Philosophical Type"?

I believe that the most important reason for Nietzsche's enthusiastic reception among the philosophers of the Russian religious and philosophical renaissance was the fact that for the first time in history a celebrated Western European philosopher, a thinker who held sway over men's minds, echoed what Russian philosophy in the person of Dostoevsky had already grasped, and thereby seemed to confirm the correctness and significance of recently emerged original Russian thought. Furthermore, as fate would have it, Nietzsche became known in Russia at precisely the moment when the most talented Marxist philosophers began to abandon that theory in search of other, more profound ideas that would answer the needs of a reality becoming more and more complex. For those brought up in the Western European philosophical tradition and at the same time nurtured on the novels of Dostoevsky and Tolstoi, an authoritative, that is to say, non-Russian spokesman was needed to confirm that Russian philosophy was indeed a way out of the spiritual and philosophical dead end humanity had reached. For the Neo-Idealists, the author of *Thus Spoke Zarathustra* was this powerful, authoritative spokesman. They saw in Nietzsche a "kindred soul." Berdiaev even wrote in his book *The Meaning of Creativity* (1916) that there was "much that was Slavic" in Nietzsche.[28] Shestov compared Nietzsche to the hero of Dostoevsky's *Notes from the Underground*;[29] Bulgakov compared him to Ivan Karamazov and to the Grand Inquisitor from *The Brothers Karamazov*.

It is in this perception of Nietzsche as "kindred soul," a "Russian and a Slav" that we see the answer to the question of why, in spite of the fact that Nietzsche was warmly received, none of the philosophers in question ever became a Nietzschean. The only ones who did were the Marxist God-builders—Lunacharsky, Gorky, Bogdanov, Bazarov, writers who were hostile to the Neo-Idealists. Although enthusiastically receiving Nietzsche's affirmation that independent Russian philosophy was on the right path,

[28] N. Berdiaev, *Smysl tvorchestva: Opyt opravdaniia cheloveka* (Moscow, 1916), pp. 317–22.

[29] Shestov, *Dostoevsky i Nitshe*, pp. 149–50.

the Neo-Idealists by no means accepted Nietzsche's philosophy. They perceived in it merely one facet of Dostoevsky's versatile and many-sided thought. This resulted in the paradoxical and constant recurrence, in articles that otherwise praised Nietzsche, of the opinion that the German philosopher "does not understand," "that he is struggling not against God, but against a false notion of God," or that he is "blind." Were it not for the sincerity with which they praised Nietzsche, the Russian Neo-Idealists' articles and longer treatises could be seen to be decidedly critical. The Marxist God-builders, who rejected Dostoevsky and his art, and, even more, Vladimir Soloviev and Leontiev, actually interpreted Nietzsche on the basis of his manifested thought, and for this reason became genuine Nietzscheans.

In short, absolutely all of the ideas that are frequently attributed to Nietzsche's influence came to the Neo-Idealist philosophers via Dostoevsky, not Nietzsche. Nietzsche's own influence was indeed very important and perhaps, at that particular moment, decisive, but solely as a catalyst for the movement of Russian philosophy in a completely different direction. The concept of a "school of suffering" that man must undergo and the idea of a historical Christianity that upholds man's freedom; the "revaluation of all values," as Nietzsche put it, or the "rebirth of all convictions" in the words of Dostoevsky; the idea that "beauty will save the world"; Nietzsche's perception of "the infinitely stupid naiveté of scientists;"[30] Dostoevsky's "dammed Bernards" (from the name of the French scientist Claude Bernard); Nietzsche's "Dionysianism," Dostoevsky's "Karamazovism," and Raskolnikov's "beyond good and evil"—were all familiar to Russian philosophers long before Nietzsche from Dostoevsky's novels. Nietzsche told them nothing, absolutely nothing new. However, the power of Nietzsche's voice was decisive. In the words of Nietzsche: "the great men of our life's epoch emerge when we have the courage to call good what we once thought to be evil."[31] The philosophers of the Russian religious and philosophical renaissance carried out just this sort of epoch-making revaluation, thanks to the *moral* support of Nietzsche.

NEO-IDEALISM

Nietzsche opened the eyes of former Marxists to the reality of personal identity, "I," the soul, and the spiritual world—as opposed to the physical

---

[30] As quoted by Shestov, *Dobro,* p. 119.
[31] *Nietzsches Werke,* 7:100.

world, the objective world. Even the titles of the greatest works of the Russian philosophers bear witness to the fact that the realization of spiritual, nonphysical reality was a most significant event and the starting point for their thought: Berdiaev, *Solitude and Society*; (*Ia i mir ob'ektov*), Shestov, *In Job's Balances* (Biblical symbolism in the contrasting of the reality of Job's sufferings with the "objective" reality of sea sand); Frank, *The Soul of Man*; Lossky, *On the Freedom of the Will*. However, as I have already said, the supreme historical originality of Russian thought, which has yet to be realized, consists in the discovery of the *third ontological layer*—unobservable reality, in which both observable levels of existence, physical and spiritual reality, are united. Frank expressed it more lucidly than anyone:

> This . . . principle of the unknowable we try to follow in three levels of existence: 1) in the world surrounding us, or to speak in a broader sense—what stands before us as the objective existence [*predmetnoe bytie*] and which we must follow in its very roots and bases; 2) in our own being—as it, on the one hand, is revealed as the "internal life" of each of us, and as it, on the other hand, appears in relation to the internal life of other people and to the deeper "spiritual" basis of our spiritual life; and 3) in that layer of reality which as first basis and all-unity, somehow unites and grounds both of these different worlds.[32]

Berdiaev expresses this three-level structure of existence in the following formula: God, the world, and uncreated freedom. Lossky builds his logic and epistemology on the recognition of the third layer of existence that unites the spiritual and physical levels. The degree to which this approach is original can be shown by the example of quantum physics, which introduced "unobservable reality" as a carrier of the "wave function" into its set of theories. Viktor Trostnikov, the Moscow mathematician and philosopher, writes: "We will proceed from the fact that quantum theory proves and makes obvious the long-suspected notion in physics of unobservable givenness as the only true ontology, i.e., the essence which possesses independent, objective status. In this theory the state of the physical system is described by *wave function* which cannot be detected by sensory perception or recorded by instruments."[33] In his fasci-

---

[32] S. Frank, *Nepostizhimoe: Ontologicheskoe vvedenie v filosofiiu religii* (Paris, 1939), p. 18.

[33] V. Trostnikov, *Mysli pered rassvetom* (Paris, 1980), p. 151.

nating book, *Thoughts before Dawn* (*Mysli pered rassvetom*), published in 1980, Trostnikov, who is not at all acquainted with Russian Neo-Idealistic philosophy and only makes use of present-day scientific data, comes to the same anti-Newtonian, anti-empirical conclusions as the philosophers of the Russian religious and philosophical renaissance. It is paradoxical that these thinkers created the philosophical basis for the present-day sciences of physics and astronomy, by starting from the realization of the reality of man's "I." If one of the constant parameters of Russian philosophy was the idea of "all-unity," which is particularly strong in Soloviev and Dostoevsky, then, in our day, as Trostnikov indicates in his book, "it is the central guiding principle in microcosmic physics, which is practically indispensable in almost any type of calculation."[34]

Russian Neo-Idealist philosophy made its most important statements thirty to forty years after it became acquainted with Nietzsche. I think it unnecessary to prove how far its teaching was from that of the author of *Zarathustra*. At first, during the last twenty years of the nineteenth century and the first decade of the twentieth, Nietzsche was perceived mainly as a moralist. The moral aspect of his thought aroused the greatest interest. Ever since the first article about Nietzsche ever published in Russia, "Friedrich Nietzsche: A Critique of the Morality of Altruism," by Preobrazhensky, which came out in 1892 in the journal *Problems of Philosophy and Psychology*, as well as in Shestov's works, Bulgakov's collections, Berdiaev's and Frank's articles in *Problems of Idealism*, and later on in *Landmarks* (*Vekhi*), everyone who wrote about Nietzsche for the most part analyzed the ethical aspects of his thought. The main conclusion was essentially that man's "I" is the sole bearer of the moral principle. This was the German philosopher's chief service in the struggle against utilitarianism. Berdiaev even began to claim that "society is a part of the individual, not vice versa."

Despite his admiration for Nietzsche, however, in his most "Nietzschean" book, *The Meaning of Creativity: An Essay in the Justification of Man* (1916), Berdiaev set about correcting Nietzsche in the following manner:

He burned with a fiery creative craving. Religiously, he knew only the law and the redemption, in which there is no creative revelation of man. And he hated the law and redemption. He hated God because he was possessed by the unfortunate idea that man's creative-

---

[34] Ibid., p. 160.

ness is impossible if God exists. Nietzsche stands on the world threshold of an epoch of creativity but he is not able to recognize the indissoluble link between the religion of redemption and the religion of the law; he does not know that religion is a whole and that in man's creativeness the same God is revealed One and Triune, as in the law and the redemption.[35]

Nietzsche talks like a religious blindman, one without the gift of seeing the final mysteries. The religion of Christ is not what Nietzsche took it for. Christian morality is not slavishly plebeian but aristocratically noble, the morality of the sons of God, of their primogeniture, their elevated birth and their elevated destination, Christianity is the religion of the strong in spirit, and not of the weak. . . . The Christian ethic is an ethic of spiritual victory rather than defeat.[36]

In opposition to the Nietzschean "will to power," Berdiaev proposes the idea that "God has no power: He has less power than a policeman,"[37] and assumes as the basis of his philosophy the idea of freedom sanctified by religion—"It is not man but God who requires man to be free."[38] Frank and Shestov understood, corrected, and supplemented Nietzsche in exactly the same way. There is nothing odd in the fact that their philosophy later came to be completely opposed to the thought of Friedrich Nietzsche, especially as it is interpreted today, for example, in Martin Heidegger:

We can see Nietzsche's thoughts on imperfect nihilism more clearly and distinctly if we say: although imperfect nihilism replaces bygone values with others, it still supposes them to be in their old location, which in some way still maintains its power as the ideal form of that which is extrasensory. Perfect nihilism, on the other hand, must do away with even the very place of values, eliminate the extrasensory as a level, and in accordance with this, lay down and revalue its values in a different way.[39]

Must we again stress that Russian thought of the religious and philosophical renaissance is directly opposed to nihilism of any kind? Must we

[35] Berdiaev, *Smysl tvorchestva*, pp. 99–100.
[36] Ibid., pp. 250–53.
[37] N. Berdiaev, *Dream and Reality*, trans. K. Lampert (London, 1950), pp. 158, 179.
[38] Berdiaev, *Smysl tvorchestva*, p. 105.
[39] M. Heidegger, *Holzwege* (Frankfurt am Main, 1957), p. 208.

repeat that this is true, to a large extent, thanks to Nietzsche's paradoxical merits?

In 1886 Nietzsche described how his book *Dawn* came to be written:

In this book you see the underground man at work—how he burrows, digs, and undermines. You see, only if your eyes have become adjusted to the depth, how slowly, carefully, with molelike stubbornness he makes his way forward, not letting anybody know too much about how hard it is for him to be without light and air for so long; perhaps we can say that he is satisfied with his dark work. It even begins to seem that some sort of faith is leading him on, that he has his own consolation. Perhaps he needs his own long darkness, perhaps he needs his own incomprehensible, mysterious, and enigmatic [existence], for he knows that his own morning awaits him, his own salvation, his own dawn.[40]

All the Russian Neo-Idealist philosophers went the route of the man "from under the floorboards" or the underground man; however, *unlike Nietzsche*, they found "their own morning, their own salvation, their own dawn."[41]

[40] As quoted by Lev Shestov, *Dostoevsky i Nitshe*, p. 116.

[41] The literal translation of "iz podpolia" commonly rendered as "from the underground," is "from under the floor," or "floorboards," as it were [AG].

PART II

NIETZSCHE'S INFLUENCE ON RUSSIAN SYMBOLISTS AND THEIR CIRCLES

6.

Blok between Nietzsche and Soloviev

Evelyn Bristol

ALEXANDER BLOK'S *oeuvre* has until now been seen primarily in terms of his concern with a Neoplatonic doctrine, that of the Divine Wisdom, or Hagia Sophia. The doctrine of the Divine Sophia is a canonical element of the teaching of the Russian Orthodox Church, but it was popularized in the 1890s by the Russian philosopher Vladimir Soloviev. Because the Divine Sophia is pictured as a feminine figure, the concept resembles that of the "eternal feminine" of German Romantics and was in some historical periods confused with cults dedicated to the Virgin. Blok's early verse is the diary of a chivalric quest for communion with Sophia and his first book was called *Verses about the Beautiful Lady* (*Stikhi o prikrasnoi dame*, 1905). In 1910 Blok wrote in a letter to a fellow symbolist, "You know the whole history of my inner development was 'prophesied' in *Verses about the Beautiful Lady*."[1]

Blok was, however, an artist, and not a thinker, and his impulses were subject to contradictions. He was impressed with the ideas of Nietzsche, and these remarks, unlike those about Sophia, have been ignored. This is perhaps because Russian critics who were sympathetic to symbolism had a tendency to connect Neoplatonism with spirituality, while linking Nietzsche's ideas with amoralism and decadence, which they deplored. Nevertheless, Soloviev's Sophian philosophy had its strongest influence on Blok's early works, while the impact of Nietzsche's thought increased during his life and finally predominated at the end.

A high point of Blok's appreciation of Nietzsche came in December of

[1] *Sobranie sochinenii*, 8 vols. (Moscow, Leningrad, 1960–1963), 8:317. Henceforth cited as *SS*.

1906, when he wrote in his writer's diary about *The Birth of Tragedy from the Spirit of Music*, "What a revelation this book is." Blok was ever after to see Nietzsche primarily as the author of this one work, in which Dionysian rites are viewed as the origin of drama, and the Dionysian principle is seen as the foundation of all art. Later in the same December, when Blok was mulling over ideas for his cycle "The Snow Mask" ("Snezhnaia maska"), he wrote in his diary, "One doesn't call with impunity on Dionysus—in this lies the whole evocation of Bacchus. . . . but, perhaps this new, fresh cycle of mine will come soon. And Alexander Blok—come to Dionysus."[2] Blok was never attracted to Nietzsche's doctrines of a superman, or individualism, or the defiance of bourgeois morals; he was drawn to the Dionysian principle seen as an elemental, orgiastic, and communal force. In fact, the older Blok became, the more he sought links with the community, which he was to perceive as the entire Russian people, and to abandon his lonely quest for Hagia Sophia.

Several of the Russian symbolists vacillated between Neoplatonic and Christian concepts on the one hand, and Nietzschean views on the other. Blok was the youngest of the group and he was readily swayed by others. Two older symbolists who had experienced this conflict were Dmitri Merezhkovsky, a poet and author of historical and philosophical novels, and Viacheslav Ivanov, who was exclusively a poet.[3] Each was in turn the dominant figure among symbolists in St. Petersburg, where Blok lived. Nietzsche's individualism and estheticism had drawn Merezhkovsky away from positivism and the civil school of Russian poetry during the 1890s. In Greece he had been won over by the cult of beauty symbolized by Aphrodite. But, when Soloviev's ecumenical ideas gained currency, Merezhkovsky began to envision an Orthodoxy enriched and reanimated by pre-Christian vitality. His novel *The Gods Resurrected: Leonardo da Vinci* (*Voskresshie bogi: Leonardo da Vinchi*, 1899) reflects his aspirations for a religion of the flesh and the spirit combined. In 1901 he and his wife Zinaida Gippius founded the Religious-Philosophic Society to popularize their views. In 1902 Blok came under the influence of Merezhkovsky's eccentric, paganized variant of Neoplatonic Christianity.

Ivanov's preoccupation with Nietzsche focused immediately on the Dionysian cult. As a student of classical studies at the University of Heidelberg, Ivanov read, in 1890, *The Birth of Tragedy*; in 1892 he moved

[2] *Zapisnye knizhki*, 1901–1920 (Moscow, 1965), pp. 84–86.

[3] Bernice Glatzer Rosenthal, *D. S. Merezhkovsky and the Silver Age* (The Hague, 1975), *passim*; Olga Deschartes, "Vvedenie," in *Sobranie sochinenii* by Viacheslav Ivanov, 3 vols. (Brussels, 1971), 1:16–18.

to Rome and became convinced that a Dionysian principle governs life in general. For Ivanov, Nietzsche's interpretation of Dionysus offered a release from conventionality and the guarantee of a life of spiritual freedom. When Ivanov met Vladimir Soloviev, who exerted an influence in the direction of Christianity, Ivanov was to waver between Dionysus and Christ for several years. In his verse, however, the Christian and pagan entities seem to coexist and even to be identified with each other. Blok began to fall under the influence of Ivanov's paganism by 1904; then the Revolution of 1905 caused him to see popular movements in a Dionysian light. By 1906 Blok was writing his anti-Solovievan plays, *The Puppet Show* (*Balaganchik*, 1906) and *The Stranger* (*Neznakomka*, 1906), and at the end of his life he sought epiphanies in the October Revolution of 1917.

Blok was an enthusiastic, even a passionate, holder of philosophical concepts. But he did not always seek to resolve conflicting ideas. From his earliest verse, contradictions, indeed, gave his work a dramatic tension. The seeds of *all* his later themes can be found in his early period, not only his devotion to the Lady Beautiful. Thus later influences on Blok reinforced one or another of his tendencies, but did not determine them. The discovery of mysteries and mystical communion were the goals of the early verse, yet his spiritual doubts and failures are more prominent even then than his attainments. As early as 1901 he had concluded the poem "I have a presentiment of you . . . ," ("Predchuvstvuiu tebia . . . ;") with the warning words, "But I am afraid: You will change your visage." Malevolent doubles (sometimes harlequins) who debased the figure of Sophia, blasphemed, and destroyed all belief and hopes appeared in 1902. In the poem "The Double" ("Dvoinik") of 1903 Blok writes: "The old one—scoffs torpidly at you, / The young one—he is your tenderly devoted brother!" In time Blok would link this countertendency with the decadent literary movement; in an article of 1910, "On the Contemporary State of Russian Symbolism" ("O sovremennom sostoianii russkogo simvolizma"), Blok was to speak of the "thesis" and "antithesis" of Russian symbolism and of the hell entailed by the antithesis. These anti-Solovievan impulses were concomitant with, if not caused by, Nietzschean views. The theme of the war-torn country, as in "Hamayun, the prophetic bird" ("Gamaiun, ptitsa veshchaia," 1899) was to become significant in his verse by 1908; this national subject would be tied closely with Dionysian, or Nietzschean concepts.

Blok indulged more intensely than did the other symbolists their common tendency to confuse life and art. Thus he was bound to live out either Solovievan or Nietzschean convictions. In his early period he sought the informal tutelage of a relative of Vladimir Soloviev (the wife of his brother Michael), Olga Solovieva, who was also a confidante of Blok's mother. She was a jealous guardian of the purity of Soloviev's ideas, and regarded the early symbolists, and even Diaghilev's innovative art journal *The World of Art* (*Mir iskusstva*, 1898–1904), as contaminated by decadence. She also rejected Nietzsche.

In their youth Blok considered Andrei Bely (Boris Bugaev) a mystical brother because of their common adulation of Sophia. But Bely's horizons were wider; in his memoirs of this period he frequently mentions Nietzsche, along with Wagner and Ibsen, as one of the liberating forces of the day.[4] In 1903 Blok wrote Bely to protest that those interests which Bely had expressed in an article called "The Forms of Art" ("Formy iskusstva") were superficial. Blok complained, "You constantly have to refer to Plato, to Nietzsche, to Wagner, to . . . Verlaine. But the 'music of the spheres' is a *mythological* profundity."[5]

Blok's marriage to Liubov' Mendeleeva, the daughter of the chemist, was the most important event of his early biography. Poems written about her are often difficult to distinguish from those pertaining to the Beautiful Lady, and the discrimination has, in any case, little purpose. Shakespeare's Ophelia, a part which she once played, became a recurrent symbol in Blok's poetry. To her astonishment and chagrin, their marriage turned out to be Platonic.

Blok's turbulent second period began with an attraction to mystical anarchism, a doctrine derived from Nietzsche's interpretation of the Dionysian principle, which was vigorously supported by Viacheslav Ivanov. Mystical anarchism, originated by the minor poet George Chulkov, was a philosophical form of populism that was welcomed by some as a response to the 1905 Revolution. According to mystical anarchists, the poet is the spokesman of his people through a shared, unconscious will. Blok helped to publicize both the theory and Ivanov in an article of 1905 called "The Work of Viacheslav Ivanov" ("Tvorchestvo Viacheslava Ivanova"). Blok's essay opens with a legend that strikes at the heart of the matter in a Nietzschean sense. Socrates was executed, Blok relates, because he failed to listen to a "spirit of music." Nietzsche felt a deep and continuous antipathy toward Socrates, Plato, and Aristotle because he

[4] Andrei Bely, *Na rubezhe dvukh stoletii: Vospominaniia* (Moscow, Leningrad, 1930), *passim*; *Nachalo veka: Memuary* (Moscow, Leningrad, 1933), *passim*.
[5] SS, 8:53.

believed they disassociated Greek culture, and consequently the whole of
Western civilization, from its earthy, Dionysian wellsprings and turned it
in the direction of logic, mechanism, and superficiality.

The poetry of Blok's second period, which lasted into 1908, was dominated by the anti-Sophian figure of the Stranger, a temptress. In a cycle
called "Bubbles of the Earth" ("Puzyri zemli") the attention shifts down-
ward from the sky, the home of Sophia in both Soloviev's and Blok's
verse, to the earth. Blok discovered in animals and folkloristic creatures
native, as well as ancient, paganism. While not called into question, the
doctrine of Sophia is surrounded by eddies of contrary thought, as well
as by ominous doubles both of the poet and of the Lady. In 1906, a
narrative poem, "The Night Violet" ("Nochnaia fialka"), was the beginning of many suggestive appearances of careless sexual infidelities on the
part of the poet. A number of the lyrics of 1904 through 1908 were to be
grouped by Blok into a section of his collected works called "The City"
("Gorod"), which contains the key poem "The Stranger" ("Neznakomka"). The city is not a community, but the sinister setting of the poet's
lonely debauchery. The figure of the Stranger, in whom he still wishes
to see metaphysical mysteries, is a parallel to himself—an always solitary,
fallen woman. The poet is the alienated doubter of Sophia who believes
"in vino veritas." In 1907 a new cycle, the thirty-odd lyrics of "The Snow
Mask," record his infatuation with the actress Natalia Volokhova. She is
pictured as an intriguing woman whose blandishments are parodies of the
attributes of Sophia.

The lyric dramas of 1906, *The Puppet Show* and *The Stranger*, epitomized for Blok's contemporaries his wayward Solovievan tendency. The
puppet show image comes directly from a poem by Soloviev: ". . . The
living language of the gods, / The sanctity of Muses—by noisy puppet
show / He has replaced and hoodwinked fools."[6] The play is peopled by
the commedia dell'arte figures Pierrot, Columbine, and Harlequin, who
are transparent representatives of Blok, the Divine Sophia (or Mendeleeva), and Bely, as well as by other doubles such as the Bride, or Death.
In *The Stranger* the Sophian figure is literally a fallen star, whose name
is identical with that of the Virgin, while her devotees, the poet and the
astrologer, cannot find her.

A closer preoccupation with Nietzsche is shown by some lesser theatrical writings of 1906. In a sketch called "On Love, Poetry, and Govern-

[6]SS, 5:433.

ment Service" ("O liubvi, poezii i gosudarstvennoi sluzhbe") Blok satirizes literature that is subservient to the state. A clown demonstrates the compatibility of literary and government service through common sense, which he calls his "gay science," a reference to Nietzsche's work dedicated to the Provençal notion of the union of a singer, knight, and free spirit. Under 29 December 1906, Blok entered in his diary fragments of an ironic play called "The Hyperborean Dionysius," which depicts a rejection of the Nietzschean superman ("This play is the collapse of the hero," wrote Blok). In all, Blok's second period is characterized by a guilty falling away from Sophia, and the beginning of an indebtedness to Dionysian theories deriving from Nietzsche.

Blok began to consider it a great sin to fuse art and life, to live and write the same story, as he wrote in "On the Contemporary State of Russian Symbolism." He believed that he had destroyed the Solovievan vision in his art by allowing it to be contaminated by life. In his first period he had deemed it natural to write and live by the same principles; he married Liubov' Mendeleeva seeing in her a distant representative of St. Sophia. Later, Blok's betrayals of Mendeleeva in actual life led to advances by Bely, and the three of them entered into a passionate love triangle, a circumstance poignantly reflected in *The Puppet Show*. Bely exiled himself to Europe, Blok's wife departed to follow an acting career and was to return in 1908, pregnant by a man whom she called only "the page Dagobert." Life, indeed, blasted Blok's dream of a Neoplatonic, Solovievan ideal. The fusion of life and art brought his overt service to the Divine Sophia to a close and left open the way for the Dionysian tendency, which Blok connected with the revolutionary movement and the national community.

Blok vacillated from 1908 until his death in 1921 between an ambivalent nostalgia for Solovievan ideals and an incomplete acceptance of Nietzschean goals. His marriage was reestablished on a new, more human, footing, as was his friendship with Bely. The personal influence of Ivanov dwindled. Blok publicly renounced mystical anarchism, at the insistence of Bely, in a letter dated 26 August 1907 to the editors of *The Scales* (*Vesy*, 1904–1909), which was then the principal literary journal of the Russian symbolist movement.[7] Nevertheless, Dionysian goals replaced the Solovievan ideals in his art to the extent that the growing revolutionary current furthered his impulse to espouse service to the

[7] SS, 5:675–76.

community. The intensity of his feeling of love for country in the cycle "On Kulikovo Field" ("Na pole Kulikovom") which opens the new period in 1908, is astonishing. True, in this cycle, which evokes the medieval past, Russia is addressed as "wife," and the relationship between poet and country is portrayed as a personal one, but his assumption of communal bonds with the people, not a "wife," became more explicit with time.

Blok's creative works reflected to the end his inability to choose between Solovievan and Dionysian principles. The works of last period were devoted to a playing out of the Solovievan topics, and amount to a reevaluation of his first love, his initial dedication and inspiration. The cycle, "Italian Poems" ("Ital'ianskie stikhi"), written in 1909 during a trip to Italy, where he and his wife had gone to rejuvenate their marriage, belongs to this group. The guiding thread of these poems appears to be the philosophical anguish experienced by the Neoplatonist in all ages. The opening poem "Ravenna" evokes Dante and his *Vita nuova*. Throughout, Christian figures such as the Virgin and Christ appear against a geographical background whose religious history goes back to pre-Christian antiquity. Vitality and death, both physical and spiritual, are everywhere juxtaposed in a random disorder that suggests no resolution, no final victory on either side.

Blok's most ambitious play, *The Rose and the Cross* (*Roza i krest*, 1912) seems to vindicate its results. The title, with its iconographic associations, recalls the title of an appreciative article on Soloviev, "The Knight-Monk" ("Rytsar'-monakh"), which Blok had written in 1910. The drama interweaves Solovievan with Nietzschean symbols, and the plot is based on Blok's private life. The representative of otherworldly beauty appears at first to be a minstrel, whose song is adored by the foolish heroine. But the minstrel is too distant from life to participate in its activities. The genuine bearer of ideal love turns out to be the old Knight, who adores, aids, and protects the beautiful but unworthy heroine in all her enterprises.

Two years later, in 1914, Blok wrote a new cycle of lyrics, "Carmen," which comes close to being a genuine celebration of earthly love. Love is here associated with art, now viewed as amoral rather than Neoplatonic. The cycle is dedicated to the singer Liubov' Delmas, and is therefore a betrayal of Neoplatonic commitment in the same sense that "The Night Violet" and "The Snow Mask" had been. A difference from the earlier infidelities is that the figure of Carmen, doomed and beautiful, becomes a symbol not only of their love, but of Delmas as musician, of her lover as poet, and even of art itself. In a lyric of 1912, "To My Muse" ("K muze"), Blok had already portrayed artistic inspiration as irresistibly beguiling but morally ambiguous: "Whether evil or good—You are wholly—unearthly. / It is complex to talk about you: / For some you are Muse and a miracle. / For me you are misery and hell." The narrative poem, "The Nightingale Garden" ("Solov'inyi sad," 1915) is also devoted to love of beauty. The garden proves to be dangerous, for it distracts a laborer with its merely physical beauty, and also cheats him of the experience of life itself; on his return he finds that his house has fallen into ruin.

The articles of Blok's third period also show enthusiasm for Nietzschean views and reflections on his Solovievan interests. In 1908 he published two articles resting on a Nietzschean, specifically Dionysian, concept of the nature of a populace. His well-known article "The People and the Intelligentsia" ("Narod i intelligentsiia") was read, as a protest, at the Religious-Philosophic Society. In it he defended Gorky, precisely as the people's champion; he considered the awakening population as more vital than the weak intelligentsia it had begun to threaten. In "The Elements and Culture" ("Stikhiia i kul'tura") Blok described the somnambulant intelligentsia as immersed in an "Apollonian dream," a term that he took from *The Birth of Tragedy*, but which here indicates a lack of awareness, rather than a lack of creativity. The populace, Blok writes, will resort to unfettered violence—is possessed of a "bomb" that will be detonated.[8] He shows an implicit sympathy for this destructiveness.

Relinquishing his servitude to Solovievan ideals was painful for Blok. In the article "Irony" ("Ironiia") published in 1908, he described an illness that causes laughter on the occasion of the deepest pain and at the expense of the most precious values; he called in Heine's irony. His article was widely thought to express a general mood of disillusionment after the failed Revolution of 1905. Blok was now irritated by Merezhkovsky. According to Blok in an article written in 1909, Merezhkovsky was more attuned to the superficial accomplishments of civilization than to religious truth—as though he were a crusader who tarried in Rome and did not see Jerusalem. About Soloviev Blok was much more generous. In the memorial piece called "The Knight-Monk" he showed that while the thinker had done much for which to be forgiven, he had been a genuine fighter for Christ and was thus more praiseworthy than his

[8] SS, 5:350–59.

heirs. A most poignant expression of regret for Solovievan ideals appeared in Blok's article "On the Contemporary State of Russian Symbolism" (1910), where he described his own change from servitor to Hagia Sophia to the originator of her double—the lavender doll (The Stranger). He generalized this betrayal, calling it merely one symptom of a European malady called decadence. "In other words, I had already made my own life art (a tendency which passes very vividly through all of European decadence). Life became art, I pronounced an incantation, and before me finally arose that which I (personally) called "The Stranger": a doll-like beauty, a blue ghost, an earthly miracle."[9]

Blok's painful nostalgia for Solovievan ideals was never obliterated by Nietzschean convictions. He believed that Nietzsche suffered from moral ailments, like himself and like Bely, who was also disillusioned. In 1909 Bely published collections of lyrics called *Ashes* (*Pepel*) and *The Urn* (*Urna*), which record his own philosophical bankruptcy. On 22 October 1910 Blok wrote in a letter to Bely that he understood people "(You, Nietzsche)" who distance themselves from their "ashes," by placing them in an "urn," that is, by writing about them, but that he, Blok, remained in "the shade, the ashes, loving perdition."[10]

It may be that Blok did not feel a compunction to make an ideological choice between Solovievan ideal and Nietzschean views because he took from Nietzsche only the Dionysian potential and not the superman, the culture hero, or free spirit. He may have even wished to combine these separate theories, although he understood their basic incompatibility. Solovievan principles never ceased to attract him because they were linked not only with philosophy, but with his private life and love. Through his adherence to Nietzschean doctrines Blok attempted to replace this private attachment with a wholehearted dedication to the wider community. Russia in his works has been seen by critics as a new face of the Beautiful Lady. But this transferral was not ultimately convincing. His devotion to Russia can more persuasively be understood as a new fusion of life and art, this time on the basis of Dionysian theories. During most of this third period, from 1910 to 1921, Blok was working on an autobiographical narrative poem, "Retribution" ("Vozmezdie"). In it he wanted to show the wellsprings of the revolution in the people. He never completed the poem to his satisfaction. The subject is the history of three generations of a radical family, the last of which is mystically predestined to change his country's

[9] SS, 5:429–30.
[10] SS, 8:317.

course. He is not aware of his mission, but it awaits him at birth. The mystical connection between hero and nation can be called Dionysian in that he is a suffering martyr; he is not a superman, or a free spirit, as in *Thus Spoke Zarathustra*.

The narrative poem "The Twelve" ("Dvenadtsat"), depicting the Bolshevik Revolution, is novel for Blok only in its setting. Its central episode is the demise of an anti-Sophian heroine; at the end of the poem Christ Himself appears before the Red soldiers, as a symbol of Russia's innate Christianity. Yet the whole piece has an air of using the Christian symbols, the twelve sections of the poem, the twelve soldiers (apostles?), for the purpose of a new, popular mythmaking. The populace is the hero here, and the poem is, essentially, a small epic of the changed times.

The articles of 1918 to 1921 are thoroughly, even fiercely, Nietzschean, or Dionysian, with the exception of an anniversary tribute to Soloviev. In "The Intelligentsia and the Revolution" ("Intelligentsiia i revoliutsiia," 1918) Blok emphasizes his dependence on Nietzsche by his constant references to music as an elemental force that expresses the will of the community, its function in *The Birth of Tragedy from the Spirit of Music*. The music of the Revolution is said to have as its message "peace and the brotherhood of nations." The artist's duty is to listen to this real music, as Blok learned from Ivanov's mystical anarchism. Socrates, he repeats as ten years earlier, perished because he disobeyed a command to "listen to the spirit of music." In 1919 Blok's article "The Collapse of Humanism" ("Krushenie gumanizma") greeted the end of the individualistic tidal wave that had flattened European civilization from the fourteenth to the eighteenth century. Kant, he believed, began the new music (a wild howl to bourgeois ears), and it was taken up by Wagner. Blok predicted that the spirit of music would conquer this superficial civilization and that the humanist would be replaced by the artist. In "On the Calling of the Poet" ("O naznachenii poeta"), his Pushkin anniversary speech in 1921, Blok asserted that because the poet can hear the universal harmony that is true culture (as opposed to civilization), his people have a right to demand service from him. This, again, is a conclusion of mystical anarchism, from which Blok must not have strayed far since 1905.

If Blok never shared with Nietzsche the adulation of the superman, neither was the world justified for him as esthetic experience; the Dionysian goal was for Blok a religious one. The idea that the world could have no meaning or be ultimately incomprehensible was repugnant to him. Blok appears never to have accepted any person or any doctrine wholeheartedly; he had passionate enthusiasms, but they were always held in check by opposing passions. In "The Collapse of Humanism" (1919), almost his last article, Blok deplored the bourgeois tendency to compromise and reconciliation. For him the vital spirit, the artistic spirit, was one that could tolerate the contradictions which frightened the bourgeoisie. This, of course, was a Nietzschean position, because it recalls the spirit of "beyond good and evil," but it also goes far toward explaining Blok's own ability to defer any ultimate choice between the Solovievan and the Nietzschean ideals.

7.

Esthetic Theories from *The Birth of Tragedy* in Andrei Bely's Critical Articles, 1904–1908

Virginia Bennett

"HENCEFORTH POETRY AND PHILOSOPHY will be inseparable."[1] Andrei Bely's statement places him among those Russian symbolists who stressed the interrelations between art and philosophy. During his formative years, he avidly studied philosophy, and he continued throughout his career to refer to it in all aspects of his writing verse, prose, and theoretical essays. Bely analyzes poetry and the other arts in the light of the fundamental questions addressed by the different branches of philosophy, such as esthetics, metaphysics, epistemology, and teleology. This remark about Nietzsche could easily be applied to himself: "Nietzsche attempted to assimilate almost all the philosophical, esthetic, and artistic schools of our time."[2]

Bely was attracted to Nietzsche's views on the metaphysical and religious origins of the arts, on the esthetic and epistemological roles of the poet, and on the origins of myth and history. In his article, "Friedrich Nietzsche" ("Fridrikh Nitsshe," 1907), Bely declared that one of Nietzsche's major contributions was his exhortation to abandon the past and to concentrate upon the future. When Bely initially became acquainted with *The Birth of Tragedy from the Spirit of Music* in 1900, he immediately

---

[1] Andrei Bely, "The Apocalypse in Russian Poetry" ("Apokalipsis v russkoi poezii"), in *The Green Meadow (Lug zelennyi)* (New York, 1967), p. 239.

[2] Andrei Bely, "Friedrich Nietzsche" ("Fridrikh Nitsshe"), in *Arabesques (Arabeski)* (Moscow, 1911), p. 73.

recognized in Nietzsche an ideological ally, hailing him as the prophet of the dawning age. "He is a symbolist and the prophet of a new life, and not a scholar, nor a philosopher, nor a poet; even though all the qualities of a philosopher, a scholar, and a poet were in him."[3] Nietzsche's influence can be discerned not only in Bely's critical articles, but also in his fiction and poetry.

Much of Bely's regard for Nietzsche stems from his first reading of *The Birth of Tragedy*. This was a major event in Bely's intellectual development, and he returned to Nietzsche's work for inspiration many times. Although Bely makes mention in passing—mainly in the article "Friedrich Nietzsche"—of some of Nietzsche's other writings, they had little influence on his theoretical works. In contrast to a number of his contemporaries who were interested primarily in Nietzsche's ethics, Bely concentrated, for the most part, upon his esthetics. He was not caught up by ethics or politics until after the Revolution of 1905. Then, he made some attempts to integrate esthetics with politics, as can be seen in his post-1905 articles.

This chapter will show the influence of *The Birth of Tragedy* on Bely's esthetics as expressed in his articles from 1904 through 1908. This influence is extensive and permeates all of Bely's writings—both critical and artistic. However, limitation of space permits little more than singling out the ideas from Nietzsche's work that occur most frequently in Bely's critical essays. During these years, different concepts from *The Birth of Tragedy* retained their validity, were abandoned, or assumed new significance for Bely as his own esthetics evolved. While he immediately welcomed some Nietzschean theories and made them the cornerstones of his own philosophy, especially his esthetics, Bely's treatment of other themes diverged from Nietzsche. This can be explained by certain external influences on Bely: the Revolution of 1905, his studies of other philosophers, and his colleagues' reactions to Nietszche.

There are several reasons for limiting the discussion of Bely's critical articles to the years 1904–1908. Even though Bely mentioned Nietzsche in an article, 'Forms of Art" ("Formy iskusstva," 1902), which was mainly on Schopenhauer, it was not until 1904 that Bely turned his full attention to him. Before then he was primarily absorbed by his exploration of the philosophy of Vladimir Soloviev, Kant, Schopenhauer, and the neo-Kantians—Heinrich Rickert (1863–1936), Wilhelm Windelband (1848–

[3] Ibid., p. 76.

1915), Herman Cohen (1842–1918), and Wilhelm Wundt (1832–1920).[4] After 1908, Bely's views became increasingly colored by theosophy as he came under influence of Ellis (pseudonym for Lev Kobylinsky); Emile Medtner; Rudolf Steiner's disciple, Anna Rudolfovna Mintslova; and then of Steiner himself—founder of the occult doctrine of anthroposophy. Steiner's ideas held great sway over Bely. After he met Steiner, it became increasingly difficult to distinguish between Bely's own interpretations of Nietzsche and Steiner's.

The Birth of Tragedy is a poetic, metaphorical treatise on a number of problems in metaphysics, epistemology, and esthetics; Bely's critical articles focus upon the same problems and frequently use the same poetic devices and metaphors. Directly responding to the metaphysical problems of defining the principles of order and chaos in the world, and of establishing man's role in the cosmos, is Nietzsche's metaphor of the Dionysian and Apollonian elements. Bely developed Nietzsche's distinction between individual versus collective perceptions of empirical realities as one of the manifestations of this dichotomy and related it to the epistemological problem of determining how knowledge is conveyed and received. He thought that Russian symbolism provided one—indeed the most important—means of obtaining a knowledge of intangible realities, because it unified the perceptions received from both the Dionysian and the Apollonian elements.

In Bely's articles he frequently referred to Nietzsche's esthetic theories: his ideas about the nature and origins of the arts; the role of myths in art and society; and the meaning and interpretation of myths and symbols in art. Like many of the other Russian symbolists, Bely viewed art as theurgy, and he shared Nietzsche's concerns about tendentiousness in all forms of art and about the invasion of science and technology into the realm of the arts. Bely expressed views similar to Nietzsche's in *The Birth of Tragedy* (Sec. 18), that the more complex our world becomes with its proliferation of factual data, the more fragmented and beyond our grasp this data will become. He insisted upon the need for access to the universal principles known to us through our emotions.

Like a number of his contemporaries, Bely hailed Nietzsche's esthetics as a spur to raise the quality of fiction and poetry, which he felt had

[4]See references to these philosophers in Bely's articles: "On Scientific Dogmatism" ("O nauchnom dogmatizme"), in *Symbolism (Simvolizm)* (Moscow, 1910), pp. 11–19, and "On the Limitations of Psychology" ("O granitsakh psikhologii"), in *Symbolism*, pp. 31–48.

diminished during the late nineteenth century. He and other symbolists attributed this to the growing predominance of critical realism and moralizing literature; they found congenial Nietzsche's attack on the "adoration of the natural and the real" (*BT*, 58). Nietzsche's remark in *The Birth of Tragedy* about the growth of secularism and politics in the domain of the arts also struck responsive chords among the Russian symbolists.

> Anyone who still persists in talking only of those vicarious effects proceeding from extra-aesthetic spheres, and who does not feel that he is above the pathological moral process, should despair of his aesthetic nature. . . . Confronted by such a public, the nobler natures among the artists counted upon exciting their moral-religious emotions, and the appeal to the moral world order intervened vicariously where some powerful artistic magic ought to enrapture the genuine listener. Or some more imposing, or at all events exciting trend of the contemporary political and social world was so vividly presented by the dramatist that the listener could forget his critical exhaustion and abandon himself to emotions similar to those felt in patriotic or warlike moments, or before the tribune of parliament, or at the condemnation of crime and vice—an alienation from the true aims of art that sometimes had to result in an outright cult of tendentiousness. But what happened next is what always happens to artificial arts: a rapid degeneration of such tendentiousness. The attempt, for example, to use the theater as an institution for the moral education of the people, still taken seriously in Schiller's time, is already reckoned among the incredible antiques of a dated type of education. (*BT*, 133–34)

The realists and the Russian press in general criticized the symbolists, because their works lacked realistic or purposeful content. Therefore it was understandable that Bely and his fellow symbolists found corroboration in Nietzsche's criticism of governments and societies that manipulated the arts, especially drama, for their own pragmatic goals. As innovators, they heartily acclaimed Nietzsche's remarks about the dead civilization of nineteenth-century Europe. Bely, speaking for his *confrères*, said: "We are decadents, because we have separated ourselves from a dead civilization."[5]

Nietzsche's theories about the origins of tragedy corresponded to a

---

[5] Andrei Bely, "Criticism and Symbolism" ("Krititsizm i simvolizm"), in *Symbolism*, p. 30.

number of esthetic or poetic canons developed in European symbolism. These include the importance of myths and symbols in art, the use of synesthesia to enable the poet to express the inexpressible and the metaphysical, and the artistic and symbolic significance of masks. Throughout *The Birth of Tragedy*, Nietzsche alludes to the synesthetic qualities of drama, and, by extension, of music, poetry, dance, and the visual arts.

> In the Dionysian dithyramb, man is incited to the greatest exhaltation of his symbolic facilities. . . . The essence of nature is now to be expressed symbolically; we need a new world of symbols; and the entire symbolism of the body is called into play, not the mere symbolism of the lips, face, and speech, but the whole pantomime of dancing. . . . Then the other symbolic powers suddenly press forward, particularly those of music, in rhythmics, dynamics, and harmony. (*BT*, p. 40)

Three other Nietzschean themes of drama examined extensively by Bely in his articles are complex and multifaceted. The first is the use of theater and drama as a metaphor for the clash between dream and reality, form and chaos. The second is chorus as metaphor for the masses and as the antithesis of the actors, who stand for individuals. Finally, Nietzsche's highly original interpretation of masks is another manifestation of the warring elements of dream versus reality, order versus chaos. Bely was particularly taken with the theme of masks, and it provided fertile soil for his explorations of the metaphysical and epistemological world. Mask imagery can be found frequently in both his critical articles and his artistic works. There can be little doubt about the direct relationship between Nietzsche's and Bely's concepts of the metaphysical significance of masks in pre-Socratic drama. For Nietzsche, masks represented the illusions created by the dream world of Apollo to shield the spectators from the harshness of reality or from outbreaks of Dionysian chaos. He calls them "Apollonian appearances in which Dionysus objectifies himself" (*BT*, 66).

The pervasive use of mask symbolism (especially French) in *fin de siècle* European art and poetry was duly noted by the Russian symbolists. These artistic precursors colored Bely's understanding of Nietzsche's view of the function and significance of masked figures in ancient Greek tragedies.[6] The French symbolists revived masked figures from eighteenth-century drama and court life, especially from the commedia dell'arte, whose characters were represented in many art forms, and by revelers at

[6]These associations are clearly stated in "The Song of Life" ("Pesn' zhizni"), in *Arabesques*, p. 52.

the *bals masqués* and Mardi gras celebrations all over Europe. In French and Russian symbolist poetry, the masked figures from the commedia dell'arte signified the alter ego or the unconscious. Symbolist poets often made the character of Pierrot the mouthpiece for their own feelings and perceptions.[7] Pagliacci figures in their works are subtle symbols not only of duality and *crise d'identité* but also of the eroticism and licentiousness of the eighteenth-century aristocracy. Bely (and Alexander Blok) tended to link commedia dell'arte masks with Nietzsche's view that masks hid the chaos and Dionysian sensuality in man which could burst forth unexpectedly.

Bely's articles on Nietzsche fall into three distinct groups, which cluster together not only chronologically, but also according to their major themes. Thus, "The Mask" ("Maska"), "A Window to the Future" ("Okno v budushchee"), and "The Green Meadow" ("Lug zelennyi")—all from 1904–1905—are concerned with many of the same problems. During those years, Bely was trying to forge his own esthetic principles and provide a philosophical basis for symbolism. The evolution of his thinking was reflected in the way in which, at this first stage, he related problems of literature and art to problems of metaphysics and epistemology. The Nietzschean themes that had the most significance for him at that time were the dichotomy between the Apollonian and Dionysian elements, as apparent in the material and spiritual-psychic worlds (for he was interested in the occult); Nietzsche's attacks upon tendentiousness and pragmatism; and his prophesies of the dawning of a new age.

The primary focus of these early essays was on symbolism as an answer to many of the problems resulting from the increasing complexity of the world, by the rapid development of the sciences and technology, and by the perceptible disintegration of outdated sociopolitical structures. The clash between reason and will struck many nineteenth-century philosophers as the most acute of these problems; they tended to argue that either reason or will must predominate. Vladimir Soloviev and Feodor Dostoevsky, however, stressed the need for balance between the two sides of human nature. Nietzsche seemed to draw the same conclusions in *The Birth of Tragedy*, but his interest lay in the manifestation of the antithetical elements (symbolized by Apollo and Dionysus) in our creative activities as well as in our psyche and mores. It is understandable,

---

[7] Robert Storey, *Pierrot: A History of the Mask* (Princeton, 1978), pp. 122–55.

therefore, that Bely readily accepted Nietzsche's approach and terminology. As one of the chief theoreticians of Russian symbolism, Bely valued most highly Nietzsche's poetic and esthetic analysis of metaphysical and epistemological problems and his emphasis on the importance of symbolism in art.

Nietzsche's metaphoric distinctions between the opposing forces in both the empirical and transcendental worlds seemed eminently suitable for expressing the symbolist esthetics that Bely espoused. Indeed, these concepts of the Apollonian and Dionysian served as symbols themselves, for they contained a number of associative meanings that coalesced with Bely's own theories. Among the principle connotations they held for Bely were: the interplay between reason and the will, intellect and feeling, logic and intuition during the process of knowing; the individual's awareness of empirical and transcendental values as opposed to that of the collective's; contemplation versus action; the expressions of human creativity in music, poetry, and drama, which at times conflict and at others merge; the divine origins and mystical functions of these opposing forces.

Particularly noticeable in the 1904–1905 articles were Bely's attempts to integrate Nietzsche's theories with those of Vladimir Soloviev. He began in "A Window to the Future" by reformulating Kantian terms of epistemology and concentrating upon our capacities for receiving knowledge. The Nietzschean terms—Apollonian for the rational and cognitive and Dionysian for our irrational and instinctual natures—were introduced there as the two channels through which we learn. Bely found them useful to convey basic functions of symbolism, where the symbol is a means of uniting the two aspects of the cognitive process. "If cognition can be raised to an idea and an image to a symbol, if a symbol is always the exterior covering of an idea, then in symbolism the link between the vertices of knowledge and intuition is established."[8]

In the same article, Bely discussed the function of a symbol, and he employed other metaphors from *The Birth of Tragedy* when he wrote of the Apollonian mask being torn off in the course of tragedies to reveal Dionysian reality.

"We looked at the drama and penetrated with a perceptive gaze," says Nietzsche, "into the inner world, agitated by its [drama's] motives, and yet it seemed to us that before us there was unfolding

[8] Bely, "A Window to the Future," in *Arabesques*, p. 140.

nothing less than a symbolic picture. The absolute clarity of the picture was not satisfying to us, for it seemed as though it was simultaneously concealing and revealing. . . ."[9] The tragic mask gazing at us with Medusa's smile causes bewilderment. What gazes at us from behind it? Is it not emptiness staring at us? What would we do if we were to snatch off the mask and discover that no one could conceal themselves there? What strength is contained in that fateful smile of Medusa the Gorgon, which is forged to the shield of Perseus who is unknown to us, if that mask is capable sometimes of turning us into horrified stone statues? At the same time, however, that horror is transparent. Is not the radiance suddenly flashing out from under the misty wraps of life capable of blinding us? Perhaps in the next moment its rays will shatter the huge black spot transparently appearing between us and the light. The white visage stares at us, the lightening success of Perseus—the new Apollo revealed to us—blazes at us. "Everywhere, where the waves stormily foam," says Nietzsche, "Apollo, hidden by a cloud, must also descend."[10]

Bely agreed with Nietzsche's opinion that the Apollonian elements in us are inherent in our imaginative, speculative, and verbal expressions, whereas the Dionysian are rooted in our passions and emotions and manifest themselves in ritual and music.

That which is inexpressible through words can be conveyed through actions. The tragic mask appearing among us summons us, the cognizant, to commonly shared action. The equally shared intoxication, which establishes a circle of psychic sparks—here is the origin of action. The whirlwind circle of separate emotions interpenetrating one another and blended together through music into the crimson Dionysian flame which carries off the inflamed into the sapphire vault of the skies—must not such a circle also create rituals having circular movements: choral and folk dances, and songs?[11]

New concerns emerged during the process of Bely's artistic and theoretical evolution, and these are reflected in the second group of articles,

[9]Compare Kaufmann's translation of this same passage: "We looked at the drama and with a penetrating eye reached its inner world of motives—and yet we felt as if only a parable passed us by, whose profound meaning we almost thought we could guess" (*BT*, 139).

[10]Bely, "A Window to the Future," p. 140.

[11]Bely, "The Mask," in *Arabesques*, pp. 132–33.

which are all dated 1907. At this time he was becoming more involved in discussions of sociopolitical problems. These articles include: "The Meaning of Art" ("Smysl iskusstva"), "The Theater and Contemporary Drama" ("Teatr i sovremennaia drama"), "Symbolic Theater" ("Simvolicheskii teatr"), "The Present and Future of Russian Literature" ("Nastoiashchee i budushchee russkoi literatury"), "On the Results of the Development of New Russian Art" ("Ob itogakh razvitiia novogo russkogo iskusstva"), "Future Art" ("Budushchee iskusstvo"), and "Friedrich Nietzsche" ("Fridrikh Nittsshe"). References to epistemological and metaphysical problems occur less frequently, though they reappear in some of the discussions pertaining to the problem of idea versus form in the arts, particularly in "The Meaning of Art." The Solovievian emphasis on the importance of religion in the arts and in the formation of a new society is intertwined with Nietzschean theories, as it had been in the earlier selections.

In 1907, a number of themes and metaphors from *The Birth of Tragedy* still had validity for Bely. In some instances, he pursued certain trains of thought introduced in earlier essays; in others, he deviated somewhat from Nietzsche's original ideas but retained their essence. He kept such concepts as the Apollonian/Dionysian polarity and the ancient mysteries, rituals, and tragedies as the origin of the arts. Bely incorporated several interconnected themes from later sections of *The Birth of Tragedy*, man's struggle against fate (Bely missed Nietzsche's ironic treatment of this theme in *The Birth of Tragedy*, perhaps because he superimposed upon it the concept of *amor fati*, which Nietzsche developed later on) and the echo in modern times of Socratic thought, which Nietzsche described as "the dialectical desire for knowledge and the optimism of science" (*BT*, 106). Bely linked the latter theme to the problem of formalism and didacticism in literature.

Art becomes inspired there, *where the summons to creation exists alongside a summons to the creation of life.*

By this life, one should understand not only its exterior, crystallized in solid forms of social, scientific, and philosophical connections, but also the source of these forms—creation. Life is creation. Moreover, life is one of the categories of creation. Life must be subordinate to creation and must be creatively reformed in those areas where it intrudes with sharp angles into our freedom. *Art is the beginning of the melting of life.* It melts the ice of life into the water of life. An artist is an artist only by virtue of the fact that as he penetrates life to the alpha and omega of life—creation, he is not subjugated by its appearance. As he creates idols (forms), he shields himself and us by these visible idols from the invisible idol—fate, which fetters our lives with what seem to be iron laws, but which in their essence are transparent. He sets up an opposition between worship of the invisible phantom and the visible forms, which he himself has created. In every art, the idol (form) is a means to an end. In every submission to the invisible idol (fate), which accepts the bloody sacrifices of the hecatomb, there is worship of the idol as end in itself.[12]

This quote from "The Theater and Contemporary Drama" seems to amalgamate a number of the abovementioned concepts into one metaphorical passage. Bely argues that great art does not focus uniquely upon conveying knowledge through empirical means, but also upon creating life. He then states that life/creation is not limited by its forms. Finally, he establishes a relationship between fate and form and art that worships form—formalist art. One more example of Bely's treatment of the problem of tendentiousness is found in his article, "The Meaning of Art."

Art speaks to us through all the indivisible wholeness of the psychic processes in which we reveal both thoughts, and emotions, and the urge to action; hence it is correctly inferred that the images of art express, incidentally, the ideas of practical reason; and further (already completely incorrectly), the meaning of art lies in the expression of ideas and tendencies. . . .

It is exactly in this way that some deduce morality from art; they are influenced by the idea that artistic images awaken will, which calls us to great deeds. But when they conclude that the mountain heights of duty and the mountain heights of creation are identical in form, then they succumb to an optical illusion, which brings those heights too close to our vision.

The haze which girdles the height of creation and seduces us disappears: in it is all the charm, all the fascination of art. Without it—art becomes too accessible; for what reason, then, does it exist, instead of a code of moral instructions?[13]

---

[12] Bely, "The Theater and Contemporary Drama," in *Arabesques*, p. 20.
[13] Bely, "The Meaning of Art," in *Symbolism*, p. 206.

There are instances too numerous to cite of passages similar to these in Bely's articles from this period.

Bely's earlier articles derive more inspiration from the first ten sections of Nietzsche's *The Birth of Tragedy*, while those of 1907 refer more often to points made in the last fifteen sections. This is related to Bely's awakening interest in history and politics. The earlier parts of *The Birth of Tragedy* were devoted to metaphysical and epistemological justifications for the existence of the Apollonian and Dionysian elements and to the importance of symbols. Nietzsche changed the focus of his later chapters to the history of philosophy, of poetics, and of drama. There he even touched upon some questions in the realm of politics and sociology. It is in the second half of the book that he raised the issues of "the theoretic versus the tragic world view" (*BT*, 106), the origins of realism in literature, and the political use of art as propaganda.

Bely's 1907 articles also treat the history of European and Russian symbolism and symbolism in nineteenth-century Russian literature. In "The Present and Future of Russian Literature," Bely attacked formalism as a barren offshoot of the Apollonian, and tendentiousness as a corruption of the Dionysian in European literature. "If literature is the weapon of the individualist, he transforms literature into elegant stylistics. When it becomes the weapon of the universalist, literature is the propagation of ideas."[14] (Here, of course, the individualist is the Apollonian and the universalist is the Dionysian.) In the same article Bely equated European symbolism with what he called "individualistic" symbolism and Russian symbolism with the irrational roots of popular creativity. "When the individualistic symbolism of the West penetrated into Russia, it came in contact with religious symbolics: the democratic tendencies of the West individually were refracted in the mass of our intelligentsia."[15] Further on, Bely says:

> It has now become clear to us that any tendency of Russian literature has sprung forth from the deeply irrational roots of popular [*narodnoe*] creation. . . . Russian literature saw the distant in what was close; in the suffering of the people, by some kind of second sight, it saw the suffering of the Diety; in the struggle with the forces of darkness, it recognized the apocalyptic struggle with the dragon of time.[16]

[14] Bely, "The Present and Future of Russian Literature," in *The Green Meadow*, p. 54.
[15] Ibid., p. 60.
[16] Ibid., p. 61.

During 1907 Bely introduced and emphasized the role of religion in the creative process (Bely's modifications of Nietzsche's remarks on the religious origins of tragedy will be discussed below); the adaptation of symbolism as a way of life to reconcile the Apollonian and Dionysian elements; symbolism as a stimulus for the creation of new art forms; and the challenge to create life through art. The latter theme may have been partially inspired by Nietzsche's comment in his later introduction to *The Birth of Tragedy*, "An Attempt at Self-Criticism," when he speaks of ". . . the task which this audacious book dared to tackle for the first time: *to look at science in the perspective of the artist, but at art in that of life*" (*BT*, 19; Nietzsche's italics). In his introductory paragraphs to "The Present and Future of Russian Literature," Bely proposes a variation of that statement. "The final goals of cognition are not rooted in cognition itself; they are rooted in action; the final goals of creation are not rooted in the creative forms of art; they are rooted in life."[17]

As he was writing these articles, Bely was struggling to create his own esthetic system, which was never to become clearly defined. Bely envisioned the development of new art forms under the aegis of Russian symbolism, because he felt it combined the Apollonian and Dionysian forces in greater equilibrium than did individualistic (European) symbolism. Collective (Russian) symbolism would be able to infuse life into what he considered to be moribund forms of art. The type of symbolism that Bely began advocating at this time could provide a solution to the political and social problems deeply troubling Bely and his fellow symbolists after 1906. It would be the instrument for uniting the individual with the masses.

The last three articles selected for discussion, "Symbolism" ("Simvolizm"), "Symbolism and Contemporary Russian Art" ("Simvolizm i sovremennoe russkoe iskusstvo"), and "The Song of Life" ("Pesn' zhizni")—all written in 1908—focus even more strongly on Bely's campaign to make symbolism a way of life, not only for the creative few, but for everyone. Having already integrated Nietzschean esthetics into his own views on literature and the arts, Bely at this point made a final attempt to hammer out a philosophy of symbolism. Thus the 1908 articles contain more elaborations on the theme of art and life—making one's own life a work of art.

Variations of characteristic Nietzschean themes pervaded this last group

[17] Ibid., p. 51.

of articles. The Apollonian/Dionysian "symbols," as Bely calls them, can be found in every selection under the appositions of contemplation versus creativity, dream versus reality, and the classical versus the romantic in literature. Bely turns to the question of the individual's (especially the poet's) "I" in relation to the people. Music as the wellspring of all creative activity and of man's struggle against fate are the central themes of "The Song of Life." (It should be mentioned here that Bely overlooked Nietzsche's criticism of the way estheticians simplified the source for the plots of ancient tragedies, i.e., man's battle with fate.)

> Of course, our aestheticians have nothing to say about this return to the primordial home, or the fraternal union of the two art deities, nor of the excitement of the hearer which is Apollonian as well as Dionysian; but they never tire of characterizing the struggle of the hero with fate, the triumph of the moral world order, or the purgation of the emotions through tragedy, as the essence of the tragic.   (*BT*, 132)

These articles contain, to a higher degree than the earlier ones, a number of metaphors and parallels from classical literature and German folklore, especially the Germanic myths used by Wagner. Bely successfully integrates them so that they do not distort Nietzsche's ideas to any degree. However, another category of borrowings would seem to be the antithesis of Nietzsche's views on religion and its role in culture, yet Bely applies them logically and convincingly. This is Bely's penchant for biblical and Apocalyptic imagery. For example, his contrapositions of consciousness versus creativity and of the individual "I" versus the masses are couched in biblical terms.

> The word of consciousness must have flesh. Flesh must have the gift of speech. The word must become flesh. The word having become flesh is both the *symbol* [Bely's italics] of creativity and the genuine nature of things. . . . the artist must become his own form: his innate "I" must merge with creative activity; his life must become artistic. He himself is the "Word having become flesh."[18]

In another passage from "The Song of Life," Bely combines biblical, folkloric, and Nietzschean terms with remarkable success.

[18] Bely, "Symbolism," in *The Green Meadow*, p. 28.

The primordial crudeness and beauty of heroism is wafted to us from "The Ring of the Niebelungen"; therein is the song of our future, when once again Siegfried will do battle with Wotan (the bear), and Wotan will rampage on earth in the guise of the Wanderer; once again heaven will unite with earth, but the gods and people will wander freely—the former on earth and the latter in heaven.

History has transformed the tree of life into the tree of knowledge of good and evil: and the hero has degenerated into the contemplator and the doer; the doer produces commodities, and the contemplator slides over him in a cloud of thoughts. . . .

The cloud of thoughts is good; the commodities of life are evil. Morality pronounced a turning away from the world. And in so doing, made man a victim of things. *"Your evil is dead and so is your good,"* exclaimed Nietzsche: and he calls us to Dionysus, i.e., to the tree of life: it is not for nothing that Betticher attributed to Dionysus the image of the spirit of the woods: Dionysus Dendrite; in the Judaic symbol (the tree of life) is resurrected the Dionysian symbol.[19]

As already indicated, Bely considered Nietzsche a poet and a symbolist as well as a philosopher. The Russian poet derived inspiration not only from the German philosopher's theories, but also from his poetic style. Although a number of articles included in this study are written in either an expository or quasi-scientific or polemical style, four of them are highly poetic, and the majority of the articles include devices normally reserved for poetry. The four articles most characterized by their poetics are "The Mask," "A Window to the Future," "The Green Meadow," and "The Song of Life." Limitation of space prevents lengthy discussion of all of the poetic images of these articles. Instead, some of the most salient of motifs and images used first by Nietzsche and then by Bely to illustrate their ideas will be noted.

The theme of masks predominates in two of the early articles, "The Mask' and "A Window to the Future." In them, Bely attributes the same significance to masks as does Nietzsche. To a lesser degree, mask symbolism can also be found in "Friedrich Nietzsche," "The Green Meadow," "The Song of Life," and "The Present and Future of Russian Literature." Another image predominating in "The Mask" and "A Window to the

---

[19] Bely, "The Song of Life," in *Arabesques*, p. 54.

Future" is that of the circle: either the term "ever-widening circle," or the circle whose periphery is intersected. Bely also favors Nietzsche's version of night as a metaphor for chaos and the unknown.

Bely seems particularly enchanted with Nietzsche's fauna, for several of his articles contain references to garlanded youths dressed in tiger, panther, or leopard skins, in connection with Nietzsche's idealization of the Dionysian. "A time will come, and again upon the flowering spring meadows admidst the violets and lilies-of-the-valley, to the accompaniment of the ecstatic groans of the wailing long trumpets, to the accompaniment of the jubilant bells, whirl naked youths in tiger skins."[20] This quote is from "The Mask," but very similar passages can be found in "The Green Meadow," and a variation of it in "The Song of Life."

Other images from the early sections of *The Birth of Tragedy* are the orgiastic flutes and trumpets of the Dionysian votaries to be found in "The Mask" (see above), and dithyrambs in "The Green Meadow." The term "abyss" as related to Nietzsche's "Dionysian abysses" (*BT*, 89) recurs in a number of articles: "The Future of Art," "The Mask," "A Window to the Future," and "Symbolism." Much of "A Window" is a study of the metaphysical question of appearances versus reality, and Bely introduces Nietzsche's contrast of "dark-colored spots" with "luminous spots to cure eyes damaged by gruesome night" (*BT*, 67). There are many more examples, but the last one offered here is Nietzsche's metaphor for logic, which "coils up . . . and finally bites its own tail" (*BT*, 98). In "The Song of Life," Bely also writes of logic "which teaches us mental somersaults; soon . . . having completed a full circle of development, like a snake will bite its own tail."[21]

An understanding of Bely's differences with Nietzsche is necessary in order to see the limits of the latter's influence and the way in which his thought was integrated into Bely's own esthetics. Bely's criticism of and departure from Nietzsche on religion is fundamental. A major theme in many of Bely's critical articles of 1904–1908 is that religion is the origin of all artistic activity. Bely first expressed this idea in "A Window to the Future," where he contended that Nietzsche introduced religion into *The Birth of Tragedy* when he linked the origins of Greek drama to the Eleusinian mystery cults. Then Nietzsche avoided the religious implications

[20] Bely, "The Mask," p. 133.
[21] Bely, "The Song of Life," p. 51.

inherent in his theories on tragedy, and failed to pursue the question of religion's place in esthetics.

> That which at the moment of the tragedy's ascendancy forced us to fix our gaze, as it were, beyond the myth in order to grasp its sacred prototypical meaning is none other than the good news about that new time, when the tragic mask will fly off the long-awaited deity who is drawing nigh to the world. Nietzsche, who invariably stresses the results which will ensue from his ideas, here is silent as the grave. All too well did he understand the danger of calling the final outcome of our culture a mystery. Such a conclusion would have placed him in the position of having to speak of religion—moreover from a completely new aspect, one which could perhaps be devastating for him. That is why he hastened in the name of Wagner to close the gap between music and poetry, omitting the fact that Wagner was only one of the pioneers heralding the confluence of music and poetry—inevitably leading to mystery.[22]

He expanded these criticisms in "Friedrich Nietzsche": "when Nietzsche restored the individual to his musical roots, he overturned the elements of religion, philosophy, and morality."[23] Bely believed that these elements are intimately related.

> Image absorbing rhythm into itself begins to be nourished by rhythm and propagates itself; the history of the development of images is the history of the development of religious cults; the laws of this development are the laws of the development of religion; the norms of development in turn generate religious dogmas; when these dogmas are adapted to cognition, they become ideas. When the idea then becomes the center of social crystalization, it becomes transformed into an idea of morals.[24]

Bely even went so far as to attribute Nietzsche's madness to his failure to resolve his religious dilemma. This occurs after a lengthy passage in which Bely compares Nietzsche's doctrines to Christ's.

> "You will be like gods," tempted the Serpent. "It is unclear what we will be," sighs John the Evangelist in sacred horror, "we know that

[22] Bely, "A Window to the Future," pp. 141–42.
[23] Bely, "Friedrich Nietzsche," p. 86.
[24] Ibid., p. 86.

we shall be like unto Him." "You are gods," Nietzsche explains to
us and goes out of his mind. "I am a god," exclaims Dostoevsky's
Kirillov and shoots himself.[25]

Another serious criticism of Nietzsche, found in Bely's discussions of
drama, deals primarily with Nietzsche's departure from the ideas of *The
Birth of Tragedy* in his later essay on Richard Wagner, "The Case of
Wagner." According to Bely, Nietzsche was led astray by his temporary
admiration for Wagner. Under the influence of the composer, Nietzsche
departed from his original analysis of the nature of ancient drama as
ritual. There Nietzsche said that the chorus of satyrs calls the initiates to
participate in real life (at least this is Bely's interpretation in "The Theater
and Contemporary Drama"). Bely wrote that Nietzsche did not understand contemporary drama.

> In the musical drama of Wagner, Nietzsche perceived a genuine
> struggle to free humankind. However, Nietzsche could not distin-
> guish the fateful contradiction of contemporary drama. He sensed in
> it a summons to life, without distinguishing that summons from the
> form in which the summons is issued. . . . worshipping the sum-
> mons to life in drama, Nietzsche also canonized the form of this
> summons—what takes place on the stage. An aberration resulted:
> the summons to life from the stage was transformed to a summons
> to life on the stage. The brilliant work of Wagner is that very un-
> natural summons. Nietzsche worshipped drama as form in the ini-
> tial period of his enthusiasm for Wagner.[26]

In other words, Bely thought that Nietzsche's comments were erroneously interpreted as a call for realistic, lifelike acting on the stage rather
than as a summons to go out and embrace life, as he seems to imply in
The Birth of Tragedy.

Criticisms related to Nietzsche's "worship of form" can be found in
"The Present and the Future of Russian Literature." There, Bely discusses how Nietzsche's focus led to the misinterpretation of the role of
music in Western symbolism.

> Rescuing emotions from empty words, literature in the West subor-
> dinated the word to melody; the individualist extended his hand to

---

[25] Ibid., p. 72.
[26] Bely, "The Theater and Contemporary Drama," p. 23.

the stylist-academician. Technique from the outside and music from the inside undermined literary prophecy in the West. Music was transformed into technique by Nietzsche, and technique was transformed into music by Stefan George.[27]

Several pages later, he continues this train of thought. "Nietzsche visualized a new heaven and earth, but threw himself into the abyss. The music of his Zarathustra passes into a tremulous prayerful scream interrupted by blasphemies."[28] In these passages Bely seems to blame Nietzsche for the development of what he termed "individualistic symbolism."

In "The Theater and Contemporary Drama," Bely turns his attention to other distortions of Nietzsche's view of drama as part of the Eleusinian mysteries. The dramatic theories of the mystical anarchists were inspired by these and by medieval mysteries.[29] Bely argued that there can be no "mystery" without religion and that attempts to resuscitate the religion of ancient Greece on the modern stage would be ludicrous.

> Whether or not they are inviting us to return to those primitive religious forms out of which drama developed, all this remains covered by the obscurity of uncertainty.
>
> If yes, then hand over to us a goat for the slaughter! But what are we to do with a goat after Shakespeare? If it is implied here that there is some kind of new religious rite, then tell us the name of the new god! Where is he, who is he![30]

A less serious criticism of Nietzsche is made in the article, "The Meaning of Art," which addresses his poetics. Bely posits a triad underlying a symbol which is made up of: 1) image (the flesh), 2) idea (the word), and 3) the living association of "word made flesh." He says that Nietzsche's symbolism is hypertrophic, because it uses only the second member of the triad (he includes the poet Valery Briusov with Nietzsche). On the other hand, Bely considers Alexander Blok an example of a poet who incorporates all three elements in his poetry.[31]

---

[27] Bely, "The Present and Future of Russian Literature," p. 57.

[28] Ibid., p. 63.

[29] For more on the mystical anarchists, see the articles of Bernice Glatzer Rosenthal, "The Transmutation of Russian Symbolism: Mystical Anarchism and the Revolution of 1905," *Slavic Review* 36 (December 1977), pp. 608–27, "Theater as Church: The Vision of the Mystical Anarchists," *Russian History* 4, 2 (1977), pp. 122–41.

[30] Bely, "The Theater and Contemporary Drama," p. 26.

[31] Bely, "The Meaning of Art," p. 226.

It can be seen from the above survey of selected articles from Bely's critical essays of 1904–1908 that *The Birth of Tragedy* made a great impact upon Bely's esthetic theories. In the early years (1904–1905), when he was presenting the symbolist point of view to the rationalist intellectuals of his time, he tended to stress the epistemological problems engaged by Nietzsche, and he saw in Nietzsche's comments an affirmation of Russian symbolism. In the middle and later period (1907–1908), Bely's articles show his awakened interest in the political and social problems brought to the forefront by the Revolution of 1905. They also express his growing interest in folklore, gnosticism, the occult, and anthroposophy. His treatment of Nietzschean themes also reflects these developments. In these years Bely's assessments of *The Birth of Tragedy* become more even-handed and even critical, for Bely was able to see how his contemporaries were misinterpreting Nietzsche's works, and the weaker points of Nietzsche's thought became clear to him. It is also understandable that Bely would find Nietzsche's antireligious stance unacceptable, for he never abandoned his religious, Solovievian approach to the role of the poet in society. He continued to believe in the prophetic, redemptive activity of the poet. Bely criticized Nietzsche's later stress on the importance of form, because he thought that preoccupation with form led to individualistic symbolism, which was divorced from the people.

In conclusion, after examining this selection of articles, one can see the consistency with which Bely either directly or indirectly referred to the themes set forth in *The Birth of Tragedy*. Of all the major philosophers of the last three centuries, Nietzsche's esthetics supported and confirmed most of Bely's own views about the role of symbolism, especially Russian symbolism, in formulating the esthetics of the future. One is struck by the creative way in which Bely integrated Nietzschean philosophy and poetry into his critical articles and how he strove to compensate for the lack of religious foundations in *The Birth of Tragedy* by stressing the links between religion, myth, and symbolism.

8.

Echoes of Nietzsche in Sologub's Writings

George Kalbouss

IN THE VARIOUS STUDIES of Russian symbolism, Friedrich Nietzsche has rarely been linked to the prose and poetic works of Fedor Sologub (1863–1927). Sologub's contemporaries shied away from making such a connection; in his wife's (Anastasia Chebotarevskaia's) collection of articles on Sologub (1911), only a few such links are made, and only in passing. The same is true regarding more recent studies, such as Andreas Leitner's extensive survey of Sologub's prose images and Ann M. Lane's doctoral dissertation, "Nietzsche in Russian Thought, 1890–1917."[1] The reason for this, no doubt, is found in Sologub's pessimistic and solipsistic poetic stance, which is more strongly reminiscent of Schopenhauer than of Nietzsche. Certainly, Sologub is the most "Schopenhauerian" of the Russian symbolists. Yet one can definitely find various moments in Sologub's works that could also be termed "Nietzschean." This chapter will focus upon some of these.

Little of a personal nature is known about Sologub; he was an intensely private person who kept even his closest friends at arm's length. He grew up a semi-orphan on an estate where his mother was a servant. Starting as a provincial schoolteacher, he rose to the rank of inspector. In the mid-1890s he befriended Dmitri Merezhkovsky, Zinaida Gippius, and

[1] Andreas Leitner, *Die Erzählungen Fedor Sologubs* (Munich, 1976). Ann M. Lane, "Nietzsche in Russian Thought, 1890–1917" (Ph.D. diss., University of Wisconsin, 1976). Bernice Glatzer Rosenthal, *D. S. Merezhkovsky and the Silver Age* (The Hague, 1975), pp. 57–79. C. Harold Bedford, *The Seeker: D. S. Merezhkovskiy* (Lawrence, Kan., 1975). James West, *Russian Symbolism: A Study of Viacheslav Ivanov and the Symbolist Aesthetic* (London, 1970).

Nicholas Minsky (N. Vilenkin), who were building part of the movement which was to be later called Russian symbolism. Sologub's mature life parallels the publication of his literary creations, which include hundreds of poems, eighteen dramas, numerous short stories, and novels, of which *Petty Demon* (*Melkii bes*, 1905) achieved great notoriety for its portrayal of a decadent provincial schoolteacher, Peredonov. Sologub lived in St. Petersburg and, after the Revolution, wrote much less but remained active in literary circles as a defender of artistic freedom. He died in 1927.[2]

Like any other symbolist, Sologub should be understood not only in his relationship to Nietzsche, whom he no doubt read, but also in light of how Nietzsche was understood in Russia at that time. Sologub would have been unusual not to have been affected by Nietzsche's philosophy; his closest friends were all excited by Nietzsche's individualism, his challenges to conventional Christianity, his concept of the *Übermensch* and his studies of the ancient Greek world. It should be emphasized, however, that the symbolists were not philosophers and that their leanings tended to the more "dramatic" and "popular" understandings of various thinkers. Sologub, in particular, wrote little of a philosophical nature; to the contrary, he prided himself upon being a poet and a creative prose writer.

It is possible that Sologub was first influenced in his understandings of Nietzsche by Lev Shestov (1866–1938) and Minsky (1856–1937), the latter a close friend.[3] Shestov's and Minsky's studies of Nietzsche divided the German thinker's works into two unequal halves: *The Birth of Tragedy* and the rest of his works. Both writers recognized that Nietzsche moved away from the Schopenhauerian pessimism of his early works toward a new and unique philosophy of individualism and morality. An admirer of Nietzsche in the early 1890s, by the turn of the century Minsky was less enthusiastic and feared that Nietzsche's ideas would lead to an outbreak of German nationalism. Shestov was powerfully influenced by Nietzsche's attack on rationalism and philosophic idealism.

Sologub borrowed selectively from understandings and interpretations

[2] Anastasia Chebotarevskaia, "K instsenirovke p'esy 'Melkii bes,' " in *O Fedore Sologube, Kritika* (St. Petersburg, 1911), p. 330; Leitner, *Die Erzählungen Fedor Sologubs*. The most complete biography of Sologub is found in F. Sologub, *Stikhotvoreniia* (Leningrad, 1975); henceforth cited as *Stikh.*

[3] Lev Shestov, *Dobro v uchenii gr. Tolstogo i F. Nitsshe (Filosofii i propoved')* (St. Petersburg, 1900); *Dostoevsky i Nitsshe (Filosofii tragedii)* (St. Petersburg, 1903). N. Minsky, *Pri svete sovesti: Mysli i mechty o tseli zhizni* (St. Petersburg, 1890); "Fridrikh Nitche," *Mir iskusstva*, nos. 19–20 (1900):139–47 (literature section).

of Nietzsche then current in Russia, to serve his own artistic purposes. These were Sologub's quest for the mystical nature of art and his desire to create a New Man character in literature, a poet-philosopher-king who could transfigure the world through an understanding of art. *The Birth of Tragedy* was the greatest single Nietzschean influence on his work.

In *The Birth of Tragedy*, Nietzsche's identification of Apollonian and Dionysian trends in Greek drama provided a framework that the symbolists could adapt to advocate a revival of theater in Russia. Virtually all of them were interested in reinfusing drama with a religious spirit as found in the Dionysian and medieval mystery plays.[4] To Minsky, *The Birth of Tragedy* combined the essence of the Greek theater with the modernistic theories of Wagner and Schopenhauer.[5] Bely sought for a new mystery play (*misteriia*) to be created in the spirit of Dionysianism, especially through musical patterns.[6] Merezhkovsky and Constantine Bal'mont translated Greek tragedies; Innokenty Annensky (1856–1909) and Viacheslav Ivanov (1866–1949) attempted to write dramas set in classical surroundings and stylized in the spirit of Greek tragedy. Bal'mont's poetic mystery play, *Three Blossomings* (*Tri rastsveta*, 1904) represented an attempt to realize what Bely was advocating, namely, a modern mystery play written in symbolist images. Set in fairy-tale surroundings, the play lasted only one performance in a theatrical venture called "The Theater of Dionysus."[7] Alexander Blok toyed with the idea of a contemporary mystery play like Bal'mont's but rejected it in favor of a parody, *The Puppet Show* (*Balaganchik*, 1906).[8] Sologub adapted ideas and images from *The Birth of Tragedy* in four works: three essays on the theater,[9] and his first play, *Gift of the Wise Bees* (*Dar mudrykh pchel*, 1906).[10]

Sologub borrowed some of his ideas on art from *The Birth of Tragedy*.

---

[4] Bernice Glatzer Rosenthal, "Theatre as Church: The Vision of the Mystical Anarchists" *Russian History* 4, 2 (1977), pp. 122–41.

[5] Minsky, *Pri svete sovesti*, p. 143.

[6] B. Bugaev, "Formy iskusstva," *Mir iskusstva*, no. 12 (1902), pp. 343–61.

[7] K. Bal'mont, *Tri rastsveta*, *Severnyye tsvety assiriiskie* (1904–1905). N. Efros, "Dionisovo deistvo." *Teatr i iskusstvo*, no. 3 (1906):41–42. N. Vsevolodsky-Gerngross, *Istoriia russkogo teatra* (Leningrad, 1929), p. 248.

[8] G. Kalbouss, "From Mystery to Fantasy: An Attempt to Categorize the Plays of the Russian Symbolists," *Canadian-American Slavic Studies* 8 (Winter 1974):488–500.

[9] F. Sologub, "Teatr odnoi voli," in *Teatr, kniga o novom teatre* (St. Petersburg, 1908); "Dressirovanyi plias," *Teatr i iskusstvo*, no. 48 (1912); "Teatr-khram," *Teatr i iskusstvo*, no. 3 (1917).

[10] F. Sologub, *Dar mudrykh pchel*, in *Sobranie sochinenii*, 20 vols. (St. Petersburg, 1913–1914), 8:57–131, henceforth cited as SS.

He liked to "rationalize" or "justify" his works by claiming that his poetry, prose, and plays were updated versions of timeless legends and myths in their spirit, images, and theoretical underpinnings. Many of his works contain entire passages from myths, legends, and folk tales. He would often actually cite these sources, claiming that the poet must render life "artistic" and therefore "beautiful" by remythologizing the eternal symbols of mankind. This is the first line of his utopian fantasy, *Legend in Creation* (*Tvorimaia legenda*, 1909):

> I take a piece of life, coarse and barren, and from it I create an exquisite legend—for I am a poet.[11]

Mythologization represents a central creative principle in Sologub's works and in this we find definite parallels with Nietzsche and Wagner. Myths, to Sologub, provide the sources for those eternal symbols that bridge the objective and subjective worlds. Each writer needs to rewrite the myths in such a way that they would make sense to his readers. Sologub, unlike the Germans, tends not to nationalize his symbols, but seeks universal ones which would speak to modern times.[12]

The play, *Gift of the Wise Bees*, constitutes precisely such an artistic "rewriting" of a legend, using *The Birth of Tragedy* as an inspiration. Based on the Greek legend of Protesilaus and Laodamia, the play dramatizes how Protesilaus, the first Athenian to die in Troy, is brought back to life by his bride of one day, Laodamia, through a Dionysian ritual. When his time is up, Protesilaus returns to Hades for the second and final time; the grief-stricken Laodamia is consumed by her passion and throws herself into a fire. It should be noted that this legend also inspired dramas by Valery Briusov, Annensky, and the Polish playwright, S. Wyspianski.[13]

This play is the only one of its time that actually presents the Dionysian–Apollonian dichotomy of *The Birth of Tragedy*; the work is sprinkled with references to it. Nietzsche's statements that refer to "oblivion," such as: "The individual, with all his restraint and proportion, succumbed to the self-oblivion of the Dionysian states, forgetting the precepts of Apollo" (*BT*, 46); and "The chasm of oblivion separates the worlds of everyday

---

[11] F. Sologub, *Drops of Blood*, trans. S. Cioran (Ann Arbor, 1979), p. 27.

[12] G. Kalbouss, "Sologub and Myth," *Slavic and East European Journal* 27 (Fall 1982), p. 440–51.

[13] Briusov, *Protesilai umershii*, *Russkaia mysl'*, no. 1 (1911). I. Annensky, *Laodamiia*, *Severnaia rech'* (1906). S. Wyspianski, *Dzieta Zebrane* [Krakow] (1958).

reality and Dionysian reality" (*BT*, 59) find their artistic restatement in the play as:

> THE LETHE'S NOISY WAVES: Oblivion, oblivion, drink eternal oblivion from our waves. We sing about one thing, only one thing, as we splash on the shores of Hell, about oblivion, about eternal oblivion, are our noisy words.[14]

Nietzsche's phraseology on joy through pain: ". . . only the curious blending and duality in the emotions of the Dionysian revelers remind us—as medicines remind us of deadly poisons—of the phenomenon that pain begets joy, that ecstasy may wring sounds of agony from us . . ." (*BT*, 40) is artistically rephrased in Aphrodite's speech to Laodamia:

> APHRODITE: I have sacrificed you to the great joy of love, which conquers Death. I shall burn you up, burn you up by the blessed flame of suffering and love.[15]

Numerous other parallels could be made as *The Gift of the Wise Bees* dramatizes the interplay between the Apollonian world of illusion and the magical, resurrective power of the Dionysian cult. Typical for Sologub, two universes exist in this play, the Apollonian world of the living and the Dionysian world of the dead. Paradoxically they are the opposite of what the portend to be: the world of the living is spiritually dead, while the world of the dead is eternally alive. Laodamia is tormented by Apollo, god of Troy, who has condemned her husband to death, while Laodamia's supernatural companion, Aphrodite—who to Sologub is both the goddess of Love and the guiding spirit of the Moirae—urges her to use the Dionysian ritual to release Protesilaus from the dead and consummate their marriage. Laodamia's ecstasy brings the dead back to life.

Laodamia still clings to the beautiful illusions of the Apollonian world. Having been given a wax statue of Protesilaus, she accepts it as reality and even when the "real" Protesilaus appears, she is reluctant to let go of the Apollonian deception. When her father throws the statue into the fire, Laodamia's passions quiet down; as the statue melts Laodamia weakens and dies.[16]

Echoes of *The Birth of Tragedy* are not confined to this play alone. In the Dionysian ritual, an essay of Sologub's argues, the participant is "no

[14] SS, 8:64–65.
[15] SS, 8:92.
[16] SS, 8:118–19.

longer the artist, he himself has become a work of art,"[17] Sologub saw the living incarnation of this idea in Isadora Duncan whose dancing, he felt, was Dionysian in spirit. In his play, *Day-Dream the Victorious* (*Mechta-pobeditel'nitsa*, 1911), a frail dancer transfigures herself into a beautiful being through her ecstatic dance. The dance, of course, was a favorite theme of Zarathustra's.

Elements from the Dionysian ritual provide Sologub with many of his favorite images: sacrificial fire (*plamia, ogon'*), the night, the ecstatic dance, the stars, the moon, and, of course, the worshipping chorus partaking of the sacrificial blood from the sacred chalice. A parody of the Dionysian ritual sacrifice is found in the slaughter of Peredonov's friend Volodin, in *Petty Demon*, the friend being referred to as a "sheep."[18] The cleansing and purifying fire, a favorite image of Nietzsche's, abounds in Sologub's works, for example:

> And in complete singular creation,
> To be cleansed by the lighting of the Fire.[19]

The sun, another of Nietzsche's favorite images, is also very frequent in Sologub's works. While the sun is a positive image to Nietzsche, it is a negative one with Sologub. To Sologub, as to certain other philosophical and romantic poets, the sun shields man's consciousness from the painful awareness of the vastness of the universe. Only when the sun's rays have disappeared and night takes over, can one sense the infinitude of the cosmos. The sun, which Sologub also terms "The Dragon" and "The Snake," symbolizes the deceptive quality of the day world. Under the sun, the world witnesses the bustle of mediocre people, which leads to suffering, perverse behavior, hypocrisy, and shallowness. In one humorous poem, "To Viacheslav Ivanov" ("Viacheslavu Ivanovu," 1906), Solugub pokes fun at Ivanov's admiration of Nietzsche's sun-image. Speaking as the World-Will, Sologub tells Ivanov that he is wrong in interpreting the sun in an Nietzschean way:

> In you I don't see an apostate,
> I call you with hope,
> The Dragon is my heart of the day,
> The Snake, my nocturnal sorrow.

[17] F. Sologub, *Mechta-pobeditel'nitsa*, *Biblioteka teatra i iskusstva* 5 (May 1912), p. 17.
[18] Charlotte Rosenthal and Helene Foley, "Symbolic Patterning in *Melkij bes*," *Slavic and East European Journal* 26 (Spring 1982):43–55.
[19] *Stikh.*, p. 210. This is, of course, also an apocalyptic image.

Later, we have:

> In vain do you glorify the Sun,
> Chasing me away from your heights—
> Laughing at your beckoning, Aldonsa
> Cuts the woolly Fleece . . .

And finally:

> I have given you and the Sun
> One commandment: Love Me. [20]

Yet, Sologub's rejection of a positive sun image does not make him anti-Nietzschean. To the contrary, Sologub has remythologized Nietzsche's interpretations in *The Birth of Tragedy* in such a way that the World-Will has become identified with the Dionysian spirit alone. The Apollonian thus opposes the World-Will, and justifies Sologub's rejection of the sun-image.

While *The Birth of Tragedy* was almost universally admired by the symbolists, Nietzsche's other works were not as unqualifiedly accepted. As stated earlier, Sologub was more of an artist than a philosopher, and therefore it is difficult to show more than reflections of and parallels with Nietzschean themes which were then "in the air" such as his rejection of Christianity, his appreciation for mythology, and his concept of the *Übermensch*.

Nietzsche's rejection of Christianity and his longing for a return to a pre-Christian past is strongly paralleled in Sologub's works. Sologub's more vital and sensuous characters are frequently linked to the life-giving spirit of the earth, to a kind of pre-Christian Slavic pantheism. Liudmila in *Petty Demon* is called a *rusalka* (water-nymph)[21] and her rituals with the youth Sasha conjure up images of pagan ones (an idea popular at this time in Russia, the greatest artistic achievement being Stravinsky's *Rite of Spring*). Many of Sologub's leading characters practice various mysterious rituals and reject the practices of a watered-down Christianity.

In many works, the religious Christian world blocks contact with the ecstasies of Sologub's ideal universe. The Christian world is but a pale reflection of the pagan. In 1898 he wrote:

> Pagan-woman! How can you compare
>   Your love with my faith?

[20] *Stikh.*, pp. 332–33.
[21] F. Sologub, *Melkii bes* (Letchworth, 1966), p. 247.

> You want to blaze away in red fire
>   While I languish in grey ashes.[22]

To Sologub, God is an indifferent force looking the other way and ignoring earthly suffering:

> Or is it for eternity from life's anxieties
>   That God has hidden himself
>   In unattainable places?[23]

Christian rituals fall upon deaf ears and are folly to perform:

> Why do we conduct masses
> And burn incense before the Lord!
> We're not needed at all,
> Having been forgotten by our God.[24]

Even Jesus' suffering is something that God has chosen to avoid:

> I only know, Lord of Heaven,
> That on Golgotha's cross of torment,
> It was man who suffered and not Thou.[25]

The novel *Legend in Creation* has a moment when the poet-philosopher
hero Trirodov meets a certain "Emmanuel Osipovich Davydov," who, of
course, is Christ:

> My design is bold and difficult. . . . Know that I will never fol-
> low you, will never accept your consoling theories. All of your lit-
> erature and preaching are, in my eyes, a complete mistake. A fatal
> mistake. I do not believe in what you speak of so rhetorically, se-
> ducing the weak. I do not believe in it.[26]

Most important, Sologub shares Nietzsche's enthusiasm for mythology.
Whether this is a direct borrowing from Nietzsche or Wagner is difficult
to determine. Sologub is the only symbolist who created his own mythological system.[27] We have already mentioned that Sologub re-
mythologizes existing legends and converts them into new tales to illus-

---

[22] *Stikh.*, p. 208.
[23] *Stikh.*, p. 241.
[24] *Stikh.*, p. 279.
[25] *Stikh.*, p. 393.
[26] *Drops of Blood*, p. 216.
[27] Kalbouss, "Sologub and Myth."

trate the veracity of his own point of view, which is also couched in mythic images. Thus, such disparate legends and fairy tales as the *chanson de geste* "Berte au grand pied (*Victory of Death*), the ballads of "Van'ka kliuchnik zloi razluchnik" (*Van'ka the Lackey and Jean the Page*) and the fairy tale by the brothers Grimm, "The Princesses and the Worn-Out Slippers" (*Nocturnal Dances*) all communicate the same message as does *Gift of the Wise Bees*, namely that the poet confronts two worlds: the Apollonian day-world of superficial deception and the Dionysian night-world of magic and intoxication. Indeed, Sologub's plays may be seen as a Russian "Ring" series, in which similar images are replayed over and over again, emphasizing the triumph of a pagan non-Christian love over the bourgeois Christian morality of the everyday world. Sologub, no doubt, knew of Wagner's ideas regarding musical drama as well as Nietzsche's reflections on Wagner; the influences here are therefore difficult to disentangle.

Sologub shared Nietzsche's disdain for the middle-class world and its ethics and morality. It should be remembered that most artists shared this kind of disdain, and thus it is specious to attribute this strictly to Nietzsche's influence. Yet, the idea of a superior being who would rise above the world, similar to Nietzsche's *Übermensch*, was certainly popular at that time. The various artists and philosophers of the Silver Age did discuss the idea of the superman. Influenced also by Vladimir Soloviev and Feodor Dostoevsky, persons in this group posited that the new man may either be Christian or non-Christian. Sologub, who was close to them, evolved the notion that the new man would be a non-Christian "super" poet-artist. The evolution of such a character took place over two decades in his novels.

Before 1896, Sologub strongly associated himself with the pessimistic spirit of the *fin de siècle*, particularly with Schopenhauer. His writings present a dyspeptic, despairing view of life where dreamers are left only to their daydreams (*mechty*), which unfortunately fail to provide them with an escape from their world of boredom and tribulations. When many of his earliest heroes attempt to put their daydreams into action, they simply perish.

By 1896, Sologub began to posit and pose as an all-encompassing "I" (*ia*) that stands over and above the world and controls it, providing a glimmer of hope that the conditions of the world will improve. In one of his earliest poems, "Ariadna" (1883), Sologub bemoans the fact that the princess will not lead the poet out of the labyrinth:

> Where are you, my Adriadne?
> Where is your guiding thread?
> Only it will help me
> Open the door out of the labyrinth.[28]

Pinpointing a relationship between Sologub's evolution of a more positive World-Will and Nietzsche is difficult. Yet it is probably more than a coincidence that the high point of his friend Merezhkovsky's Nietzscheanism is 1896, the same year that Sologub changed his poetic stance. In 1896, in a poem ("Tsarevnoi Mudroi Ariadnoi") using the same Ariadne-labyrinth imagery, Sologub introduces a ray of hope. At the last moment, "Fate" (Sud'ba) provides the poet with the lifesaving thread:

> And anew I'll walk out into Freedom
> To die under the clear sky
> And, while dying, to look upon nature
> With clear eyes.[29]

Obviously, the Fate of this poem is the same as the World-Will. The World-Will becomes the poet:

> I closed my eyes,
> I turned off the entire world.[30]

And:

> It is because there is no other
> Existence, than only I;
> The joy of blue happiness
> The sorrow of evil languor,
> In everything, in everything, you can find my soul.[31]

Thus the progression: 1) The World-Will indifferent to the world, 2) the World-Will slightly aware of the world, 3) the World-Will as the poet, 4) the World-Will as expressed through a person of action. The latter two steps in Sologub's evolution of his new man are Nietzschean to some degree. Superior people can change the world if they are part of the World-Will;

[28] *Stikh.*, p. 80.
[29] *Stikh.*, p. 163.
[30] *Stikh.*, p. 216.
[31] *Stikh.*, p. 171.

I'm the god of a mysterious world,
The entire world is in my daydreams.[32]

Through the Will, the daydreams of the poet can transfigure the world:

The bitter languor of the day
Will be transfigured through daydreams,
And everything that was evil and fearful
Will now become humble prayer . . .[33]

Sologub's evolution of a superior fictional hero follows this same kind of pattern. As early as 1894, Sologub entertained the idea of a Russian type of *Übermensch* who rejects the morality of his society. While Merezhkovsky and Gippius later sought a remythologized new Christian man, Sologub's *Übermensch* remained outside the bounds of Christianity. Yet, at least in his early fiction, Sologub does not allow his heroes to succeed in creating their own worlds. He was still too much a realist and "child of the Eighties" to produce such a fantasy.

In his first novel, *Bad Dreams* (1896), his main character Login (a schoolteacher like Sologub) does attempt to create his own world but fails, being too much a victim of the social environment and unable to assert his will over the tremendously degenerate powers of evil society.[34] Throwing off the shackles of bourgeois morality, he considers the pursuits of pleasures and pains rejected by the self-righteous. Sadism, with the joy it brings through others' suffering, is a part of Login's pleasure-spectrum of intense feelings which Sologub believes modern, bourgeois people lack. Sexual abandonment converts men and women into gods, hence the connection with the superman. As Login states in *Bad Dreams*:

Love is stronger than anything that people have created by piling up barriers against each other. Let us love each other and we, *like gods*, will create and conceive new heavens and a new earth.[35]

To Sologub, the way to become godlike is to participate in an ecstatic and erotic ritual. The shedding of middle-class values is symbolized by the resolute abandonment of disrobing in preparation for lovemaking and oneness with the Will:

[32] *Stikh.*, p. 176.
[33] *Stikh.*, p. 241.
[34] SS, vol. 2.
[35] Italics mine. SS, 2:337. Note also the apocalyptic allusion.

. . . Suddenly an expressive resolution and great calmness fell
across her paling face; she slowly uplifted her calm arms, quietly
unfastened a metallic clasp on her left shoulder, and said in a passionless voice:

My gift to you—is myself.

Her dress fell to her feet. Nude and cold did she stand before him
and with anticipation did her unsinning eyes look at him. [36]

Sologub's "superior" characters are constantly challenging social ta-
boos. Again, his earlier works show that they are not successful in doing
so. The hero of his narrative poem *Kremlev* (1894) decides to engage in
incest with his niece. She, however, is in love with a young man her
own age. In a fit of melancholy, he kills himself. [37] In later works, however, the obstacles are overcome. In the play *Loves* (*Liubvi*, 1907), the
new man, Reatov, has just suffered the loss of his wife. At her funeral,
he asks his daughter Alexandra if she possibly could love him not as a
father but as a lover. Obviously upset by the question, she is speechless.
He then proposes a hypothesis: would it be easier for her to consider him
a lover if she were only his adopted daughter? Could she then admit to
such a feeling? He makes it appear that, indeed, she is adopted and not
his natural daughter. Claiming that the circumstances of her birth should
make no difference in her feelings for him, he encourages her to reveal
them. He proposes that she first reveal her feelings and then he will tell
her whether or not she is adopted. She admits that she has erotic feelings
for him; he then states that she is indeed his natural daughter, but that it
makes no difference when a man and a woman are attracted to each
other. Having become the new woman, she states:

My beloved! Why should I care about those evil, deceitful people
who do not believe in the truth. We know. We are happy. [38]

This ending must have created a furor, since Sologub altered it for his
collected works, making Alexandra the adopted daughter rather than biological. Yet the final line remained the same: the bounds of bourgeois
morality can be ignored by superior people. These ideas may derive from
Beyond Good and Evil and *Genealogy of Morals*, but no evidence of
direct influence exists.

[36] SS, 2:405.
[37] *Stikh.*, pp. 128–29.
[38] SS, 8:155.

After 1907, Sologub's new man attempts to merge mythology, poetry, and science, and, out of them, make a new utopia. Trirodov, in *Legend in Creation*, is the most "superior" of all of Sologub's heroes. Educated in the occult sciences, he is both magician and scientist; he can resurrect the dead as well as conquer gravity. At the end of the novel, Trirodov enters the world of politics to become king of the beleaguered Balearic Islands, its magician-scientist-philosopher ruler, and promises the advent of a new era on earth. In the play *Hostages of Life* (*Zalozhniki zhizni*, 1912), Sologub's new man is an engineer, who dreams of creating a utopia through science and technology. Like Ibsen's Solness in *Master Builder*, he wishes to build his new world in a beautiful way. Perhaps the inspiration here is also the Brooklyn Bridge:

> I will build bridges, roads and high towers. . . . A new beauty will come into being out of what I build, a beauty of lines so light and so simple. . . . Ecstatic glances will be cast on the cobwebs of steel cables and people will glorify my name, and I shall be crowned and glorified for you [for Katia, his wife-to-be]. . . . Together we shall build a new, happy, and free life, not like this one. Life shall become as light as the bridge which hangs over the abyss by its cobweb of steel cables.[39]

In his later works, Sologub's characters devote their lives to improving the lot of their fellow man. Ironically, these more positive heroes are also some of Sologub's dullest ones, and thus are not as interesting and colorful as his demented perverts and child-torturers. As Blok once stated, Sologub's later characters "have ceased to love Death and hate Life in the Sologubian way."[40]

In summation, it is simple to find various Nietzschean themes in Sologub's works but difficult to show discrete influences. The simplest parallels can be found between *The Birth of Tragedy* and *Gift of the Wise Bees* where Nietzsche's Apollonian–Dionysian dichotomy is remythologized to fit Sologub's Neoplatonic universe of day and night worlds. Like Nietzsche, Sologub shared with the other symbolists an interest in the idea of a new man who rejects the world of bourgeois morality and who might explore the mysterious world beyond the senses. In Sologub's "superior" characters we find the closest parallels to the *Übermensch*, although they are never called this; in them we see a new breed of poet-

---

[39] F. Sologub, *Zalozhniki zhizni, Al'manakh Shipovnik*, no. 18 (1912):25.
[40] A. Blok, *Sobranie sochinenii* (Leningrad-Moscow, 1963), 7:185.

priests who are bringing a world yet to come into being. They represent Sologub's answer to the symbolist quest for the "transfiguration of the world through beauty" (*preobrazhenie mira krasotoi*). Sologub is indebted to Nietzsche for at least some significant inspirations in the development of his own ideas. Indeed, Minsky's observation of Nietzsche's own creative development can likewise apply to Sologub: after sharing a closeness to Schopenhauer, he departed along his own path, searching for a new kind of individualism.[41] It may be added that even when Sologub shared this path with Nietzsche, he picked and chose those ideas that would reinforce his own theories of myth-creation.

[41] Minsky, "Fridrikh Nitche," p. 144.

9.

Bal'mont and Skriabin:
The Artist as Superman

Ann M. Lane

THE EARLY MODERNIST CULT of the individual reached its apogee
in Bal'mont's and Skriabin's celebration of the Nietzschean superman,
particularly in their conception of the artist as the superman par excel-
lence—the destroyer of old worlds and creator of new worlds. They longed
to achieve greatness, taking to heart Nietzsche's exclamation: "If there
were gods, how could I endure not to be a god!" (Z, 110). The primary
Nietzschean influences upon both were *The Birth of Tragedy* and *Thus
Spoke Zarathustra*. Bal'mont and Skriabin were prominent figures; Bal-
mont's exposition of ultra-individualism was especially significant in the
"revaluation of values" that began in the Russian literary world in the
1890s.

BAL'MONT

The estheticism of Constantine Bal'mont (1867–1942) was the product
of both Nietzsche's call for new values based upon strength and creativity,
and of French symbolism with its sense of the individual's ability to perceive impressions in a highly personal way. Initially the French symbolist
influence was the stronger; later on the Nietzschean influence came to
predominate in his most acclaimed works. Bal'mont drew upon Nietzsche's
ideas and imagery; as will be seen, there are many textual parallels.

Bal'mont can be considered the crown prince of Russian modernism.
Among those who paid tribute to his talents as an innovator were Andrei
Bely, who dedicated the first poem in his first collection to him. Valery

Briusov, recalling the literary ferment of the early 1890s, wrote, "That was the time when the sun of Bal'mont's poetry rose. Bal'mont possessed the souls of all those who really loved poetry, and made everybody fall in love with his resonantly melodious poetry." Bal'mont, he added, is "above all, the 'new man.' "[1] Alexander Blok (1880–1921), perhaps the greatest symbolist poet, felt that he had learned much from Bal'mont's poetic innovations.[2]

Although Bal'mont's first poetic collections *Under a Northern Sky* (*Pod severnym nebom,* 1894) and *In Boundless Space* (*V bezbrezhnosti,* 1895) were tinged by the melancholy characteristic of the French symbolists, his next collection, *Silence* (*Tishina,* 1898), announced a new theme, the celebration of himself as artistic genius: "I am a disturbing specter, I am an elemental genius" (from the poem "Snow Flowers").[3]

The reference to the Nietzschean "elemental genius" suggests that Bal'-mont knew of Nietzsche in the late 1890s. Bal'mont's familiarity with Nietzsche by this time is also indicated by an entry in Briusov's diary from late 1897: "We [Briusov and Bal'mont] spoke about Christ. Bal'-mont called him a lackey, a philosopher for beggars,"[4] an obvious allusion to Nietzsche's thought. Bal'mont probably learned of Nietzsche from both Briusov and Prince Alexander Urusov, a Moscow lawyer and well-known promoter of Western literary modernism, who in the early 1890s gave a lecture on Nietzsche to a St. Petersburg literary circle.[5] Briusov, in turn, learned about Nietzsche from, among other sources, Max Nordau's *Degeneration.*[6] Briusov's poetry also contains Nietzschean themes.

> Oh, heart! in these shadows of the century,
> Where there are no truths, believe in something else!
> Love the superman in yourself
> Appear, our god and half-animal![7]

[1] Valery Briusov, *Dalekie i blizkie: Stat'i i zametki o russkikh poetakh ot Tiutcheva do nashikh dnei* (Moscow, 1912), pp. 107, 73.

[2] Blok wrote: "Bal'mont—he is entirely a many-stringed lyre." Aleksandr Blok, *Sobranie sochinenii,* 8 vols. (Moscow and Leningrad, 1960–1963), 5:528.

[3] From "Snezhnye tsvety," in *Tishina, Polnoe sobranie stikhov,* 10 vols,. 3rd ed. (Moscow, 1909–1914), 1:163. Henceforth cited as *PSS.*

[4] Briusov, *Dnevniki 1891–1910* (Moscow, 1927), p. 30.

[5] Z. Gippius-Merezhkovskaia, *Dmitry Merezhkovsky* (Paris, 1951), pp. 62–63. See K. Bal'mont, "Kniaz' A. I. Urusov: Stranitsa liubvi i pamiati," in *Gornye vershiny* (Moscow, 1904), p. 105.

[6] Briusov, *Iz moei zhizni* (Moscow, 1927), p. 27. Nordau's *Entartung* appeared in 1892; a Russian translation, *Vyrozhdenie,* appeared in 1893, 1896, and 1901.

[7] Briusov, *Urbi et Orbi* (Moscow, 1903), p. 44.

Bal'mont's *Silence* has other Nietzschean references. In the poem "Edelweiss," the Nietzschean imagery of the heights is used to express a sense of life's vast possibilities. The poem echoes Nietzsche's conviction that man is lord of the universe (indeed, the setting of the poem is Nietzsche's favorite habitat, the Swiss Alps) and also Baudelaire's *le goût de l'infini* (yearning for infinity).

I look upon the earth from the blue heights,
I love the edelweiss—unearthly flowers
That grow far away from ordinary eyes,
Like the sky dream of snow preserves.

From the blue heights I look upon the earth
And in my soul I speak with a voiceless dream,
With that unseen Soul that shimmers within me
In those hours when I go to the unearthly heights.

And slowly I go down from the blue heights
Leaving not a trace in the snows behind,
But only one hint, a white snowy flower,
Reminds me that the earth is infinitely wide. [8]

Similar sentiments are expressed in "Snow Flowers": I am the lord over the kingdom of earthly visions, / Always free, always alone."[9] The poet, "The brilliant-eyed genius [who] seeks unknown shores," describes himself as going "Beyond the bounds of both truth and lie."[10]

Bal'mont brings Nietzsche and Baudelaire together again in the poem "Chords," using for the epigraph a line of Baudelaire: "C'est un phare allumé sur mille citadelles" ("This is a beacon set alight over a thousand citadels"). The piece speaks of the artist's power to create worlds, to gain the "infinite," and of the artist as superman:

I saw the Magi of revelations; the beloved of future times,
The appeals to battle, the powerfully bright banners.

Hints of the superman, the fragments of unearthly worlds,
The chords of fathomless words. [11]

The poem expresses a Baudelairean sense of mysterious *"correspondances"* between this world and the world of the poet's dreams, shown,

[8] Bal'mont, "Edel'veis," *PSS*, 1:170.
[9] "Snezhnye tsvety," *PSS*, 1:166.
[10] Ibid., 1:164, 165.
[11] "Akkordy," ibid., p. 203.

for example, in the synesthetic linking of words with paintings as "chords." Artists, the "Magi of revelations," however, are not confined to dreams; they are the forerunners of the superman.

This sense of the artist as the lord of the world, free and uncontrollable, became more intense in Bal'mont's next collection, *Burning Buildings* (*Goriashchie zdaniia*, 1900). In 1899 he had written in a letter, "I have changed my understanding of the world. No matter how odd my phrase sounds, I will say: I have understood the world. For many years, perhaps forever."[12] While *Silence* still contained much of the passive, languid mood of his earliest poetry, *Burning Buildings* portrays the artist as a fierce warrior whose strength masters the world. In the poem "Daggerlike Words," prefaced by Hamlet's "I will speak daggers," Bal'mont's warrior persona exclaims:

> I am tired of tender words,
> Of the ecstasies of these whole
> Harmonious feasts
> And of cradle refrains.
> I want to rip the azure of peaceful dreams.
> I want burning buildings,
> I want screaming storms!

> The rapture of repose
> Is the sleep of the mind.
> Let the sea of hot heat flare up,
> Let darkness shudder in the heart.

> I want other clangings
> For my different feasts.
> I want dagger words
> And death's exclamations![13]

The collection is subtitled "Lyrics of the Modern Soul." The modern soul (meaning himself) as he depicts it, reaches out to life, color, light, sound, sensation, and especially to fire as the symbol of life's intensity; the poet, as elemental genius, is a creature with the force and spontaneity of nature.

Bal'mont expressed another Nietzschean theme, love of fate (*amor fati*), in the poem "The Scorpion."

---

[12] As quoted by Vl. Orlov, "Bal'mont: Zhizni i poeziia," in *Stikhotvoreniia*, by K. D. Bal'mont (Leningrad, 1969), p. 50.

[13] *Goriashchie zdaniia: Lirika sovremennoi dushi* (Moscow, 1900), p. 7.

I am surrounded by a circle of fire,
It comes closer, I am condemned to death,—
Because I was born hideous
Because I am the evil scorpion.

My enemies look on from all sides,
A nightmare fateful and inevitable—
There is no escape, death encircles me,
The flame fixes me.

But though all is more and more horrible for me
The breath of the relentless fire—
I am full only of painless transport.

I will perish. Let it be. I challenge fate.
I found my death in myself.
I will perish as the scorpion—proud, free.[14]

In a letter of 1900, he said, "Oh, I love life and bless it with all its tortures![15] Using specifically Nietzschean imagery and phraseology he confesses:

> I give myself to the world, and the world enters into me. I am close to the stars, the waves, and the mountains. I am close to beasts and heroes. I am close to the beautiful and the ugly. . . . I understand all and hold it dear. I understand the heights—I have climbed on them. I understand the low—I have fallen low, and I understand also what is outside the bounds of high and low.[16]

The poet-as-warrior theme is continued in "Like the Spaniard."

> Like the Spaniard dazzled by faith in love and faith in gods,
> And intoxicated by his own and others' red blood,
> I want to be first in the world, on earth and sea,
> I want crimson flowers I have created everywhere.
> I will see the sun, the sun, the sun—red like blood.[17]

The red blood shed by the warrior and the crimson flowers created by the poet both come from the sun, celebrated as the symbol of life, a

---

[14] Ibid.
[15] As quoted by Orlov, "Bal'mont," p. 52.
[16] "Iz zapisnoi knizhki" (1904), PSS, 2:13.
[17] "Kak ispanets," PSS, 2:3.

Nietzschean theme Bal'mont will explicitly develop in his next collection, *Let Us Be Like the Sun* (*Budem kak solntse*, 1903).

In the numerous lyric heroes through which Bal'mont presents himself in *Burning Buildings*,[18] the artist-superman becomes and does anything he wishes. The power of his "elemental genius" goes "beyond all bounds." Bal'mont expressed this faith in his own limitless powers as an artist in the poem "In Souls There Is All":

> Only to my soul do I sing a prayer,
> Only boundlessness alone do I love,
> Only my soul![19]

This part of the poem is similar to Nietzsche's long ode to his soul in *Thus Spoke Zarathustra*: "Oh, my soul, I gave you back freedom over created and uncreated things; and who knows as you know the delight of things to come?" (Z, 238). Bal'mont continues speaking to his soul:

> In you greatness is born,
> You can roar with storms,
> From the white abyss of indifference
> You can extract both gold and copper.[20]

Zarathustra says to his soul, "With the storm that is called 'spirit' I blew across your surging sea . . ." and calls his soul "the golden marvel around whose gold all good, bad, marvelous things leap . . ." (Z, 238–40). In the same poem Bal'mont refers to the idea of eternal recurrence, using Nietzsche's symbols, the snake and ring:

> You are brilliancy, you are the genius of infinity,
> In you is all the magnificence of existence.
> But your sign, the fearful symbol of Eternity
> Is the ringlike snake.[21]

The poem touches yet another aspect of Nietzsche's thought, the esthetic redemption of the dark side of human nature:

---

[18] As quoted by Orlov, "Bal'mont," pp. 51–52. Not only is Bal'mont the poet speaking of daggers, the warrior Spaniard, the proud scorpion, but also the fearless sentry who alerts his comrades to battle ("The Cry of the Sentry"), the ballad singer ("Death of Dmitri the Red"), the dawn ("Words of Love"), the prisoner ("In Jail"), the pupil of Baudelaire ("To Baudelaire"), a Scythian ("Hyperboreans"), the Indian sage ("Indian Wiseman"), the Tatar, and the sun ("The Chosen One").

[19] "V dushakh est vse," *Goriashchie zdaniia*, pp. 81–82.

[20] Ibid., p. 82.

[21] Ibid.

But the wild horror of crime,
But the ugly traits—
And all these your visions,
Is this the new that frightens you?

The world must be entirely justified,
So that one can live![22]

Nietzsche, of course, in *The Birth of Tragedy*, had said that this world can be justified only as an esthetic phenomenon, and had insisted on a revaluation of all values. "I blew all clouds away;" Zarthustra said. "I killed even that killerbird called sin" (Z, 238).

Another striking reference to Nietzsche appears in *Burning Buildings*:

Both *yes* and *no*—all this is mine,
I accept pain—as a blessing,
I bless existence,
And if *I* created the desert,
Its magnificence is mine![23]

Zarathustra says: "Oh my soul, I gave you the right to say No like the storm and to say Yes as the open sky says Yes: now silent as light you stand, and you pass through denying storms" (Z, 238). Nietzsche had also referred to his pain and illness as a blessing (GS, 35–37); he associated pain with the "primordial Dionysian joy" in *The Birth of Tragedy* (BT, 141). In this poem, too, Bal'mont treated solitude and its anguish much as did Nietzsche: the superman transforms the pain of solitude into proud joy. Because he has created solitude, he is not its victim but its master.

Bal'mont's next collection of poetry, *Let Us Be Like the Sun* (1903), revolves around sun imagery. On the cover is a picture of a naked man standing exultantly before a brilliant sun, arms uplifted. This theme has explicit correspondence to Zarathustra: "Oh my soul, I washed the petty shame and corner-virtue away from you and persuaded you to stand naked before the eyes of the sun" (Z, 238). In his literary criticism, Bal'mont discusses Nietzsche in terms of the sun, calling him an Icarus. Writing of his own generation, Bal'mont links it to Nietzsche:

A decadent, in the true sense of this word, is a refined *artist, perishing because of his refinement*. As the word itself shows, decadents

---

[22] Ibid., pp. 82–83.
[23] *Goriashchie zdaniia*, p. 86.

are the representatives of an era of degeneration. These are people who think and feel on the border of two periods, one ended, the other not yet born. They see that the sunset is not yet extinguished, but that the dawn still lingers beyond the horizon; thus the songs of the decadents are the songs of twilight and darkness. They dethrone the old because it has lost its soul. But they can only sense, not see the new, therefore they feel ecstasy but also much anguish. Such a person is the hero of Ibsen's drama: he falls from the tower he himself built. The philosopher of decadence is Friedrich Nietzsche, the perished Icarus, who was able to make himself wings but not able to give his wings the strength to endure the heat of the scorching sun.[24]

The imagery of twilight also recalls Nietzsche. In *Human, All Too Human*, he describes his own generation similarly: "The best in us has perhaps been inherited from the feelings of former times. . . . The sun has already set, but our life's sky glows and shines with it still, although we no longer see it" (*HH*, 137). Bal'mont uses the imagery of sunset with its promise of the dawn to convey this same thought in "The Voice of Sunset":

The golden fire behind the tapestry of branches
Changes in its finery.
It burns, like the flame of splendid charms,
The lilac-yellow-pink fire.

I am the day going away.
Not many such days can you remember, my dreaming brother.
I am the evening luminary,
The victorious-fiery sunset.

I burn so brilliantly, so joyously
Sliding through the airy clouds so fierily,
That to be more beautiful
And to be more blessed is impossible.[25]

But whether or not Bal'mont took this particular imagery from Nietzsche (and the similarity is striking), echoing another passage from Nietzsche referring to the sun moving toward the constellation of Hercules, he used

[24] *Gornye vershiny*, p. 78.
[25] *Budem kak solntse: Kniga simvolov* (Moscow, 1903), pp. 5–7.

the sun as the symbol of the Nietzschean joyful acceptance of earthly life with all its pain, pleasure, and passion.

> He who revolts against the full power of desire revolts against life. And what could be sweeter than life in all its tortures, in all its burning pain, linked with each pleasure. God loves day and night. Let us be like God, let us love light and darkness. Let us eternally contemplate infinity and beauty. Let us be like the Sun, with all its stars is carried off to the far-away constellation of Hercules, but living for itself.[26]

Sun and fire are two frequent motifs in Bal'mont's poetry; indeed, Bal'-mont wrote, "My favorite element is Fire. I pray to fire."[27] Fire, as in Nietzsche, was for Bal'mont a symbol of creation and of the destruction necessary and inherent to creation. For Nietzsche, the sun is a symbol of renewal and power:

> Is it our fault that we were born for the air, clean air, we rivals of the beams of light, and that we wish we could ride on ethereal dust specks like these beams—not away from the sun but *toward* the earth, be "the light of the earth"! And to that end we have our wings and our speed and our serenity; for this we are virile and even terrible like fire. (GS, 236)

Finally, Nietzsche used the sun as the ultimate symbol of life:

> If one could burden one's soul with all of this—the oldest, the newest, losses, hopes, conquests, and the victories of humanity; if one could finally contain all this in one soul and crowd it into a single feeling—this would surely have to result in a happiness that humanity has not known so far: the happiness of a god full of power and love, full of tears and laughter, a happiness that, like the sun in the evening, continually bestows its inexhaustible riches, pouring them into the sea. (GS, 268)

Let Us Be Like the Sun opens with an epigram from Anaxagoras, "I came into this world to see the sun" and its first poem enlarges on this epigram, celebrating the sun as the symbol of life:

> I came into this world to see the sun
>   And the deep blue horizon.

[26] *Gornye vershiny*, pp. 40–41.
[27] "Iz zapisnoi knizhki" (1904), *PSS*, 1:viii.

I came into the world to see the sun
  And the high mountain.

I came into this world to see the sea
  And the flourishing flowers of the valley.
I took in worlds in a single ken,
  I am the sovereign.

I conquered cold oblivion:
  I created my dream.
Every moment I am full of revelation,
  Always I sing.

Sufferings awoke my dream,
  But I love, no matter.
Who can equal my singing strength?
  No one, no one.

I came into this world to see the sun.
  And if the day dies,
I will sing, I will sing of the sun
  In the hour of death![28]

The title poem (the second poem in the collection) further expresses Bal'-mont's feeling that he is a sovereign like the sun:

Let us be like the sun. Forget
Who leads us along the golden way.
Let us always pray
In our earthly desires
To the unearthly!
Let us remember only
That we strive in the golden dream brightly
For the other—
The new, the strong, the good, the evil.

Let us be like the sun always young,
Tenderly caress the fiery flowers,
The limpid air and everything golden.
Are you happy? Be twice as happy,
Be the incarnation of the sudden dream!

[28] Ibid., p. 1.

Only do not delay in motionless calm,
Further still to the cherished boundary,
Further, the fateful hour beckons us
To eternity where new flowers take fire.
Be like the sun, it is young,
In this is the precept of beauty![29]

The subtitle of the collection is "Book of Symbols." Bal'mont described symbolism as a "mighty force, striving to guess the new combinations of thought, colors, and sounds, and not rarely guessing them with irresistible conviction."[30] He and his fellow symbolists expected a new world, in which beauty would be the prevailing value.

An image taken from Nietzsche serves as the epigram of the poem "White Fire": "Hier stehe ich inmitten des Brandes der Brandung" ("I am standing here amidst the blaze of the surf").

I stand on the sand, in the blaze of the breakers,
And the wave, rippling whiteness at the top
Just like a horse heated from running and battle
Rushed to me in its pre-death surge.

And behind it others, like white horses,
Shaking their manes, are borne on, run,
They die from the horror of the wild chase
And consume themselves in their haste.

They toppled over, they flared up—right and left,—
And sighing before death and shining brilliantly,
They die on the sand in trembling rage
Tongues of spent white fires.[31]

Bal'mont expressed his vision of life, intense as white fire and brilliant as the sun, in poems depicting the artist as a solitary superman justifying his existence by creating himself through his art. Not only does this artist-superman create himself, but he is eternally re-creating himself in deriving the full intensity, novelty, and beauty of each moment as he moves on the next moment: "I am eternally new."[32]

Briusov noted this quality of Bal'mont's poetry. "And really, what is

[29] Ibid., p. 2.
[30] *Gornye vershiny*, p. 95.
[31] *Budem kak solntse*, p. 24.
[32] Ibid., p. 90.

Bal'mont's poetry if not the impression of moments," he said, pointing out that Bal'mont rarely used past or future tenses, usually only the present tense.[33] In his notebooks, Bal'mont wrote of his need to live intensely, moment by moment. "I have too rapid a life, and I don't know anyone who would so love the moment as I do. . . . I give myself to the moment, and it again and again reveals fresh meadows to me. And new flowers eternally bloom for me."[34] Nietzsche too, celebrated the moment:

> "Soft! Soft! Has the world not just become perfect?" and "O happiness! O happiness! Would you sing, O my soul? You lie in the grass. But this is the secret solemn hour when no shepherd plays his flute. Take care! Hot noontide sleeps upon the fields! Do not sing! Soft! The world is perfect. Do not sing, you grass-bird, O my soul! Do not even whisper! Just see—soft!—old noontide sleeps, it moves its mouth: has it not just drunk a drop of happiness—an ancient brown drop of golden happiness, of golden wine?" (Z, 238)

To Bal'mont, like Nietzsche, a focus on the present means acceptance of the passions:

> Fate itself decrees our descent
> To the world of passion.
> We do not know a higher happiness—
> And love and want—we must.
>
> And does not life love the present?
> And do not the stars shine behind the mist?
> And does not the burning sun want
> To unite in love with the earth?
>
> And does not the transparent moisture breathe
> Accepting the rays into the depths?
> And does not the newly wed earth await?
> So love. And kiss. And be silent.[35]

Nietzsche used almost the same image to express the intensity of life and its passions in *Thus Spoke Zarathustra*:

[33] Briusov, *Dalekie i blizkie*, p. 74.
[34] "Iz zapisnoi knizhki" (1904), *PSS*, 2:13.
[35] "Otpadenie," *Budem kak solntse*, p. 141.

All sun-love is innocence and creative desire. . . . Just look how it
comes impatiently over the sea! Do you not feel the thirst and the
hot breath of its love? It wants to suck at the sea and drink the sea's
depth up to its heights: now the sea's desire rises with a thousand
breasts. . . . It wants to become air and height and light's footpath,
and light itself.   (Z, 146)

As with Nietzsche (and the French symbolists), Bal'mont's emphasis
upon passion led to a tendency to *épater le bourgeois*. In the poem "In
the House," dedicated to Gorky, Bal'mont scorned bourgeois commitment to duty.

> In the tortuously crowded heaps of houses
> Live ugly pale people,
> Chained by the memory of faded words,
> Who have forgotten about the creative miracle.
>
> All is boring in their lives. If they fall in love,
> Immediately heavy chains are laid on.
> "Well, are you happy?" "It does not matter."
> Oh, yes, nothing could be worse!
>
> And they wither away, locked in their coffins.
> And somewhere birds float through the air.
> What are birds! Wiser than human visions
> Are beetles, spiders, and lice. [36]

He challenged the conventional concepts of good and evil in the same
deliberately provocative tone as Nietzsche, expressing his contempt for
the "good" unequivocably:

> I hate all holy people,—
> They worry tortuously
> About their petty little plans,
> Only about salvation.
>
> They fear for their soul.
> They fear the abysses of dreams,
> And they put to death without pity
> The poisonous snake.

[36] "V domakh," ibid., pp. 80–81.

I would hate heaven.
Among shades with a mild smile,
Where an eternal holiday, an eternal May
Goes along with a measured gait.

I would not want to live in heaven,
Putting to death the snake's cleverness.
From my youth, I loved the Snake,
And admired it, a picture.

I would not want to live in heaven
Amidst exalted dullards.
I perish, perish, and I sing,
An insane demon of lyric dreams.[37]

This poem is in the spirit of Nietzsche's contempt for good little people. The Snake is a reference to Satan's temptation of Eve, and to Nietzsche's Snake as the symbol of Eternity, which Bal'mont prefers to "heaven." Bal'mont approved of Nietzsche's anti-Christian statement: "The saint in whom God takes pleasure is the ideal castrate. Life is at an end where the 'kingdom of God' *begins*" (TI, 45).

In Bal'mont's last collection of poetry before the revolution, *Sonnets of the Sun and the Moon* (*Sonety solntsa, meda i luny*, 1917), there are other references to Nietzsche; "The Birth of Music," for example, echoes Nietzsche's belief that the terrifying impulses of man cannot be separated from man's creative nature.[38]

In sum, we may agree with the poet Innokenty Annensky (1856–1909), who said that there is really no defined philosophy in Bal'mont save his intense estheticism.[39] But it is not the estheticism of Baudelaire or the French symbolists, the idea of *l'art pour l'art*—art as retreat from the world, a concept strongly critized by Nietzsche—which motivated Bal'-mont. Rather it is the idea of the artist-superman who creates himself and the world through the total acceptance of life and the intense experiencing of all of life's passion, pain, and pleasure that dominated Bal'-mont's estheticism. Although Bal'mont's poetry is highly musical and he was aware of Nietzsche's theory of music as the primary vessel of the world force, Bal'mont said little about it. Skriabin, on the other hand,

---

[37] "Golos d'iavola," ibid., p. 180.
[38] *Sonety solntsa, meda i luny: Pesnia mirov* (Moscow, 1917), p. 218.
[39] I. F. Annensky, "Bal'mont-lyrik," in *Kniga otrazhenii* (St. Petersburg, 1906), p. 193.

emphasized this idea. As musician and composer, Skriabin naturally found much of interest in Nietzsche's treatment of music as the embodiment of the heroic, Dionysian force of the universe.

SKRIABIN

In the music and poetry of Alexander Skriabin (1872–1915), the theme of the superman is central. But in Skriabin, Nietzsche's ideas are combined with theosophy. Skriabin began to compose in the 1890s, and by the mid-1900s he was already well known. Around the turn of the century Skriabin became acquainted with Nietzsche's work. One of his friends later recalled that Skriabin was then "greatly attracted" to Nietzsche's concept of the superman: *"Thus Spoke Zarathustra,"* was a phrase often heard from him.[40] Skriabin himself acknowledged the influence of Nietzsche upon his thought. The German journalist Ellen von Tiedebohl recalls that she and Skriabin often spoke of Nietzsche while on concert tour along the Volga in 1910. She was then reading *The Birth of Tragedy.* Skriabin told her of his indebtedness to the book for its treatment of the Dionysian concept of abandon, pleasure, and rapture. "It strengthened my own doctrine," he said.[41] A highly sensual, self-idolizing individual, Skriabin felt an intuitive closeness to Nietzsche's Dionysian superman, in much the same way as Bal'mont conceptualized him: the artist-superman creating himself and the world. This was the major motif of Skriabin's early work. Whether Nietzsche merely strengthened Skriabin's own ideas, or indeed suggested them, is not clear. Wagner also influenced the composer, probably reinforcing the impact of Nietzsche or vice versa. To delineate the precise extent of influence is always a difficult task, but Skriabin himself specifically acknowledged his debt to Nietzsche. Boris Pasternak, a youthful worshipper of Skriabin, whose family lived near the Skriabin family in 1903, remembered the long talks Skriabin had with his father, Leonid Pasternak, a well-known portrait painter. "He argued with Father about life, about art, about good and evil, he attacked Tolstoy, preached the Superman, amorality, Nietzscheanism."[42] Thoroughly conscious of his own great talent, Skriabin sought to express

[40] Iu. Engel', "A. N. Skriabin: Biograficheskii ocherk," *Muzykal'nyi sovremennik*, nos. 4–5 (1916):49.

[41] As quoted by Fabian Bowers, *Scriabin: A Biography of the Russian Composer 1871–1915*, 2 vols. (Tokyo and Palo Alto, 1969), 2:214–15.

[42] Boris Pasternak, *I Remember*, trans. David Magarshack (New York, 1960), p. 37.

the concept of genius in his work. Early in his career, when working on his now well-known "Poem of Ecstasy," Skriabin would often exclaim, as one of his students recalled, "This will be something the world has never known, what I now see and feel will be a great joy, a great celebration."[43] It is easy to see why Skriabin was attracted to the superman Nietzsche preached.

Boris Schloezer, Skriabin's brother-in-law and a music critic, stressed the centrality of the idea of Dionysian ecstasy—from both Nietzsche and Viacheslav Ivanov's interpretation of Nietzsche—in Skriabin's work. Skriabin the man, the artist, and the thinker, Schloezer said, strove to bring mankind to a state of ecstasy through "orgiasm, the way of Dionysus: Through ecstasy and destruction."[44] Interested in philosophy, Skriabin read extensively in the field and owned a large collection of books. Judging from his annotations, he was especially interested in Kant, Fichte, Nietzsche, and Schopenhauer. On Plekhanov's urging, he also read some of Marx's writings but was unimpressed. However, he was fascinated by Helene Blavatsky's doctrine of theosophy. He made copious annotations on his copy of her five-volume work.[45]

As the Soviet scholar Al'shvang noted, Skriabin was unique in the extent of his attempt to express philosophical concepts in music.[46] The librettos show this. N. Vol'ter, who analyzed the music itself, states that there are five basic philosophical themes in Skriabin which have a "real musical content." These are themes of 1) the will; 2) movement, creative play; 3) languishing; 4) contemplation; 5) mysterious forces. Vol'ter came to these conclusions by analyzing Skriabin's very extensive musical directions, comparing certain themes to others whose meaning is known, by studying memoirs and remarks, and by comparing Skriabin's works with the works of other composers.[47] L. Danilevich found eight basic themes in Skriabin's "Poem of Ecstasy": 1) languishing; 2) the dream; 3) the flight; 4) arising creations; 5) anxiety; 6) the will; 7) self-assertion; and 8)

[43] M. Nemenova-Lunts, "Otryvki iz vospominanii o A. N. Skriabine," *Muzykal'nyi sovremennik*, nos. 4–5 (1916):104.

[44] Boris Shletser, "Ob eksatze i deistvennom iskusstve," *Muzykal'nyi sovremennik*, nos. 4–5 (1916):146–49.

[45] See A. Al'shvang, "O filosofskoi sisteme Skrabina," pp. 153–54, and S. Markus, "Ob osobennostiakh i istochnikakh filosofii i estetiki Skriabina," pp. 184–88 in *Aleksandr Nikolaevich Skriabin, 1915–1940: Sbornik k 25 letiiu so dnia smerti* (Moscow and Leningrad, 1940).

[46] Al'shvang, "O filosofskoi sisteme," p. 145.

[47] N. Vol'ter, "Simvolika Prometeia," in *Aleksandr Nikolaevich Skriabin*, p. 116.

protest. The themes of the will and of self-assertion, Danilevich argues, have special significance for the whole; they "personify the heroic principle." In the beginning of the work, the "anxious rhythms," he maintains, symbolize darkness and tragedy in opposition to the heroic themes, but toward the end of the work these rhythms change their emotional significance and gradually unite with the heroic themes.[48]

Skriabin kept secret notebooks, which were published after his death by Michael Gershenzon, a literary critic and historian, in 1919. One of the earliest entries, written about 1900, has a Nietzschean cast: "In order to become an optimist in the true sense of the word, one must experience despair and conquer it."[49] Compare this to Nietzsche in the *The Birth of Tragedy*, where he admires the ancient Greeks for their optimism born of despair: "Is pessimism necessarily a sign of decline, decay; degeneration, weary and weak instincts—as it once was in India and now to all appearances among us, modern men and Europeans? Or is there a pessimism of strength?" (*BT*, 17).

The entry continues as Skriabin addresses life, that unknown force which has deceived him and destroyed his youthful illusions, and speaks of his personal genesis of "tragic philosophy":

> I forgive you and do not murmur against you. I am nevertheless alive, I so love life, love people, I love them all the more because they too suffer because of you. I am going to tell them about my victory over you and over myself. I am going to tell them not to hope in you and not to expect anything from life except what *they themselves can create for themselves*. Thank you for all the horrors of your trials, by this you revealed my infinite power, my limitless might, my inconquerable nature, you gave me victory.[50]

The inspiration for this might well be Nietzsche's *amor fati*: "Affirmation of life even in its strangest and sternest problems, the will to life rejoicing in its own inexhaustibility through the very sacrifice of its highest types . . . (TI, 110).

Indeed, some of Skriabin's entries seem to be borrowed directly from Nietzsche.[51] Some lyrics came directly from out of the Nietzschean jot-

---

[48] L. Danilevich, "Poema ekstaza," in ibid., p. 87.

[49] "Zapiski A. N. Skriabina," *Russkie propilei*, vol. 6, ed. M. Gershenzon (Moscow, 1919), p. 121.

[50] Ibid.

[51] Al'shvang, "O filosofskoi sisteme," p. 152.

tings of his notebooks. In the chorus of the *First Symphony* (1900), Skriabin praises the heroic, uplifting, healing nature of music, much as
Nietzsche did in *The Birth of Tragedy*. Part of Skriabin's libretto is an
ode to music:

> You summon miraculously to life
> The forces fallen in battle,
> In the tired and sick mind
> You give birth to new thoughts.
>
> Your free and mighty spirit
> Reigns omnipotently on earth,
> Man elevated by you
> Gloriously achieves great feats.[52]

Nietzsche's influence is much more apparent, however, in the unfinished opera Skriabin worked on between 1900 and 1903, in which the
hero was to be a combination of Siegfried and the superman. While
Skriabin was working on the opera, he frequently mentioned *Thus Spoke
Zarathustra*. Skriabin's friend, Yuri Engel', a well-known musicologist
and critic, later recalled that the hero of the opera was to have been the
creator-artist who dominates and masters the world, but that Skriabin
constantly changed the plan, which grew larger and more unwieldy as
time went on. Another friend who knew the libretto of Skriabin's "philosophical opera" later recalled it expressed a Nietzschean outlook, but
found it bombastic and extremely sentimental.[53] Although the music has
not survived, part of the libretto is extant. It represents the first manifestation of that constant persona of Skriabin, the artist-superman. The opera opens as a bored, unhappy young princess yearns for the "free spirit"
and the "great bearer of genius." Suddenly a young "philosopher-musician-poet" appears, who says:

> The tender deception of religions
> Does not lull me
> And their tenderly shining mist
> Does not darken my mind.
> My reason, always free,
> Tells me: you are alone;
> You are the slave of cold chance,

[52] *Russkie propilei*, p. 122.
[53] Engel', "A. N. Skriabin," p. 49.

You are the master of all the universe.
Why, oh pitiful mortal,
Do you trust your fate to the Gods?
You can and you yourself must
Bear on your luminous face
The glorious stamp of victory.[54]

The "philosopher-musician-poet" modeled on Zarathustra teaches the princess ecstasy through dance. He calls himself the "apotheosis of the world," the "goal of goals, the end of ends," he has "for a long time possessed the world by [his] strong, daring thought." He is what the princess longs for, the "genius."

The earliest public display of Skriabin's Nietzscheanism appears in the program notes to a concert given in 1901 at which his *Third Piano Sonata* (1898) was performed. The author of the program notes is not known, but that Skriabin knew the text of the notes is certain;[55] it is possible that Skriabin may have himself interpreted the music for the unknown writer of the program notes, since the interpretation given here of the *Third Sonata* corresponds so closely to Skriabin's own notes and to the lyrics Skriabin wrote for the later "Poem of Ecstasy." The program notes to the sonata explain it as an "attempt to incarnate musically certain ideas and aspirations of the human spirit—I would say, the history of moods from Byron to Nietzsche." The first three movements deal with despair, protest, and longing, while the fourth movement culminates in the birth of the "man-god" who will become an "external ideal for strong people."

> . . . from the bowels of the spirit of unhappy, sorrowing mortal man, abandoned by God and alone here on the earth, there arises all that is elementally immortal and powerfully mighty and explodes into freedom out of the darkness of the ages, the darkness of superstition, deception and falsehood which chained the free mind of man, the darkness fostered by slavery and teachings which extinguished joy in his heart; those forces explode, break out, grow into the Man-god—you hear there in the realm of light, a brilliant construction of mighty chords, it rings and resounds with triumph, glorying in the immortal name of fateful centuries!—and, it breaks, the Man-god perishes, struck down by a blind and cold, passionless force—inevitable death. Yes, by death, but the Man-god, condemned to

[54] *Russkie propilei*, pp. 128–29.
[55] A. N. Skriabin, *Pis'ma*, ed. A. V. Kashnerov (Moscow, 1965), p. 259.

death, has the power to tame death, to live and die free! Thus: from the chaos of despair and the doubts of Byron, from the sorrow and the fear of death of Maupassant, from the hopelessness and craving for Nirvana of Leopardi, there grew up a bright, clear, eternally joyous and mighty attitude—grew up, developed, shone through the murk of life, and showed people the single way out of the slavish condition of suppression and submission, and it was borne along and created a place for the new moods that for a long while will be born in the languishing breast of man. But it will shine eternally, the faraway star, the ideal for all strong people who do not want to submit to unknown forces. . . . This last image was conceived in the Alps, at night, during a storm in the mountains.[56]

The idea of the creative genius engendering the universe through Dionysian ecstasy is the central motif of the "Divine Poem" (*Third Symphony*, 1904). Like the "Poem of Ecstasy" (1907), it is imbued with the idea of the individual, creative genius whose Dionysian life instinct creates the world. When Skriabin composed the "Divine Poem" he was vehemently expounding the superman. First performed in Paris in 1905, the piece was accompanied by program notes that had Skriabin's sanction.[57] Again, the theme is the liberation of the human spirit and its engendering of the universe through Dionysian ecstasy. The origin of the world in the "sole power of the creative will" is called "divine play."[58]

The notes written soon before his "Poem of Ecstasy" (originally called "Poème Orgiaque") reveal his musings on the idea of the primacy of the creative genius that he first tried to realize in his unfinished opera. Only "free creation" can destroy the feeling of constraint imposed upon us by time and space; even these, he says, are only processes created by the self. "Everything is my creation. . . . I am only what I create. Everything that exists, exists only in my consciousness."[59] In his rough draft of the "Poem of Ecstasy," he sketched out some preliminary poems: "I am the fire. I am the chaos," one poem reads. He talks to the world, to life, and to his soul much as Nietzsche does in *Thus Spoke Zarathustra*.

You, the cliffs of my rage, you, the tender lines of my caresses, you, the sole twilight of my dream, you, the stars, the lightning flashes

---

[56] Ibid., pp. 258–59.
[57] Engel', "A. N. Skriabin," p. 58.
[58] Ibid.
[59] *Russkie propilei*, pp. 133–37.

of my dreams, you, the sun of my bliss—you are the special expressions of my temporal sensations. . . . Oh, life, oh creative upsurge, / All-creating desire: / You are all. You are the bliss of suffering, and the bliss of joy, and I love both of you equally. You are the ocean of passions, raging, calm. I love your moans. I love your joy (I do not love only despair.) / I am free. I am *nothing*. I want to live. / I want the new, the uncreated. I want to create. I want to create freely. I want to create consciously. I want to be on the heights.

Continuing his half-prose, half-poetry, Skriabin desires to capture and conquer with his creativeness and wild beauty, to be the very brightest light, to be the very greatest sun, to illuminate the universe with his light, to include the whole world in his self. He wants to create the world—past, present, and future—with his feelings. "I am nothing. I am only what I want, I am God."[60]

The sun imagery, the use of the word "height," the acceptance of all suffering and joy, the emphasis on beauty, the desire to be God indicate that Skriabin was echoing Nietzsche's thoughts. Who could not wish to be God, Nietzsche said, shocking his contemporaries—but inspiring Skriabin. In the first sketch of the "Poem of Ecstasy," almost every line begins with the word "I."[61] His preoccupation with his own psyche was reinforced by Nietzsche's writing on the moral validity of egoism.

Skriabin's notebooks also illustrate his ruminations on several Nietzschean topics: the will to power, the individual as the mover of history, the strong over the weak, the "noble enemy," and the perils of *ressentiment*. They express delight in the concept of "ecstasy," derived from Nietzsche's treatment of the Dionysian ecstasy in *The Birth of Tragedy*, and from Ivanov's interpretation of the Dionysian rites. Skriabin exclaims, "I hold dear everything in ecstasy! At last I have found myself. What flights, what a force of expression!"[62] Absolute being, he says, is the "striving for ecstasy."[63]

The "Poem of Ecstasy" is the most intense expression of Skriabin's belief that the world is created by the self, the individual genius, the man-god, whose power is released through the Dionysian forces of ecstasy. The images in the "Poem of Ecstasy" are sensate—flowers, fra-

[60] Ibid., p. 137.
[61] Ibid., pp. 141–43.
[62] Ibid., pp. 159–60.
[63] Ibid., pp. 169–70.

grances, fire, a physical sensation of power. As poetry it is mediocre, but it helps to clarify the meaning Skriabin saw in his music. Creation here, in Skriabin's interpretation of Dionysian ecstasy, has a definite sexual meaning; it is, in fact, procreation. The poem ends with the artist-creator speaking to his world:

I have created you many times,
and I have elevated you,
Legions of feelings,
Oh pure strivings,
I create you,
The complex unity
The feeling of bliss
Which seized all you.
I am the moment, radiating eternity,
I am affirmation.
I am ecstasy.
Fire
Embraces the universe.
Spirit is on the heights of life.
And it feels
The infinite surge of
Divine power,
Of free will.
It is all daring.
What threatened
Now is stimulation.
What horrified
Now is delight,
And the bites of panthers and hyenas
Now are a new caress,
A new torture,
And the snake's sting
Is a burning kiss.
And the universe resounds
In a prolonged cry,
I am![64]

[64] Ibid., pp. 199–201.

In all of these works Skriabin celebrated the heroic feats of the superman-creator, but by the time of his last symphony, "Prometheus" (1910) his focus had shifted from the personal, creative will to the creative principle in general. Now the influence of theosophy with its idea of unseen spiritual forces is manifest as the whole world becomes transformed into the abstract concept of the Creative Principle. Fabian Bowers believes that Skriabin may have joined a secret theosophical cult, the Sons of the Flames of Wisdom, whose members worshipped Prometheus and fire.[65] In the program notes to the symphony written by a close friend and approved by Skriabin, Prometheus and Satan represent the creative energy of the universe.[66] Dionysian ecstasy, associated with the rise and triumph of the creative principle, continues to play an important role.

Toward the end of his life Skriabin planned to write a gigantic communal musical that would celebrate and embody the creative principle of the universe. He originally called this grandiose plan "Mysterium," but gradually, as he worked on it, the preface grew and the work became "Preparatory Activity." Schloezer, who spent much time with Skriabin in this period, writes that the "Mysterium" was to represent the history of the "macrocosmos and microcosmos, the evolution of the worlds and of the human race and of the separate personality."[67] Skriabin worked first on the text, which is extant, and planned to work on the music in 1915. He conceived of his "Preparatory Activity" as a liturgical, theatrical rite in which the spectators would be participants, performing Dionysian dances. This conception was influenced by the theories expounded by Viacheslav Ivanov, then a close friend. Ivanov, inspired by Nietzsche's *Birth of Tragedy*, dreamed of turning the theater into a temple in which the spectators would be like Dionysian participants in the early Greek rituals.[68]

Skriabin's inclination to see grandiose mystical protents was revealed in his reaction to the beginning of the World War I. He viewed it as an event that would renew the spiritual life of mankind and later as the evidence of a spiritual shift occurring on a mystical plane of being.[69] In

[65] Bowers, *Scriabin*, 2:206.

[66] Ibid., pp. 206–207.

[67] B. F. Shletser, "O Predvaritel'nom Deistvii," *Russkie propilei*, pp. 104–105, 107–108, 118.

[68] See chap. 6 in Ann M. Lane, "Nietzsche in Russian Thought 1890–1917" (Ph.D. diss., pp. 215–255, University of Wisconsin, 1976) and Bernice Glatzer Rosenthal, "The Transmutation of Russian Symbolism: Mystical Anarchism and the Revolution of 1905," *Slavic Review* 36 (December 1977), pp. 608–27; and "Theater As Church: The Vision of the Mystical Anarchists," *Russian History* 4, 2 (1977), pp. 122–41.

[69] Shletser, "O Predvaritel'nom Deistvii," p. 112.

"Mysterium" Skriabin hoped to depict the history of the human race as the process of disintegration and absorption of the "Spirit" into matter and its reverse transformation into a triumphant unity, a key theosophic tenet.[70] However, he apparently maintained some remnant of his earlier Nietzschean belief in the "heroic feat" of the individual, for he would often say: "It is absolutely necessary to reveal the cosmic meaning of each personal experience; the history of one feeling, of one aspiration is the history of the universe."[71] Here also, ecstasy has the same meaning as in his earlier works, a liberating, creative force:

> I am the bright joy of the final feat
> I am the scorching diamond in white flame
> I am the unspoken bliss of dissolving
> I am the joy of death, I am freedom, I am ecstasy.[72]

The various voices and choirs represent the Dionysian creative principle, but here it is presented as a cosmological force, not the will to power of the individual personality (as in his earlier works except for "Prometheus"). Skriabin shared in the widespread apocalyptic mood of the time. He spoke of "world conflagration" and he hoped through the "Mysterium" to literally bring on the apocalypse.

Like Bal'mont, Skriabin in his early works emphasized the idea of the hero and superman, and, like Viacheslav Ivanov, Skriabin wanted to revive the Dionysian rituals. Like so many others, Skriabin fell under the spell of Nietzsche's *Birth of Tragedy*, and the charm was not broken by any realization that Nietzsche himself had been dissatisfied with this book in Nietzsche's more rationalistic and self-deprecating moods. Even in an age when extravagant ideas were common, Skriabin, with his vision of himself as Dionysus, superman, and God, was considered by many to be a megalomaniac. Unlike the premonitions of a great and agonizing cataclysm sensed by Blok, Skriabin's vision of the final conflagration was pure celebration.

[70] Ibid., p. 114.
[71] Ibid.
[72] *Russkie propilei*, p. 236.

10.

Art for Philosophy's Sake: Vrubel against "the Herd"

Aline Isdebsky-Pritchard

THE INFLUENCE OF Friedrich Nietzsche (1844–1900) on modern art mirrors his extraordinarily wide-ranging appeal. The Vienna Secession and Barcelona Modernista groups in the 1890s, and in the twentieth century German expressionism, Italian futurism, and the New York School are just a few of the movements that absorbed Nietzschean principles at their inception.[1] The Russian painter Michael Vrubel (1856–1910) belonged to no such movement but was one of the isolated artists who responded to Nietzsche's call for a fierce individualism. He remained something of an outsider and did not consider himself an integral part of any artistic community, even though he participated in such groupings as the Mamontov circle and the World of Art, discussed below. His own productive life was fertile and varied, resulting in a following among both symbolist and formalist Russian artists.

Philosophical issues were among the most pressing in Vrubel's life. One of the major ways in which he changed the course of Russian art was to replace his nineteenth-century predecessors' rhetorical, descriptive, and polemical subjects with metaphysical speculation. He explored the relationship of individual consciousness to a timeless and boundless real-

[1] Carl E. Schorske, *Fin-de-Siècle Vienna* (New York, 1981), pp. 213–45. Ronald W. Johnson, "Picasso's 'Old Guitarist' and the Symbolist Sensibility," *Artforum* 13 (December 1974):56–62. Werner Haftmann, *Painting in the Twentieth Century*, trans. Ralph Manheim, 2 vols., (New York, 1965), 1:87, 103–106. Frederick Levine, *The Apocalyptic Vision* (New York, 1979), pp.11–13, 21–22, 93–108. Dore Ashton, *The New York School* (New York, 1973), pp. 124–29, 185–88.

ity, drawing his inspiration as much from Russian and world literature as from the philosophies of Kant, Schopenhauer, and eventually Nietzsche. The object of this chapter is to define Nietzsche's contribution to Vrubel's work.

Vrubel belonged to the educated upper class. The son of a Russian mother of partly Tatar descent and an officer of Polish extraction in the Russian army, he tended toward Slavophilism. Simultaneously, he assimilated contemporary changes in the artistic climate of the West. He had originally entered the St. Petersburg Academy of Arts as an evening student ca. 1877, then became a full-time student in 1880. By 1882 Paul Chistiakov (1832–1919) became his only professor; the latter insisted on a Renaissance type of form analysis, that is, a study of the underlying geometric structure of volumes, and also retained a classical ideal of subject-matter. Vrubel's determination to apply these principles was the basis of his persistent classicism—which did not prevent his strong objection to traditional dogmas. As he wrote to his sister Ann in 1893, any tradition, "even if it is only fifteen years old like the tradition of our Wanderers [*Peredvizhniki*] is a threat of absolutism."[2] The Wanderers, an artistic association founded in 1870, dominated Russian art at the time of Vrubel's apprenticeship in the 1870s and 1880s. Its members were known as the Travelers or, in a more common translation, the Wanderers, from their traveling exhibits, which were intended to take art directly to the people.[3] Founding members included Nicholas Gay (a French name like Benois), Ivan Kramskoi, Basil Perov, and Ivan Shishkin. They sought to promote social justice by depicting scenes from Russian life and painted in a naturalist version of realism.[4] From the outset, Vrubel repudiated their style, their objectives, and their genre subjects.

While he was still at the Academy, Vrubel received an invitation to design icons and mural paintings, including restoration work, for Kiev's twelfth-century church of St. Cyril's. Work on this commission, 1884–1885, gave Vrubel the opportunity to bypass ordinary Western modes of painting. This event significantly shaped the direction of his art, as he combined the training under Chistiakov with his experience of Byzantine conventions to arrive at a very personal style.[5] His commission com-

[2] E. P. Gomberg-Verzhbinskaia, Iu. V. Novikov, and Iu. N. Podkopaeva *Vrubel, perepiska, vospominaniia o khudozhnike* (Leningrad, 1976), p. 59. Henceforth cited as *Vrubel*.

[3] Their formal name was Association of Traveling Exhibits (Tovarishcheestvo peredvizhnykh khudozhestvennykh vystavok).

[4] See Elizabeth Valkenier, *Russian Realist Art* (Ann Arbor, 1977).

[5] For Vrubel's artistic development see my monograph, *The Art of Mikhail Vrubel* (Ann Arbor, 1982).

pleted, Vrubel remained in Kiev until his move to Moscow in late 1889. Then, he successfully completed a subject which he had abandoned on several previous occasions since 1885, *The Seated Demon* (1890). In this monumental painting, Vrubel made use of his newly developed style in conjunction with archetypal subject matter. For, in addition to an innovative style, the experience of religious painting furthered Vrubel's interest in elemental themes.

During his early years in Moscow Vrubel became part of the circle of the art patron Savva Mamontov (1841–1918), which provided him with a wider scope of activities, such as dramatic production and theater design, ceramics, and even architecture. The circle included members of an older generation such as Basil Polenov and his sister Elena Polenova, Ilia Repin, and Victor Vasnetsov, as well as younger artists such as Constantine Korovin and Valentin Serov, who were among Vrubel's earliest admirers. It was a Slavophile environment where the use of folk motifs and subject-matter were encouraged; however, among Vrubel's extant work, only one watercolor of this type, *The Snow-Maiden* (ca. 1892), probably belongs to the early 1890s.

Many of Vrubel's best-known works, among them the ones to be discussed in relation to Nietzsche's possible influence, belong to a later phase of Vrubel's Moscow period, which came to a tragic close with his mental and physical breakdown. His state first became evident in 1902 and culminated in total blindness in February 1906. In spite of his illness and his confinement in psychiatric clinics, Vrubel continued to be active as an artist until the blindness prevented it. Among his last works is the well-known *Portrait of the Poet Valerius Briusov* (1906).

The similarity between Vrubel's and Nietzsche's catastrophic decline is only one of the parallels in their lives and temperaments. Both lost a parent and a younger brother at an early age and remained intensely loyal to the memory of the absent parent—his mother in Vrubel's case. Their difficult relationship with the surviving parent in maturity, in each instance, set their spirited quests for individuation into sharp relief. Both died in their mid-fifties after many years of deteriorating health, possibly caused by syphilis.[6] Among the differences between them was Vrubel's more sociable disposition and his love of women. At the age of forty he

---

[6] Diagnoses of both Nietzsche and Vrubel are inconclusive. Kaufmann states that Nietzsche suffered "almost certainly" from atypical general paralysis. Ronald Hayman is less certain and speculates on the possibility of congenital syphylis or even self-induced psychosis. Walter Kaufmann, *Nietzsche: Philosopher, Psychologist, Antichrist* (Princeton, 1974), p. 69. Ronald Hayman, *Nietzsche, a Critical Life* (1980; rpt. Harrisonburg, Va., 1982), *passim*. Vrubel's case is equally complex: *Art of Vrubel*, pp. 11–18, 30–32.

married the talented young opera singer, Nadezhda Zabela (1868–1913). Vrubel shared more than personal traits with Nietzsche, however. Born only twelve years later, he also belonged to a generation confronted with the implications of Darwin's treatises (especially *The Origin of Species*, 1859, and *The Descent of Man*, 1879), which dislodged God and humanity from their central cosmological positions. For Vrubel as for Nietzsche, in *Thus Spoke Zarathustra* for example, all life became imbued with a consciousness of process, of evolution, of transfiguration. Vrubel's fascination with the artistic process meant that he often left behind him, destroyed, or overpainted works of art in search of new ideas. Metamorphosis became Vrubel's subject in works such as *Lilacs*. His working method was grounded in experimentation. As early as 1883, while still at the Academy but painting independently in his own studio, he considered artistic activity to be an elucidation of "a series of interesting, clearly defined, and resolved problems."[7]

Experimentation was among the most fundamental attitudes shared by Nietzsche and Vrubel. Nietzsche writes of life as "an experiment of the seeker for knowledge." (GS, 225). Elsewhere, this concept pervades his writings as advocacy of the "free spirit," of self-overcoming and self-creation, of the revaluation of values and the creation of new ones. For Vrubel the experimental resources at his disposal were summed up in the word "technique." For many years he believed that the artistic value of a subject depended more on the validity of its expressive form, or technique than on content. No one with some interest in the arts could ignore the question in Russia, since the influential Wanderers and their mentor, the critic Vladimir Stasov, had dedicated art to social progress.[8] As a twenty-year-old law student in St. Petersburg, Vrubel joined other young members of his family circle in debating this issue. The two theoretical works that Vrubel mentions in his correspondence to his parents coincide broadly with the opposing viewpoints represented in their group.[9] One attitude, shared by most of Vrubel's relations, supported the Wanderers' "utilitarian view of art," and echoed the anarchist thinker Pierre Proudhon's *Du principe de l'art et de sa destination sociale*. The book, published in Russia in 1866 only a year after its original appearance, was a tribute to Proudhon's friend the painter Gustave Courbet, whose working-class subjects he interpreted politically, praising them as "socialist

[7] Letter to his sister, in *Vrubel*, p. 43.
[8] Valkenier, *Russian Realist Art*, pp. 56–73.
[9] *Vrubel*, p. 65.

painting." In view of Vrubel's later violent opposition to Tolstoi's stand on art, as the antithesis to Nietzsche's, it is revealing to find passages in Proudhon that anticipate Tolstoi. He considered "art for art's sake" to be a frivolous deception, myth, and mirage. On the other hand, Courbet's *Stone-Breakers* (now destroyed) was "morality in action," and worthy of being set up on a church altar.[10]

In these debates Vrubel was "almost alone in defending the cause of 'art for art's sake.'" The second text he mentions, Gotthold Lessing's *Laocoön* (1766), also discusses the function of the artist but from an internal rather than a social standpoint. Lessing maintained that Horace's motto "*ut pictura poesis* (as is art, so is poetry)," which for centuries had validated the subjects of painters by equating them with those of poets, was quite flawed. The poet, he pointed out, appeals to the ear and to the imagination, while the sculptor and the painter use "forms and colors in space" to show the "visible properties [which] are the peculiar subjects of painting," and it is their skill of execution in these areas that is significant.[11] Vrubel, as it happens, had a rare gift for evoking visually those spheres which Lessing reserved to poets, namely imagination and the passage of time. Nonetheless, for well over two decades following these debates he insisted on his unique interest in "art for art's sake," which he interpreted as formal experimentation. He first expressed this experimental quest in letters of 1883, before he could have read or even known about Nietzsche. He characterized the modern artist as "an independent adult who insists energetically on the independence of his rights" instead of imitating the past.[12] In his view, the artist was a specialist whose function was to celebrate and share with the public "nature as form," in all its subtle "infinitely harmonious, marvellous details."[13] Above all, form was "the most important content of plastic art."[14] Even in 1890, while preparing to paint one of his most introspective subjects, *The Seated Demon*, he was still writing: "only one thing is clear to me, that my quest is exclusively in the area of technique. This is the arena where the specialist must exert himself."[15]

[10] Linda Nochlin, ed., *Realism and Tradition in Art 1848–1900* (Englewood Cliffs, N.J., 1966), pp. 50–53.

[11] Lorenz Eitner, ed., *Neoclassicism and Romanticism 1750–1850*, 2 vols. (Englewood Cliffs, N.J., 1970), 1:26.

[12] Letter to his sister, in *Vrubel*, p. 39.

[13] Ibid., p. 37.

[14] Ibid.

[15] Ibid., p. 55.

By 1890 Vrubel had perfected the crystalline compression of planes and bold synthesis of volumes that were the most characteristic features of his style, as examplified by *The Seated Demon*. He nevertheless always retained his experimental attitude toward technique, even after abruptly reversing his exclusive emphasis on formal expression. While he was working on *The Demon Cast Down* (1901–1902), the dialectical balance of his thinking suddenly veered toward content as his sister-in-law, Katherine Gay (1859–1918) recorded in her diary on 2 March 1902. "His tastes have completely changed. Now he despises artists who are not interested in subject-matter or even in words, whereas before, he recognized only 'art for art's sake.' "[16]

This shift in opinion, corresponding as it did to the period when Vrubel commented on his admiration for "the German genius," Nietzsche, undoubtedly derived from his reading of the philosopher. While the details of Vrubel's knowledge of Nietzsche remain obscure, it can be assumed that a primary text was *The Birth of Tragedy*, which has been of exceptional interest to visual artists, despite its emphasis on drama and music. Nietzsche's claim that "it is only as an *aesthetic phenomenon* that existence and the world are eternally *justified*" (BT, 52) was certainly one of the primary reasons. Furthermore, Nietzsche reversed a previous assumption, that art echoes national character. Instead, he assigned to it— or to the creators of Greek tragedy—the more dynamic function of actually transforming life. He suggested that if Greek artists of the past had assumed the supreme task of creating new values, artists of the present and future could duplicate this feat. They had the possibility of redeeming modern life through the regenerative powers of art. "I am convinced," wrote Nietzsche, "that art represents the highest task and the truly metaphysical activity of this life" (BT, 31–32). In this context, Vrubel no longer had any reason to deny the metaphysical content, which had permeated his art from the beginning. Even his first major independent painting, *Hamlet and Ophelia* (1884), had examined questions of "consciousness of the infinite."

Vrubel's knowledge of Nietzsche, like much else in his ideology, is not documented by systematic statements but only through fragmentary evidence derived from correspondence, rough notes for his own use, mem-

---

[16]Katherine Gay, "The Last Years of Vrubel's Life" ("Poslednie gody zhizni Vrubelia"), in V*rubel*, p. 279. The painter Nicholas Gay had been the father-in-law of Katherine Gay, Vrubel's wife's sister. The Vrubels spent their summers with Katherine and her husband Peter at the painter's former country home in the Ukraine.

oirs about him, and the context of his work. In all probability, Vrubel's awareness of Nietzsche precedes the few references to him of 1901 and 1902 which are now available. Although he lived mainly in Moscow, Vrubel often came in touch with St. Petersburg personalities for whom Nietzsche was a great source of interest at an earlier time. In the mid-1890s, while he was part of the circle of the art patroness Margaret Morozova, he may have met the writer Dmitry Merezhkovsky who also attended her salon. If he did not, as a voracious reader he is certain to have known the works of this literary symbolist, who treated Nietzschean themes as early as 1890.[17] Members of the World of Art (Mir Iskusstva) group whose publication and exhibitions prominently displayed the work of Vrubel, and whose journal included articles on Nietzsche from its first year of publication in 1899, were part of Vrubel's entourage from late 1897. The founder of the group, Serge Diaghilev, at that time chose Vrubel's decorative panel *Morning* as the centerpiece of a major exhibition that opened in January 1898.[18] As a result of these contacts, it seems likely that Vrubel read the Russian translations of Nietzsche when they appeared in 1898, since his considerable linguistic accomplishments did not include ease in reading German.[19]

Vrubel's recorded allusions to Nietzsche, which do not occur until the approach of his first mental breakdown in 1902, project all the more clearly the centrality of Nietzsche's teachings in the inner conflicts that perturbed his emotional life at that time. A letter of February 1902 to Gay, referring to Nietzsche not by name but as "the German genius," implies earlier conversations on the subject.[20] His praise of Nietzsche is followed by an attack on Christianity as well as on Tolstoi and his followers. This message is couched in strange, intemperate language.

> While science is disclosing the widest horizons of "necessities" and the German genius has shown how impotent and wretched are invented "possibilities" as opposed to "necessity," the dear herd with Tolstoi at its head finds it timely to regurgitate one of the "possibilities" and chews over this rough leftover gruel which once had the quality of true nourishment. . . . [The herd] is trying with rigid malice to protect its half-vision from the bright light. Faced with the

[17] Bernice Glatzer Rosenthal, *D. S. Merezhkovsky and the Silver Age* (The Hague, 1975), pp. 56–68.

[18] Exhibition of Russian and Finnish Artists, St. Petersburg.

[19] Letter to his sister, in *Vrubel*, p. 41.

[20] Ibid., p. 95. The letter is undated but the content makes its chronology clear.

pathetic, it longs for its dear belchings and for the cud of the commonplace minutiae of naturalism.

Vrubel, who had previously expressed a sense of obligation to his public,[21] now considered his unresponsive viewers a Nietzschean "herd." He
blamed its addiction to Christianity and to the commonplaces of naturalism on the leadership of Leo Tolstoi, who had published his polemical
article "What is Art?" in 1898. Tolstoi's position in that essay is that only
art that is easily understood by the masses is not "counterfeit."[22] Works
of some complexity such as the writings of Shakespeare, Goethe, and
Ibsen, all revered by Vrubel, were false "brainspun, invented works."[23]
According to Tolstoi, only two criteria applied to the evaluation of art,
and, as he noted himself, they amounted to only one, a moral criterion:
the work of art should inspire either a religious perception of universal
brotherhood, or a lay feeling of common humanity.[24]

Vrubel's letter clearly addresses these criteria when referring to Christianity as an outworn creed now being spewed out by Tolstoi and his
followers, who also cling to their artistic half-vision. Definitions of Vrubel's special philosophic terminology, used in this letter, occur in notes
of the same period used in preparation for a lecture at the Stroganov Art
School, Moscow.

> "Necessity" is portentous and infinite. It is an attribute of "object."
> "Subject"—consciousness—flops around in this boundless ocean and
> imagines that it can swallow it. Each gulp is a "possibility." Count
> up the number of little gulps.
>
> And how foolish man is when he thinks that one of his pitiful
> "possibilities" is welded to "necessity": (love your neighbor as your-
> self, equality in relations). Toys.[25]

According to these notes "necessity" is eternal and infinite but "possibilities" are countless. One of these pitiful possibilities, Vrubel explains with
Nietzschean contempt, is the Christian maxim "love your neighbor as
yourself." Vrubel's outlook on Christianity as an obsolete mass delusion

---

[21] Ibid., pp. 37–38, 50.
[22] Lev N. Tolstoi, "What is Art?" *The Novels and Other Works,* trans. Aylmer Maude,
22 vols. (New York, 1902), vol. 19.
[23] Ibid., p. 450.
[24] Ibid., pp. 487–93.
[25] P. Suzdalev, "On Vrubel's Worldview" ("O mirovozrenii Vrubelia"), *Art (Iskusstvo)* 11
(1976) p. 59. The undated notes belong to the 1901–2 period.

combined his rejection of Tolstoi's criteria of art with his attraction to
Nietzsche.

Vrubel's attitude had been rather different in 1887, when he first realized that his Christian faith was waning in the absence of his family. A
letter to his sister at that time, indicating sadness at his loss of faith,
contrasts with his later angry rejection of Christian values.[26] The unrealized watercolor projects of the same year for the decoration of the new
cathedral of St. Vladimir, Kiev, including several versions of *The Lam-
entation over the Body of Christ*, imply a high degree of religious empa-
thy, as they are masterpieces of Christian transcendental art. It is evident
that the virulent anti-Christian bias that Vrubel later acquired was the
result of a serious inner crisis, which was never resolved. However readily
Vrubel consciously accepted Nietzsche's harsh judgment of Christian values, the specter of religious sin and guilt subconsciously haunted him,
quite literally in the form of voices, after his breakdown of 1902. During
interludes of health and artistic activity he continued to borrow iconog-
raphy from biblical archetypes such as *The Six-Winged Seraph* (1904),
The Vision of the Prophet Ezekiel (1906), and even the figure of Christ
in *The Meeting at Emmaus* (1904).

The rejection of "equality in relations," Vrubel's second example of
"possibilities" mistaken for "necessity," is closely related to his denunci-
ation of the Christian golden rule and also contrasts with his former behavior. While it is true that he had sometimes taken pleasure in stressing
his virtuoso facility as an artist over that of his friends, the position taken
here is of a different order, unlike the earlier innate gentleness and egalitarianism described by his contemporaries. Now, his resolutely antidemocratic stance even brought him to blows.[27] Aside from a heightened
irritability and lack of control, Vrubel's new stand demonstrates his read-
iness to test previous assumptions "beyond good and evil," to the point
of accepting Nietzsche's distinction between higher and lower men. Once
again, this may have been prompted by Tolstoi and his insistence on
judging art according to its ability to unite "all men in one common
feeling."[28] Vrubel, like Nietzsche, believed in intensely cultivating individual differences. Individual psychology was explored in depth in his
1890–1891 illustrations to the narrative poem "The Demon" by Michael
Lermontov and later, under Nietzsche's influence, in the painting *The*

[26]*Vrubel*, p. 50.
[27]Gay, "Last Years," pp. 277–78.
[28]"What is Art?" p. 495.

Demon Cast Down. This Demon, as Vrubel explained to Gay, represented "much that is strong, even elevated in man . . . which people consider it a duty to cast out as the result of Christian Tolstoian ideas.[29]

In "What Is Art?" Tolstoi also savagely attacked symbolist art and poetry as bad art "absolutely unintelligible both in form and substance."[30] Vrubel's indignation with these views comes to light in a key passage of his "German genius" letter to Gay.

> At a time when art is trying with all its might to illusionize the soul [*illuzionirovat*, a Vrubel neologism], to awake it from the trifles of the commonplace through powerful imagery, [the herd] is trying with rigid malice to protect its half-vision.

This text assigns an entirely new role to the artist, whose task is no longer limited to the transmutation of nature into form as Vrubel had concluded earlier. Now, art must illuminate and transform the soul of the viewer through powerful imagery.

In practice, however, the change was more theoretical than real. Just as formal problems continued to function prominently in Vrubel's art, so from the earliest days of his artistic independence in St. Petersburg, he had been engrossed in the exploration of new iconographic content. His oil painting of 1884, *Hamlet and Ophelia* (Fig. 1), introduced some of the themes he elaborated over the years. Like many of Vrubel's works, it was left unfinished, and this allows the present-day viewer to read the artist's notes to himself; these are inscribed directly into the background paint and would certainly have been covered over if the picture had been completed. His words give ample proof of his immersion in metaphysical questions at that time—questions that he did not hesitate to transform into imagery. As transcribed by the Russian art historian P. Suzdalev, the inscription reads in part:

Consciousness
1   of the infinite. confusion of the notions about human dependence.
2   of life. The infinite and dogma, the infinite and science . . .[31]

These words clarify the relationship between Vrubel's metaphysical interests and his often tangential use of subject-matter.[32] Instead of dramatiz-

[29] Gay, "Last Years," p. 276.
[30] Cf. Nietzsche on symbolism in *The Birth of Tragedy*, p. 40.
[31] Suzdalev, "On Vrubel's Worldview," p. 59.
[32] For a detailed discussion of *Hamlet and Ophelia* see *Art of Vrubel*, pp. 61–65.

Fig. 1 HAMLET AND OPHELIA, 1884. Oil on canvas, 120 × 89 cm. The Russian Museum, Leningrad.

ing the action of Shakespeare's play, as earlier artists had done—Dela-
croix is the best known—Vrubel borrows its characters in order to speculate
on the nature of consciousness. Hamlet's introspection and his questioning proclivity become a paradigm for the artist-philosopher. Vrubel's own
fascination with Kant's philosophy in that period focused upon the interplay between individual consciousness and the nature of reality. As the
inscription demonstrates, however, his concerns reached beyond Kant's
own emphasis on observable phenomena to encompass also "the infinite." In his painting Vrubel investigates both of these factors. The keen
attention that the visual artist pays to the outside world is represented by
Hamlet as a painter at work; he sits in the foreground, looking out to his
surroundings while he draws on a pad. Ophelia, on the other hand,
stands immobile beside him with her eyelids lowered in a dreamlike trance
as she contemplates an inner vision. Together, Hamlet, whose glance
analyzes the surrounding world, and Ophelia, who penetrates inner reality (the infinite), reach out to the essence of existence; the inscription's
primary concern with consciousness forecasts also Vrubel's lasting attention to its obverse, the unconscious, as portrayed by Ophelia. Vrubel's
related preoccupation with the infinite, knowable only through the inner
life, as the essential reality against which all else must be measured,
lasted even after he came under Nietzsche's influence.

The continuing importance of the infinite for Vrubel is clearly stated
in his Stroganov School lecture notes of 1902, where the ultimate goal
of artistic activity is defined as the contemplation of the infinite or all-
encompassing "necessity." Such contemplation was not part of Nietzsche's
philosophical position, but he accepted some such intuitive knowledge
on the artistic level. Even though Nietzsche later ceased to give art the
dominant position it held in his first book, *The Birth of Tragedy*, his
initial faith in art as "the truly metaphysical activity of this life" was
always retained by Vrubel.

In 1888 Vrubel again took up the subject of *Hamlet and Ophelia* in a
small oil painting that is nevertheless monumental in conception. He
again bypassed the Shakespearean text but abandoned his earlier concern
with the duality of consciousness and the unconscious. Instead, he anticipated the unified primeval world to be found in his paintings of ca.
1900. This painting differs from the later ones such as *Pan* or *The Swan-
Princess* in portraying a couple. A Dionysian rapture is conveyed by the
two lovers who face one another at a slight distance. As Hamlet and
Ophelia seem to rise slowly out of the ground, their dark-blue silhouettes

and silvery faces set against the sea and moonlit sky cohere with the elemental forces of nature. There is no question here of influence, as Vrubel could not yet have known Nietzsche or his interpretation of the Dionysian ecstasy. Rather, this painting, as well as *The Seated Demon*, painted two years later, whose body merges in similar fashion with its natural surroundings, suggest an affinity of spirit that Vrubel nurtured in later paintings.

Having completed his task at St. Cyril's in 1885, Vrubel embarked upon a search for a substantial iconographic theme which resulted in his choice of the Lermontov poem, or group of poems, "The Demon.' The subject proved to be so rich as a symbol of the process of individuation and all its metaphysical connotations which Vrubel wished to probe, that it remained a major part of his art until 1905.[33] With the Demon, as he explained to his friends, Vrubel wished to embody his conception of the human soul. "It incarnates the eternal struggle of the mutinous human spirit seeking the reconciliation of its stormy passions with a knowledge of life; it finds no answer to its doubts either on earth or in heaven."[34]

These inner conflicts, with their resulting ambiguities and contradictory actions described in Lermontov's poems, are vividly depicted by Vrubel in his illustrations to the Kushnerev jubilee edition of the poet's work (1891). In all his images of the Demon over the years, Vrubel resolved the problem of this soul's divided nature, unquestionably masculine in the poem, by representing it as androgynous.[35] The Demon of the book illustrations is a disjointed, frenzied being.[36] On the other hand, the large canvas of 1890, *The Seated Demon* (Fig. 2), offers a very different image. Although, once again, there is every reason to assume that Vrubel was not yet acquainted with Nietzsche,[37] his *Seated Demon* curiously anticipates Nietzsche's thesis in *The Birth of Tragedy*. One might surmise that, as in that book, the soul's reconciliation between the Apollonian spirit of "measured restraint" and "freedom from the wilder emotions," and a Dionysian immersion into nature's "mysterious primordial unity" (*BT*, 35–37) is the subject of the painting. The thoughtful *Seated Demon* has

[33] Ibid., chap. 5.

[34] N. A. Prakhov, "Mikhail Aleksandrovich Vrubel," in *Vrubel*, p. 195.

[35] C. G. Jung writes: "Perhaps the majority of cosmogenic gods are of a bisexual nature." With time, their function "has become a symbol of the creative union of opposites." *Psyche and Symbol*, ed. Violet S. de Laszlo (Garden City, N.Y., 1958), p. 139.

[36] *Art of Vrubel*, pp. 95–114.

[37] S. Iaremich reports that just then, in 1890–1891, Vrubel was full of enthusiasm for Schopenhauer. *Mikhail Aleksandrovich Vrubel* (Moscow, 1911), p. 116.

Fig. 2 THE SEATED DEMON, 1890. Oil on canvas, 115 × 212.5 cm. Tretiakov Gallery, Moscow.

Apollonian qualities of quiet self-containment in spite of his profound sadness. At the same time, his fusion with the ground, his vegetal hands, and the magnificent flowers that enfold him indicate that he is a Dionysian Demon, closely bound to elemental earthly powers. The "demonic" soul, which Vrubel wanted to project in his painting, still depicted the interplay between two types of knowledge, that of consciousness and of the infinite.

Vrubel was even then planning a larger and more definitive statement on the subject of the Demon, but he kept postponing its execution from year to year. He might possibly never have returned to it at all, had it not been for Nietzsche's concept of the overman, which he portrayed in two colossal canvases, neither of them ever completed. Nietzsche's influence as the source of Vrubel's two paintings, *The Flying Demon* and *The Demon Cast Down*, can be deduced from the Nietzsche–Tolstoi polarity which agitated Vrubel during this period, the end of 1898 to the spring of 1902.[38] The evidence includes the anti-Tolstoi comments concerning the meaning of *The Demon Cast Down*, already cited. Also significant is a passage in a letter dated 24 September 1901, where Vrubel's wife, with whom he shared his artistic ideas, wrote with disappointment that the painting no longer represented Lermontov's Demon but some extraordinary "contemporary Nietzschean being."[39]

Vrubel first returned to the subject with *The Flying Demon* (Fig. 3), a painting of unusual format (138.5 × 430.5 cm, or approximately 4½ ft. high × 14 ft. wide), on which he worked intermittently from the last month of 1898 to early 1901. This impressive composition, which shows the Demon with wings and body spread out at intersecting diagonals across the canvas as the figure surges forward, high above the Caucasian peaks, was unfortunately abandoned at a relatively early stage. Vrubel's correspondence contains few references to the painting and no commentary; but its link to the better-documented painting that followed is clear. When Vrubel subjected this next painting, *The Demon Cast Down*, to constant, seemingly compulsive changes, the Demon was often shown again as flying rather than cast down.[40] The image of flying stems directly from Lermontov's narrative poem. In the opening stanzas he describes the Demon's alienation from the universe, symbolized by relentless flight. Vrubel reflects this alienation in the Demon's rigid features but he also shifts

[38] Letter to his sister, in V*rubel*, pp. 55–56.
[39] P. Suzdalev, V*rubel and Lermontov* (V*rubel i Lermontov*) (Moscow, 1980), p. 172.
[40] Gay, "Last Years," p. 278.

the meaning from an image of self-revelation to a Nietzschean assertion of the self. The Demon's high altitude becomes an affirmation of the struggle needed to rise over the herd and over oneself, to become the *Übermensch*. Nietzsche, who uses the metaphor of mountain heights repeatedly, describes the process specifically on several occasions as learning to fly (Z, 68, 213, 236; GS, 100–101). Yet, the Demon's features are anguished. He does not suggest the Apollonian calm of the *Seated Demon* and, inevitably, he has lost Dionysian rootedness. It was perhaps Vrubel's difficulty in visualizing the state of perfection attained by the overman which prompted him to seek a new interpretation.

In *The Flying Demon* and later representations, Vrubel retained his previous motif of androgyny to represent the soul. Since the German *Übermensch* has connotations of the "overhuman" or "more than human," rather than being linked to male gender as might appear to be the case in English translation, Nietzsche's word image and Vrubel's visualization coincided in this respect.

The Demon Cast Down (Fig. 4) occupied Vrubel continuously from the fall of 1901 to the spring of 1902. It is about a foot shorter in width than the preceding canvas but otherwise identical in format. The Demon is no longer soaring over the world; instead, he has crashed down into the mountainous depths. He nonetheless remains embattled and enmeshed in an astonishing range of emotions. Though his body is laid back against the wings, like that of a helpless insect, it is still diagonally set for flight. His distended features, even while reflecting anger, suffering, and anxiety, also show an imperious pride of being. Knowing that Vrubel welcomed all contradictory aspects of existence in his own life, the Demon's spirited reaction to his fall into the abyss appears to be a manifestation of Nietzschean *amor fati*.[41] In this version of the painting, the Demon no longer dominates the viewer's total field of vision. His slim, rigid, misshapen figure is caught in a huge primordial mass of chaotic forms which surge beneath and around him in endless movement. Nor is the Demon entirely alone: his isolation is coupled with the presence of unseen adversaries. One implicit enemy is Milton's God from *Paradise Lost*—whose image of the fallen Satan Vrubel borrowed for his rebellious Demon. The others, as Vrubel's comments to Gay indicate, are Tolstoi and his herd of followers. Though the mountainous masses threaten to engulf his slender body, an innate majesty and "the will to

---

[41] Iaremich, *Vrubel*, pp. 173–74.

power" maintain his head in an upright position, raised high in defiance of his enemies. The image thus strangely blends moral victory with a measure of defeat. Vrubel had concluded that, in Russia at least, "the strong" and "the elevated in man" were being cast down by Tolstoi's championing of mediocrity. He felt acutely isolated as an artist and perhaps Nietzsche's books fostered a perception of futility in his struggle as a "free spirit" even as they encouraged him to renew the conflict. Nietzsche's praise of the creator's tragic sense of life coincided with Vrubel's vision of the Demon. The philosopher's principle of the revaluation of values finds an echo in Vrubel's denial of outworn Tolstoian "possibilities" in religion and art. This response is translated visually into the prominent, brightly colored spiky crown that circles the Demon's head. The counterpart to Christ's crown of thorns, it marks the Demon as Nietzsche's Antichrist. The Antichrist's values of joy in struggle, in resistance, and "the preservative instincts of strong life" (A, 115–17), are all reflected in *The Demon Cast Down*.

The depth of emotion invested in the painting is evident in its expressionist energy of thickly built-up, deeply textured pigments and glowing hues, despite much color fading. Directly and vividly, they accentuate the fragmented movement of the heaving shapes that reflect the psychological turmoil tearing apart the world of the Demon—and Vrubel's. The sad fact is that Vrubel's feverish work on the painting coupled with his adoption of Nietzsche's values proved to be very harmful to him. While he was at work on *The Demon Cast Down*, his always fragile emotional balance gave way to a disintegration of the personality, which led to his first psychiatric hospitalization in April 1902. The poet Alexander Blok, one of Vrubel's most perceptive admirers, was awed, grateful, and alarmed for all symbolist artists by Vrubel's example. He realized that Vrubel's free access to infernal inner "lilac twilight worlds," what we post-Freudians would more prosaically call a surrender of ego restraints, had endangered his very life.[42] Whether or not the painting was, in actuality, a cause or an effect of the coming emotional collapse, it is certain that the two were inextricably entangled.

The Demon Cast down with its allusions to later principles of Nietzsche—his overman, his Antichrist—reflects the darkest aspect of the philosopher's legacy to Vrubel: an obsessively self-absorbed will to power. As noted previously, one may speculate that the earlier *Birth of Tragedy*,

[42] Alexander Blok, "On the Present State of Russian Symbolism" ("O sovremonnom sostoianii russkogo simvolisma"), *Apollon* 8 (1910):21–30.

Fig. 3 THE FLYING DEMON, 1898–1901. Oil on canvas, 138.5 × 430.5 cm. The Russian Museum, Leningrad.

Fig. 4 The Demon Cast Down, 1901–1902. Oil on canvas, 139 × 387 cm. Tretiakov Gallery, Moscow.

with its affirmation of the artist's fundamental role in national consciousness, represents a happier facet of Nietzsche's influence. It is tempting to
conclude that the book also affected Vrubel's accelerated turn to folk
material in the late 1890s. During this period Vrubel further developed
the folk imagery that differs so markedly both from the descriptive and
imitative folk motifs of his associates in the Mamontov circle and from
the anecdotal fauns and naiads of such Westerners as von Stuck and
Böcklin. By contrast, Vrubel, in the spirit of Nietzsche's comments in
The Birth of Tragedy, presented his folk figures as manifestations of primordial myth. Moreover, in many instances these primordial figures move
in an environment that reflects another Nietzschean theme: the interde-
pendent flow of time and life. At the very least, these analogies once
more suggest a genuine affinity in temperament between Nietzsche and
Vrubel. It is more probable that the folk images that Vrubel had been
using for some years now emerged as a major subject under the impetus
of his readings of Nietzsche, just as the Demon, always on his mind, was
now taken up again and used in new ways.

Vrubel first expressed interest in folk material when he joined the Mamontov circle. In 1896, he chose the heroes of the epic tale *Mikula
Selianinovich and Volga* as the subjects of a gigantic mural painting on
canvas, now lost, for the Nizhnii-Novgorod fair. In 1897 the monumental painting *Morning,* now known as *Russalky* (Water Nymphs), marked
a totally original approach to the subject. It depicts the nymphs merging
with the surrounding fluid habitat and its vegetation. In 1898 Vrubel, in
his zeal to confirm his new friendship with the composer Rimsky-Korsa-
kov, in whose operas his wife performed major roles, attributed to his
influence the decision to devote himself to folk subjects.[43] Rimsky-Kor-
sakov did in fact inspire numerous works, including two important paintings derived from Zabela's roles in *Tsar Saltan* and in *Sadko: The Swan-
Princess* (Fig. 5), and *The Sea-Princess Volkhova.* but this was only part
of the story. There were other folk subjects.

Vrubel's *Bogatyr* (Fig. 6), or Russian epic hero (1898–1899), whose
huge mass is welded to that of his flying horse, further explores the implications suggested in *Russalky.* The particular *bogatyr* represented here
is Ilia Muromets, celebrated in a twelfth-century chant, a hero with magical powers whose strength springs directly from the earth. The horse,
which is suspended over treetops, forms a single unit not only with its

[43] *Vrubel,* p. 88.

Fig. 5 THE SWAN-PRINCESS, 1900. Oil on canvas, 142.5 × 93.5 cm. Tretiakov Gallery, Moscow.

Fig. 6 Bogatyr, 1898. Oil on canvas, 321 × 222 cm. The Russian Museum, Leningrad.

rider but also with the colors and textures of tree bark, foliage, and even birds. In spite of his position in the sky, this powerful hero is not the overman, the rebellious man of the future who has revalued all values, but rather his opposite, a personification of the eternal values of Dionysus. The vitality of the figure and his mount was a deliberate message Vrubel intended to convey to his public, as we learn from a letter of January 1899. Vrubel was certain, he wrote, that the values inherent in his *Bogatyr* would refute the assumption of the critics and the public that "I am, after all, a certified decadent. But this is a misunderstanding."[44] This may be understood in two senses. First, Vrubel's critics had labeled his work decadent, a term which they associated with all symbolist styles in Russia. Furthermore, Nietzsche's own target throughout his writings was the decadence of modern man, his institutions, and art. Vrubel's life-affirming intentions were directed here at portraying a hero whose potency, like that of the followers of Dionysus, derived from chthonic energies.

The interaction between nature and the various forms that it assumes becomes a metaphor, in many paintings, for eternal flux. Again, this tendency in Vrubel's art did not originate with Nietzsche's influence. Even as early as 1886 the figure represented in *Girl against the Background of a Persian Carpet* seems to be contained within a vortex of elusive metamorphic forces in motion. Vrubel was no doubt encouraged to explore this motif by Nietzsche's doctrine of eternal recurrence, as reflected in *Thus Spoke Zarathustra,* whose third part concludes with the sevenfold refrain: "For I love you, O eternity!" In describing the eternal recurrence, Nietzsche writes: "the complex of causes in which I am entangled will recur—it will create me again! . . . I shall return eternally to this identical and self-same life" (Z, 244–47, esp. 237).

A very similar celebration of invisible forces at work—mysterious forces that dissolve nature's entities only to reunite them just as silently again— pervades Vrubel's paintings and ceramics of ca. 1900 and later. One example is his large *Lilacs* (1900) (Fig. 7), a study in latent metamorphosis. The figure of a young girl hovers in the foreground plane, in front of masses of blooming lilacs. Her features are faint, her colors less substantial than those of the blossoms. It seems as if she will instantly recede

---

[44] Letter to his sister, in *Vrubel,* p. 62. In April 1898, Vrubel had toasted Princess Tenisheva for patronizing "the so-called decadence, which I hope will soon be recognized as a renaissance." Gay, "Last Years," p. 272. The triangular top of *Bogatyr* was not part of its composition; it was cut down by an early owner to fit a "Gothic" frame.

Fig. 7 LILACS, 1900. Oil on canvas, 160 × 177 cm. Tretiakov Gallery, Moscow.

and vanish into the flowering bushes where she has just materialized. In *Toward Night* (1900), a masculine presence and horselike creatures, equally mysterious, rise out of the steppe against the dusky sky. Examples could be multiplied, but it is water, the primal fluid, even more than earth, that inspires such subjects. Among them the previously mentioned like-linesses of Zabela in her roles as *Princess Volkhova* (1899) and *The Swan-Princess* (Fig. 5) offer particularly striking suggestions of evanescent substance incarnated into womanly visions. The opalescent colors that play over the two figures and enhance their fragile, transient reality are further explored in *The Pearl* (1904), where two naiads emanate from a seashell. Other playing *Naiads* and several versions of the magic sea-dwelling *Thirty-Three Heroes* from Alexander Pushkin's "Tsar Saltan," are among related figures whose existence originates in water.

One subject stands out as clearly in the spirit of *The Birth of Tragedy*, where Nietzsche lavishes praise on the "sublime and divine" folk satyr of ancient Greece in words that might almost describe Vrubel's major painting *Satyr* (1898–1899) (Fig. 8), now known as *Pan*.

> The satyr, like the idyllic shepherd of more recent times, is the offspring of a longing for the primitive and the natural; but how firmly and fearlessly the Greek embraced the man of the woods, and how timorously and mawkishly modern man dallied with the flattering image of a sentimental, flute-playing shepherd! Nature, as yet unchanged by knowledge . . . the satyr was the archetype of man, the embodiment of his highest and most intense emotions, the ecstatic reveler enraptured by the proximity of his god . . . a symbol of the sexual omnipotence of nature which the Greeks used to contemplate with reverent wonder.(*BT*, 61)

Vrubel's immediate source was a tale in which Anatole France's millennia-old "Saint-Satyre" endures over the centuries on the same Roman site; Vrubel suggests an equivalent sense of the passage of time as he integrates his satyr with the surrounding natural rhythms of the locale near Smolensk which inspired this subject. His rugged hero, truly a "man of the woods," rises treelike from the ground. His broad shoulders seem to have been carved into muscles by the elements. His dark, ancient, craggy face is lightened by blue eyes that duplicate the colors of the stream behind him. The fingers resting on the barklike texture of the knee are as gnarled as twigs. Such an organic identification of "the sexual omnipotence of nature" with human archetypes is nowhere else as clearly stated.

Fig. 8 SATYR (PAN), 1899. Oil on canvas, 124 × 106 cm. Tretiakov Gallery, Moscow.

The prophet is a subject that can be traced with even more confidence to Nietzsche. Vrubel's interest had originally been aroused in 1884 by his experience at St. Cyril's, where he depicted *Moses*, not in the traditional guise of a patriarch, but as a young prophet. This was another subject which he had planned to pursue but abandoned until the period of Nietzsche's influence. In 1899, among his several illustrations to poems by Pushkin for another Kushnerev jubilee edition, he included "The Prophet." The illustration and a related painting of the same subject also represent, in addition to the Prophet Isaiah, the Six-Winged Seraph who is God's messenger in the poem. From that time to the end of his artistic activity, Vrubel returned to both these figures, shown singly or together, in numerous drawings and a major painting of 1904, *The Six-Winged Seraph* (Fig. 9). The seraph's features, his pride, and evident suffering recall those of the Demon. But his splendor, erect bearing, and the dagger raised in a symbolic gesture of inner power reflect a victory that the Demon had never attained. His heavy jeweled crown, worn instead of thorns, may indicate that he remains the Antichrist whose individuality has triumphed over the herd. An exultant mood, still mixed with sorrow, also pervades a drawing of the same year, *Head of the Prophet* (Fig. 10), whose inspired features and posture call to mind the spiritual elevation of Zarathustra. The head incarnates Nietzsche's statement in *The Gay Science*: "To 'give style' to one's character—a great and rare art!" (*GS*, 232). The mixed emotions expressed by these two figures reflect Vrubel's own moods and his existential position at that time, with his health ever more precarious but his prophetic artistic message at last attracting a faithful and vocal following.

The rise of Russian modernism owes much to the activity of these young admirers of Vrubel, who first emerged as a distinct group with the exhibition "The Crimson Rose" in 1904. Participants in that group and like-minded painters responded at first primarily to Vrubel's images of elemental forces at work behind familiar appearances.[45] In the process they reduced recognizable shapes and color modulations to near-abstract swirls of movement. Later on, partly under the impact of Western movements, these and other artists came under the influence of Vrubel's ex-

---

[45] Crimson Rose and Blue Rose artists whose symbolic canvases derived from Vrubel were Paul Kuznetsov (1878–1968), Nicholas Milioti (1874–1962), Martiros Sarian (1880–1972), and Serge Sudeikin (1882–1946). Others include Nathalie Goncharova (1881–1962), Michael Larionov (1881–1964), Kuzma Petrov–Vodkin (1878–1939), and Nicholas Roerich (1874–1947).

Fig. 9 THE SIX-WINGED SERAPH, 1904. Oil on canvas, 131 × 155 cm. The Russian Museum, Leningrad.

Fig. 10 HEAD OF THE PROPHET, 1904–1905. Pencil, charcoal, watercolor, gouache on paper, 43.2 × 33.5 cm. Tretiakov Gallery, Moscow.

perimentation with technique and with unorthodox traditions such as the Byzantine. During that period Nietzschean values of rebelliousness and provocative behavior also gained ground among artists.[46] The course of Russian art between 1904 and 1914 was transformed by all these factors, and Vrubel's distinct legacy of metaphysical speculation combined with experimental technique was of special importance.[47]

Vrubel's own thinking and artistic activity had been decisively affected by Nietzsche's writings. They intensified an earlier quest for individuation, his tragic view of life, his intuitive understanding of the unconscious and of the phenomenal world's timeless flux. Moreover, Vrubel's work and comments starting in 1898 reflected new attitudes. He now repudiated compromises with Christianity and with an uncomprehending public, and he abandoned his role as gifted craftsman. He accepted Nietzsche's metaphysics: the void left by the death of god would be filled by the self-creation of the overman—"God is a supposition. . . . But you could transform yourselves into forefathers and ancestors of Superman: and let this be your finest creating!" (Z, 110). Vrubel acquired a new vision of himself: as a great artist attaining to the stature of overman, he became a prophet who shares his higher values, his deeper insights, and his integrative primeval nature with society. This new faith was achieved at a dreadful cost to Vrubel the man, who never recovered his mental equilibrium. As an artist, he unquestionably profited from the experience.

[46] Valkenier, *Russian Realist Art*, p. 174. Purposeful outrageousness is a well-known trait of Russian modernist behavior. The membership of pre-Revolutionary groups such as the Donkey's Tail and the Cubo-Futurists often overlaps. The most active organizers among them were Goncharova, Larionov, and David Burliuk (1882–1967). See John E. Bowlt, "Chronology," in *Russian Avant-Garde Art, The George Costakis Collection*, ed. Angelica Rudenstine (New York, 1981); Charlotte Douglas, *Swans of Other Worlds* (Ann Arbor, 1976).

[47] See, for example, Gabo's comment, in *Art of Vrubel*, p. 163.

PART III

NIETZSCHE'S INFLUENCE
ON RUSSIAN MARXISM

11.

Gorky and Nietzsche:
The Quest for a Russian Superman

Mary Louise Loe

WHEN MAXIM GORKY'S first two volumes of collected stories were published in 1898, numerous critics accused the unknown writer of being a "Nietzschean"—a philosophy which, for many Russians at the time, was synonymous with immorality and nihilism. Gorky was accused of creating a Russian version of the superman: a superhobo (*über-bosiak*) and supertramp (*über-brodiag*) who advocated "provincial Nietzscheanism" and "demonism."[1] Gorky's hobo indeed condemned all aspects of Russian society: its religion, morality, government, and culture, but other writers had been making similar attacks for over one hundred years. Yet Gorky's works evoked an extraordinary and unprecedented public response because he had also condemned—as did Nietzsche's Zarathustra—the current ideologies and behavior of radical intellectuals. He called on Russian youth to reject the traditional role of the intelligentsia—the role of sacrificing oneself for the masses—and become aggressive individualists. Even though Gorky never used Nietzsche's term "superman" in these early stories, critics noted the strong resemblance between the philosophy preached by his hoboes and the teachings of Zarathustra. While there is no question that Gorky had rejected much of Russian society long before reading Nietzsche, the German philosopher provided him

---

[1] N. M. Minsky, "Filosofiia toski i zhazhda voli," in *Kriticheskie stat'i o proizvedeniiakh Maksima Gor'kogo*, ed. S. Grinberg (St. Petersburg, 1901), p. 21. The words *bosiak* and *brodiag* present problems of translation. They may both be translated into English as hobo, tramp, vagabond, bum, vagrant, and wanderer, each having its own connotations. I have chosen to translate *bosiak* as hobo and *brodiag* as tramp, although I will use the other terms as well, depending on the context.

nonetheless with philosophical arguments to bolster that rejection as well as with a concrete vision of what man could become in the future.

Inspired by Nietzsche's belief in man's power to "overcome" himself, Gorky was determined to show Russian youth how this could be done. His Zarathustra was not a foreign hermit descending from the mountain heights, but a rough, ragged, and violent Russian hobo who proudly revealed the scars of his own rebellion and challenged the young to become Russia's new warrior-leaders. It was Nietzsche, however, more than any other writer, who gave Gorky the cogent arguments for condemning the Russian intelligentsia. Nietzsche's influence on Gorky was a dominant and lasting one, remaining with him even after he had joined the Bolsheviks and had gone on to become the most important literary figure in the Soviet Union. Yet, there has been no attempt to explain why the young Gorky found Nietzsche's philosophy so appealing and how his vision of the new man differed from Nietzsche's own. This chapter will address some of these questions by focusing on Gorky's early quest for a Russian superman and his attempt to create one in his early stories.

From the early nineteenth century, the Russian intelligentsia had dedicated itself to changing Russia and to liberating the masses from their social, economic, and political oppression. At the time Gorky appeared on the scene, the crucial question was how this was to be done. While Populists and Marxists agreed that socialism was the solution to Russia's ills, they had differing views both of the socialist future and of the best means of achieving it. Whereas Populists believed in the revolutionary nature and socialist goals of the peasants, Marxists argued that Russia's recent industrialization and enlarged working class were signs that Russia was following the inevitable historical development predicted by Marx and that it was indeed only a matter of time before the socialist revolution occurred. In spite of their disagreements, both were convinced that the Russian intellectual, as a member of a privileged group, had the moral obligation to devote himself to overthrowing the existing order and to liberating the lower class.

It was into the midst of this debate that Gorky appeared. Neither Populist nor Marxist, Gorky expressed total disdain for all ideologies and suggested that the intellectual's first step toward self-liberation should be the rejection of his traditional obligation (*dolg*) to help the lower classes. Gorky's stories were populated by a long gallery of tough and hardened hoboes, dressed in tattered clothes and living on the fringes of society.

These men ridiculed the Russian intellectual's devotion to the people, and revealed that the Russian folk, contrary to the intellectual's view, were greedy, selfish, servile, and fearful. Although these hoboes were outsiders and outcasts, they boasted that they were the only men in Russia who were truly free.

Undoubtedly, Gorky would have received a very different reception from the Russian reading public had he been an intellectual, but he was one of Russia's first writers from the lower classes, a man with no formal education who had spent years working among migrant laborers, social outcasts, and drifters, whose numbers had dramatically increased in the 1890s as a consequence of Russia's rapid industrialization. Although Gorky has been working as a journalist since 1892, he affected the coarse mannerisms of these men and deliberately exaggerated his association with their underworld in his autobiographical sketches published at the time.[2] The inevitable result was that the Russian literary public identified him with the characters in his stories; virtually overnight he became the most famous writer in Russia and the hero of its rebellious youth. Fascinated by Gorky's unusual background and experiences, the literary public flocked to him with queries about his views, his life, and the underworld he had portrayed.[3] Like Nietzsche's Zarathustra, Gorky seemed to have appeared in the marketplace out of nowhere. Moreover, he knew how to play his role for all it was worth and dressed in an outfit that was a combination of wanderer and magician: he had long hair and a mustache and wore a flowing cape, a wide-brimmed black hat, a peasant-style tunic, pants, and high boots, and carried a cane. He condemned, insulted, and preached to the intelligentsia on its vices and folly, but they listened to him like children following the pied piper because he was a dynamic, charismatic man from the people.[4]

Yet Gorky remained difficult to classify. Critics called him not only a

[2] See M. Gorky, "Avtobiograficheskaia zametka 1897 goda," in *Russkaia literatura xx veka, 1890–1910,* ed. S. A. Vengerov, 3 vols. (Moscow, 1914–1916), 1:190–92; Gorky, "Avtobiograficheskaia zametka iz zhurnal 'Sem'ia'," in ibid., 1:192–94.

[3] Iv. Bunin, "Gor'kii, Otryvki iz vospominanii," *Don,* no. 3 (1968):169–70, quoted in A. Ninov, *M. Gor'kii i Iv. Bunin* (Leningrad, 1973), p. 44; L. Andreev, "Vpechatleniia," *Kur'er,* no. 317 (15 November 1900), in *Literaturnoe nasledstvo,* vol. 72: *Gor'kii i Leonid Andreev: Neizdannaia perepiska* (Moscow, 1965), pp. 472–75; M. Gorky to E. P. Peshkova, 18 October 1899, in M. Gorky, *Sobranie sochinenii v tridtsati tomakh* (Collected Works in Thirty Volumes) (Moscow, 1959–1965), 28:95–96. Henceforth cited as SS 30.

[4] Gorky attributed his popularity to the public's knowledge of his past. See M. Gorky to A. P. Chekhov, 1–7 October 1900, in SS 30, 28:135. See also K. Stanislavsky, "A. P. Chekhov v khudozhestvennom teatre," in *Chekhov v vospominaniiakh sovremennikov,* 2nd ed. (Moscow, 1954), p. 366.

Nietzschean, to them the most opprobrious of labels, but also a proletarian, a humanist, a misanthrope, an anarchist, a Marxist, and even an advocate of sadomasochism. As one reviewer noted, Gorky offered something to everyone,[5] and Russians of all ages and political persuasions welcomed and idolized him, seeing in him a confirmation of their own rejection of contemporary society and the promised fulfillment of their dreams. Speaking in the voice of the Russian people—the free wanderers of its past—and demanding a resurgence of Russia's discarded warrior traits of strength, courage, and freedom, Gorky called for the creation of a new man. He was a leader in search of disciples—Nietzsche's Zarathustra transformed into a Russian hobo.

It was precisely because Gorky became known as Russia's first self-made writer, and later, during the Soviet period, as the father of socialist realism, that Nietzsche's influence upon his thinking has been seriously underestimated. When several contemporary critics, including the noted Populist N. K. Mikhailovsky, pointed out the strong parallels between the teachings of Zarathustra and that of Gorky's hoboes, and directly questioned whether Gorky had read Nietzsche,[6] Gorky did not publicly respond, choosing to represent himself as a rough diamond whose writings derived almost entirely from his own experiences. Marxist critics accepted and further elaborated Gorky's image as an original writer. V. A. Posse, who was responsible for the initial publication of Gorky's works and obtained positions for him on the journal *Life* (*Zhizn'*), and in the Znanie Publishing Cooperative, made no mention of Nietzsche's influence in his early article on Gorky, yet, years later, in his memoirs, he discussed Gorky's strong enthusiasm for Nietzsche when he first met him in the 1890s.[7] It is likely that Marxist critics did not want to admit that Gorky agreed with a philosopher who attacked socialism and egalitarianism because they were trying to bring him into their camp, and silently hoped that he would soon cast off these unpopular views.

Soviet critics have followed the pattern established by Marxists prior to the October Revolution. Particularly because Nietzsche has become associated with the Nazis, there has been a determined effort to deny all Nietzschean influence on the first proletarian writer, the father of social-

[5] E. A. Liatsky, "Maksim Gor'kii i ego rasskazy," *Vestnik evropy* 11 (1901):282.

[6] N. K. Mikhailovsky, "Literatura i zhizn'; Eshche o Maksim Gor'kom i ego geroiakh," *Russkoe bogatstvo*, no. 10 (1898):84.

[7] V. A. Posse, "Pevets protestuiushchei toski," in *Kriticheskie stat'i*, pp. 1–16; Posse, *Moi zhiznennyi put'* (Moscow, 1939), p. 151. See also the review by the Marxist "A. B." (A. I. Bogdanovich), "Mir bosiakov v izobrazhenii g. Gor'kogo," in *Kriticheskie stat'i*, pp. 27–43.

ist realism. Since acknowledgment of a philosophical affinity between Gorky and Nietzsche might imply an ideological affinity between the Soviets and the Nazis, Soviet critics have dismissed the Gorky–Nietzsche connection, even though the result is an inaccurate representation of Gorky's early views.[8] Moreover, Gorky himself contributed to this attitude by denouncing Nietzsche as a protofascist in articles written in 1932 and 1934, although he had admitted Nietzsche's influence on his writing elsewhere.[9]

Until recently, Western scholars have either ignored Nietzsche's influence or treated it as insignificant.[10] Then, in the past fifteen years, a number of studies, focusing on different periods of Gorky's writing and from different perspectives, have convincingly demonstrated Gorky's debt to Nietzsche.[11] The definitive study of the nature of this debt is yet to be written, however.

While there are many examples in Gorky's correspondence and in memoirs by his friends that document Gorky's early interest in Nietzsche's writing, a brief summary of only the most important evidence will be offered here. The exact date of Gorky's initial contact with Nietzsche is uncertain. In 1930–1931, Gorky published an essay entitled "Conversa-

[8] V. V. Vorovsky, "O M. Gor'kom," in *Literaturno-kriticheskie stat'i* (Moscow, 1956), pp. 66–67; B. V. Mikhailovsky, "Stanovlenie sotsialisticheskogo realizma v tvorchestve A. M. Gor'kogo," in *Russkaia literatura kontsa XIX–nachala xx v.: 1901–1907*, ed. B. A. Bialik, E. B. Tager, and V. R. Shcherbina (Moscow, 1971), pp. 65, 73; A. Makarov, "Izmyshlenie i deistvitel'nost': Razoblachenie burzhuaznoi legendy o nitssheanskikh uvlecheniiakh Maksima Gor'kogo," in *Estetika i Zhizn'*, no. 3 (1974), pp. 334–76, cited in Betty Y. Forman, "Nietzsche and Gorky in the 1890s: The Case for an Early Influence," in *Western Philosophical Systems in Russian Literature: A Collection of Critical Studies*, ed. A. M. Mlikotin (Los Angeles, 1979), p. 153.

[9] M. Gorky, "O starom i novom cheloveke," *SS* 30, 26:281; M. Gorky, "Sovetskaia literatura," *SS* 30, 27:313; M. Gorky, "Besedy o remesle," *SS* 30, 25:319–22.

[10] See F. M. Borras, *Maxim Gorky: The Writer* (London, 1967); Irwin Weil, *Gorky: His Literary Development and Influence on Soviet Intellectual Life* (New York, 1966); Dan Levin, *Stormy Petrel: The Life and Work of Maxim Gorky* (New York, 1965); Richard Hare, *Maxim Gorky: Romantic Realist and Conservative Revolutionary* (London, 1962); Rufus W. Mathewson, Jr., *The Positive Hero in Russian Literature* (Stanford, Ca., 1958); Filia Holtzman, *The Young Maxim Gorky: 1868–1902* (New York, 1948); Alexander Kaun, *Maxim Gorky and His Russia* (New York, 1931).

[11] See Forman, "Nietzsche and Gorky in the 1890s"; Mary Louise Loe, "Maxim Gorky and the Sreda Circle, 1899–1905" (Ph.D. diss., Columbia University, 1977); Ann M. Lane, "Nietzsche in Russian Thought, 1890–1917" (Ph.D. diss., University of Wisconsin, 1976); George L. Kline, "Nietzschean Marxism in Russia," in *Demythologizing Marx*, ed. Frederick J. Adelmann, Boston College Studies in Philosophy, vol. 2 (Chestnut Hill, Mass., 1969); George L. Kline, "The God-Builders: Gorky and Lunacharski," in *Religious and Anti-Religious Thought in Russia* (Chicago, 1968), pp. 103–26.

tions of the Craft" ("Besedy o remesle") in which he stated that he became familiar with Nietzsche in the winter of 1889–1890 through a Russian translation in manuscript form of *Thus Spoke Zarathustra* by his
friend N. Z. Vasiliev. Even though Gorky condemned Nietzsche's philosophy from a Marxist perspective in this article, he nonetheless also
admitted that he had attributed Nietzschean philosophy to the hoboes
and tramps in his early stories, and to the merchant Iakov Maiakin in his
novel *Foma Gordeev*.[12] In a letter to his Soviet biographer I. A. Gruzdev,
also written in 1930, Gorky said that Vasiliev translated *Zarathustra* in
1893, not in 1889–1890, and that he overwhelmed Gorky with Nietzsche's
philosophy—in Gorky's words: it was like being hit over the head with
"the blunt edge of an ax"—but Gorky nonetheless "survived."[13] Thus
Gorky's initial introduction to Nietzsche's writings was no earlier than
1889–1890 but no later than 1893. Even if we accept the later date, it
can be affirmed that Gorky was familiar with *Thus Spoke Zarathustra* at
the time he was publishing his early stories, if not his very first story,
which was published in 1892. He refers to *Zarathustra* most frequently
in his early correspondence, although he also owned translations of *Beyond Good and Evil* and *Twilight of the Idols*, and probably read other
Nietzschean works as well.[14]

From Gorky's published correspondence we know that he was familiar
with works written about Nietzsche as well as those incorporating his
ideas.[15] In 1901 he wrote that he was "deeply interested in the ideas" of
Merezhkovsky's novel, *Julian the Apostate*, first published under the title
The Outcast (Otverzhennyi) in 1895, and described by Bernice Glatzer
Rosenthal in her study of Merezhkovsky as "essentially a Nietzschean
tract."[16] The first time Gorky met Merezhkovsky in 1899, they spent the
evening discussing Nietzsche's philosophy.[17]

[12] Gorky, "Besedy o remesle," pp. 319–21.

[13] Gorky to Gruzdev, 7 January 1930, in *Arkhiv A. M. Gor'kogo*, vol. 11: *Perepiska A. M. Gor'kogo s I. A. Gruzdevym* (Moscow, 1966), p. 211.

[14] D. A. Balika, "Lichnaia biblioteka A. M. Gor'kogo nizhegorodskikh let," in *Trudy Gor'kovskoi oblastnoi biblioteki im. Lenina*, no. 1 (Gorki, 1948), cited in Forman, "Nietzsche and Gorky in the 1890s," p. 157.

[15] Gorky to Piatnitsky, 18–19 June 1900, in *Arkhiv A. M. Gor'kogo*, vol. 4: *Pis'ma k K. P. Piatnitskomu* (Moscow, 1954), p. 10; Gorky to Andreev, early April 1901, in *Literatur-noe nasledstvo*, vol. 72, p. 88; *Perepiska Gor'kogo s Gruzdevym*, p. 208.

[16] *Literaturnoe nasledstvo*, vol. 72, p. 116; Bernice Glatzer Rosenthal, *D. S. Merezhkov-sky and the Silver Age: The Development of a Revolutionary Mentality* (The Hague, 1975), p. 62.

[17] *Literaturnoe nasledstvo*, vol. 72, p. 116.

Gorky repeatedly expressed his enthusiasm for Nietzsche to his friends and protegés in the Wednesdays (*Sreda*) circle, which was formed in 1899 and rapidly came under his leadership. Gorky advised the young writers in his group, which included, among others, Leonid Andreev and Alexander Kuprin, to read Nietzsche's works.[18] Moreover, the influence of Nietzsche's philosophy on the members of Gorky's circle—known to the public as the *Znanie* writers—is evident in the stories they published under his editorship in the *Anthologies of the Znanie Cooperative (Sborniki tovarichestva "Znanie")*, beginning in 1904.[19]

Since Gorky downplayed the significance of literary influences, and especially Nietzsche's influence, it is necessary to turn to his autobiography for the origins of Nietzsche's appeal. This three-volume work—*Childhood (Detstvo), In the World (V liudiakh)*, and *My Universities (Moi universitety)*—was begun in 1912 when Gorky was past forty, living in exile, his popularity in a temporary decline. He wrote the work not just to expose the violent and savage life of Russia's lower classes—as he explicitly claimed—but also to refurbish his own image as an outcast and rebel who had overcome the great suffering and hardships of his youth to become a major writer and leader of men. The autobiography ends when Gorky's literary career begins, offering only a brief and superficial discussion of literary influences on him. Yet, in spite of its limitations as an objective historical source, it offers important insights into Gorky's family life and early experiences and reveals why he found Nietzsche's teachings so compelling.

In *Childhood* Gorky indicates that his father died of cholera after catching the disease from the three-year-old Gorky. The young Gorky, whose real name was Alexei Peshkov, was raised in the home of his maternal grandfather Vasily Kashirin, the owner of a dye shop. Kashirin had never approved of his only daughter's marriage to Gorky's father, Maxim Peshkov, and never accepted his grandson as one of his own. Virtually abandoned by his willful mother to his despotic grandfather, the young Alexei felt that the only person in his family who truly loved him was his grand-

[18] Gorky to Andreev, 2–4 April 1900; early April 1901; Andreev to Gorky, 11–14 February 1904, *Literaturnoe nasledstvo*, vol. 72, pp. 69, 88, 195–97; "Skitalets" (Stepan Gavrilovich Petrov), "M. Gorky," in *Povesti, Rasskazy, Vospominanii* (Moscow, 1960), p. 289; see my article "Maksim Gor'kii and the *Sreda* Circle: 1899–1905," *Slavic Review* 44 (Spring 1985):49–66.

[19] *Sbornik tovarichestva "Znanie,"* 40 vols. (St. Petersburg, 1904–1913); see also Loe, "Maxim Gorky and the Sreda Circle" diss.; and Lydia Weston Kesich, "Gorky and the *Znanie* Volumes 1904–1913" (Ph.D. diss. Columbia University, 1967).

mother, Akulina. The gentle old woman filled Alexei's vivid imagination with romantic tales about his father, portraying him as a tragic figure, a solitary wanderer and loner who possessed the heroic characteristics of strength, wisdom, compassion, and integrity which the male Kashirins so evidently lacked. These early feelings of loss, rejection, and isolation would later lead the young Gorky to search for a male hero who possessed the traits he attributed to his father.[20]

Yet, while Gorky condemned his grandfather for being mean, tyrannical, and brutal, his grandfather nonetheless was the man who had raised him; Gorky respected certain aspects of Kashirin's character, and adopted many of his views. Grandfather Kashirin had trained the young Alexei to be a warrior, initiating him into his own violent world with harsh beatings, but he had not provided his grandson with a satisfactory philosophical rationale for the warrior role. Moreover, his grandparents had created for him images of male heroes that were contradictory. Their colorful tales of ancient Russian warriors, religious martyrs, and wise men contained two kinds of heroes: his grandfather's heroes were rebellious, selfish, and fearless warriors, lacking compassion or pity, men "who had broken idols, or quarrelled with Roman emperors, for which they had been tortured, burnt, and flayed"; while his grandmother's heroes were submissive, humane, and self-sacrificing martyrs, men who had "turned the other cheek" and continued to go on helping others.[21]

When he was only eleven, Gorky was kicked out of his grandfather's home, since the bankrupt, miserly old man decided he could no longer afford to support him. Gorky spent the next years working in odd jobs along the Volga. During this period, he was trying to decide what to do with his life, and looked to other men to provide him with a role model he could follow. Not surprisingly he was disappointed; he did not find any heroes either among the hoboes, tramps, and migrant workers he met in his many odd jobs or among the excessively cerebral intellectuals, writers, and poets he met in Nizhny-Novgorod, Kazan, and Samara.[22] His need for a meaningful, creative life led him to begin writing, but he did not consider himself an intellectual and continued to seek a role that would combine the intellectual and moral characteristics of his grand-

[20] Gorky, "Detstvo," in *Polnoe sobranie sochinenii: Khudozhestvennye proizvedeniia v dvadtsati piati tomakh* (Complete Collected Works: Artistic Productions in Twenty-Five Volumes) (Moscow, 1968–1976), 15:15, 68–69, 171. Henceforth cited as *PSS 25*.

[21] Gorky, "Detstvo," pp. 89–93.

[22] Gorky, "Moi universitety," in *PSS 25*, 16:16–17, 80, 156, 163–66.

mother's heroes with the manly courage and strength of his grandfather's warriors. Gorky later revealed that his conflict between the different roles of knight-errant and monastic recluse led him to seek psychiatric help, and contributed to his suicide attempt after his grandmother's death.[23] It was during this period, when Gorky was in his early twenties and first starting out on his literary career, that he first read *Zarathustra*, and it is likely that it had such a strong impact on him because of his own intense feelings of isolation and alienation.

To be sure there were many Russian poets, artists, writers, and philosophers who were also influenced by Nietzsche's philosophy in the 1890s and incorporated certain of his ideas into their work. Nietzsche offered them, as he did Gorky, a rationale for rejecting contemporary society and culture, and a new individualistic role as creators and artists. Yet Gorky approached Nietzsche from a very different perspective. Because of his lower-class background and experiences, Gorky did not feel comfortable in intelligentsia circles nor could he accept their ideologies. Not having received any formal education, except for six months in an elementary school, he had educated himself in a rather unsystematic and eclectic way. Although he read voraciously he was neither a speculative nor profound thinker; he was searching, nonetheless, for "his own truth." When he first began associating with intelligentsia circles in Nizhny-Novgorod and encountered their Populist and Marxist views, Gorky found both ideologies unacceptable. He considered the Populists' idealization of Russian peasants to be totally unfounded and a reflection of their alienation from the people. Having grown up and worked among members of the provincial urban petty bourgeoisie, working class, and unemployed poor, many of whom were children and grandchildren of peasants, he found Populist notions about the "folk" odd, curious, and unrealistic. They may have believed that peasants were pure, innocent, wholesome, and cooperative, but Gorky knew better: peasants were superstitious, fearful, greedy, and violent. They had their pride, their dreams, and hopes for the future, but few of them ever succeeded in attaining what they desired. In addition, Gorky was shocked by these intellectuals' expressed desire to sacrifice themselves for the people. Having only recently succeeded in emerging from the lower depths himself, he certainly did not share the intelligentsia's guilt about its privileged past—particularly strong among

---

[23] Gorky, "V liudiakh," in *PSS* 25, 15:522; Gorky, "Moi universitety," pp. 57, 83–84, 147, 207.

those who came from the gentry—nor their need to immerse themselves among the folk.[24]

Gorky was also introduced to Marxist ideas at this time, but he considered Marxism too impersonal and deterministic.[25] After he had achieved popularity, Gorky would join the Bolshevik party, but in the early 1890s Marxism did not offer him the challenge and inspiration he was looking for.

Gorky thus became interested in Nietzsche's philosophy only after he had summarily rejected the two major ideologies of the Russian intelligentsia. Zarathustra's command that men must be warriors and recognize that conflict is of value in itself echoed his grandfather's teachings. Moreover, Nietzsche provided an image of a heroic male who was both a courageous warrior and a moral leader. His superman would lead others not by self-sacrifice, love of one's neighbor, or pity, but by overcoming, self-denial, and struggle. Nietzsche offered Gorky not only a confirmation of his grandfather's beliefs, but also specific reasons for rejecting the current ideologies of the Russian left, and for condemning the weakness, flabbiness, and effeminacy of male intellectuals. Like Nietzsche, Gorky associated passivity and weakness with effeminacy, and condemned intellectuals for not demonstrating the masculine traits of aggressiveness and strength. Of the many teachings in *Zarathustra*, it is the section "Of War and Warriors" which must have influenced Gorky most of all, for his early stories and letters repeatedly echo these words of Zarathustra:

> And if you cannot be saints of knowledge, at least be its warriors. They are the companions and forerunners of such sainthood. . . .
>
> You should be such men as are always looking for an enemy— for *your* enemy. And with some of you there is hate at first sight.
>
> You should seek your enemy, you should wage your war—a war for your opinions. And if your opinion is defeated, your honesty should still cry triumph over that!
>
> You should love peace as a means to new wars. And the short peace more than the long. . . .
>
> War and courage have done more great things than charity. Not your pity but your bravery has saved the unfortunate up to now. . . .

[24] For his descriptions of intellectuals, see Gorky, "Moi universitety," pp. 16–17, 147, 155–56.
[25] Posse, *Moi zhiznennyi put'*, p. 126.

But you should let me commend to you your highest idea—and
it is: Man is something that should be overcome. (Z, 74–75)

Nietzsche's call for young men to become warriors was especially appealing to young intellectuals rebelling against their elders and against
the positivism of the late nineteenth century, but there was a strongly
anti-intellectual as well as anti-ideological strain in Nietzsche's thought.
This attitude deeply appealed to Gorky, because he was not an intellectual himself and because at this time in his life he did not fully understand nor respect intellectuals. He found them to be weak, passive, ef-
feminate, and virtually schizophrenic in their ascetic denial of their physical
needs. He agreed with Nietzsche that intellectuals overestimated the power
of the mind and the ability of ideas to bring about change. Moreover,
Gorky observed the Russian intelligentsia's deep alienation from the masses
and recognized that their relationship was a problematic one, far more
problematic, to be sure, than that between European intellectuals and
the masses. Yet at the same time that Gorky feared that intellectuals were
not the warriors Russia needed, he believed that they alone had the moral
qualities to become Russia's supermen.[26]

Like Nietzsche, Gorky believed that the only significant social change
would come from the striving actions of individual men. Gorky felt that
intellectuals were too passive and did not appreciate, as he did, the importance of physical strength. Having lived and worked among laborers,
tradesmen, and small entrepreneurs, Gorky appreciated difficult physical
labor and the daily testing of a man's cunning, intelligence, and strength,
which he observed among the dock workers and bargemen of the Volga.
Like Gorky's grandfather, these men were coarse, cruel, and greedy, but
they were also extreme individualists, who loved to prove their manliness
and courage in the often vicious and competitive world of trade. Gorky
deeply respected them for their warrior traits, while recognizing that they
did not have the moral characteristics of leadership that the intelligentsia
possessed.[27]

Although Nietzsche condemned intellectuals for cultivating one aspect
of themselves to the neglect of others, he expressed even more contempt
for sensualists and hedonists. Gorky indicates that he shared this contempt when he described the confusion he felt as a child for the drunken,
violent behavior of his uncles, and his disappointment in discovering,

[26] Gorky, "Moi universitety," pp. 155–56.
[27] Ibid., pp. 27–29.

once he left home, that many Russians behaved in a similar way, lacking the ability to control their desires and passions and pursuing their immediate selfish needs without any higher personal goal. Gorky was repelled by this lack of self-control and direction, reflecting an asceticism in him which had a strong affinity to Nietzsche's own, and which became more pronounced as he matured. Moreover, Nietzsche did not hold any illusions about the masses either, and his cynical view of the crowd as weak, cowardly, and submissive certainly confirmed what Gorky had experienced himself.[28]

Although Nietzsche's writings contain a wealth of ideas and suggestions, Gorky was not a subtle, philosophical thinker. He was looking for quick and simple answers and solutions, and in Zarathustra's superman he found the hero he was looking for. Not particularly interested in Nietzsche's theories of esthetics, his view of eternal recurrence, or his interpretations of history, Gorky seized upon those Nietzschean views which he found to be accurate, and adopted them for himself. Most frequently he presented these views as his own, although he infrequently admitted his debt to Nietzsche. As he wrote to his editor in 1898:

> I think that the meaning of life is in man, that "the true epitome is man" as Zarathustra says; I believe that man is something that must be overcome, and I believe, I do believe—he will be overcome![29]

The impact of Gorky's works would not have been so explosive had he not combined Nietzsche's teachings with his own ideas and attitudes and offered a vivid and dramatic portrayal of Russia's violent underworld. The interesting question is why Gorky chose the Russian hobo to express Zarathustra's teachings. First, it should be noted that not all of Gorky's hoboes are romantically portrayed and not all are Nietzschean prophets. The Marxist critic A. I. Bogdanovich divided Gorky's characters into two types: the "former people" (*byvshie liudi*: by this term Gorky meant outcasts who had lost their social status) and "the restless seekers of freedom." While he argued that the men in the first group were dangerous, violent, and uncontrollable, he believed that men in the second group, the seekers of freedom, had "an elemental and unconscious drive" that united them with revolutionary intellectuals.[30] Bogdanovich was correct

---

[28] Gorky, "Detstvo," pp. 33–51, 54–55; Gor'ky, "Moi universitety," pp. 102–4, 130–32, 156, 163–65.

[29] Gorky to F. D. Batiushkovu, 8 or 9 October 1898, *SS* 30, 28:33.

[30] "A. B." (A. I. Bogdanovich), "Mir bosiakov," p. 31.

in suggesting that the tramps in the first category were dissatisfied, frustrated, and violent. These characters are portrayed in such stories as: "Emel'ian Piliai" ("Emel'ian Piliai," 1893), "Zazubrina" ("Zazubrina," 1897), "Out of Boredom" ("Skuki radi," 1897), "In the Steppe" ("V stepi," 1897), "The Orlovs" ("Suprugi Orlovy," 1897), "Mal'va" ("Mal'va," 1897), "Former People" ("Byvshie liudi," 1897), and "Companions" ("Druzhki," 1898).[31] They are alcoholics, tramps, prisoners, and criminals. Although their rebellion from society may have been justified, they have failed in their attempt and have ended up living in flophouses, jails, or on the road. Occasionally they preach to their companions in passages that echo Zarathustra, expressing their yearning for freedom and glory, but it is evident that they are doomed to fail. All critics found these men most threatening; Nicholas Mikhailovsky, for example, described them as "dangerous barbarians" threatening to destroy the contemporary social order.[32]

The characters who emerge as Gorky's heroes are strong individualists who have succeeded in their rebellion. Like Zarathustra, these men and women have left the cities and sought the "raw and rough air." They live in the steppe region or along the seacoast, close to nature, and as far from the crowd as possible. They have broken all ties to society and are willing to make whatever sacrifices are necessary in order to retain their independence. Although they are dissatisfied and restless and occasionally look back on their past with nostalgia, they will not exchange their freedom for the security and material rewards conformism provides. The price is simply too high. These rebels appear in the following stories: "Makar Chudra" ("Makar Chudra," 1892), "The Old Woman Izergil" ("Starukha Izergil'," 1895), "Chelkash" ("Chelkash," 1895), "Konovalov" ("Konovalov," 1897), and "The Rogue" ("Prokhodimets," 1898).[33] They are romanticized characters, modeled both on their literary predecessors, the

---

[31] Gorky, "Emel'ian Piliai," PSS 25, 1:34–45; "Druzhki," PSS 25, 4:62–77; "Zazubrina," PSS 25, 3:166–73; "Skuki radi," PSS 25, 4:7–24; "V stepi," PSS 25, 3:174–86; "Suprugi Orlovy," PSS 25, 3:219–77; "Mal'va," PSS 25, 3:343–94; "Byvshie liudi," PSS 25, 3:278–342.

[32] N. K. Mikhailovsky, "Literatura i zhizn'; O g. Mak. Gor'kom i ego geroiakh," Russkoe bogatstvo, no. 9 (1898):55–75; idem, "Literatura i zhizn'; Eshche o Maksim Gor'kom i ego geroiakh," Russkoe bogatstvo, no. 10 (1898):61–93; M. A. Protopopov, "Propadaiushchiia sily, M. Gor'kii—Ocherki i rasskazy," Russkaia mysl', no. 5 (1899):146–62; no. 6 (1899):187–204; M. Men'shikov, "Krasivyi tsinizm'," in Kriticheskie stat'i, pp. 181–209.

[33] Gorky, "Makar Chudra," PSS 25, 1:13–26; "Starukha Izergil'," PSS 25, 1:76–96; "Chelkash," PSS 25, 2:7–41; "Konovalov," PSS 25, 3:7–60; "Prokhodimets," PSS 25, 4:25–61.

wanderer-primitive who appeared in Russian literature from the time of Pushkin, and on the real hoboes and tramps whom Gorky met on his travels.

With the exception of Makar Chudra, these hoboes are introduced to the reader by a narrator-intellectual. He too has left the city, seeking a new life. The two men meet, become temporary partners, and after a short time separate. They are drawn to one another because of their common feelings of alienation, but the differences between them eventually drive them apart. Yet during their brief alliance, the hobo-gypsy-wanderer serves as teacher to the intellectual who has not yet broken all his ties to society. Even though these stories do not offer the close structural and textual parallels to *Thus Spoke Zarathustra* provided by Gorky's story "Song of the Falcon" ("Pesnia o Sokole," 1895)—a parallel that has been perceptively analyzed by Betty Y. Forman—there are, nonetheless, many echoes of Zarathustra's voice in the teachings of these hoboes.[34]

The hobo challenges the intellectual to become a free man, advising him that he can only succeed if he has the courage to reject all duties and obligations to others. Zarathustra told his followers: "Unlearn this 'for,' you creators: your very virtue wants you to have nothing to do with 'for' and 'for the sake of' and 'because.' You shall stop your ears to these false little words" (Z, 301). The Caucasian gypsy Makar Chudra laughs at the intellectual's desire to help others, to sacrifice himself for the people. He asks:

> Life? Other people . . . Hmm. Why should that worry you? Aren't you life? Other people live without you and will live their lives without you. Do you imagine anybody needs you? You're neither bread nor a stick and nobody wants you.[35]

The hobo Promtov describes to the intellectual the sense of freedom he feels because he has broken his ties to others, and refused to follow their rules:

> You must understand this: in the vagabond life there is something absorbing, devouring. It is great to feel yourself free of responsibilities, of the various petty little ties which bind your existence among people . . . of all the little trifles clinging to your life so that it is no longer a pleasure, but becomes a tedious burden . . . a heavy

---

[34] Forman, "Nietzsche and Gorky in the 1890s."
[35] Gorky, "Makar Chudra," p. 13.

basket of obligations . . . like the obligation to dress oneself . . . respectably, as they say, respectably . . . and to do everything as is acceptable, and not as you wish. . . . But in the vagabond life you live outside of this nonsensical waste of time. . . . The very fact that you have refused the various comforts of life without regret and are able to exist without them somehow raises you in your own eyes.[36]

Attempting to convince the intellectual that his need to sacrifice himself for the folk is absurd, Makar Chudra argues that Russian peasants are weak, servile, and vicious men whose greed for land and fear of God prevent them from understanding what freedom is. He portrays the peasant as a slave:

Do you mean to say he was born to dig the earth and die without having managed to dig a grave for himself? Does he know what freedom is? Has he any idea of the vast and glorious steppe? Does the music of the steppe gladden his heart? He's a slave, from the moment he is born, a slave all his life long, and that's all! What can he do for himself? All he can do is hang himself, if he learned a little sense.[37]

Makar blames the servility of the peasant not on Russia's socioeconomic system nor political oppression, but rather on the peasant's weak character. He suggests that religion only teaches moral hypocrisy:

Huh! I spoke to a man once. He was a serious man, one of yours, a Russian. You must live, he says, not the way you want, but according to the way of God. Obey the Lord and he will give you everything you ask for. He himself was all in rags and holes. I told him to ask God for a new suit of clothes. He fell into a rage and drove me away, cursing. And he'd just been telling me that one should forgive and love his fellow creatures.[38]

All of Gorky's hoboes try to convince the intellectual to accept the truth about the peasant. Rather than sacrifice his life for them, the intellectual must learn to be a daring and courageous man himself. Self-liberation must come first. Makar Chudra recounts a story about two

---

[36] Gorky, "Prokhodimets," p. 52.
[37] Gorky, "Makar Chudra," p. 14.
[38] Ibid., pp. 14–15.

young defiant gypsies who fall in love. They choose to die rather than give up their personal freedom by submitting to one another, and the moral of the tale is clear: even death is preferable to a life of submission. Just as Zarathustra suggested that men in the past have always valued courage above all: "Courage, however, and adventure and joy in the unknown, the unattempted—*courage* seems to me the whole prehistory of man" (Z, 313), so the old Moldavian gypsy Izergil tells the young Russian that there are no heroic men any longer, and that if he wants to find out why, he must look into the past. She explains that people today "don't know how to live" and "bemoan their fate." "What's fate got to do with it?" she asks. "Everybody decides his own fate! I see all sorts of people nowadays, but I don't see any strong ones! What's become of them?"[39]

Izergil tells the intellectual two legends that illustrate her belief that men must become strong leaders once again. In the first tale the eagle-man Larra refuses to recognize the rules and laws of his tribe. The tribe punishes him by rejecting him and refusing to grant his wish for death.

In the second tale she portrays the story of Danko, described by a contemporary critic as Gorky's only true Nietzschean superman.[40] Danko is a young, courageous man who sacrifices himself for his tribe, not out of pity, for he recognizes that the people are weak, cowardly, and ungrateful, but rather because he recognizes what has to be done and that he alone can do it. His tribe has fled to a dark, swampy forest to escape an alien tribe, and is lost and perishing in the forest. Realizing their need for a leader, Danko tears out his heart and holds it up as a torch to lead his people out to the light, and to life. The people condemn and attack Danko even as they follow him; and after he successfully leads them out of the forest, one man crushes Danko's heart out of fear. Danko is dead, but the sparks from his heart continue to appear whenever a storm approaches.[41] The fate of the heroic and courageous Danko echoes Zarathustra's words: "You must be ready to burn yourself in your own flame: how could you become new, if you had not first become ashes!" (Z, 90).

In these folktales the gypsies Makar Chudra and Izergil advise the intellectual to perform feats of courage, not out of duty nor pity, but because they are men. There is, however, an unresolved ambivalence in their teachings, as distinct from Nietzsche's. Izergil, like Gorky's own

---

[39] Gorky, "Starukha Izergil'," p. 92.

[40] M. Gel'rot, "Nichshe i Gor'kii," *Russkoe bogatstvo*, no. 5 (1903):63.

[41] Gorky, "Starukha Izergil'," p. 96.

grandmother, advocates loyalty to the tribe—Danko's self-sacrifice is made, after all, to help his people—whereas the selfish rebellion of the eagle-man Larra leads to eternal suffering. Makar Chudra, in contrast, advo-cates a position taken up by the male hoboes and reflecting that of Gor-ky's grandfather: men must be completely selfish and individualistic.

For Nietzsche, the tension between the individual and the collective also exists, but he suggests that the individual must pursue his own goals, and that his acts will benefit men in the future. Gorky offers the same teaching in his allegory, "About the Siskin Who Lied, and the Wood-pecker, Lover of Truth" ("O Chizhe kotoryi lgal, i o Diatle-Liubitele istiny," 1893), which contains passages that seem to be taken directly from *Thus Spoke Zarathustra*.[42] Yet in his hobo stories, which are more realistic, he remains ambivalent about the individual's relationship to the group. While his hoboes preach to the intellectuals to become strong, heroic rebels, they themselves have suffered because of their own individ-ualistic rebellion. In the story "Konovalov," the narrator-intellectual Maxim suggests that these hoboes are the natural "blood brothers" of Stenka Ra-zin, the seventeenth-century Cossack rebel leader. They have succeeded in breaking their ties to society, but they are still angry, restless, and frustrated by their inability to reach their goals. Moreover, they refuse to accept the intellectual's sociological explanations for their moods and be-havior. Konovalov tells Maxim that he will not blame "external circum-stances"; he refuses to be categorized according to a class analysis.[43]

While Gorky indicates that his hoboes are not Russian supermen and have not achieved complete freedom and self-fulfillment, they nonethe-less are portrayed as the strongest men in Russia because they at least have had the courage to follow their own desires. Moreover, Gorky sug-gests that their dissatisfaction is inevitable. Zarathustra made a similar prediction to his followers, teaching them that only mediocre men were satisfied, and that the higher they strove, the greater their chance of fail-ing. He told them to accept failure; they had to be able to laugh at themselves, to never submit to despair, and to look toward the future (Z, 303–305). He predicted that they would be ostracized by other men pre-cisely because they had the courage to be different, to refuse to submit to any laws or people, and to strive ceaselessly. Weak men would envy them: "And he who flies is hated most of all" (Z, 89).

Gorky's rebels experience what Zarathustra predicted. They have re-

---

[42] Gorky, "O Chizhe, kotoryi lgal, i o Diatle-liubitele istiny," *PSS* 25, 1:46–53.
[43] Gorky, "Konovalov," pp. 23–24.

belled against society, and seek to be left alone, but whenever they come in contact with men who conform, their lives are in danger. Their greatest enemies are peasants. Although the hobo survives by exploiting the peasant's greed, cowardliness, and fear—Promtov claims he only needs the "sun, air, water, and the peasant" to survive—he realizes nonetheless that the peasant will destroy him, if he gets the chance.[44] The peasant Gavrila is portrayed by Gorky as a typical representative of his class. Even though the thief Chelkash has given him work, Gavrila admits to Chelkash that he had planned to kill him for his money because he knew that Chelkash would not be missed and is "not needed on earth." Only his fear of God, he claims, prevented him from attempting the murder.[45] The hobo Promtov brags about "the wall" that separates him from other men, yet he admits to the intellectual that if he is ever caught by others, they would "not just mutilate, but kill" him.[46]

Gorky's hoboes may have preached to Russian intellectuals to rebel and become new Russian supermen, but they could not be role models for Russian youth—a living person, possessing the strength, courage, and rebelliousness of Gorky's literary characters was needed, and Gorky filled the bill. Soon after the publication of Gorky's stories in 1898, young intellectuals seized him as their hero, assured that he possessed not only the worldly experience and courage of his hoboes, but also the rationality and creativity of intellectuals. Gorky certainly did not expect the fame and power that the public rapidly thrust upon him, and realized that he was not the heroic figure portrayed by the press, but he rose to the occasion nonetheless and soon became the culture hero of Russia's youth.[47]

A controversy immediately developed in the press because of Gorky's many attacks on Russian society and culture, particularly those on the intelligentsia and the peasants. Non-Marxist critics accused Gorky of preaching a "very dangerous" Nietzschean amoralism, of glorifying the strong and condemning the weak, and of romanticizing violent and criminal behavior.[48] Marxists were the only critics not to call Gorky a Nietz-

---

[44] Gorky, "Prokhodimets," p. 60.

[45] Gorky, "Chelkash," pp. 38–40.

[46] Gorky, "Prokhodimets," pp. 37, 60.

[47] Loe, "Maksim Gor'kii," pp. 50–54.

[48] See A. Andreevich (E. A. Solov'ev), "Ocherki tekushchei Russkoi literatury," *Zhizn'*, no. 4 (1900):311; Menshikov, "Krasivyi tsinizm," pp. 206–209; Minsky, "Filosofiia toski i zhazhda voli," pp. 24–25; Mikhailovsky, "O g. Mak. Gor'kom i ego geroiakh," pp. 55–75.

schean. V. A. Posse, for example, acclaimed him as an "authentic," "spontaneous" voice of the Russian people, who expressed the "soul of the working masses," "the soul of the lumpen proletariat."

> Gorky is a living protest against the boredom and peacefulness of communal-rural Russian life. Gorky is a reaction against Slavic dullness, flabbiness, and submissiveness.[49]

Other Marxists took the position established by Posse who realized that Gorky could be a leader of young intellectuals and workers and gave him considerable support. They too accepted Gorky's harsh portrait of the Russian peasants as an accurate one, and pointed out the similarities between his energetic, rebellious heroes and Russia's intellectuals and workers.[50] Ignoring the accusations that Gorky was a Nietzschean, they seemed to condone Gorky's voluntarism and antipositivism.

Populists and conservatives were surprised and confused by the Marxists' response to Gorky. The conservative M. A. Protopopov noted that it was "naive" and "odd" for Marxists to claim Gorky "as one of their own" since his hoboes were very different from "hard-working" and "well-behaved proletarians,"[51] while the Populist A. Skabichevsky accused Marxists of idolizing Gorky simply because of his ignorant, unfounded, and biased attack on Russian peasants.[52] Yet Marxists were not the only ones to give Gorky special treatment. With the exception of Populists, critics of varied political persuasions tolerated Nietzschean views in Gorky's works, which they would not accept from Nietzsche himself, nor from other Russian writers who were not intellectuals. Gorky was forgiven for overstepping the acceptable limits of criticism, for preaching a philosophy that condemned the basic morality of the intelligentsia, only because he was not an intellectual and just starting out on his literary career. Nonetheless, he was given repeated warnings in the press: he must stop romanticizing criminals and outcasts; get rid of his Nietzschean views; and adopt the traditional views of the Russian intelligentsia.[53]

Gorky was very quick to respond to the critics' attacks. Within months

---

[49]V. A. Posse, "Pevets protestuiushchei toski," in *Kriticheskie stat'i*, p. 14.

[50]"A. B.," "Mir bosiakov," pp. 40–43; "A. B.," "Krepnushchii talant'," in *Kriticheskie stat'i*, pp. 146–48.

[51]Protopopov, "Propadaiushchiia sily," no. 6, pp. 202–204.

[52]A. Skabichevsky, "M. Gor'kii, ocherki i razskazy," in *Kriticheskie stat'i*, pp. 106–31; idem, "Novye cherty v talante g. M. Gor'kogo," in *Kriticheskie stat'i*, pp. 125–45.

[53]Mikhailovsky, "Eshche o Maksim Gor'kom," pp. 91–93; Skabichevsky, "M. Gor'kii," pp. 106–21; "Novye cherty," pp. 125–45.

of the publication of the two-volume collection, he wrote a story entitled "The Reader" ("Chitatel' ") which condemned intellectuals and particularly writers while arguing that they had to become Russia's new leaders. Gorky described this story to his future wife as "his own truth" and predicted that he would "suffer a great deal" for his truth because people would not accept it and would condemn him for it for a long time. [54]

Gorky's editor F. D. Batiushkov advised Gorky to revise this story since it bore such a strong resemblance to "The Siskin Who Lied, and the Woodpecker, Lover of Truth" (the story that contains numerous parallels to *Thus Spoke Zarathustra*). Batiushkov noted, however, that when he read the story to an audience of "sympathetic" listeners the younger members felt it corresponded to their own mood, while the "more mature" members of the audience believed that Gorky should not publish "his confession" until he resolved its contradictions. [55] Gorky insisted, however, on publishing the story just as it was, defiantly responding to his editor that he hoped his attack (on Russian writers) was sufficiently strong. [56]

It is evident that Gorky had no intention of casting off his Nietzscheanism; on the contrary, in "The Reader" he tells Russian writers how they can become Russian supermen by adapting Nietzschean philosophy to the particular conditions in Russia.

"The Reader" is a dialogue between a writer and a shadowy figure called the Reader, who accosts him on the street. He accuses the writer of failing to fulfill his responsibilities. The Russian writer must become a "self-appointed apostle," "sense the future," and awaken man from his "indifference, cynicism, and beastliness." Instead the writer has not assumed this role, but "digs in the mire of reality," reflecting the evils of the real world, rather than offering man "a way out to the light, to truth, to beauty, to a new life." Preaching to the writer in words that directly echo those of Zarathustra, the Reader says: "The idea of life is in the beauty and strength of striving toward a goal, so that every moment has its own high purpose." [57] Striving distinguishes men from beasts, and gives

[54] Gorky to E. P. Peshkova, 25 February 1896, in *Arkhiv A. M. Gor'kogo*, vol. 5: *Pisma k E. P. Peshkovoi* (Moscow, 1955), p. 13. Gorky had begun working on "The Reader" in 1895. He completed it, however, between April and September 1898. *PSS* 25, 4:571.

[55] F. D. Batiushkov to Gorky, 4 October 1898, in *M. Gor'kii: Materialy i issledovaniia*, ed. S. D. Balukhatyi and V. A. Desnitskii, 4 vols. (Moscow and Leningrad. 1936–1951), 2:269.

[56] Gorky to F. D. Batiushkov, 19 or 20 October 1898, *PSS* 30, 28:38.

[57] Gorky, "Chitatel'," *PSS* 25, 4:126.

meaning and purpose to life. But men have lost their purpose: they are "slaves of life" rather than "tsars of the earth." They have lost pride in the knowledge that man was "the firstborn." Instead of recognizing their own potential they bow before facts—facts that have been created by them and then become "immutable law." But man must find faith in himself; his search for perfection is equivalent to the search for God:

> Those who make mistakes on the path to truth will perish! But leave them be, don't pity them—for there are many people. Striving is what is important, the desire of the soul to find God, and if there are souls who are seized with a striving toward God, He will be with them and revitalize them, for He is the eternal striving for perfection.[58]

Russian writers must become the prophets of this truth; they must be able to inspire men to respect themselves and to develop their strengths, but they have failed in this task because they themselves do not know how to live and are psychologically and physically weak.

But while the intellectual lacks vitality and an integrated personality, the masses have other weaknesses: they lack strength of character and ideals. The Reader explains that because people have known only violence, they respect its power alone, and will never listen to reason. The intellectual-writer must have the strength and courage to "create levers," to "create new freer forms of life." "Anger, hatred, courage, shame, repulsion, and sinister despair" are the levers needed to destroy "everything on earth." The Reader tells the writer he must have the courage to take the whip to men. Man needs the whip and the fiery caress of love after its blow: "Do not be afraid to make him ill; if you beat him loving him, he will accept your blows and his scar as one who deserves it."[59] He calls upon intellectuals to become Russia's new Dankos:

> Above life floats an odor of decay; cowardliness and servility saturate the heart; laziness binds the mind and hands in soft chains. What are you bringing into this abominable chaos? How insignificant you all are! How pitiable you all are! And how many of you there are! Oh, if only a rigorous and loving man with a flaming heart and a powerful comprehensive mind would appear! Into the oppressiveness of shameful silence, powerful words would ring out

[58] Ibid., p. 119.
[59] Ibid., p. 126.

like the tolls of a bell, and, perhaps, would shake up the despicable souls of the living corpses.[60]

There are numerous passages in this story that parallel *Thus Spoke Zarathustra*: the condemnation of contemporary society, particularly positivism; the distinction between "lords" and "slaves" of the earth; the condemnation of intellectuals for failing to be courageous men of action; the portrayal of the masses as servile, bestial, and cowardly; the call for ceaseless striving and for working toward a glorious, though undefined, future. These concepts may all be found in Nietzsche (Z, 55, 75–78, 82–84, 87, 136–39, 218–32, 312–13), and yet Gorky interprets Nietzsche according to his own past experiences. Whereas Zarathustra advised his followers to go to women with the whip (Z, 91–93), Gorky says the strong leader must take the whip to Russian men and women alike, for both are in need of tough and strong leaders. Gorky evidently applied his own experiences among the lower classes to Nietzsche's philosophy, including the lesson he had learned from his grandfather—that you teach people first by whipping them and then, by caressing them with love.[61]

In a letter to the artist I. E. Repin, Gorky described "The Reader" as a conversation he was having with himself: "I, as a man, am dissatisfied with myself—the writer, for I have read too much and books have robbed my soul."[62] To be sure, it was a conversation which Gorky would have with many other writers as well. Throughout his letters to his friends and to his protégés in the Wednesdays circle, Gorky would repeat the words expressed by Zarathustra, advising Russian writers to become warrior-leaders, leading the people by example and with the whip, rather than with pity and self-sacrifice.[63]

It is evident that by 1898 Gorky had decided that Russian supermen would not be found among the hoboes and tramps portrayed in his early stories, and hoped, though with many reservations and much skepticism, that intellectuals would be able to assume that role. In future years he would try to get his protégés to become fellow warriors with him, but would meet with little success. Moreover, after 1898, he began to gravitate toward the Marxists. Though he never fully accepted many of their views, he joined the Bolshevik section of the Marxist Social Democratic

---

[60] Ibid., p. 125.
[61] Gorky, "Detstvo," pp. 29–31.
[62] Gorky to I. E. Repin, 23 November 1899, SS 30, 28:100.
[63] Loe, "Maksim Gor'kii," p. 59.

Labor party in 1904. Gorky's newly placed Marxist hope in the Russian worker would be reflected in many of his later works, such as his play, *The Philistines* (*Meshchane*, 1902), and his novel, *Mother* (*Mat'*, 1907). Still he never fully gave up his early Nietzschean philosophy; he simply combined it with his new views. Thus, it is not surprising that in 1908 he joined A. V. Lunacharsky and A. A. Bogdanov (a pseudonym for A. A. Malinovsky) in attempting to establish a "God-building" school for Russian workers in Italy, whose goal was the creation of a new man-god. George Kline has aptly called these thinkers, including Gorky, "Nietzschean Marxists," and indicated how each succeeded in combining these two philosophies.[64] Even though Lenin quickly crushed the God-building school because of its heretical teachings, Gorky continued to preach his philosophy. Once he had found "his own truth," first expressed in his story "The Reader," he also found the role he was seeking and became a warrior-leader himself. This role proved especially satisfactory to him because it enabled him to combine the teachings of his grandfather with the philosophy of Friedrich Nietzsche.

Gorky never fully resolved his ambivalence toward the individual's relationship to the group, although he gradually gave up the strong Nietzschean individualism which Russian critics had found so objectionable in his early stories. On the other hand, he never fully accepted the Bolshevik, and later Stalinist, view that the individual must subordinate himself to the collective and often defended writers and other intellectuals from the authoritarianism of the Soviet government. To be sure, the complex and controversial story of Gorky's problematical relationship to the Soviet regime cannot be told here, but it should be noted that Gorky retained many of his early Nietzschean views into the Soviet period, and that these influenced that relationship. Moreover, certain of them in particular, such as his conviction that the Russian people needed strong, aggressive leaders, his intolerance for "weak" intellectuals, and his belief that harsh actions were justifiable in man's struggle to create a better future, help to explain both Gorky's admiration for Lenin and his later cooperation with Stalin. Gorky's quest for a Russian superman—a quest that bore strong resemblance to the Bolsheviks' own determination to create a new Communist man—may be traced back to Gorky's childhood, but its philosophical rationale derived from his reading of Friedrich Nietzsche.

[64] George Kline, "The God-Builders," 103–16.

12.

Lunacharsky: A "Nietzschean Marxist"?

A. L. Tait

"THE GLOOMY POWER of Nietzsche's brash pessimism, black romanticism, and the evil pathos of his strong, belligerent personality seemed at times to mesmerize Lunacharsky. The voice of Nietzsche cast the same spell over him as did the music of Wagner."[1] That A. V. Lunacharsky— an associate of Lenin from 1904, a leading member and ideologist of the Bolshevik Vpered group who exercised much influence on Maxim Gorky's outlook in the years after the Revolution of 1905, the brother-in-law of Alexander Bogdanov, and from 1917 to 1929 commissar of enlightenment of the Russian Republic with responsibility for education and the arts—should have been enthusiastically receptive to the influence of Nietzsche is the cause of consternation among many critics. Nevertheless, little serious effort has gone into analyzing the reasons for this.[2] Little attention has been paid to the wider intellectual context, to the critical reactions of Lunacharsky's contemporaries, to the influence of Nietzsche on Lunacharsky as a dramatist and as a major cultural policymaker during the Soviet period, or to the striking evolution of Lunacharsky's public pronouncements on Nietzsche.

---

[1] A. A. Lebedev, *Esteticheskie vzgliady A. V. Lunacharskogo: Ocherki*, 2nd ed. (Moscow, 1970), p. 39.

[2] The only thoroughgoing assessment is contained in a recent West German monograph. See Raimund Sesterhenn, "Nietzsche als Gotterbauer," in his *Das Bogostroitel'stvo bei Gor'kij und Lunačarskij bis 1909* (Munich, 1982), pp. 101–11. Much useful information is also to be found in Dora Angres's annotated bibliography *Die Beziehungen Lunačarskijs zur deutschen Literatur* (Berlin, 1970); and in Richard Davies, "Nietzsche in Russia: A Preliminary Bibliography," *Germano-Slavica* 2, no. 2, (1976):107–46; 2, no. 3 (1977):201–20; reprinted without annotations as Chapter 16 in this volume.

The extent of Nietzsche's influence on Lunacharsky has been obscured by the circumstance that Lenin, in combating the Vperedists, parenthetically attacked Lunacharsky's ideology, which he nicknamed "God-building" (*bogostroitel'stvo*), in *Materialism and Empirio-criticism* (1908). Subsequently, Soviet critics have in general accepted his contention that Lunacharsky was a member of a group of empirio-critical "Machists," assembled around Lenin's rival for the Bolshevik leadership, Alexander Bogdanov, and this has distracted critical attention from Nietzsche's contribution.[3] Lenin evidently wished to concentrate his fire on the antimaterialism of such empirio-criticists as Avenarius and Mach in order to disqualify the Russian group as Marxists, and for this reason disregarded their Nietzscheanism. Western critics on the other hand speak in general not of "Machists" but of "Nietzschean Marxists."[4] Raimund Sesterhenn supports George Kline's terminology, noting that, at least until about 1915, the designation of Lunacharsky as a "Nietzschean Marxist" is entirely apposite.[5] This can have curious consequences, as when Philip T. Grier comments that "the 'Nietzschean' group as a whole had suffered a strenuous attack by Lenin in the form of his *Materialism and Empirio-criticism*."[6] In fact there is not a single mention of Nietzsche in the work.

Let us look in more detail at Lunacharsky's intellectual context.[7] His schooldays in Kiev coincided with a rise in the popularity of Marxism and with a corresponding decline in the fortunes of Populism. The lull

---

[3] A. Krivosheeva writes that "Bogdanov's eclectic philosophy, radically opposed to Marxism, produced its poisoned offshoots; under Bogdanov's influence Lunacharsky studied E. Mach and F. Nietzsche." Thirty years later Alexander Lebedev comments that "Bogdanov's apostasy from Marxism struck Lunacharsky as innovation and as representing a critical attitude to the traditions of revolutionary philosophy. The philosophical doctrines of E. Mach and afterwards of F. Nietzsche increasingly occupied Lunacharsky's thoughts." See A. Krivosheeva, *Esteticheskie vzgliady A. V. Lunacharskogo* (Leningrad and Moscow, 1939), p. 8; Lebedev, *Esteticheskie vzgliady A. V. Lunacharskogo*, p. 39. Sesterhenn's monograph is devoted in part to discrediting this stereotype.

[4] Thus George L. Kline writes that "When, in the early 1900's, some of the early Russian Marxists (especially Lunacharsky and Vol'sky) became dissatisfied with the impersonalism and anti-individualism of Marxian historical materialism (a lineal descendant, in this respect, of Hegelianism), they turned explicitly to Nietzsche for support in their 'deviation.'" See George L. Kline, "Changing Attitudes towards the Individual," in *The Transformation of Russian Society*, ed. Cyril E. Black (Cambridge, Mass., 1960), p. 608.

[5] Sesterhenn, *Das Bogostroitel'stvo bei Gor'kij und Lunačarskij bis 1909*, p. 110.

[6] Philip T. Grier, *Marxist Ethical Theory in the Soviet Union* (Dordrecht, 1978), p. 77.

[7] Lunacharsky's early intellectual development is chronicled in my *Lunacharsky: Poet of the Revolution (1875–1907)*, Birmingham Slavonic Monographs, no. 14 (Birmingham, 1984).

in revolutionary activity following the assassination of Alexander II in 1881 was followed by a sharpening of the intelligentsia's antagonism toward the government in the wake of the famine of 1891–1892—a catastrophe on a scale that seemed to beggar the benign homespun solutions of Tolstoi and of Populist utopianism. Reacting against the deliberate classicism of the tsarist school curriculum, Lunacharsky and his school friends, who included Lunacharsky's lifelong philosophical opponent, the religious thinker, Nicholas Berdiaev (1874–1948), eagerly seized upon any positivist literature that came their way, legally or illegally. John Stuart Mill, Herbert Spencer, Charles Darwin, and Karl Marx were prominent on their reading lists. In locally organized debates the Social Democrats took on the Populists and, at least in their own recollection, won. By 1894 the Social Democrats of Kiev were splintering over tactics into the followers of Peter Struve (1870–1944), who favored leaving the workers to develop their own socialist consciousness, and the "Plekhanovites," who, following the precepts of the "father of Russian Marxism", G. V. Plekhanov (1857–1918), favored more widespread agitation with ultimate political rather than economic goals. By 1899 a reaction was evident among the various Marxist groups that sought to come to terms in a variety of ways with some of the previously rejected strengths of Populism and earlier Russian religious and intellectual traditions. Marxism's "scientificness," its economic determinism, which had seemed so European and so powerful, seemed now on the one hand to have excluded Populism's "critically thinking individual" from the historical process only too successfully, to the detriment of revolutionary morale. On the other hand, its passionless acceptance of the social horrors of industrialization, its willingness to sacrifice one generation for the good of another, seemed wholly to undermine the indispensable socialist ethic of altruism. In these debates Lunacharsky, while remaining unambiguously a Social Democrat, ranged himself against both the "Struvists," with their neo-Kantian critique of the ethics of Marxism, and against Plekhanov with his scholastic objectivism, which seemed only to justify the charges of the "Struvists." Lunacharsky's principal buttress in ethics is undoubtedly Nietzsche.

Lunacharsky's unexpectedly strong and enduring interest in myth and religious values, in ethics and esthetics, predates his familiarity with Nietzsche's teachings. If we ignore his desecration of an icon in early childhood, we find him already in 1896, at the age of twenty, developing an interest in the ethical side of socialism after a conversation with Plekhanov.[8] His interest in religion and myth was strengthened by his acquaintance in the same year with the sociologist, Maxim Kovalevsky (1851–1916). Living in 1896–1898 in Paris, Lunacharsky spent much of his time in the library of the Musée Guimet, which specialized in religious history.[9] When in these years he met the aged Populist leader Peter Lavrov, the topic of conversation was the origination of kindred myths among widely separated peoples, and the laws governing the evolution of myths.[10] Up to this time, however, Lunacharsky had made no reference to Nietzsche.

In April 1900 Lunacharsky was arrested while giving a lecture in Kiev on "Henryk Ibsen as a Moralist." His notes for this talk include a first reference to Nietzsche, along with Dostoevsky and Tolstoi, in the context of the instability of *fin de siècle* norms of social morality.[11] He later gave 1900 as the year in which he translated Nietzsche, although without naming the work or works he translated.[12] In 1901, detained in Kaluga on a conspiracy charge, he passed the summer months agreeably enough on boating trips with young ladies declaiming his own poetry and a long "Dithyramb to Dionysus," which clearly owes its inspiration to Nietzsche's *Dionysian Dithyrambs*.[13] In 1902 he is stoutly defending Nietzsche's amoralism, and by 1903 his Nietzscheanism is immoderate.[14]

The initial impetus for Lunacharsky's "God-building" came from a question posed in 1901 by Serge Bulgakov (1871–1944). Does not philosophical materialism or positivism lack the ethical momentum essential for socialism to be seen as an ideal worth struggling for?[15] Lunacharsky's attempt to formulate a combative Social-Democratic ideology in response

[8] A. V. Lunacharsky, *Velikii perevorot (Oktiabr'skaia revoliutsiia)*, pt. 1 (St. Petersburg, 1919), pp. 17–18.

[9] *Museum Guimet* (Paris, 1976), p. 4.

[10] Lunacharsky, *Velikii perevorot*, pp. 18–19.

[11] "Genrik Ibsen kak moralist: Konspekt referata," in A. V. *Lunacharsky: Neizdannye materialy*, Literaturnoe nasledstvo, 82 (Moscow, 1970), p. 280.

[12] Ibid., p. 557.

[13] Lunacharsky, "Muzyka: Difiramb bogu Dionisu: Poema" (Manuscript in Institut mirovoi literatury imeni A. M. Gor'kogo, Moscow, fond 16, opis' 1, ed. khr. 30, 46 pp. [Dated 10–26 June 1901]); E. Gnesina, "Vospominaniia o Lunacharskom," *Sovetskaia muzyka*, no. 3 (1967):71.

[14] See, for example, his articles "Russkii Faust" (1902) and "Pered litsom roka" (1903), reprinted in Lunacharsky, *Etiudy kriticheskie i polemicheskie* (Moscow, 1905), pp. 179–90 and 36–110 respectively.

[15] This is asserted in Sergei Bulgakov, "Ivan Karamazov (v romane Dostoevskogo 'Brat'ia Karamazovy') kak filosofskii tip" (1902), in *Ot marksizma k idealizmu* (St. Petersburg, 1903), p. 109.

to this question was scorned by Berdiaev in *Landmarks* (*Vekhi*, 1909): Nietzsche, he wrote, had died in the belief that nobody needed him and that he was stranded alone on his mountain peak, but suddenly he was very much in demand to refreshen and reinvigorate Marxism. While on the one hand whole herds of Nietzschean individualists were on the move, on the other "Lunacharsky has concocted a Russian salad of Marx, Avenarius, and Nietzsche which many have found piquant and to their taste."[16] Marx the economic determinist, Avenarius the antimaterialist, and Nietzsche the antisocialist are not the most obviously compatible of ingredients even for a vinaigrette, but they are indeed the main contributors to his philosophy. Lunacharsky propagated his "God-building" ideology in numerous newspaper articles, in his two-volume study, *Religion and Socialism* (*Religiia i sotsializm*, 1909–1911), at the Social Democratic Party schools for worker activists of Capri (1909) and Bologna (1910), and through a proletarian culture circle that he ran in Paris in 1911–1915. Lunacharsky persisted until the mid-1920s, only to then abandon his ideology abruptly and to pour ridicule on members of the intelligentsia who had been attracted by Nietzsche.

What are the Nietzschean elements of Lunacharsky's God-building? The revolutionary acts as he does, Lunacharsky tells us, for his own gratification. With Nietzsche, Lunacharsky renounces the sense of duty as a motivator in favor of the creative will.[17]

> Tell me, what has an artist to do with altruism? . . . He works primarily in order to sense his own strength, for the freedom of his creative genius. Can the social activist not work in the same way? To him the people, society are a lump of marble from which he creates a beautiful humankind in accordance with his ideal. . . . Is he an altruist? He is not interested in your happiness, reader. It may be that he would not sacrifice a fingernail for your happiness. On the contrary, if you get in his way he will destroy you.[18]

[16] Nikolai Berdiaev, "Filosofskaia istina i intelligentskaia pravda," in *Vekhi*, 2nd ed. (Moscow, 1909), p. 16.

[17] Cf. Nietzsche: "Yes, a sacred Yes is needed, my brothers, for the sport of creation: the spirit now wills *its own* will, the spirit sundered from the world now wins *its own* world" (Z, 55).

[18] Lunacharsky, "Pered litsom roka: K filosofii tragedii" (1903), in *Etiudy kriticheskie i polemicheskie*, pp. 104–105.

Marxian acceptance of the principle that the individual may be sacrificed in the interests of society does not therefore deter the social reformer, as Bulgakov had suggested. Nietzsche provides the ready answer that humane concern and compassion do not enter into the matter since "social creativity" is an end in itself.

While Marx and Nietzsche agree on the expendability of the individual where necessary, a trickier problem concerns the question of the status of the "critically thinking individual" in history, with its implications for the role of the intelligentsia in the revolutionary process. Marx's great strength, after all, had been his ability to point to the invincible masses rather than the vulnerable hero as the prime mover of history. There is an immense gulf here between Marx and Nietzsche, and Lunacharsky has no illusions about Nietzsche's elitism. He writes that where for Marxism the struggle is that of a class instinctively fighting for its rights and for a life worthy of man, the attractive aspect of Nietzsche is "the declaration of the right to complete self-determination, the proud challenge to society and its pillars, emphasis of the rights of the individual to perfect himself and to the joy of life and creativity."[19] Whereas Lunacharsky describes himself as a "democratic amoralist," he unambiguously acknowledges Nietzsche as an "aristocratic amoralist" who believes it is fair enough to force a thousand mediocrites to live in the swamp of a servile existence in order that one genius should be enabled to move even marginally forward. The problem, Lunacharsky explains, is to persuade such aristocrats as Nietzsche himself that a democratic order best serves the aspirations of the exceptional individual, "but this," he admits, "is far from easy."[20]

Lunacharsky devoted a good deal of energy to arguing this case. In a long treatise of 1909 he considers ways in which the intelligentsia may find its way to the cause of the proletariat.[21] Temporary destitution, political opportunism, and philanthropy are all seen as less than satisfactory bases for conversion. The fourth way is the path of the "ultra-individualist" to collectivism, and it is here that Lunacharsky resolves the problem of his individualism and collectivism. A great creative personality cannot but rise above the shortsighted pettiness of individualistic philistinism. He cannot fail to see how irrationally society is organized or to understand

[19] Lunacharsky, "Opyt literaturnoi kharakteristiki Gleba Uspenskogo" (1903), in *Sobranie sochinenii*, 8 vols. (Moscow, 1963–1967), 1:289. Henceforth cited as *SS*.

[20] Lunacharsky, "Voprosy morali i M. Meterlink" (1904), in *Etiudy kriticheskie i polemicheskie*, p. 158.

[21] Lunacharsky, "Meshchanstvo i individualizm" (1909), in *Meshchanstvo i individualizm* (Moscow and Petrograd, 1923), pp. 5–136.

why. He must comprehend his own position as a link between the past and the future human culture, and precisely the striving toward happiness will dictate actions that will lead, not to wolfish self-betterment, but to the progress and development of humanity of which he is a conscious part, even if this means forgoing certain possibilities for personal development. Among the attributes of the "ultra-individualist" are:

a profound sympathy and admiration for any force that is raising itself up to its full height; a feeling bordering sometimes on complete infatuation with the beauty of the man of the future, my brother, the continuer of my work; a drive to build the edifice of culture, gigantic and eternal—because the joy of creating something vast many times exceeds the joy of working at something small, complete in itself, and capable of fitting within the limitations of an individual's abilities.[22]

Lunacharsky's explicit sources are Nietzsche's superman as a cultural ideal, but adapted to socialist purposes, Gorky's "Man, with a Capital Letter" (Lunacharsky was living on Capri with Gorky at this time), and Ernst Mach's meditations on the theme of the Dionysian in the life of the natural scientist. Lunacharsky quotes him:

The content of our consciousness, to the extent that it unquestionably breaks down the barriers of the individual and of his links with other people, leads a supra-individual life, more general, impersonal, independent of the individual who elaborated it. To collaborate in this is the supreme joy of artists, scholars, and politicians.[23]

Lunacharsky's play *Faust and the City* (*Faust i gorod*, 1918), which he wrote 1906–1916 and by which he set great store, is devoted precisely to the problem of "genius, with its drive to enlightened absolutism, on the one hand, and democracy on the other."[24]

More perplexing for critics even than Lunacharsky's Nietzscheanism is his fascination with religion. Much the same emotional magnetism is at the root of both. "The very soul of religion," he writes, "is hope of the triumph of beauty and grace, of bliss and power on the one hand, and a

---

[22] Ibid., pp. 127–28.

[23] Ibid., p. 135.

[24] Lunacharsky, "Vmesto predisloviia," *Faust i gorod* (1918), in his *P'esy* (Moscow, 1963), p. 133. The prehistory of the play is discussed in my "Lunacharskii's Russian *Faust*," *Germano-Slavica* 3, no. 3 (Spring 1980):189–203.

joyful devotion to the sublime which breaks down the shutters of the isolated life, which raises its ephemerality to eternal significance."[25] We recognize the Dionysian tendency of ultra-individualism to breach its banks and overflow into enthusiastic collectivism. Certain aspects of the religious tradition, together with certain aspects of Nietzsche, could be used by Lunacharsky in his search for an ideology that would swell the ranks of those prepared to fight to the last for a socialist future. The compound is evident in the *loci classici* of his God-building: God is dead and the universe is without meaning. Where is man to find a firm foundation on which to build? How is he to retain his dignity in an empty cosmos?

> To overcome one's fear of suffering, that fear that sometimes causes a man to screw up his eyes and long for a strong and stable culture founded on the granite of philosophical truth rather than on the uncertain supports of fictions—to overcome that fear, according to Nietzsche, should be the pride of man.[26]

> Nietzsche taught that man is free to create illusions and fantasies providing they lead him forward along the path of creative achievements, to the growth of his powers, to the sovereign joy of power over Nature. Even if the vision should prove unrealizable, even if the ideal should prove to be beyond his powers, all that matters is that man should be bold and should struggle to advance. Take away from a man such an illusion and, if he is strong, he will create another, even more beautiful, for himself. And who knows but that what awaits him may not be more beautiful than any vision.[27]

The motivating illusion that man has lost is God, and the even more beautiful illusion with which Lunacharsky proposes to replace him is a collectivist version of the superman.[28] By humanizing the environment, by creating a rationally organized society, the socialist can see himself as preparing the way for the full realization of the potential of man, for the collective superman of the future.[29]

Lunacharsky had no illusions about his standing as an academic phi-

---

[25] Lunacharsky, "Ateizm," in *Ocherki po filosofii marksizma: Filosofskii sbornik* (St. Petersburg, 1908), p. 157.

[26] Lunacharsky, "Dachniki" (1905), SS, 2:9.

[27] Ibid., p. 10.

[28] Lunacharsky, "Ateizm," p. 157.

[29] Lunacharsky, "[Novye] dramy," (1907), in *Kriticheskie etiudy (Russkaia literatura)* (Leningrad, 1925), p. 167.

losopher. He knew he was a propagandist, and quotes with delight from *Thus Spoke Zarathustra*, "Let us divinely strive *against* one another!" (Z, 125)—adding for himself a Darwinian aside, "And let not logic decide, but . . . natural selection!"[30] Ultimately, it is a matter of class ideals, and Lunacharsky hints as clearly as was possible under the tsarist censorship that "natural selection" will ultimately take the form of armed struggle. The democratic amoralists will confront their class opponents with clear *proofs* that will owe nothing to logic or rhetoric.[31]

Lunacharsky's Nietzscheanism drew criticism from both orthodox Marxist and Populist contemporaries. Plekhanov irritably proclaimed that "gospodin" Lunacharsky was not a Marxist but a bourgeois philosopher, and that his constituency was not the proletariat but the modish pessimists of the bourgeois intelligentsia.[32] N. Grabovsky (1863–1925), in a lengthy analysis of Lunacharsky's philosophy, written from a generally Leninist viewpoint, likewise wrote him off as a non-Marxist. In the case of Lunacharsky his "Nietzscheanism and all the rest of it is firmly bound up with his bourgeois individualism. His mystical 'collectivist philosophy' is the philosophy of a repentant individualist seeking immortality through the agency of a supernatural Macro-Ego (just as Bulgakov and Co. want a transcendent God to realize their immortality)."[33]

Populists were unhappy about his moral relativism and rejection of compassion as the mainspring of social action. Lunacharsky's "Nietzschean Marxism," they claimed, made explicit what was only implied by Marx: the proletariat no less than the superman stands beyond conventional norms of good and evil. The long-term dangers of this, later only too amply demonstrated under Stalin, were apparent enough to Russian liberal critics who predicted that the time might come when Lunacharsky and his fellow "ethical positivists," having rent the garments of duty, morality, religion, and altruism, might find that their "fatalistic cult of reality" and their faith in the spontaneous morality of "life" failed to live up to expectations.

[30] Lunacharsky, "O 'Problemakh idealizma' " (1903), in *Etiudy kriticheskie i polemicheskie*, p. 249.

[31] Lunacharsky, "Voprosy morali i M. Meterlink," pp. 160–61.

[32] G. V. Plekhanov, "O tak nazyvaemykh religioznykh iskaniiakh v Rossii" (1909), in *Literaturnoe nasledie Plekhanova*, 8 vols. (Leningrad, 1930–1940), 7:85.

[33] N. Grabovsky [V. F. Gorin-Galkin], *Doloi materializm! (Kritika empiriokriticheskoi kritiki)* (St. Petersburg, 1910), p. 276.

Deep down in this amoralism there is always concealed a firm conviction that the principle that "Everything is permitted" will ultimately lead back nonetheless to the "safe stronghold," to the proxy of morality, and that because of this, and only because of this, amoralism is not dangerous: "And it doesn't matter if Smerdiakov himself hears it!"[34]

Interestingly enough, humane concern for the individual informs the criticism of the Marxist Grabovsky, whose acceptance of the inexorable determinism of Marx seems creditably grudging. He makes the point that where Marx has in mind a real society with future happiness for real people, Nietzsche and Lunacharsky are concerned with nebulous "supermen" whose value is not even in themselves, but in an abstract strength or beauty that they embody. In this sense the ideal is not social or socialist but abstractly esthetic.[35] In this respect Lunacharsky does indeed follow not Marx but Nietzsche.

Soviet criticism is neither extensive nor detailed. The most widespread view is that Lunacharsky was "blind" to the antisocialist aspects of Nietzsche's teaching.[36] Neither Soviet nor Western critics refer to a very early review by Lunacharsky of Hans Vaihinger's *Nietzsche als Philosoph*.[37] This review appeared in 1903, within one year of his earliest published reference to Nietzsche. In it he imperturbably lists seven tendencies that Vaihinger identifies in Nietzsche, including the *antisocialist*, the *antidemocratic* and *antifeminist*, and the *anti-intellectual*. He does not question the correctness of Vaihinger's generalizations, and notes only that one might question whether they are the *principal* tendencies in

[34] Volzhsky [A. S. Glinka], "Torzhestvuiushchii amoralizm (Po povodu 'Russkogo Fausta' A. Lunacharskogo)," *Voprosy filosofii i psikhologii*, no. 4 (September–October 1902):903, 905.

[35] Grabovsky, *Doloi materializm!*, pp. 299–300.

[36] Often some predisposition is identified that made Lunacharsky susceptible to Nietzsche's influence. Lebedev himself suggests that it was his earlier enthusiasm for the German Romantic philosophers: even in 1920 Lunacharsky "seemed not to notice" such aspects of Nietzsche's romantic ideal as the idea of eternal recurrence or his "racist ravings." Lebedev, *Esteticheskie vzgliady* A. V. Lunacharskogo, p. 41. Krivosheeva finds him "naive" (*Esteticheskie vzgliady*, p. 34), while S. F. Oduev finds him gullible (S. F. Oduev, *Reaktsionnaia sushchnost' nitssheanstva* [Moscow, 1959], p. 35). I. P. Kokhno claims that "As far as Nietzsche's misanthropy and pessimism, his antidemocratism and hatred of socialist doctrines are concerned, Lunacharsky seemed not to notice these highly characteristic features of Nietzscheanism." I. P. Kokhno, *Cherty portreta: Stranitsy zhizni i deiatel'nosti* A. V. *Lunacharskogo* (Minsk, 1972), p. 30.

[37] Lunacharsky, "Gans Faiginger: Nietsshe kak filosof" [Review], *Obrazovanie*, no. 4 (1903):127–29.

Nietzsche. Lunacharsky regrets the emphasis on "antis" to the detriment of Nietzsche's positive features. He writes of Nietzsche (whom A. A. Lebedev, while supporting the "blindness" theory, describes as Lunacharsky's "unchallengeable authority"),[38]

> Nietzsche's criticism of democracy and socialism is dreadfully superficial; the very fact that he could equate them with Christianity is enough to show its insubstantiality. Only a man who has not bothered to get to the bottom of the matter could confuse equality before the law with a tendency to standardize people, or could confuse socialism with hyperstatism.[39]

Nietzsche's antidemocratic stance, he continues, is "wholly based on misunderstanding, on the confusion of democracy with the weak, the pathetic, the meek, on the absurd equating of strata of the population with castes of racial origin."[40] Clearly, if Lunacharsky's belief that he could utilize Nietzsche in a Marxist philosophy is symptomatic of a disability, then it is not blindness to what he himself terms "the dubious aspects" of Nietzsche's teaching.[41] We may agree at least with I. P. Kokhno when he writes that "in the works [of Mach, Avenarius, and Nietzsche] he was seeking ideas that fitted with his own outlook, and the sources of his outlook were to be found in the social life of pre-Revolutionary Russia."[42]

Before the Revolutions of 1917 Lunacharsky was not only a prolific journalist and lecturer but also a prolific playwright. Current estimates suggest he wrote in excess of seventy plays. Several, including one titled *The Superman* (*Sverkhchelovek*, 1906), deal with various aspects of "pseudo-Nietzschean" zoological individualism.[43] Others deal with particular philosophical notions, like the non-existence of objective truth and the temporary beneficence of this or that delusion or half-truth,[44] or the need

---

[38] Lebedev, *Esteticheskie vzgliady* A. V. *Lunacharskogo*, p. 79.
[39] Lunacharsky, "Gans Faiginger: Nietsshe kak filosof," p. 128.
[40] Ibid.
[41] Ibid.
[42] Kokhno, *Cherty portreta*, p. 30.
[43] Lunacharsky, "Sverkhchelovek" (1906), in *Piat' farsov dlia liubitelei* (St. Petersburg, 1907), pp. 3–21; and, for example, his *Korolevskii bradobrei* (St. Petersburg, 1906), and the post-Revolutionary *Iad* (Moscow, 1926).
[44] "Vavilonskaia palochka" (1911), in *Idei v maskakh* (Moscow, 1912), pp. 75–110.

for activism in the face of an indifferent universe.[45] Three plays written in 1919 during the Civil War stand out from the rest stylistically for their complete nonrealism. The most notable of these is the mythological *The Magi (Magi).*[46]

Nietzsche's influence on Lunacharsky received a boost during the First World War. Lunacharsky resided in Switzerland in 1915–1917, and there made the acquaintance of Nietzsche's erstwhile protegé, Carl Spitteler (1845–1924). Studying Spitteler's literary works Lunacharsky was amazed: "I can hardly recollect a fact to parallel this, a similar feeling of delight and happiness on reading any other poetic works."[47] He settled down for eight months to translate Spitteler into Russian. In an article of 1916 Lunacharsky quotes with approval the view that Spitteler synthesizes individualism and socialism. In his works he portrays the synthesis of individualism and socialism through "voluntary, natural service to a pan-human task from an individual who, in accordance with his every instinct, can do no other, who shines as does the sun with complete spontaneity, hating evil, and altruistic only as a result of the urge to be true to himself, his soul, and his inner uniquely personal duty."[48] In Spitteler's heroes we see Nietzsche's superman freely serving the cultural growth of humanity.[49] Lunacharsky began to imitate Spitteler in his own plays, and this is why the Civil War plays with their mythical or legendary characters are so strikingly different from his other, predominantly historical or contemporary plays. In Lunacharsky's words, they "bear on them the impress of Carl Spitteler's influence."[50]

The Magi (1919) is one of Lunacharsky's more successful plays. As it is written in verse the intellectuality and "wordiness," which are often obtrusive in his plays, are in accord with the prominence of the dialogue. Despite the speed with which the play was written (Lunacharsky asserts that he wrote it in eleven nights after grueling days of work at the Commissariat of Enlightenment in the winter of 1918–1919), the principles for which the characters stand are clearly enunciated.[51] Appropriately

[45]"Tri putnika i Ono" (1911), in Ibid., pp. 111–44.
[46]Lunacharsky, *Magi* (Moscow, 1919); the others are *Ivan v raiu* (Moscow, 1920), and *Vasilisa Premudraia* (Petrograd, 1920).
[47]Lunacharsky, "Karl Shpitteler" (1916), SS, 5:362.
[48]Lunacharsky is quoting the critic Herman Stegemann. Ibid., p. 365.
[49]Ibid., pp. 365–66.
[50]Lunacharsky, *Velikii perevorot*, p. 56.
[51]Lunacharsky, Foreword to *Magi*, in his *Dramaticheskie proizvedeniia*, 2 vols. (Moscow, 1923), 2:228.

enough he turns for the play's underlying philosophy to Nietzsche's precursors, Fichte and Schelling, for whom he had nurtured an enthusiasm in the 1890s. Publishing it in 1919, he emphasized that he had long since affectionately relegated his outlook of those years "to the treasury of my artistic myths," but considered the poet free to choose his materials where he would.[52] The plot illustrates a number of familiar "Nietzschean" tenets, and centers on the intrusion into a community of Magi of the Eternal Feminine in the form of the prophetess Manessa. She is invited by the leader of the Magi to waken them from sluggishness. The fundamental principle of their community, as distinct from that of the neighboring ascetic Christian community, is full realization of the individual's potential. At the end of the play the God Dionysus proclaims the unity of the universe:

> Those descending understand:
> Motion, action, God transcend;
> And like rainfall bless the chasms.
> My path, a circle, never ends.[53]

The public attitude of Soviet critics to *The Magi* has been predominantly negative on the grounds that it is linked with Lunacharsky's "philosophical errors." Lunacharsky himself was evidently so pleased with the style that he soon began work in the same manner on a mythological trilogy, *Song of Hope (Pesnia nadezhdy,* unfinished?).[54]

Nietzsche's influence on Lunacharsky is evident in a number of areas of the latter's cultural policy. As has been mentioned, his play *Faust and the City* depicts the path of an "ultra-individualist" or aristocratic amoralist to collectivism. This concept was behind Lunacharsky's whole policy of seeking reconciliation as commissar of enlightenment with the most

---

[52] Ibid.

[53] Ibid., p. 304.

[54] The three parts were to have been V*asilisa Premudraia, Mitra spasitel'*, and *Moisei Kon—vozhd' narodov.* See V. Ash[marin], "Mitra spasitel'," *Izvestiia*, 12 July 1919, p. 2. These plays, of which the third may never have been completed, have been neglected in subsequent criticism, although Valery Briusov considered V*asilisa Premudraia* Lunacharsky's best play to date when it appeared, and Gorky, too, was anxious that it should be produced. See A. V. *Lunacharsky: Neizdannye materialy*, p. 563; and "Pis'mo A. V. Lunacharskogo v Revoliutsionnyi Khudozhestvennyi teatr v Tiflise," *Literaturnaia Gruziia*, no. 2 (1961):76.

talented members of the intelligentsia: Blok, Briusov, Gorky, Stanislavsky, and others. He surmised that the rank and file would follow the bellwethers. Lunacharsky's God-building ideology played its part in his highly effective pro-Bolshevik oratory in Petrograd in 1917, and in his exertions on behalf of the Proletarian Culture movement, of which he was a founding member. The nurturing of the proletariat's cultural development can be seen as part of the process of paving the way for the future God.

As commissar, Lunacharsky favored experiments in musical drama. He writes in 1917 that opera was likely to be of only marginal interest to the Revolution.

> We need not subscribe to such extreme judgements as those of Wagner and Nietzsche, but one cannot but express the hope that the new era will create a new form of musical drama in place of the really rather absurd mongrel which is what the typical opera has been up to now.[55]

He saw the circus as having a potential (abundantly realized in the U.S.S.R. subsequently) for esthetic ceremonies and mysteries.[56] Along with his enthusiasm for mythological plays, he developed a belief in the future of melodrama and of a new opera. He writes approvingly of Fedor Kommissarzhevsky's view that opera and drama should come closer together and notes that similar views were put forward in the past by Gluck, Wagner, and Nietzsche.[57]

Lunacharsky was an unwavering Wagnerophile, and saw Wagner's early work in unreservedly Nietzschean terms. Speaking at the opening of an Institute of Musical Drama in 1920, he referred to Nietzsche's *The Birth of Tragedy* as "a work of genius," and elaborated the ideal of a musical drama where the stage depicts an "Apollonian dream" of the spirit of the music. "Music is tragic in its essence. And even as Dionysus is raging there should unfold on the stage, as if in a visionary dream, an approximate concrete representation of what the orchestra is, much more broadly, depicting."[58] He found Mussorgsky the only creator of truly musical drama,

---

[55] Lunacharsky, "O zadachakh gosudarstvennykh teatrov" (1917), in *O muzyke i muzykal'nom teatre*, 3 vols. (Moscow, 1981–   ), 1:212.

[56] Lunacharsky, "Zadachi obnovlennogo tsirka," *Vestnik teatra*, no. 3 (1919):5–6.

[57] Lunacharsky, "Teatral'nye voprosy" (1919), in *O muzyke i muzykal'nom teatre*, 1:229.

[58] Lunacharsky, "O muzykal' noi drame," in *V mire muzyki* (Moscow, 1958), pp. 51–52.

rivaling even Bizet.[59] In 1925, defending the continued existence of the Bolshoi Theater in Moscow, he claims that Nietzsche demanded of Wagner "not, of course, proletarian opera, but at all events a profoundly meaningful opera."[60] The imperialist bourgeoisie had evidently lacked the cultural energy to create this Nietzschean opera. In 1933, writing on the fiftieth anniversary of Wagner's death, Lunacharsky held him up as an example of a philosopher-musician, a philosopher-poet, and playwright who had achieved the highest synthesis of music and literature to date. He castigated Soviet musicians and playwrights for their inadequacy in this area, and their inability to create a major opera of the revolutionary emotions and the worldwide revolutionary struggle.[61]

Never one to preach what he did not himself practice, Lunacharsky made a number of attempts over the years to create "Apollonian" visions to accompany particular musical works he loved. He describes various reactions to music of the listener, of which his own is evidently the most sophisticated:

on the repeated hearing of a piece of music, having understood its basic idea, one works over the stream of images so that they receive an Apollonian dimension, in Nietzsche's terminology. That is, pure music receives that supplementation which, in a crude form, it receives on the operatic stage, in a tremendously subtle performance which man's fantasy unfolds before him to the accompaniment and at the dictation of the music.[62]

As precedents for his own efforts Lunacharsky cites Heine's *Florentine Nights*, where Heine "translates" Paganini's music, and works by E. T. A. Hoffmann in which he does the same for passages of Beethoven, Mozart, and Gluck.[63]

In addition to passages in his pre-Revolutionary stories in which he conveys musical ideas in highly colored prose,[64] Lunacharsky tried to translate Debussy's quartets into four interconnected prose pieces. Dissat-

[59] Lunacharsky, " 'Boris Godunov' Musorgskogo" (1920), in V *mire muzyki*, p. 59.

[60] Lunacharsky, "Dlia chego my sokhraniaem Bol' shoi teatr?" (1925), SS, 3:347.

[61] Lunacharsky, "Rikhard Vagner" (1933), in *Stat'i o teatre i dramaturgii*, 2 vols. (Moscow, 1958), 2:507–508.

[62] Lunacharsky, "O poezii kak iskusstve tonal'nom" (1925), SS, 7:429.

[63] Ibid.

[64] See Anatoly Aniutin [Lunacharsky], "Arfa," *Russkaia mysl'*, no. 11 (1902):52–53; "Skripach," ibid., pp. 50–52; "Voskresen'e," *Kievskaia mysl'*, no. 100 (1911):3; "Vremena goda," *Kievskaia mysl'* no. 96 (1914):6–7.

isfied with the result in prose, he tried to capture the rhythm in verse, but again remained dissatisfied with the results. He was much better pleased with verse "translations" of Schubert's *Impromptus* in A Major and of J. S. Bach's *Fantasia in A Minor*, and indeed had planned to publish them in 1924.[65]

As far as Lunacharsky's public critical assessment of Nietzsche is concerned, it was inevitable that it should grow increasingly negative. Whether or not as a result of Nietzsche's (or Marx's) moral relativism, Lunacharsky was not a believer in absolute truth, and as time passed Lunacharsky the politician demonstrated considerable elasticity of judgment. The superman, who in 1908 had been one of those supra-individual entities that are "in the eyes of a true human being the essential,"[66] was by 1923, after the Civil War and Intervention, merely an ideological front concocted by Nietzsche for the "virtuosos of the world of big business,"[67] and by 1928, with Mussolini ensconced in power in Fascist Italy, the superman became the center of a "cult of power, arrogant and exulting in its own strength." "Truth to tell it is to a new barbarism, highhanded, pitiless and self-confident, that the mind of those turns who wish to smash Communism and stride firmly to the apex of the pyramid of humanity in order to trample it underfoot."[68]

Nietzsche himself became tainted with philistinism. In 1920 Lunacharsky saw him as deriving his belligerence from Bismarck's regime, but still argued that "it would be pure primitivism to imagine that Nietzsche was a pure apologist for the military." There is the blond beast, but there is also Zarathustra, invigorated by the air of imperialism but an admirable human being. Indeed, the same spirit of combativeness can serve to fuel the fighting spirit of the working class.[69] In 1923, however, before a student audience in Moscow, the scales come down on the other side. Nietzsche, "distilling feudal sentiments, indirectly supported the megalomania of the bourgeoisie by propounding his superman. This is really quite disgraceful because you simply can't suppose that the figure of the

[65] Lunacharsky, "O poezii kak iskusstve tonal'nom," pp. 429–31.

[66] Lunacharsky, *Religiia i sotsializm*, 2 vols. (St. Petersburg, 1908–1911), 1:132.

[67] Lunacharsky, "Kul'tura v kapitalisticheskuiu epokhu" (1923), in I: *Idealizm i materializm, II: Kul'tura burzhuaznaia, perekhodnaia i sotsialisticheskaia* (Leningrad, 1924), p. 64.

[68] Lunacharsky, "Parizhskoe iskusstvo na Prechistenke" (1928), in *Ob izobrazitel'nom iskusstve*, 2 vols. (Moscow, n. d.), 1:357.

[69] Lunacharsky, "Rikhard Shtraus," in *V mire muzyki*, pp. 70–71.

hermit Zarathustra, soaring above the joys and sorrows of life, can be used to exculpate some fat banker driving off to enjoy himself in the restaurants and brothels of the metropolis at the expense of the workers and those he has robbed on the stock exchange."[70]

Lunacharsky's attitude to his own Nietzscheanism also evolved. In 1926 the tone is one of unrepentant detachment as he looks back on what it was in Nietzsche that attracted him: "His combativeness was very appealing—his spirit of exultation, his contempt for petty bourgeois morality and Christian romanticism." Plekhanov had been right to tell him off, but Nietzsche could still delight Marxists even though his was a bourgeois rhetoric. An imperialist military march could stir proletarian blood. "But Nietzsche was, in spite of everything, extraordinarily rewarding. He was a man of great culture, and unraveling the complex threads of his moods is a very important task."[71] In 1929 times had changed. With the political upheavals of the late 1920s Lunacharsky was obliged to relinquish his post as commissar of enlightenment. A month later, in February 1929, personally vulnerable to attack for "philosophical errors" of earlier years, he declared in a lecture to the Communist Academy,

> It is interesting that Nietzsche, who is correctly classified as a precursor of imperialism, started out spitting at the petty bourgeoisie, at the same time viewing the Revolution as we understand it with hatred. He proclaimed the freedom of the individual and exulted haughtily in his triumph over the petty bourgeoisie. Sundry intellectual renegades, miscellaneous cultured and hypercultured nervous people, fell in love with him.[72]

Presumably he included his former unregenerate self.

Lunacharsky had an eventful life. In 1933, after holding a succession of academic posts, he was appointed Soviet ambassador to Republican Spain, which he evidently saw as something of a sinecure, at least relatively speaking. He was looking forward, after a lifetime's polemics, to at last systematizing the vast amount of knowledge he had acquired. We find

---

[70] Lunacharsky, "Iskusstvo i ego noveishie formy" (1923), SS, 7:347–48.

[71] Lunacharsky, "Simvolisty" (1926), in *Ocherki po istorii russkoi literatury* (Moscow, 1976), pp. 443–44.

[72] Lunacharsky, "Sovremennaia literatura na Zapade," in A. V. *Lunacharskii: Neizdannye materialy*, p. 323.

him in scholarly mood, protesting before his departure at the omission of Nietzsche from the *Great Soviet Encyclopaedia*'s entry on "Esthetics,"[73] and at his initiative the Academia publishing house was to have issued a translation of *Thus Spoke Zarathustra*.[74] He died at the age of fifty-eight, in December 1933, so that neither the translation nor the hoped-for transition to scholarliness occurred.

Nicholas Berdiaev, who ended his days in emigration, deported by the government of which Lunacharsky was a member, concluded philosophically that "he was a very erudite and a very gifted man, but he remained rather unserious."[75] This is unjust. His superficiality derived from and made possible his political activity in the cause of the superman. In the words of the ancient Chinese curse, it was Lunacharsky's misfortune, if indeed it is a misfortune, to have lived in interesting times. And, we might add, to have left his mark on them.

[73] Lunacharsky, Letter to the Editors of *Bol'shaia sovetskaia entsiklopediia* [1933], in ibid., p. 540.

[74] Lunacharsky, Letter to Academia publishing house [1933], in ibid., p. 525.

[75] Nikolai Berdiaev, *Samopoznanie (Opyt filosofskoi avtobiografii)* (Paris, 1949), p. 131.

13.

A. A. Bogdanov:
In Search of Cultural Liberation

Zenovia A. Sochor

ALEXANDER BOGDANOV (1873–1928), political thinker and activist, rose to the top ranks of the Bolshevik faction of the Social Democratic Party and then, in a bitter showdown with Lenin, was ousted from the Bolshevik Center in 1908. He promptly organized a new political group, Forward (Vpered), which included such well-known figures as A. V. Lunacharsky and Maxim Gorky. This group, earning Lenin's epithet as "Left Bolsheviks," emphasized the cultural-educational tasks of a revolutionary movement, and established two Party schools for the Russian proletariat with this end in mind (Capri, 1909 and Bologna, 1910–1911). Following the October Revolution, Bogdanov helped organize the Proletarian Culture organization (Proletkult), which was dedicated to the proposition that socialism required not only political and economic transformation but also "cultural liberation." This could best be achieved, according to Bogdanov, by first subjecting "bourgeois culture" to critical scrutiny and then by developing values and attitudes specifically suited to the working class and the new society, that is, by creating a "proletarian culture."

The questions that arise are: Where did Bogdanov derive these ideas? Why was Bogdanov intrigued by the notions of revaluation of values and of "cultural liberation"? Was Nietzsche a possible source of influence?

Bogdanov is difficult to pinpoint on the philosophical spectrum. Although the primary influence on him was Marxism, he never hesitated to look elsewhere for insights. An early philosophical endeavor, *Empiriomonism* (1904–1906), contained non-Marxist influences, contributing to friction within the Bolshevik faction and ultimately prompting Lenin to write a harsh critique in *Materialism and Empirio-Criticism* (1909). Bogdanov himself acknowledged his intellectual debt to positivist philosophers such as Ostwald, Mach, and Avenarius; they were important to the development of his concepts of empiriomonism and of a "universal organizational science," the latter being a pioneering effort in systems thinking (*Tectology*, 1913–1929).

And yet, heresy, or at least unorthodoxy, in the Marxist camp does not necessarily place Bogdanov in the Nietzschean camp. Bogdanov did not attribute his ideas to Nietzsche. Indeed, Bogdanov and Nietzsche, on the face of it, seem to stand at opposite poles in their views of history and of human beings, in general, and of socialism, in particular.[1]

Nietzsche perceived an innate drive in human nature, the "will to power," which contemporary society attempted to subdue in favor of the weak and the mediocre. Such a society earned nothing but scorn from Nietzsche and he envisioned that history would eventually lead to the emergence of superior individuals who would question the values of the "herd" and construct new values.

In contrast to Nietzsche's exaltation of elites, of "supermen," Bogdanov, as a Marxist, focused on the common man, the worker. He readily acknowledged that the worker was weak and debilitated but believed that this same ordinary person would rise to the occasion and, together with other workers, as part of a mass, would overthrow the society that suppressed and exploited them.

Clearly then, the agent of history was entirely different for Bogdanov and Nietzsche, the working class being emphasized by the former and the superior individual by the latter. Moreover, the critical actors of history were linked to diametrically opposed notions of historical progression. Nietzsche maintained a concept of change that was based on "eternal recurrence," that is, human triumphs and setbacks would be repeated endlessly; even though a higher state, or a new level of culture, was possible, a perfected "end-state" could not be attained. To Nietzsche, history did not come to a dramatic finale with the creation of "supermen" because inferior individuals would in time replace superior ones in the

---

[1] For a discussion of Nietzsche's views, see, among others, R. J. Hollingdale, *Nietzsche* (London, 1973); Malcolm Pasley, ed., *Nietzsche: Imagery and Thought* (Berkeley, 1978).

For a summary of Bogdanov's views, see Alexander Vucinich, "A Blend of Marxism and New Positivism: A. A. Bogdanov," in his *Social Thought in Tsarist Russia* (Chicago, 1976), pp. 206–30. For a more comprehensive treatment, see Zenovia A. Sochor, "Modernization and Socialist Transformation: Leninist and Bogdanovite Alternatives of the Cultural Revolution" (Ph.D. diss.; Columbia University, 1977).

inescapable cycle of life. This was both the tragedy and challenge of life since it offered humans innummerable opportunities for self-affirmation.

Bogdanov, on the other hand, persisted in expounding the Marxist theory of social change. Each society contained within itself economic and political contradictions that burst asunder and gave way to new social formations dialectically. Moreover, history was not just a record of the new but of development from lower to higher stages; social changes, in other words, implied progress. The ultimate and desirable end-state, to Bogdanov, was socialism.

Nothing drew Nietzsche's ire so much as the question of socialism; he was both vehement and vitriolic in rejecting it. Socialism was based on false premises insofar as history, to Nietzsche, was not the result of anonymous social forces or economic impetus but the product of conscious and active human beings. Socialism, Nietzsche argued further, incorrectly assumed continuous progress toward some inevitable goal; this was contrary to the lessons of history. "Mankind is not a whole: it is an inextricable multiplicity of ascending and descending life-processes—it does not have a youth followed by maturity and finally by old age; the strata are twisted and entwined together" (WP, 84). More importantly, socialism held out false promises insofar as it predicted an end to exploitation. According to Nietzsche, appropriation, suppression, and exploitation would persist throughout history because they were intrinsic to human nature. Exploitation was the inevitable consequence of the will to power and the struggle for life. From Nietzsche's point of view, it was "a disgrace for all socialist systematizers to suppose there could be circumstances—social combinations—in which vice, disease, prostitution, distress would no longer grow." That would mean condemning life and the "growth of life" (WP, 25). Finally, and perhaps most importantly, socialism represented to Nietzsche the very opposite of his ideal, because it meant not a society of superior individuals but one reduced to smug mediocrity. "Socialism [is] the logical conclusion of the *tyranny* of the least and the dumbest, i.e., those who are superficial, envious, and three-quarters actors" (WP, 77).

Need the contrast between Nietzsche and Bogdanov be drawn any stronger? As a socialist, Bogdanov supported and defended much of what Nietzsche reviled and repudiated. And yet, as noted above, Bogdanov was a rather peculiar Marxist. He refused to be bound by what he called the "Holy Scriptures of Marx and Engels"; he sought answers to the questions that troubled him from among a host of philosophical creeds. Nietzsche's influence, even if indirect, was to draw Bogdanov's attention to those aspects of Marxism that were unclear or treated in a derivative fashion. In responding to critics, especially those who turned from Marx to Nietzsche, Bogdanov was forced to think about the role of culture, of ideology, and of the superstructure as a whole. Ultimately, Bogdanov addressed some of the same questions that Nietzsche did and suggested similar responses.

BOGDANOV AND NIETZSCHE: CULTURAL LIBERATION

Bogdanov and Nietzsche were both agitated by the large philosophical question: What would promote the liberation of human beings? For their answers, both focused on the cultural sphere, the creation of new values, and "cultural liberation."

Despite Bogdanov's commitment to socialist thought, he expressed doubts about any automatic or inevitable liberation. That is, he believed in the progressive movement of social history and in economic factors as the propellant of change, but remained skeptical about the ease of transition, especially from economic to cultural levels of change. Reigning ideas and values, even if properly classified as "remnants of the past," were remarkably tenacious and would resist change unless deliberate and specific measures were adopted.[2] Indeed, a revolution could even prove to be "retrogressive" if prior preparation in the ideological and organizational spheres had not taken place.[3] Thus, some degree of cultural change was necessary as a prelude and not simply as an aftermath of revolution. Economic and cultural factors had to be considered side by side.

Bogdanov, in fact, felt that this dimension of social change was slighted by Marx. According to Bogdanov, Marx had devoted himself to an analysis of economic factors but treated ideology in a cursory fashion. Bogdanov took it upon himself to fill in this gap in Marxist thought.[4]

Bogdanov was not alone in discovering gaps in Marxism. Several Marxists of the time questioned the adequacy and completeness of Marx's thought. One of the first groups of revisionists, the "legal Marxists," accepted the scientific explanation of historical materialism but believed it was compatible with different philosophies and epistemologies. Indeed, they consciously turned to other philosophers because they felt that Marxism "did

[2] A. A. Bogdanov, *Nauka ob obshchestvennom soznanii* (Moscow, 1914), pp. 32–33.
[3] Ibid., p. 11.
[4] A. A. Bogdanov, *Iz psikhologii obshchestva* (St. Petersburg, 1904), p. 37.

not account for moral principles."[5] By 1903, this group became ex-Marxist, and in their declaration of principles in *Problems of Idealism (Problemy Idealizma,* 1903), specifically invoked Nietzsche in support of their views, "scanning his philosophy for condemnation of moral utilitarianism, eudaemonism, slave-morality, and the sacrifice of personal creativity to the 'welfare of the masses.' "[6]

Bogdanov's own intellectual collaborators, while maintaining adherence to Marxism, proved to be susceptible to Nietzschean influence, as witnessed by Lunacharsky (Bogdanov's brother-in-law) and the "God-builders" (1908).[7] Much of the critical intelligentsia began to turn away from philosophic "rationalism" toward idealism, esthetism, even religious mysticism.[8] Indeed, scientific materialists found themselves on the defensive throughout the early 1900s. The Neo-Idealists introduced different questions into the realm of philosophical debate and "brought about changes in the ideas of their opponents."[9]

Bogdanov, while disputing the Idealists' philosophical position, was himself infected by their probing outlook; he conceded that positivism could leave a "young inquiring philosopher" unsatisfied because the "eternal" (and cursed) questions (e.g., "What is the essence of things?") were brushed aside. He seemed to think he could transcend both Kantian idealism and positivism by developing a collectivist viewpoint. A collectivist, claimed Bogdanov, was the historical successor to the positivist, a realist from the Marxist school.[10]

Such open-mindedness toward philosophy did not sit well with orthodox Marxists such as Plekhanov or Lenin. It was not long before Bogdanov was accused of philosophical errors and thrown in with the unlikely

[5] Leszek Kolakowski, *Main Currents of Marxism,* vol. 3: *The Golden Age,* trans. P. S. Fallo (Oxford, 1978), p. 362.

[6] Ibid., p. 421.

[7] According to one author, the God-builders were at least in part "a response to idealist taunts that socialism ignored philosophical questions" and were inspired by such diverse sources as Christ, Marx, and Nietzsche. See Christopher Read, *Religion, Revolution, and the Russian Intelligentsia, 1900–1912* (London, 1979), p. 77. For a comparison of Lunacharsky's and Bogdanov's views, see Kendall Eugene Bailes, "Philosophy and Politics in Russian Social Democracy: Bogdanov, Lunacharsky, and the Crisis of Bolshevism, 1908–1909" (Master's thesis, Columbia University, 1966).

[8] Richard Pipes, "The Historical Evolution of the Russian Intelligentsia," in *The Russian Intelligentsia,* ed. Richard Pipes (New York, 1961), p. 56.

[9] Christopher Read, "New Directions in the Russian Intelligentsia: Idealists and Marxists in the Early Twentieth Century," *Renaissance and Modern Studies* (1981):4.

[10] A. A. Bogdanov, *Novyi mir,* 3rd ed. (Moscow, 1920), p. 123.

company of his ideological opponents, Berdiaev and Struve.[11] Even with the passage of time, some analysts remained uncertain how to characterize Bogdanov's thought: it contained idealist as well as materialist elements; it was eclectic; it was revisionist. "In his overall philosophical scheme, Bogdanov, in some fanciful manner, managed to combine Marx, Mach, Avenarius, partly Bergson," concluded one critic of the 1920s.[12]

Bogdanov never gave up his underlying belief in rationalism and empiricism, but he clearly was caught up in the intellectual ferment of the times. In comparison to the doctrinaire orientation of Lenin and Plekhanov, Bogdanov shared the new mood of philosophical inquiry and iconoclasm. According to one analyst, Bogdanov, not unlike Ivanov, Skriabin, or Blok, was animated by "Prometheanism: the belief that man— when fully aware of his true powers—is capable of transforming the world in which he lives."[13] Another writer asserts that all the "Nietzschean Marxists," including Volsky, Lunacharsky, Bogdanov, and Bazarov, were "sensitive to the problems of artistic creativity and freedom. It was natural that they should have found in Nietzsche—philosopher-poet, 'esthete,' and furious critic of normative morality—a congenial support for their own revisions of Marxism."[14]

Bogdanov considered his work an updating or expansion of Marxism rather than its abandonment, although he had little sympathy for ortho-

[11] See L. I. Akselrod, *Filosofskie ocherki* (Moscow, 1925); V. I. Lenin, *Materialism and Empirio-Criticism* (New York, 1927); G. V. Plekhanov, *Izbrannie filosofskie proizvedeniia v piati tomakh*, vol. 3: *Materialismus militans* (Moscow, 1957).

[12] A. Udal'tsov, "K kritike teorii klassov u A. A. Bogdanova," *Pod znamenem marksizma*, nos. 7–8 (July–August 1922):100.

A more contemporary Soviet assesment suggests that some of Bogdanov's early critics simply did not understand his innovations in systems analysis. See M. I. Setrov, "Ob obshchikh elementakh tektologii A. Bogdanova, kibernetiki i teorii sistem," *Uchenye zapiski kafedr obshchestvennykh nauk vuzov g. Leningrada. Filosofia.* no. 8 (1967):56. The problem, largely unresolved among Marxist philosophers, is when "creative Marxism" stops being Marxism.

Western analysts tend to conclude that while Bogdanov was obviously a "revisionist," he nevertheless remained a Marxist. See, for example, S. V. Utechin, *Russian Political Thought: A Concise History* (New York, 1964), pp. 207–13; or V. V. Zenkovsky, A *History of Russian Philosophy*, vol. 2, trans. George L. Kline (New York, 1953), pp. 741–44.

[13] James H. Billington, *The Icon and the Axe* (New York, 1966), pp. 478, 488. Also see Bernice Glatzer Rosenthal, "Eschatology and the Appeal of Revolution: Merezhovsky, Bely, Blok," *California Slavic Studies* 11 (1980), pp. 105–39.

[14] George L. Kline, " 'Nietzschean Marxism' in Russia," *Boston College Studies in Philosophy* 2 (1969):170. Another author also suggests a resemblance between some of Nietzsche's ideas and empiriocriticism, the revisionist philosophy associated with Bogdanov. See Aileen Kelly, "Empiriocriticism: A Bolshevik Philosophy?" *Cahiers du Monde Russe et Sovietique* 22 (January–March 1981):89–118.

dox labels. In describing human potential, Bogdanov did not hesitate to quote from the Bible, from Marx, and from Nietzsche—a rather revealing choice of authorities. Bogdanov seemed to find the following equally inspiring: "God created man in His image . . . ," or "Social being determines social consciousness," or "Man is the bridge to the superman."[15] The task at hand, according to Bogdanov, was to develop new concepts that depicted human beings "not only as a whole world of experiences but also as an unfolding world, not confined by any *absolute* limits."[16] Such absolute limits consisted, among other things, of norms and values that suppressed the creative powers of humans and contributed to "authoritarian thinking" (or in Nietzschean terms, to a "slave-morality"). A whole range of "fetishisms" created boundaries to development and freethinking, such as "sacred traditions, class honor, absolute duty, simple justice."[17] Bogdanov rejected any Kantian "categorical imperatives." On the contrary, he preferred to see himself as an "amoralist."[18]

Thus far, there are distinct similarities between Bogdanov and Nietzsche. Both railed against morals and authority; both called for a revaluation of values; both sought a new, creative, unrestricted human being. Bogdanov, however, parts company with Nietzsche insofar as he sees liberation through collectivism while Nietzsche holds to a radical individualism.[19]

COLLECTIVISM VERSUS INDIVIDUALISM

Bogdanov's argument for collectivism is based on sociological analysis while Nietzsche's advocacy of individualism tends to be based on philo-

[15] Bogdanov, *Novyi mir*, p. 5.

[16] Ibid., p. 8.

[17] Bogdanov, *Iz psikhologii*, p. 73.

[18] In an autobiographical account, Bogdanov reveals that the local Marxist organization in Kharkov, which he joined in 1896, was engaged in "furious debates . . . on 'freedom of the will' [and] on the absolute principle of morality." Since Bogdanov adopted the position that moral principles were a "social fetishism conditioned by the relations of production," he says that he was almost "expelled for immorality." As cited in James D. White, "Bogdanov in Tula," *Studies in Soviet Thought* 22, no. 1 (February 1981):54. In one of his science fiction novels, Bogdanov labels Lenni, his alter ego, an "amoralist." See A. A. Bogdanov, *Krasnaia zvezda* (Moscow, 1918), p. 10.

[19] Kline divides the Nietzschean Marxists into "individualistic" (Lunacharsky, Volsky) and "collectivistic" (Bazarov, Bogdanov) groups. In addition to the citation in n. 14, see George L. Kline, "Changing Attitudes toward the Individual," in *Transformation of Russian Society*, ed. C. E. Black (Cambridge, Mass., 1960), pp. 618–19. Kelley argues against this division and considers the label "Nietzschean Marxists" misleading insofar as all the writers identified with this philosophy were "unanimously opposed to the individualism which was central to Nietzsche's ideal." See Kelly, "Empiriocriticism," p. 101.

sophical, even personal, exhortations. This difference can be amply seen in how the two authors trace the origins of norms and how they relate them to individualism versus collectivism.

According to Nietzsche, history records the development of two types of morality, a master morality, which is expressed by noble individuals and implies power and self-glorification, and a slave morality, which emanates from the lower elements of society and denotes timidity and plebeianism. Over time, the "bearers of the instincts of decline" succeed in discrediting master morality; by promoting equality, the "social hodgepodge" make all the noble qualities appear to be vices and all the weak qualities appear to be virtues. The "herd mentality" asserts itself and whoever wants to retain power must flatter the mob by expressing its values—"sympathy, even reverence, for all that has lived a life of suffering, lowliness, contempt, and persecution." In this way, "the center of gravity necessarily shifts to the mediocre" (WP, 461). Nietzsche's call for individualism thus becomes a call for a renewed master morality, for values associated with "the great emotions, the passions of power, love, revenge." These are values that provide the glorious battles of life, test the will, and forge remarkable individuals.

In a far more pedantic vein, Bogdanov views norms as the product of heightened social interaction. Primitive societies, for example, do not have norms; they are guided, rather, by an instinct of self-preservation, by habits or customs. Norms, according to Bogdanov, differ from simple habits because they already assume a certain level of consciousness and imply the possibility of transgression; they reflect a new phase of human development. "Norms are necessary," concludes Bogdanov, "only when relations become complex and contradictory." It is then that the notion arises of "establishing boundaries of transgression."[20] Norms, consequently, assume an essential role in society; they help regulate human interactions, soften contradictions, and introduce some degree of organization into an increasingly intricate and potentially anarchic social existence.[21] Indeed, without norms, society would disintegrate "as a cask without hoops."[22]

It is interesting to note that Bogdanov's concept of norms is embedded entirely in societal needs, as something that stands outside, or above, the individual. He specifically refutes any Kantian philosophy of morality as

[20] Bogdanov, *Novyi mir*, pp. 42–45.
[21] Ibid., pp. 51–52.
[22] Ibid., p. 54.

inherent in a human being. To Bogdanov, even "pangs of remorse" are not internally or autonomously derived but are the "individualistic-psychological expression of a social reaction to contradictory norms of conduct."[23] Grasping the fact that norms are socially induced is for Bogdanov an immensely important step. To him, liberation itself is a process of revelation. Humans must begin to discern the social nature of norms. They must shed the idea that norms belong to the realm of "metaphysics"; they must come to realize that norms are not dark, abstract, and spontaneous forces dominating humans, but simply the elements of social regulation and control. Only then can humans undertake the task of transforming society and themselves.

In this process of liberation, Bogdanov, coinciding with Nietzsche, readily gives credit to the rise of individualism. He perceives that insofar as the "I" is affirmed as an absolute, becoming the subject and not merely the object of history, individualism performs an emancipating task. Moreover, it does so not only at a personal level but also at social and political levels. In other words, the assertion of the individual involves a discriminating reappraisal of relations within society, which, ultimately, leads to discarding of all forms of authoritarianism.[24]

Individualism, however, is not a culminating point in the process of liberation; rather, it marks a transitional stage of human development. Capitalism, which spawns individualism, requires a division of labor and strict specialization in order to operate. This produces, argues Bogdanov, a unidimensional human being, and, at the same time, creates a nagging yearning for all-around development, for internal harmony. Only collectivism, Bogdanov insists, can hope to fill this need. In the new society, "where the divisive forces of competition and class struggle will disappear, together with the accompanying psychological disconnectedness," a human being can begin to feel "an integral part of the great whole."[25]

Bogdanov believed that the "authoritarian division of labor" and extreme specialization, typical of capitalism, could also be overcome. This would become possible because of changes in technology, in organizational methods, and in educational goals under socialism. According to Bogdanov, rapid advances of technology would allow transfer of the odious, detailed tasks to machines, freeing men and women for more demanding, creative tasks. Indeed, a new class of workers, a "new psychologycal type,"

[23] Ibid., p. 53.
[24] Ibid., pp. 21–22.
[25] Ibid., p. 90.

would arise. Workers would be oriented toward mobility and diversity; their activities would combine previously divided dimensions of labor, for example, organization (challenging) and implementation (perfunctory).[26] Work would be organized on the basis of "comradely cooperation," meaning that "everyone, according to their degree of knowledge and experience, participates in developing a collective will."[27] Finally, a "new ideal of education" would complement these technological and organizational changes, Bogdanov maintains. Although specialized training and knowledge would continue, great care would be made not to "suppress the psyche" but to expand the spheres of knowledge, to transmit comprehensive knowledge and universal methods.[28] The "old philistine-specialist" would no longer be admired; a new type of scholar would arise—"widely educated, monistic in thought, socially alive."[29]

CONTRADICTIONS OF COLLECTIVISM

Needless to say, Bogdanov's predictions for the new society contain a considerable amount of wishful thinking and more than one pitfall. Quite apart from the question of whether or not technology is progressive and emancipating, a belief typical of Bogdanov's time, is the question of whether collectivism, as Bogdanov conceived it, was an adequate response to the problem of liberation. One analyst, in fact, discerns a "doctrinal tension" in the collectivism that Bogdanov so admired. Bogdanov and his adherents were "genuinely concerned to free the individual from the constraints of coercive norms and abstract obligations; yet they proceed[ed] to dissolve the 'emancipated' individual in an impersonal social collective".[30] Even a contemporary Soviet writer accuses Bogdanov of "excessive collectivism." Bogdanov and his ideological collaborators "obliterated the individual personality in the name of a collective 'we.' "[31]

What was Bogdanov's position on this question? Was he aware of the potential contradictions of collectivism? Bogdanov was forced to clarify

[26] Ibid., p. 28–29.

[27] Ibid., p. 133.

[28] Ibid., p. 134.

[29] Ibid., p. 32. By monism, Bogdanov meant a world-view guided by a single comprehensive principle, which provided a key to understanding, was applicable to the natural as well as the social sciences, and suggested that reality was one unitary organic whole, with all its parts interrelated.

[30] Kline, "Attitudes toward the Individual," p. 621.

[31] N. V. Dement'eva, "O nekotorykh osobennostiakh estetiki i gnoseologii proletkul'ta," *Pisatel' i zhizn*, no. 6 (1971):131, 135.

his ideas when one of the contributors to the Proletkult journal, A. K. Gastev (1882–1941), proclaimed the epitome of collectivism to be the transformation of the proletariat into an "unprecedented social automaton." Bogdanov, as a founder and one of the chief ideologists of Proletkult, had to react to this contention.

Certainly Gastev, founder of the Central Institute of Labor, which produced the Russian version of Taylorism, shared Bogdanov's zeal for technology and for a new proletarian culture. From this common point of departure, Gastev's views diverged considerably from Bogdanov's.[32] To Gastev, the automobile and airplane factories of America and Europe would serve as "gigantic laboratories for creating the psychology, and for producing the culture, of the proletariat." This would be a culture marked by collectivism, but a "mechanized collectivism," one that was at odds with any personal connotations. The new collectivism, Gastev predicted, would be anonymous to such a degree that "the movement of the collective-complexes [would] resemble the movement of things, as if there were no longer human individual features, but even, standardized strides, faces without expressions, spirit, devoid of lyricism, emotions, measured not by shouts, laughter, but by the manometer and taxometer."[33]

Bogdanov was dismayed at this eulogy to anonymity; in fact, his reaction was Nietzschean in character. In his rebuttal to Gastev, Bogdanov argued that his projected images were entirely those of a crowd, a herd, but certainly not those of a collective. Bogdanov shunned any identification between collectives and the masses as a whole. The term "masses" to Bogdanov seemed to connote peasant backwardness and "militaristic drill." A proletarian collective, on the other hand, was associated in Bogdanov's mind with competence, participation, and comradely relations. Moreover, he denied that collectivism had to mean depersonalization. While Bogdanov believed that individualism would be replaced by collectivism, he insisted that individuality would remain. By individuality he meant "the distinctiveness of personal experiences and abilities, thanks to which separate individuals complement each other in a whole."[34]

[32] One analyst, in fact, maintains that the Central Institute of Labor was "a more or less illegitimate child of Bogdanov's theory of organization." See Peter Scheibert, "Lenin, Bogdanov, and the Concept of Proletarian Culture," in Lenin and Leninism, ed. Bernard W. Eissenstat, (Lexington, Mass., 1971), p. 53.

[33] A. Gastev, "O tendentsiakh proletarskoi kul'tury," Proletarskaia kul'tura, nos. 9–10 (June–July 1919):43–45.

[34] A. A. Bogdanov, "O tendentsiakh proletarskoi' kul'tury (Otvet A. Gastevu)," Proletarskaia kul'tura, nos. 9–10 (June–July 1919):50–51.

There was a further implication in Gastev's collectivism that troubled Bogdanov. Underlying Gastev's idea of a collective, "created in the image and likeness of a backward mass, drawn into industry through mobilization," there was, in Bogdanov's view, an "invisible sense of leading authorities." According to Bogdanov, Gastev failed to appreciate a critical feature of the unfolding, industrializing economy, namely, who was going to carry out the planning and organizing of production? Gastev focused only on the "mass of mechanized robots," a form of raw energy that responded to norms, standards, regulations. But who would supply the "artistic-scientific creativity" and the "precise engineering calculations" needed for technological and economic development? In response to his own question, Bogdanov declared that Gastev overlooked a key social group, "not one deprived of individuality, but one full of originality and talent, of educated engineers, who will take the initiative and assume the general leadership over the anonymous-spontaneous collective."[35]

Comments such as these opened Bogdanov to a different round of criticism. If critics of the 1970s accused Bogdanov of obliterating the individual in a collective, critics of the 1920s claimed that Bogdanov espoused the opposite—a cult of heroes. According to one author, Bogdanov's new society would be led by a "technical intelligentsia." There would arise a "kind of cult of 'organizers' . . . social 'heroes' " who would "stand in contrast to the 'crowd,' to the masses who implement [tasks]."[36]

Undoubtedly there is some truth to the charge that Bogdanov's view of a well-ordered and planned socialist society implies some sort of an "organizational elite." His emphasis on organizational skills stands in sharp contrast to his disparaging remarks about the spontaneous (i.e., unorganized) backward masses. This type of elitism reflects a Nietzschean tinge. As one author notes, "The idea of the proletariat as the organizing force of the future machine age" implies a "unified progressive will," and the workers' collective becomes "something like a superman."[37]

And yet, in the final analysis, Bogdanov's "organizers of production" are closer to James Burnham's "managerial class" than to Nietzsche's "supermen."[38] An admiration for "precise engineering calculations" seems

[35] Ibid., p. 52.
[36] Udal'tsov, "K kritike," p. 95.
[37] Scheibert, "Lenin, Bogdanov," p. 54.
[38] Burnham was one of the first to forecast the rise of a new class, a "managerial class," which differed from the traditional owners of capital and which would play an important role in capitalist economies. See James Burnham, *The Managerial Revolution* (New York, 1941).

mundane and bloodless in comparison to an exultation of the "redeeming man of great love and contempt, the creative spirit." Although Nietzsche also appreciated the "ability to organize" in the establishing of a new order, his organizers have an inherent superiority; they are masters by nature. "They do not know what guilt, responsibility, or consideration are, these born organizers; they exemplify that terrible artists' egoism that has the look of bronze and knows itself justified to all eternity in its 'work' " (GM, 87).

Bogdanov was extremely sensitive to this egoist brand of authority and saw it arising from the same gulf that Nietzsche did—the gulf between backward masses and arrogant elites. Rather than embracing elites as did Nietzsche, or glorifying the faceless masses as did Gastev, Bogdanov sought a solution in collectivism. He believed that a combination of advanced technology and cultural transformation would pave the way to more fluid and more equitable human relations. Ultimately such changes would redefine the nature of authority and remove the potential contradiction of collectivism.

Of particular interest is Bogdanov's endorsement of cultural transformation to upgrade the proletariat, purging meekness and apathy, and, in their place, cultivating self-assurance and self-reliance. In one specific attempt to describe the desired features of the new culture, Bogdanov adopts some distinctly Nietzschean positions. Proletarian culture, Bogdanov argues, should be guided by "laws of the new conscience." Perhaps conscious of the surprising use of terms, Bogdanov hastens to add that these laws are not "commandments" in the old sense of the word but simply "expedient norms" for the collective. The following are Bogdanov's Ten Commandments (paraphrased and abbreviated):

1. There shall be no herd instinct.

    A passive, submissive attitude has more to do with the petty bourgeois fear of being different than with true collectivism. A faceless being brings nothing to a collective but mechanical force, thereby increasing its inertia. In rejecting the herd instinct, a collectivist coincides with the individualist; he differs, however, insofar as the individualist thinks only of "me and mine," whereas the collectivist attempts to elevate and perfect the collective, and, in so doing, to maintain and develop his individuality together with the collective.

2. There shall be no slavery.

    Slavery, and its complement, authoritarianism, consists of a blind submission to a higher individual or in the demand for such submission. Although members of a collective should have confidence in their leaders, this confidence should be based on proven competence, not reduced to the worship of authority. Leadership requires repeated acknowledgement and verification; only in this way can it preserve the character of comradely relations, free of slave-authoritarian elements.

3. There shall be no subjectivism, neither of a personal nor group nature.

Personal subjectivism is individualism; group subjectivism is clannishness, guild narrow-mindedness, professionalism, patriotism, nationalism. All of these orientations lead to a waste of collective energy in anarchistic confrontations.

4. There shall be no Hottentotism.[39]

Essentially this means 'it is good, if I steal, it is bad, if someone steals from me.' Although class struggle evokes double standards, the proletariat must eventually become the representative of mankind as a whole. To maintain the logic of the soldier is to lower the proletariat to the level of inimical classes, undermining the force of idealism.

5. There shall be no absolute norms.

Higher culture is marked by objective norms which can never be absolute because they are an expression of life; development, struggle, and creativity cannot be shackled into absolute formulas. To accept eternal truths is to adopt a path of conservatism and reaction.

6. There shall be no inertness.

Herd instinct, slavery, group restrictiveness all inevitably have the propensity to halt movement. Any striving toward the new and the higher threatens established harmony and the authority at the center of that harmony. Movement forward cannot be attained along smooth tracks; creativity is not only joyful but also painful, as in birth. The proletariat must learn and relearn to create a new culture.

7. There shall be no violation of the purity of purpose.

Although the revolutionary proletarian, the conscious socialist,

---

[39] Bogdanov may have employed this term because of its common use in German politics at the time. In 1906–1907, a decision by the Reichstag not to allocate funds to suppress an uprising of the Hottentots in a German colony in Africa was reversed when a new coalition, called the "Hottentot bloc," was formed. See *Bol'shaia Sovetskaia entsiklopedia*, Vol. 18 (1930), p. 542.

looks to the future, much of his soul remains rooted in the past. At times, the past contaminates large goals with petty motives—especially those of comfort and of vengeance. These motives have a way of disguising themselves as idealistic goals, giving birth to a peculiar form of self-deception, where the lower presents itself as a manifestation of the higher.

8. All-mastery [*vseovladenie*]—the greatest goal.

The collective seeks to organize the world, to gain mastery over everything, to bind everything into a harmonious whole. Toward this end, it is necessary to master techniques from past labor as well as to seek new paths, new sources of energy.

9. All-understanding—the higher ideal of the new consciousness.

A collective must be marked by mutual understanding among participants, a continuous deepening of unity of will, mind, and feelings. This constitutes the soul of a collective, its common consciousness. Words such as respect, care, and love for fellow workers can only partially express the binding elements.

10. Pride of the collective—the supreme stimulus of will and thought of the worker.

In previous epochs, there was a pride of serving the higher will (authoritarianism), or truth and duty (individualism). In the development of the collective, everything that requires submission or worship is unmasked. Instead, the worker develops a consciousness of self as a living link of the great all-conquering whole. [40]

Nowhere is there a more striking similarity between Bogdanov and Nietzsche than is this list of exhortations. The Nietzschean indictment of socialism as a society of "harmless lambs" seems to haunt Bogdanov and to compel a response. Indeed, several of the "commandments" could just as easily have been written by Nietzsche, whether in the terms used or in the message conveyed. Both Bogdanov and Nietzsche express revulsion at the herd instinct and it is Nietzsche who first denounces "slave instincts, the instincts of cowardice, cunning and *canaille*" that emerge in the aftermath of revolution. Bogdanov's urging of the workers to shed their sluggishness, not to settle into inertness, bespeaks of his fear that the revolutionary dynamic cannot be maintained; it also echoes Nietzsche's warnings of recurring decadence or of the inherent "instincts of decline."

[40] A. A. Bogdanov, *O proletarskoi kul'ture, 1904–24* (Moscow and Leningrad, 1925), pp. 333–43.

While Bogdanov admonishes against the petty motives of comfort and vengeance, Nietzsche, with a good deal more sarcasm, ridicules the "hearth-squatters," the "shrewd sloths," and the "long etcetera of the small virtues." Both denounce the meanness of spirit found in what Bogdanov calls the "logic of the soldier," and Nietzsche counsels hating but not despising enemies. Bogdanov (and Marx, for that matter) wants for the proletariat what Nietzsche wants for the "new nobility," that they become "procreators and cultivators and sowers of the future," rather than being weighed down by the past, by absolute norms or "old illusions . . . called good and evil." Even the idea of "laws of the new conscience" finds its parallel in the "new values on new tables" that Nietzsche's supermen would write.[41] Both Bogdanov and Nietzsche use birth as a symbol of creativity, although Marx, too, saw the new society emerging from the womb of the old.[42]

Perhaps it is also not surprising that in criticizing passivity, anonymity, and submissiveness, Bogdanov should suggest individualism as the counterpoint. Nietzsche too assumed that the rise of individualism had a liberating impact, and provided freedom from the "overpowering domination by society (whether that of the state or of the church)." Both, moreover, saw individualism as a way station. For Nietzsche, "individualism is a modest and still unconscious form of the 'will to power' "; it is succeeded by strife and "power friction" with the assertion of "an order of rank." Bogdanov, it is worth remarking, saw exactly the same scenario. The individualist, says Bogdanov, is "permeated with the spirit of competition" and his goal is personal victory, which implies the "enslavement of others."[43]

The difference between Bogdanov and Nietzsche, however, is that Nietzsche accepts, and indeed welcomes the emergence of superior individuals, whereas Bogdanov denounces this course of events and hopes to prevent it by elevating the cultural level of the proletariat. In addition, Bogdanov looks to advanced technology to promote new skills and new

[41] Most of the parallels can be found in Friedrich Nietzsche, *Thus Spoke Zarathustra*, especially in "Of Old and New Law Tables," pp. 214–32. The author is indebted to the editor, Bernice Glatzer Rosenthal, for drawing attention to the resemblance of Bogdanov's "laws" to Nietzsche's "tables." Both, of course, are reacting to the original Ten Commandments, with Bogdanov making a specific effort to substitute "Ten Laws."

[42] There is also a similarity between Nietzsche and Bogdanov in their attitudes toward death. Nietzsche's declaration "Die at the right time!" in *Thus Spoke Zarathustra* is echoed in Bogdanov's "suicide rooms" in his science fiction novel, *Red Star*, ed. Loren R. Graham and Richard Stites, trans. Charles Rougle (Bloomington, Ind., 1984).

[43] Bogdanov, *O proletarskoi kul'ture*, p. 336.

organizational methods, thereby laying down the basis for comradely collaboration. Nietzsche, in contrast, remains a skeptic on the virtues of technology, admitting on one hand, that modern technology requires "intellect, discipline, and scientific imagination," but arguing, on the other hand, that "machine *Kultur*" leads to routinization, "impersonal enslavement," and a "despondent boredom of the soul."[44]

CONCLUSION

In response to the question posed at the outset—what is the source for Bogdanov's preoccupation with ''cultural liberation"—it is, at the very least, plausible to point to Nietzsche. True, there is no direct evidence (e.g., citations) that Bogdanov incorporated Nietzsche's ideas. At the same time, it is quite clear that Bogdanov was familiar with Nietzsche's work, either at second hand or through direct reading. Bogdanov was exposed to people who read and quoted Nietzsche, whether it was the Neo-Idealists, whom Bogdanov refuted, or Lunacharsky and Gorky, with whom he collaborated closely. It is probably fair to say that, among the critical intelligentsia, Nietzsche was in the air.

Bogdanov is not an obvious candidate for receptivity to Nietzsche's ideas, given their divergent political and philosophical points of view. Even Bogdanov's severest critics did not readily suggest a Nietzschean influence. Also, Bogdanov himself found the work of Mach and Avenarius, with their scientific bent, more congenial to his style and more intellectually exciting because they seemed to him closer to the "wave of the future." It is to them that he looked when he drew up plans for the new order, which would be guided by science, mathematics, and "tektology."

There is, nevertheless, another Bogdanov that emerges from his writings—one that fits poorly within the framework of technological optimism and rationality, one whose ideas cannot be easily traced either to positivism or to Marxism. This is the Bogdanov who worried about the "torment of a fragmented life" and alienation, closer in spirit to the young Marx, whose *Economic and Philosophic Manuscripts of 1844* were not yet known in Russia.[45] This is the skeptical Bogdanov, conscious of the

[44] For this discussion and citation, see Robert E. McGinn, "Nietzsche on Technology," *Journal of the History of Ideas* 41, no. 4 (October–December 1980):679–92.

[45] See James D. White, "The First *Pravda* and the Russian Marxist Tradition," *Soviet Studies* 26, no. 2 (April 1974):195–96.

missing links in socialist transformation. This is the Bogdanov who prescribed "cultural liberation" as the fundamental goal of the revolution,
founded Proletkult, and urged the worker to become an artist. It is this
Bogdanov who coincides with Nietzsche in a number of important views.

Most striking among Nietzsche's thoughts in this regard is his challenge to Marxism on the question of human emancipation. Whereas
Marx believed that alienation and suppression were the result of socioeconomic factors, Nietzsche focused on the human being itself. As one
analyst notes, "it is characteristically Nietzschean that he holds the workers as well as the capitalists responsible for the workers' plight . . . .
Their assent or passivity is a condition for the possibility of the continuation of this system."[46] Similarly, another writer contrasts Marx's assumption that the proletariat was a historically effective agent, pursuing
"material interests with some degree of foresight, calculation, and hence
rationality," with Nietzsche's portrayal of human beings as being driven
by fear, craving "security, order, certainty, the familiar, tried-and-true
routine that seems to provide a steady foundation for life."[47]

Bogdanov, although retaining his ultimate faith in progress and the
Marxist vision of society, seems to have been affected by Nietzsche's taunts.
A critical observer of the emerging Bolshevik society, he was troubled by
the relatively easy imposition of authoritarianism. As Berdiaev, one of his
"idealist" opponents, noted: "Bogdanov behaved with great nobility during the Bolshevik revolution. He was a veteran Bolshevik and for a time
a trusted collaborator of Lenin. . . . But when Bolshevism came into its
own, he was strongly repelled by some of its uglier by-products and did
not conceal his reactions."[48] The more disenchanted Bogdanov became
with Lenin and the authoritarian tendencies within the Bolshevik Party,
the more likely he was to express Nietzschean doubts, both before and
after the October Revolution. He sensed that human vulnerability, whether
at the level of the leader or the masses, contributed to this state of affairs
as much as "objective conditions." A revolution at the political and economic levels, consequently, was not sufficient to produce human emancipation. Bogdanov concluded that a socialist revolution had to be accompanied by "cultural liberation," a conscious, direct effort at transforming

[46] McGinn, "Nietzsche on Technology," p. 687.

[47] James Miller, "Some Implications of Nietzsche's Thought for Marxism," *Telos*, no. 37
(Fall 1978):24, 32.

[48] Nicolas Berdiaev, *Dream and Reality: An Essay in Autobiography* (New York, 1951),
p. 130.

ingrained attitudes of submission and passivity, ultimately involving the creation of a new "proletarian culture" and a "new human being."

In essence, Bogdanov brought to his analysis a Nietzschean skepticism toward any automatic or spontaneous transformation in consciousness, a questioning whether cultural change was simply a byproduct of changes in the socioeconomic sphere. Bogdanov remained, however, far more optimistic than Nietzsche in his belief that cultural liberation was possible and that collectivism was the antidote both to the herd imperative and to the preeminence of superior individuals.

PART IV

OTHER ASPECTS OF
NIETZSCHE'S INFLUENCE
IN RUSSIA

14.

Literary Reception as Vulgarization: Nietzsche's Idea of the Superman in Neo-Realist Fiction

Edith W. Clowes

STUDENTS OF LITERARY and cultural influence have come to view their subject in terms of a mutual transaction between two parties: the"receiving" author/reader and the "received" work.[1] This transaction, as it has been worked out by critics such as Norman Holland and Harold Bloom, consists of a number of stages. The first is usually the author/reader's imitation of the work. Next comes a deeper confrontation and transformation. Finally, the receiving author, in an attempt to create literary "space" for himself, frequently denies the impact of the received work.[2] Such a model has been used to great advantage to illuminate the creative interaction between two major writers. However, it is not so successful when analyzing the impact of a work upon a large cultural framework. Here, the reception is often mediated by one or more intervening works. These intermediaries interpret and help to assimilate the work into a cultural tradition. This transformation can show a great deal about social and moral values of the receiving culture. For example, Alfred Kelly, in his book, *The Descent of Darwin*, shows how in middle-class German society of the late nineteenth century Darwinian theories were

---

[1] See Louise Rosenblatt, "Toward a Transactional Theory of Reading" in *Influx: Essays on Literary Influence*, ed. Ronald Primeau (Port Washington, N.Y., 1977), pp. 121–36.

[2] See Harold Bloom, *The Anxiety of Influence: A Theory of Literary Influence* (New York, 1973); Norman H. Holland, "Literature as Transformation," in *Influx*, ed. Primeau, pp. 137–53.

popularly interpreted through the prism of idealist *Naturphilosophie*.[3] In his book, *Nietzsche in England, 1890–1914*, David S. Thatcher discusses the refraction of Nietzsche's philosophy through Darwin's ideas about natural selection.[4] Likewise, in the early stages of its reception in Russia, Nietzsche's *Thus Spoke Zarathustra* and its idea of the superman were popularly interpreted in terms of the world-views of Dostoevsky's "nihilist" heroes, naturalist ideas taken from Darwin and Spencer, and contemporary physiological and psychological theories.[5] In this chapter I am concerned with analyzing three aspects of mediated reception: how fiction and literary criticism functioned as vehicles for the popular dissemination of interpretations of Nietzsche, what the effect was on Nietzsche's public image in Russia, and how these interpretations revealed cultural values. We will focus particularly on two pieces of fiction, Leonid Andreev's "Rasskaz o Sergee Petroviche" ("The Story of Sergei Petrovich," 1900) and Michael Artsybashev's *Sanin* (1907).[6]

My analysis centers on one type of mediated reception, vulgarization. This phenomenon is best defined in terms of the related and more familiar phenomenon of popularization. Popularization may be defined as a simplified but largely accurate explication of an abstract idea or theory. The purpose of a popularizing work is to make the idea comprehensible to nonspecialist readers. The author's tone is generally sympathetic and balanced. He summarizes essential points, using examples familiar to a reader from a particular social and cultural background.

Fiction often serves a popularizing function. A character in a novel who reads a certain thinker and uses his ideas often makes those ideas acceptable to his readers. For example, the German novelist Hermann Hesse helped to popularize Nietzsche's works in the years following World War I. Emil Sinclair, the hero of Hesse's novel *Demian* (1919), reads Nietzsche and is led to deny traditional Christian morals and rethink his own personal values. The novel appealed strongly to the generation that

---

[3] Alfred Kelly, *The Descent of Darwin* (Chapel Hill, N.C., 1981), p. 52.

[4] David S. Thatcher, *Nietzsche in England, 1890–1914: The Growth of a Reputation* (Toronto, 1970), pp. 23–30.

[5] For a lengthier treatment of this subject see Edith W. Clowes, "A Philosophy 'for All and None': The Early Reception of Friedrich Nietzsche's Thought in Russian Literature and Society, 1892–1912" (Ph.D. diss., Yale University, 1981), pp. 35–111.

[6] Henceforth page numbers from these works will be cited parenthetically in the text. Leonid Andreev, "Rasskaz o Sergee Petroviche," *Sobranie sochinenii v 8-i tomakh* (St. Petersburg, 1908) will be cited as *SP*. Mikhail Artsybashev, *Sanin* 1907; reprint, Letchworth, 1972) will be cited as *VS*.

fought in World War I, and it gave Nietzsche new significance for that readership.

Vulgarization is more elusive than popularization because it often requires a value judgment on the part of the reader. I will define vulgarization as negative, distortive popularization. Here an idea is presented without regard for the author's original intention. It is identified with superficially similar, but essentially different phenomena—whether situations, stereotypes, or ideas—which bring about its ultimate discrediting. A good example of deliberate vulgarization is found in Max Nordau's *Entartung* (*Degeneration*, 1892), a much-read treatment of "decadent" nineteenth-century European culture. Nordau consistently concretizes, personifies, and dramatizes abstract ideas, such as Nietzsche's "master" or "superman," linking them to clearly abhorrent theories, situations, and character types.

It should be noted, however, that vulgarization can be inadvertant. For example, most readers of Nietzsche now recognize his sister's attempts to edit his works as a blatant exercise in distortion. Förster-Nietzsche, however, considered that she was giving an accurate presentation of her brother's life and ideas.[7] Her misinterpretations exerted a very strong influence for over three decades.

In the present chapter I will focus on vulgarizations of an idea that attracted public attention early in the dissemination of Nietzsche's thought in Russia: the superman. This idea naturally lends itself to multiple interpretations because of its vague character. The term "Übermensch" can be understood only in relation to other key words (some of them neologisms) in Zarathustra's vocabulary that have the prefixes "über-" ("over-", "super-"): "überfliessen" ("to overflow"), "überreich" ("overrich"), "überdrussig" ("disgusted"), and, most importantly, "überwinden" ("to overcome").[8] These words, as they are used in *Thus Spoke Zarathustra*, point to a state of the spirit: the superman is a symbol of man's psychic urge to subordinate necessity to some higher goal. As Zarathustra presents the idea, it is associated with the loftiest aspects of human nature: the desire to know and perfect oneself, to strive beyond material goals, to reach into the unknown, and, finally, to create new goals and vistas for the spirit. Still, unlike Nietzsche's psychological "types," for example, the "last man," the "higher man," the "slave" mentality, or the "master"

[7] See Walter Kaufmann, *Nietzsche: Philosopher, Psychologist, Antichrist* (New York, 1968), pp. 3–9.
[8] Ibid., pp. 307–309.

mentality, which are all pictured in colorful language, the superman remains abstract and elusive.

Nietzsche, however, is quite clear about the kind of person who is capable of continual inner searching. Few people have the power to divine their own higher goal in life and to live by that goal. Such a person is alone and does not enjoy the support of other people. The ultimate danger, as Nietzsche sees it, is spiritual emptiness and despair. In all European history, Nietzsche picks out only a handful of such people, for example, Julius Caesar, J. W. Goethe, Stendhal, Heinrich Heine, and Arthur Schopenhauer.

A new generation of Russian intellectuals emerging at the turn of the century believed it had found in Nietzsche's idea of the superman a solution to social, moral, and spiritual ills. This concept was most closely bound with a kind of "individualism"; with renewed attention to the value of individual will, subjective perception, self-reliance, physical, sexual liberation and artistic creativity. In the 1890s and 1900s a faith in the creative self replaced the predominant self-denying ethic of social service. The generation as a whole turned inward, attempting to find new directions in following their own desires—the more exotic, the better—rather than dedicating themselves to the poor. The new faith gave added legitimacy to "higher" heroic natures, the artist, the political leader, the philosopher, and their "works." But ironically, this form of individualism emphasized the mediocrity, the banality of "normal" humanity, of human nature as it is, and it led eventually to renewed denial of self and the reestablishment of a variety of world-views that posited human nature as bad, weak, contemptible. The widespread association of the superman with Dostoevsky's nihilist heroes helped to exacerbate the underlying mood of self-denial and the denial of earthly existence.

Older intellectuals mistrusted the philosophy of the superman from the start. They generally saw him as a moral anarchist. Confusing him with Dostoevsky's rebel heroes, Raskolnikov and Ivan Karamazov, some critics claimed that Nietzsche's essential morality was: "All is permitted."[9] The Nietzschean concept of the superman was viewed as an apotheosis of arbitrary human will.[10] Other critics mixed up Nietzsche's idea with the

[9] See Nikolai Grot, "Nravstvennye idealy nashego vremeni Fridrikh Nitsshe i Lev Tolstoi," *Voprosy filosofii i psikhologii* 16 (January 1893):145. Petr Boborykin, "O nitssheanstve," *Voprosy filosofii i psikhologii* 54 (September–October 1900):543.

[10] See F. I. Bulgakov, "Iz obshchestvennoi i literaturnoi khroniki zapada," *Vestnik inostrannoi literatury* 5 (1893):206–207; V. Chuiko, "Obshchestvennye idealy Fridrikha Nitsshe," *Nabliudatel'* 2 (1893):247.

naturalist view of man advanced by Turgenev's hero, Bazarov, in *Ottsy i deti (Fathers and Sons)*.[11] They felt that the German philosopher exalted physical drives, animal necessity over spiritual striving.

Perhaps the most influential vulgarizer of Nietzsche was the Austrian critic, Max Nordau. His book *Degeneration* enjoyed special authority as the only uncensored European treatment of Nietzsche to reach the lay Russian readership in the period before 1898. It was published in three inexpensive editions in 1893, 1896, and 1901 and was widely read and discussed. Nordau views his subject as an insane megalomaniac. Sadistic hedonism, Nordau argues, is at the center of Nietzsche's thought. In his opinion, all Nietzsche's ideal "types"—the master "type," the superman, the free spirit—are essentially the same: all are "bullies" motivated by a desire for self-gratification at the expense of the helpless. Nordau tells us that the free spirit and, by association, the superman, "judges his impulses and actions by how they help him, not by how they help other people, the herd: he does what gives him pleasure even when, especially when, it torments and harms . . . others."[12]

Another type of intentional vulgarization that prejudiced many readers against Nietzsche took the form of literary criticism and satires on Nietzsche's first Russian followers. These young men and women quickly gained a bad reputation at the hands of older, influential intellectuals. Nietzsche's philosophy became identified with all kinds of moral profligacy observed in the younger generation, with petty egoism, criminality, sexual depravity, and spiritual confusion. The aging Leo Tolstoi criticized Maxim Gorky for creating Nietzschean heroes who have no clear idea of good and evil.[13] In his satires, the popular novelist Peter Boborykin characterized Nietzsche's Russian adherents as effete, self-worshipping pseudo-intellectuals.[14] The well-known literary historian Nestor Kotliarevsky, writing in 1900, recognized the vulgar "Russian Nietzschean" in a whole gallery of offensive persons:

> Anyone who is sometimes tormented by his own moral insignificance; anyone who indulges all possible appetites, and sometimes very base ones; anyone dissatisfied with the way things are, who seeks something for which he does not hold himself accountable;

[11] Ivan Bichalets, "Chelovek-Lopukh i Chelovek-Zver'," *Kievskoe slovo* 1873 (3 April 1893):1.

[12] Max Nordau, *Entartung* (Berlin, 1895), p. 318.

[13] L. N. Tolstoi, *Polnoe sobranie sochinenii*, vol. 57 (Moscow, 1952), p. 175.

[14] See particularly Boborykin's novels, *Pereval* (*The Pass*, 1893), *Zhestokie* (*The Cruel Ones*, 1901), and his play, *Nakip'* (*Scum*, 1899).

any neurotic nature that yearns for the sublime, but has no ability
to create it; and finally, anyone prevented by . . . a neighbor from
doing things in a big way—all these people prefer now to say that
they are "Nietzscheans" instead of calling themselves by their real
name.[15]

Russian readers were typically limited in access to Nietzsche's actual ideas.
Although Nietzsche's works were circulated among small groups of intellectuals, they were officially banned from publication until 1898. Likewise, with the exception of Nordau's book, all European criticism was
proscribed until the same year. Thus, casual readers were led to believe
if not the negative judgment then at least the general approach of the
only available interpretations, those of Nietzsche's vulgarizers.

Vulgarized Nietzscheanism was based on the premise that anyone could
be an "individual" if only he would work to liberate himself spiritually
and physically.[16] The first example discussed here deals with spiritual
liberation while the second addresses the issue of free love and sexual
liberation. Both works served the dual function of reflecting a widespread
social phenomenon and helping to channel and focus it. And finally,
both of them hint at the reasons for the failure of this type of individualism and the return to an ethos of self-denial.

A variety of young writers read Nietzsche's work, but they got their
interpretation of his thought from the journals and from discussion within
their literary circles. What the vulgarizers had disliked, the young people
modified and cast in a positive light. Such is the case with Leonid Andreev. Andreev read *Thus Spoke Zarathustra* at the very start of his career, but, as Gorky noted, really did not understand it. Gorky praised
Andreev's Nietzschean tale, "The Story of Sergei Petrovich," but urged
Andreev to buy and read a newly published, reliable exegesis of Nietzsche's
thought by the French writer, Henri Lichtenberger.[17] Andreev, like many
others, mistook Nietzsche's ideas for those of Feodor Dostoevsky. In a
later conversation with Gorky, Andreev confused Nietzschean views of
Christ with Dostoevsky's.[18] Andreev's interpretation of the superman in

---

[15] Nestor Kotliarevsky, "Vospominaiia o Vasily Petroviche Preobrazhenskom," *Voprosy
filosofii i psikhologii* 54 (September–October 1900): 532.

[16] K. F. Golovin, *Russkii roman i russkoe obshchesvo* (St. Petersburg, 1904), p. 488.

[17] *Gor'ky i Leonid Andreev: Neizdannaia perepiska, Literaturnoe nasledstvo,* vol. 72
(Moscow, 1965), p. 88.

[18] Ibid., p. 395.

"The Story of Sergei Petrovich" combines elements of Dostoevsky's "man-god" with the vulgarized view of Nietzsche's thought.

"The Story of Sergei Petrovich" is about a "superfluous man," an ordinary university student who discovers the superman philosophy and is inspired to remake himself into a true hero. As Andreev entered in his diary for 1 April 1900, it is:

> a story about a person typical of our time, who has realized that he has a right to everything that other people have and rebels against nature and the people who try to take away his last hope for happiness. He commits suicide, inspired by Nietzsche's notion of "free death" . . .[19]

Two Nietzschean characters appear in "The Story of Sergei Petrovich": Sergei Petrovich's best friend, Novikov, and Sergei Petrovich himself. Novikov, who introduces Sergei Petrovich to Nietzsche's philosophy, is a copy of Boborykin's vulgar Nietzschean antiheroes. He is inconsiderate, arrogant, and often cruel. He disdains the people closest to him, especially Sergei Petrovich. When Sergei Petrovich, inspired by a vision of the superman, wants to transform his own character, Novikov scoffs at the irony of Sergei Petrovich's infatuation with Nietzsche. Nietzsche, he says, "who so loved the strong, has become the teacher of the weak and the poor in spirit" (SP, 225).

After reading *Thus Spoke Zarathustra*, Sergei Petrovich becomes disenchanted with Novikov's view of Nietzsche. He feels that his friend misinterprets the idea of the superman.

> [Novikov] spoke of Nietzsche's precursors in philosophy, about the connections between his doctrine and the economic and social trends of the age, and he affirmed that Nietzsche's basic thesis of individualism, "I want," came a thousand years ahead of its time. sometimes he would make fun of the obscure style of [*Thus Spoke Zarathustra*] . . . and Sergei Petrovich would try feebly to object. Novikov's remarks seemed very original to him, . . . but somehow they did not quite correspond to the truth. (SP, 245)

Andreev thus rejects the vulgar Nietzschean stereotype of the egotistical pseudo-intellectual created in the 1890s by Nietzsche's detractors. However, Sergei Petrovich himself embodies another vulgar Nietzschean ste-

[19]L. A. Iezuitova, *Tvorchestvo Leonida Andreeva, 1892–1906* (Leningrad, 1976), p. 92.

reotype: the inward-looking type, characterized by Kotliarevsky as being "tormented by his own moral insignificance." Sergei Petrovich is spiritually lost. His reading of Nietzsche leads him to a self-destructive mania. When Sergei Petrovich first reads about the superman, his own spiritual emptiness becomes obvious to him:

> When Sergei Petrovich read a piece of *Thus Spoke Zarathustra*, it seemed to him that a sun rose in the night that was his life. but it was a sad, midnight sun, and it illuminated . . . the cold, deathly, mournful desert of [his] soul.   *(SP, 243–44)*

And instead of finding a new, "burning and vital faith, the kind that moves mountains, Sergei Petrovich sees in himself a "foul lump of ritual mixed with cheap superstition."   *(SP, 249)*

Sergei Petrovich's view of the ideal self reflects the commonly held identification of the superman with Dostoevsky's idea of the man-god. The goal of Sergei Petrovich's life is to transform himself into an independent and spiritually elevated person. His tragedy is that he succeeds in overcoming personal mediocrity only by ending his life. In despair, he recalls a line from *Thus Spoke Zarathustra*, a line he misquotes twice: "Esli zhizn' ne udaëtsia tebe, esli iadovityi cherv' pozhiraet tvoë serdtse, znai, chto udastsia smert' " ("if you do not succeed in life, if a poisonous worm eats at your heart, know that you will succeed in death") *(SP, 250)*. Sergei Petrovich interprets the line to mean that he will find ultimate freedom and victory in death. When he cannot overcome his own nature, his only alternative is suicide.

Sergei Petrovich's "motto" comes from the section entitled "On Free Death" in which Zarathustra reveals his ideas about the meaning of death. He says, "Die at the right time" *(Z, 97)*. Death should be fitting denouement to a rich life. In dying, Zarathustra argues, a man should affirm his own life and urge others to live. Suicide is never mentioned in this section; indeed, the subject is raised only once in *Thus Spoke Zarathustra* when Zarathustra attacks his enemies, the Christian "preachers of death." He feels that the kernel of their message is "Kill yourselves!"[20] These alleged ministers of true faith hate life because their own lives are miserable. They resent happy people and secretly want to punish them for their happiness. They claim knowledge of a "true" life, a life after death, when all people will be judged and punished. For such people, death

---

[20] *Also Sprach Zarathustra, Werke II* (Frankfurt, 1976), "Von den Predigern des Todes," p. 548; cf. Z, 72.

has become a way to avenge a wretched life. The quotation Sergei Petrovich cited from "On Free Death" refers to these people, the "preachers of death." Zarathustra says in German: "Manchem missrät das Leben: ein Giftwurm frisst sich ihm ans Herz. So möge er zusehn, dass ihm das Sterben um so mehr geräte" ("For a certain kind of man life turns out badly: a poisonous worm eats at his heart. So let him take care that dying turns out well for him").[21] Zarathustra acknowledges that some people have miserable lives. He urges them to view death not as revenge, but as a form of self-fulfillment. Even here, Zarathustra does not advocate suicide: he feels that death is the completion of life, not its bitter and vengeful discontinuation.

Sergei Petrovich's interpretation of Zarathustra's idea of "free death" is derived from the views of one of Dostoevsky's heroes. In *Besy (The Possessed)*, Aleksei Kirillov believes that freedom can be gained for all humanity if one person can freely will his own death. People, he says, suffer because they anticipate and fear death. Kirillov dreams fervently of a "man-god" who is indifferent to death:

> man is not yet what he will be. A new man will come, happy and proud. To whom it won't matter whether he lives or not. He'll be the new man! He who conquers pain and fear will himself be a god.[22]

Kirillov conceives of a paradoxical solution to his dilemma: he must sacrifice the very life he loves—or wishes to love—in order to prove that he is free and to liberate all people. He is compelled to commit suicide. Sergei Petrovich thus follows Kirillov, not Zarathustra, in believing that freedom is found through suicide.

While the central issue in "The Story of Sergei Petrovich" is spiritual liberation, the issue in our second example is physical liberation. Artsybashev's hero, Vladimir Sanin, embodied for contemporary readers a specific Nietzschean stereotype, this time the superman as a moral hedonist. Published in the aftermath of the Revolution of 1905, *Sanin* dramatized the focus on personal life and particularly on physical love which characterized that period. Nietzsche was seen as a major influence on the new mores. As K. F. Golovin put it, Russian society "welcomed" Nietzsche as "the liberator of flesh."[23]

[21] Ibid., "Vom freien Tod," p. 608; cf. Z, 98.
[22] F. M. Dostoevsky, *The Devils*, trans. David Magarshack (London, 1969), p. 126.
[23] Golovin, *Russkii roman*, p. 516.

Sanin was an immediate sensation both in Russia and abroad. Its near-pornographics descriptions, among the first to appear on the open Russian market, were scandalous. The novel soon became the Bible for a whole generation of young people disillusioned with social and political activism.[24] Although a few critics recognized Sanin's philosophy of the flesh as a vulgarization, many viewed it as a free but faithful representation of Nietzsche's thought.

It is interesting to note that the author of *Sanin* claimed never to have read Nietzsche "beyond the beginnings of his books." Artsybashev remarked in an autobiographical profile from 1915 that the German philosopher was a "brilliant thinker," but that he "diverged from me both in his ideas and the bombastic form of his works."[25] It is not surprising that Artsybashev should have disclaimed direct influence; it was a vulgarized interpretation of Nietzsche in the air at the turn of the century that helped to form the world-view of his hero, Vladimir Sanin.

In *Sanin*, Artsybashev advances a philosophy of physical pleasure. The main characters, all young men and women, question traditional values and goals, trying to find valid new ones. Some cling to social utilitarianism, but the only acceptable philosophy appears to be the hedonism expounded by Vladimir Sanin.

Several cues tell the reader that Sanin's philosophy should be seen as "Nietzschean." Although the hero himself is "irritated and bored" by Nietzsche, he is viewed by others as a kind of superman (VS, 26). His admirers read Nietzsche. His sister Lida keeps a copy of *Thus Spoke Zarathustra* by her bedside. His drunken friend, Ivanov, is ironically called a "superman." Opponents see Sanin's adherents as the "triumphant swine of Zarathustra" (VS, 155).

Sanin's personal appearance and behavior echo in positive tones what Max Nordau perceived as Nietzsche's negative and dangerous ideal. Nordau identified Nietzsche's ideal man with an image used by Nietzsche in *The Genealogy of Morals*: the "magnificent beast of prey," the "laughing lion." This type, Nordau said, wanted to satisfy all his urges without consideration of others. Sadistic voluptuousness, Nordau said, was the foundation of Nietzsche's philosophy. Sanin's appearance exudes the great health and energy of the "magnificent beast of prey." "There were no

[24] D. S. Mirsky, *Contemporary Russian Literature, 1881–1925* (1926; reprint, New York, 1972), pp. 139–40.

[25] Michael Artzibashef, "Introduction," *The Millionaire*, trans. Percy Pinkerton (London, 1915), p. 9.

signs of weariness or excitement in his tall, fair-haired, broad-shouldered figure, or in the tranquil, slightly mocking expression of his face" (VS, 3). He is completely self-reliant, aloof and reserved in society. Yet Sanin is fundamentally a kind of "natural" man. Although restrained among his friends, he vents his primal instincts when alone. During a thunderstorm, "feeling life and strength with his entire being, Sanin spread his arms and gave out a . . . prolonged and happy cry" (VS, 250).

Sanin's world-view is simple, indeed primitive. He believes that an individual should "experience the pleasure and happiness of which [he] is capable" (VS, 26). "Paradise," he says, "is a synonym for absolute pleasure" (VS, 27). Of all human pleasures, Sanin thinks sexual gratification is the greatest. He strives to be the "completely sincere and natural man" who satisfies his sexual desires.

> If [the natural man] sees a thing which does not belong to him, but which is pretty, he takes it: if he sees a gorgeous woman who will not give in to him, he takes her by force or deceit. It is completely natural to do so because the need for and the understanding of pleasure is one of the few qualities which sets the natural man apart from the animals.   (VS, 26–27).

Sanin feels that people are at last ready for such liberation; they have passed through a period of "revaluation of all their feelings, needs, and desires" and now know that they must have physical freedom (VS, 275). "People," he proclaims, "must enjoy love without fear or taboo, limitlessly." He dreams of a time when man will fully liberate his body, "when nothing will stand between man and happiness, when man will give himself freely and fearlessly to all pleasures accessible to him" (VS, 276–77).

This vulgar Nietzschean philosophy of hedonism gains credibility in a general atmosphere of moral and spiritual despondency. The older generation offers no alternatives and no direction. Sanin himself grew up without moral guidance. When his moral character was forming, "Sanin was living away from his family. No one watched after him, no hand shaped him, and the spirit of this man formed freely and uniquely, like a tree in the field" (VS, 3). Hedonism is juxtaposed to other moral alternatives: one person is a Social Democrat, another is a Tolstoian. The first appears weak and self-deprecating, the second is shown to be hypocritical. Neither achieves the goal of social enlightenment he sets for himself. Sanin's philosophy appears stronger than any other because it offers the ideal of a self-assured, aggressive individual who pretends to no higher goal than the attainment of personal pleasure.

Both Andreev and Artsybashev created interesting and in some ways sympathetic heroes, using as thematic material some widespread misinterpretations of Nietzsche's superman. It is important to ask what effect such heroes, themselves popularly held representatives of Nietzschean thought, had on Nietzsche's public image. In my view, they helped to discredit the German philosopher. The texts themselves and the critical discussions surrounding them called into question the validity of the idea of the superman. Because very few critics distinguished Nietzsche's actual idea from its vulgarizations, Nietzsche's reputation suffered as well.

Several aspects of both narratives encourage the reader to doubt the new Nietzschean heroes. In "The Story of Sergei Petrovich," for example, the narrator is unsympathetic to Sergei Petrovich and his dilemma. He makes the aspiration of this dull person to such a high and heroic state of being seem both ludicrous and sad. Although his honest self-appraisal and his desire to strive toward a higher existence make him appealing, the obvious incongruity between actuality and ideal are laughable. Sergei Petrovich knows that he does not have the profundity of spirit to reach a new level of being. To escape self-contempt, he learns to be contemptuous of other people. He begins to think of himself as a superman. He isolates himself, scoffing at his classmates at the university. Such pretentiousness is worthy only of disdain.

When Sergei Petrovich decides to commit suicide, he experiences a brief, uplifting burst of joy and strength. The narrator makes light of this final outburst, calling his sense of victory the "arrogant and unreasoned delirium of megalomania" (SP, 277). After Sergei Petrovich's death, the narrator devotes his attention to grotesque details, such as a decomposition of Sergei Petrovich's body and the poverty of his funeral. Sergei Petrovich, we are led to believe, has not found a new sense of heroism.

In *Sanin*, the narrator's discrediting of the hedonist philosophy is not so clear. This philosophy can, however, be judged by its effect on others: Sanin's practices bring unhappiness to everyone but himself. During the summer in the province Sanin's "disciple" Ivanov drinks himself into oblivion. His sister, Lida, a devout reader of *Thus Spoke Zarathustra*, gives herself up to a night of passion with a soldier. When she learns that she is pregnant, she tries to commit suicide. Sanin saves her only to marry her off to a boring, but trustworthy young man. Lida's life is saved, but her vitality is lost. Sanin himself ruins the life of the book's heroine, Zina Karsavina, by raping her. Soon after, another of Zina's admirers, who really cares for her, commits suicide. In the autumn, Sanin goes off in search of a new adventure, leaving behind friends he has destroyed. A philosophy that appeared to promise new vitality has ruined the lives of the best young people in town.

Critical discussion also helped to discredit the Nietzschean "solutions" to life devised by such individualist heroes. Some critics recognized these works and others like them as vulgarizations of Nietzsche. They lamented the unfortunate reception of such a brilliant thinker. For example, the critic Iury Aleksandrovich viewed Andreev's story as the reduction of the lofty "illusion" of the superman to a "sanctified idol.[26] The critic Arsky similarly argued that Sanin "vulgarized" Nietzsche.[27]

Other critics accepted the vulgarized reflection as truly Nietzschean. The outstanding editor and critic, S. A. Vengerov, argued that Sanin's new "theory of the strong man, to whom all is permitted, is basically taken from Nietzsche's doctrine of the superman."[28] Another critic, F. Beliavsky, noted in a discussion of Nietzsche and contemporary literature that "self-love, egoism will always bring divisiveness and enmity, no matter what sauce you serve it with."[29] Nietzsche's influence, both men felt, was negative and destructive.

Although a number of critics recognized that such works as Andreev's and Artsybashev's misrepresented Nietzsche's philosophy, they generally failed to outline another more accurate and equally accessible interpretation. Thus, the casual reader was left only with the vulgarization, wrong as it might be. The critic Evgeny Anichkov called in 1912 for an end to the vulgarized "cult" of Nietzsche.[30] He suggested that most readers and writers should simply put Nietzsche aside if they could not read and interpret him carefully and seriously. Indeed, in these few years before World War I, interest in Nietzsche dropped sharply. A full academic collection of his works begun in 1909 was never finished. Fewer critical

[26] Iury Aleksandrovich, *Posle Chekhova: Ocherk molodoi literatury poslednego desiatiletiia, 1898–1908* (Moscow, 1908), p. 42.

[27] Arsky, "Motivy Solntsa i Tela v sovremennoi belletristike (M.P. Artsybashev)," *Voprosy pola* 2 (1908):28.

[28] S. A. Vengerov, "Etapy neo-romanticheskogo dvizheniia," in *Russkaia literatura XX veka* (Moscow, 1914), p. 22.

[29] F. Beliavsky, "Gor'kaia pravda," *Slovo* 157 (22 May 1905):5.

[30] Evgeny Anichkov, "Doloi Nitsshe," *Novaia zhizn'* 9 (1912):139.

works were published. Although Nietzsche's literary impact remained very strong among a handful of writers and thinkers, it was certainly less blatant and less accessible to the lay reader.

One of Nietzsche's most devoted admirers, Nikolai Berdiaev, remarked in 1907:

> One can imagine nothing more tragic . . . than Nietzsche's posthumous fate. This person suffered his whole life from the anxiety of isolation, he was neither understood nor recognized. The whole meaning of his spiritual struggle, the whole essence of his remarkable ideas, lay in the fact that Nietzsche was alone, raised himself above any crowd, challenged the world and was rebuffed. Nietzsche's success after death is a great and terrible insult to a life full of suffering, an outrage against his agony. Nietzsche had every reason to think that almost no one would recognize him, but almost everyone ended up recognizing him, they stole his [ideas] little by little, everyone needed him, all his ideas were vulgarized and debased. Nietzsche was a great phenomenon of the world spirit, yet Nietzscheanism [*Nitssheanstvo*] gives off a foul odor, this phenomenon grows more vulgar with every day.[31]

Nietzsche's difficult philosophy, in Berdiaev's view, should have been read and studied only by a few caring devotees. It is perhaps a great irony that it should have become so popular. However, the Nietzschean fashion lasted only a very short time: the idea of the superman, at first hailed as the panacea of the age, soon became its sickness. It became a name for every bad trend among Russian youth. And because the public—most writers, critics, and readers— could not distinguish Nietzsche's real thought from the various vulgarized images of the superman, Nietzsche's popular reputation soon failed as well. It would take a different generation to unmask the vulgarization and find a fresh approach to Nietzsche.

The discreditation of vulgar Nietzscheanism helped to undermine the belief of young people in the pre-1905 era that each self-conscious, searching person is valuable. The individual, with his own perceptions, needs, creative will, became equated with arbitrariness, arrogance, impotence. Vulgar Nietzschean works, ironically, undermined the view that they set out to support. These stories were pervaded by a mood of contempt for the ordinary person who tries to distinguish himself. Sergei

---

[31] Nikolai Berdiaev, "Bunt i pokornost' v psikhologii mass" (1907), in *Dukhovnyi krizis intelligentsii* (St. Petersburg, 1910), p. 77.

Petrovich's quest is put in the worst possible light by the narrator. In Artsybashev's novel, Sanin is the source of contempt. He puts himself above the others and feels only scorn for people who "abuse" his hedonist philosophy. In the years before World War I, people drew away from the morality of self-reliance and creative initiative that had been so appealing and looked for ways to lose the individual self in the collective, in nature, in the elements, in some "higher" principle.

15.

Michael Bakhtin, Nietzsche, and Russian Pre-Revolutionary Thought

James M. Curtis

As Michael Holquist put it, there was a hex on the life and work of the critic Michael Bakhtin (1895–1975).[1] Bakhtin had a long and productive career, but much of his work was either published long after it was written, or it was lost and never published at all. Born in 1895, Bakhtin belonged to the generation of Osip Mandelstam, the generation that grew up in the exciting milieu of Russian modernism, and then spent its adult life dealing with the horrors of post-Revolutionary existence. Like Mandelstam, Bakhtin attended St. Petersburg University during World War I, where he studied with the great Polish-born classicist Tadeusz Zieliński (1859–1944). Zieliński was unique among European classicists in that he hailed *The Birth of Tragedy* as a great work, and it was he who taught Bakhtin to think in Nietzschean terms.

Bakhtin spent the turbulent years from 1920 to 1924 in the Belorussian city of Vitebsk, which Marc Chagall has lovingly depicted in so many paintings, and then returned to Leningrad, where he published his first major work, *Problems of Dostoevsky's Art* (*Problemy tvorschestva Dostoevskogo*, 1929).[2] Although the title sounds innocuous enough, the author-

---

[1] I take this biographical information on Bakhtin from Michael Holquist's "Introduction" in M. M. Bakhtin, *The Dialogic Imagination*, trans. Caryl Emerson and Michael Holquist (Austin, Texas, 1981). I regret that the following major works on Bakhtin appeared too late for consultation in the preparation of this essay: the Bakhtin issue of *Studies in 20th Century Literature* (Fall 1984); and Michael Holquist and Katerina Clark, *Mikhail Bakhtin* (Cambridge, Mass., 1984).

[2] Mikhail Bakhtin, *Problemy tvorchestva Dostoevskogo* (Leningrad, 1929). Translated as *Problems of Dostoevsky's Poetics* by R. W. Rotsel (Ann Arbor, 1973).

ities considered the book subversive, and exiled him to the obscure town of Kustanai for six years. After defending a very controversial dissertation on François Rabelais (ca. 1490–1553) at Moscow State University in the late Forties, he taught in the Mordovian city of Saransk, where he remained until his retirement due to ill health in 1961.

Whether because of the censorship, bad luck, his difficult expository style, or a combination of all three, Bakhtin began to acquire the recognition he had long deserved only in the Sixties. A second edition of his book on Dostoevsky appeared in 1963, and a revised version of his dissertation on Rabelais appeared in 1965.[3] In addition, two anthologies of collected essays, which included some major theoretical statements from the Twenties, were published in the Seventies: *Questions of Literature and Esthetics (Vosprosy literatury i estetiki,* 1975)[4] and *The Esthetics of Verbal Creativity (Estetika slovesnogo tvorchestva,* 1979).[5] Bakhtin died in 1975.

When Bakhtin became another of the fashionable names in the debates about literature in the Sixties and Seventies, most critics associated him with semiotic theory because of his longstanding interest in language and dialogue. However, I wish to argue here that we can best understand Bakhtin in a historical context by relating him to Nietzsche. This chapter thus deals with three inter-related topics. First, it takes up the Nietzschean features of Bakhtin's criticism. A juxtaposition of his statements about the principles he believed in and the images that he used shows a remarkable, and remarkably consistent, similarity to those of Nietzsche. The second topic follows logically from the first: From whom did Bakhtin assimilate the Nietzschean principles and the philosophical modes of thought and exposition that inform his work? Answering this question requires a discussion of Tadeusz Zieliński's work and the works of others in pre-Revolutionary Russia. Something that Ivan Vinogradov said about the formalist critics Victor Shklovsky (b. 1893), Boris Eichenbaum (1886–1959), and Iury Tynianov (1894–1943) applies to Bakhtin as well: "The formalists grew up on the soil of subjective-idealistic philosophy. One has only to flip through the bourgeois philosophical journals of the 1900s and 1910s to see the spiritual food on which the formalists were nour-

---

[3] Mikhail Bakhtin, *Tvorchestvo Fransua Rabel* (Moscow, 1965). Translated as *Rablelais and His World* by Helene Iswolsky (Cambridge, Mass., 1968).

[4] Mikhail Bakhtin, *Voprosy literatury i estetiki* (Moscow, 1975). Henceforth cited as *Vle.* This volume has been translated as *The Dialogic Imagination* (see n. 1).

[5] Mikhail Bakhtin, *Estetika slovesnogo tvorchestva* (Moscow, 1979). Henceforth cited as *Est.*

ished."[6] Although I do not believe that the philosophers in question were subjective idealists and I do not wish to denounce Bakhtin, as Vinogradov wished to denounce the formalists, I do think he hit upon something essential about the intellectual origins of the major critics of the Twenties. The books and articles that they read and the lectures they heard while at the university during World War I gave them an intellectual orientation which they later applied in their criticism. It now seems clear that Bakhtin and the three principal formalist critics were the most important Russian critics of the Twenties, but Bakhtin had substantive disagreements with them, and thus the third questions arises: How does an understanding of the Nietzschean features of Bakhtin's criticism help to clarify his relationship to the formalists?

This chapter treats literary criticsm as intellectual history. I propose to establish continuity between the pre- and post-Revolutionary periods in Russia by articulating a common intellectual paradigm, while renouncing any concern with the issues of originality or truth. That is to say, I will not deal with the origins of Nietzsche's ideas about the Apollonian and Dionysian, for instance; likewise, I will not evaluate any of the books and essays under discussion. The question of whether Bakhtin's statements about Dostoevsky are true or verifiable offers no help in understanding those statements as part of a coherent larger paradigm, and therefore this essay does not raise the question.

As a general prefatory comment, I might note that especially during the second and third decades of this century, European critics took an active interest in philosophy, and applied philosophical precepts when they wrote about literature. T. S. Eliot (1888–1965) wrote his Harvard doctoral dissertation on the British idealist philosopher F. H. Bradley (1846–1924), and the French critic Albert Thibaudet (1874–1936) was a prominent Bergsonian. I interpret Bakhtin as belonging to this group of well-educated, multilingual men caught in a great historical upheaval that forced them to think through their principles with the help of philosophy.

In his writings published so far, Bakhtin makes three references to Nietzsche, all of which refer to style. Apparently alluding to *Thus Spoke Zarathustra*, Bakhtin speaks of "Nietzsche's estheticized philosophy." It would apper that Bakhtin is making a distinction between himself and Nietzsche, for his own writing is certainly not "estheticized." During a

---

[6]Ivan Vinogradov, *Bor'ba za stil'* (Leningrad, 1937), p. 395.

discussion of the classification of biographies, he says, "A philosophical conception that arose on the basis of the essential elements of the first type of biography is the estheticized biography of Nietzsche."[7] Bakhtin seems to be referring here to the poetic qualities of Nietzsche's style, which culminated in *Thus Spoke Zarathustra*. It was in the interest of these qualities that made Nietzsche regret that he had written *The Birth of Tragedy*; he said of his voice in that book, "It should have *sung* (*BT*, 20).

Bakhtin's writing does not sing, and perhaps he thought Nietzsche's should not have. For all the force and originality of Bakhtin's work, it is clearly that of a scholar trained in a Germanic tradition of *Wissenschaft* that Nietzsche despised. If we seek for an early twentieth-century analogy, it would be with the seminal figure in the phenomenological movement, Edmund Husserl (1859–1938). Bakhtin uses the word "adequate" as Husserl does, in the sense of "semantically or ontologically equivalent," and this fact gives us a clue to his affinity with Husserl. Like Husserl, Bakhtin seeks general, suprapersonal principles, not individual peculiarities. But whereas Husserl concerned himself with the nature of transcendent being, Bakhtin concerned himself with the nature of literary works. This difference presumably explains why their most significant affinities are stylistic, rather than thematic.

Like Husserl's, Bakhtin's work abounds in long sentences with complex syntax and abstruse terminology. (He has a special fondness for abstract neologisms and compound adjectives.) It deals with abstract classifications, not personalities nor the specifics of history or biography. While Bakhtin's style has the denseness of German philosophical prose, and lacks the dance of paradoxes and images that animates Nietzsche's, his erudition and perspicacity keep it from becoming turgid and self-indulgent.

When Europeans in the early twentieth century thought about art and values, they often thought as Nietzsche taught them to think. They did not have to read a great deal of Nietzsche to revaluate their values; indeed, the first part of the first sentence of Nietzsche's first major work, *The Birth of Tragedy*, states an essential principle: "We shall have gained much for the science of aesthetics, once we perceive not merely by logical inference, but with the immediate certainty of vision, that the continuous development of art is bound up with the *Apollonian* and the *Dion-*

---

[7] Bakhtin, *Est*, p. 140.

ysian duality. (*BT*, 33). The translator renders the German *Duplizität* as "duality" here, but the term does not have its usual philosophical meaning. Rather, it means something like "interaction." Since Nietzsche spoke so often about the Dionysian, we may easily forget that the Dionysian was not important in and of itself. He believed its resurgence in Wagner's music heralded a great change in European consciousness because it redressed the balance which Socrates had upset by emphasizing Apollonian inquiry. The crucial theme of *The Birth of Tragedy*—and indeed of Nietzsche's theory of art—is that great art derives its greatness from the *interaction* of Apollonian and Dionysian elements. Therefore, it makes more sense to think of Nietzsche as a pluralist, rather than as a voluntarist. Thinking of Nietzsche as a pluralist makes it possible to connect *The Birth of Tragedy* with *Thus Spoke Zarathustra*, for one can interpret his career as one long polemic against monism, as represented by Kant and Socrates, among others. (As an aside, I might note that popular interpretations of Nietzsche, such as those which associate him with the theory of the superman and leave it at that, ignore his pluralism and make him out to be a monist.)

Bakhtin believed that Nietzsche was arguing for pluralism, and that his pluralistic ontology, not his provocative attacks on Christianity or his extravagant individualism, constituted the essence of his thought for the serious critic. As a result Bakhtin took over Nietzsche's defense of pluralism and applied it to the theoretical esthetic questions that concerned him in the Twenties. Although he did not use the terms "Apollonian" and "Dionysian," he concluded that understanding a work required understanding that its structure was the result of the interaction of two different elements. In an early essay from 1924, ponderously titled "The Problem of Content, Material, and Form in Verbal Artistic Creativity," he attempted to resolve the nineteenth-century dichotomy of form and content into one unified whole. He failed to do so, but he offered the following principle:

> In an artistic work there are as it were two powers and two legal orders defined by these powers: every element can be defined in two value systems—content and form, for in every signifying element both these systems are in an essential value-charged interaction.[8]

The presence of a crucial Nietzschean word, "values," signals Bakhtin's concern to relate works of art to the nature of the societies in which they

---

[8] Bakhtin, *Vle*, p. 36.

arose. Although he never managed to do this in a satisfactory way, he maintained throughout his long and difficult life his belief in the pluralistic structure of works of art as manifested through the interaction of heterogeneous elements in them.

Notice that Bakhtin refers in the title of his essay to "verbal artistic creativity." We call the verbal interaction of two people a dialogue, and Nietzsche has this to say about dialogue in *Human, All Too Human*:

> A dialogue is the perfect conversation, because everything that the one person says acquires its particular color, sound, its accompanying gesture *in strict consideration of the other person* to whom he is speaking; it is like letter writing, where one and the same man shows ten ways of expressing his inner thoughts, depending on whether he is writing to this person or to that. In a dialogue, there is only one single refraction of thought: this is produced by the partner in conversation, the mirror in which we want to see our thoughts reflected as beautifully as possible.   (*HH*, 191–92)

Just as it takes the interaction of the Apollonian and the Dionysian to create a great work of art, so it takes the interaction of one person with another person to create dialogue.

"Dialogue is the perfect conversation." This phrase might well stand as the dominant theme of Bakhtin's criticism of the Twenties, which culminates in the book on Dostoevsky. In a long, unfinished, Husserlian essay from the early Twenties, Bakhtin worked on something like a phenomenology of the encounter between the self and the other in the pluralistic experience of dialogue. Unlike Nietzsche, he emphasized the separateness of the two people even during their interaction.

> When we look at each other, two different worlds are reflected in the pupils of our eyes. One can, by adopting a corresponding position, reduce this difference of *outlooks*, but it is necessary to merge into one, to become one person, in order to destroy it entirely.[9]

In his *Problems of Dostoevsky's Art*, Bakhtin maintained that Dostoevsky never allowed this merger to occur, thereby sustaining the interaction that characterizes (by implication at least) all great art.

Bakhtin denounced the monism of previous Dostoevsky criticism. For Bakhtin, the irreducible pluralism of the self–other encounter in dialogue

[9] Bakhtin, *Est*, p. 22.

offers a model for Dostoevsky's work as whole. "It is not the multiplicity of fates and lives in a single objective world in the light of a single authorial consciousness that develops in his work, but precisely *the multiplicity of equal consciousnesses with their worlds* which is combined here, preserving their own integrity into the unity of a certain event."[10] Just as two people do not merge during dialogue, so Dostoevsky's characters do not merge—either with each other, or with the author, "the single authorial consciousness," as Bakhtin puts it. Such a merger would create the homogeneity of monism. This issue will return in another context.

Dostoevsky created "the multiplicity of equal consciousnesses," Bakhtin tells us, because "he could hear two quarreling voices in every voice."[11] He imputes to Dostoevsky the capacity that Nietzsche denounced in his self-criticism of *The Birth of Tragedy*. Nietzsche later decided that the problem with his first book was stylistic; that it spoke "in a *foreign* voice." (*BT*, p. 20; Kaufmann translation "in a *strange* voice"). But where Nietzsche rejected this voice, Bakhtin repeatedly affirmed its necessary presence. In the chapter "The Types of the Prose Word, the Word in Dostoevsky," Bakhtin used the word "foreign" (*chuzhoi*)—an exact translation of Nietzsche's *fremde*—no less than eight times, in various combinations such as "a foreign style,"[12] and (three times) "a foreign word."[13]

Bakhtin loved terms, so he invented a new one that would characterize the distinctive features of Dostoevsky's work. "Dostoevsky is the creator of the *polyphonic novel*. He created an essentially new novelistic genre."[14] Although Nietzsche does not seem to have used the term "polyphony" himself, Bakhtin's use of this term partakes of the general predilection of European Nietzscheans for musical imagery. As it happens, the literary use of "polyphony" began with the French symbolists who were reading Nietzsche and listening to Wagner. It occurs in this sense in an essay by Tristan Visan (1878–1945), to cite only one example.[15]

[10] Bakhtin, *Problemy*, p. 9.

[11] Ibid., p. 152.

[12] Ibid., p. 113.

[13] Ibid., pp. 134, 139, 147.

[14] Ibid., p. 9.

[15] Visan speaks of "all the rich polyphonies of the soul"; see Tristan Visan, *L'Attitude du lyrisme contemporaine* (Paris, 1911), p. 461.

For a brief discussion of the metaphorical uses of the word "polyphony" in the early twentieth century, see James M. Curtis, *Culture as Polyphony* (Columbia, Mo., 1978), p. vii. In 1933, and almost certainly independently of Bakhtin, the Austrian novelist Hermann Broch concluded his essay "The World Picture of the Novelist" with this comment: "For the writer's task as such is not new; it is an eternal and immortal wish-picture [*Wunschbild*]

Nietzsche said a great deal about the effects of the eruption of the Dionysian, of course, but one of his most evocative passages about it occurs in the first part of *The Birth of Tragedy*, when he asks us to imagine the choral ending to Beethoven's Ninth Symphony, Schiller's "Ode to Joy," as a painting. Thinking of the famous line, "All men become brothers," he writes:

> Now the slave is a free man, now all the rigid hostile barriers which necessity, whim, or "imprudent convention" have set between man and man are broken. Now, with the gospel of world harmony, each one feels himself not only united, reconciled, fused with his neighbor but also one with him, as if the veil of Maya had been torn aside and was now merely fluttering in tatters before the mysterious-primordial unity.   (BT, 37)

People who emphasize the elitism of Nietzsche's later work usually forget this passage with its strongly democratic qualities. Although I certainly do not wish to make Nietzsche out to be a populist, I do wish to make the point that Bakhtin's populism is not necessarily inconsistent with the argument of *The Birth of Tragedy*.

Bakhtin became interested in the carnival revelry which preceded Lent,[16] a period of abstention, which provided him with yet another example of the interplay of opposites—opposites that expressed values in a social setting. He certainly sounds as though he has *The Birth of Tragedy* in mind when he describes the democratizing effects of carnivalization:

> Any *distance* between people is abolished, and a particulate carnival category—*free familiar contact between people*—goes into effect. This is a very important element of the carnival world-feeling. People

---

in the soul of man. It has long been in existence in all its polyphony, but the instrument which literature has created in the modern novel is of such organlike dimensions, the moden novel in its rational and irrational polyphony is so magnificent an instrument, that in its organ tone the intoxication of the future resounds for each one who wishes to hear." Hermann Broch, *Dichten und Erkennen: Essays*, vol. 1 (Zürich, 1955), p. 238.

[16] But we should not forget the *Soviet* carnivals that were organized after the Revolution and that Bakhtin had surely seen. Indeed, Bakhtin could have written the opening lines of an interesting book about them, which came out in 1930: "The carnival procession has existed in various forms for a long time. Predicated on the movement of crowds occuring in squares and streets, demanding that its spectator be an active participant, that is, demanding immediate self-activity, it has always been a truly class-oriented, truly collective celebration." B. Zemenkov, *Oformlenie sovetskikh karnavalov i demonstratsii* (Moscow, 1930), p. 5.

separated in life by impenetrable hierarchical barriers, enter into a free familiar contact on the carnival square.[17]

Although we will never know for sure, Nietzsche may have suggested to Bakhtin the appropriateness of medieval carnivals for this purpose when, also in the first part of *The Birth of Tragedy*, he comments on the singers and dancers of medieval Germany: "In these dancers of St. John and St. Vitus we rediscover the Bacchic choruses of the Greeks" (*BT*, 36). In his book on Rabelais Bakhtin cites the "feasts of fools" during the Middle Ages as an example of carnivalization. "These feasts of fools basically had the character of a parodic travesty of the official cult, and were accompanied by masquerades and improper dances."[18] Bakhtin's "feasts of fools" resemble Nietzsche's dances in that both of these hedonistic activities threatened propriety. Even if this analogy is coincidental, it nevertheless suggests an intellectual affinity between Nietzsche and Bakhtin.

Parodic travesties evoke laughter, of course, and in *The Gay Science* and *Thus Spoke Zarathustra* Nietzsche continually returns to laughter as an experience that places one beyond good and evil. Zarathustra asks, "What has been the greatest sin here on earth? Was it not the saying of him who said, 'Woe to those who laugh!' " (Z, 304). If the denial of laughter was the greatest sin, then laughter takes on a religious quality, and constitutes an essential part of what Zarathustra wishes to teach. "This crown of him who laughs, this rose-wreath crown to you my brothers, do I throw this crown! Laughter I have pronounced holy; you Higher Men laugh for my sake!"[19] Laughter expresses an affirmation of life, an affirmative interchange between the self and the world that is possible only for those who have a good conscience and who do not live in guilt.

Nietzsche was a visionary, and Bakhtin was a scholar. Naturally, Bakhtin's discussions of laughter lack the ecstatic rhetoric of Nietzsche's, but they share a common set of attitudes about laughter and its importance. Just as the emphasis on laughter appears in Nietzsche's later work, so it appears in Bakhtin's later work, on Rabelais. In the first chapter, "Rabelais in the History of Laughter," Bakhtin rejects Bergson's conception of the effect of laughter (from his book, *Laughter*), as removing the encrus-

---

[17] Mikhail Bakhtin, *Problemy poetiki Dostoevskogo*, 3rd ed. (Moscow, 1972), p. 208.

[18] Bakhtin, *Rable*, p. 83.

[19] Translation mine. Nietzsche, *Werke im fünf Banden* (Frankfort am Main, 1981), 2:805. Cf. Z, 306. Hollingdale translates the last phrase as "learn to laugh" but this construction of the imperative of *lernen* is very idiomatic.

tation of the mechanical on the organic, and he does so for very Nietzschean reasons.

> Let us emphasize once more that for the Renaissance theory of laughter (as well as for its classical sources characterized by us) it is precisely the recognition of a positive, renewing, *creative* significance that is characteristic. This sharply distinguishes it from subsequent theories and philosophies, including Bergson's conception, which principally bring out in laughter its negative functions.[20]

The laughter of satire, Bakhtin tells us, "shifts the center of gravity to the abstractly significant, 'moral' content of the images."[21] Such "moral" content derives from abstractions about good and evil; Bergson's emphasis on satire is thus consistent with the abstract quality of so much of French thought. And it is just this abstraction that makes it unacceptable to Nietzsche and to Bakhtin as well. Bakhtin thus interprets carnival laughter "primarily as a victory over moral fear, which fetters, oppresses, and clouds a person's consciousness."[22]

Yet in this important chapter, the difference between Nietzsche the visionary and Bakhtin the scholar appears again, as when Bakhtin says that the Janus face of folk laughter (an indicative image) "emphasized precisely the element of *change* and *renewal*, yet in a social-historical setting."[23] Bakhtin wishes to apply Nietzschean ideas to the interplay between Rabelias's work and its social setting. Remarkably, he does so by utilizing its antagonism toward Christianity (which Nietzsche shared with Marx, for very different reasons, of course). During the horrors of the Soviet repression of the Thirties, he can use Nietzschean ideas—and remain faithful to his material—by presenting the medieval carnival, and carnivalization, as an illegal, proletarian, anticlerical phenomenon. He discusses its parodies of the mass, its blasphemous qualities, and the like.

What it comes to is that Bakhtin takes Marx and Lenin at their word; they had denounced the abstractions of Christianity and imperialism and had proposed to replace them with a practical, egalitarian doctrine. Bakhtin says that carnival life, with its attack on hierarchies, did this as well, although he takes pains to note its limitations as a revolutionary movement. He thereby acquires the right to associate carnival with the earth, and with fertility rites.

[20] *Rable*, p. 80.
[21] Ibid., p. 71.
[22] Ibid., p. 102.
[23] Ibid., p. 71.

We have said that medieval laughter overcame the fear of that which was more frightening than the earth. All that was unearthly and frightful was turned into the *earth*; it was the native mother which engulfed in order to give birth anew, to give birth to something bigger and better.[24]

This sounds revolutionary enough, but it is revolutionary in Zarathustra's sense, not Lenin's.

The theme of establishing an affinity with the earth and on drawing one's strength from it as a way of overcoming the weakness of abstract thought recurs in *Thus Spoke Zarathustra* as often as the theme of laughter, to which it is related. At the very beginning of the book, when Zarathustra announces that he will speak of the Superman, he says:

The Superman is the meaning of the earth. Let your will say: The Superman *shall be* the meaning of the earth! I entreat you, my brothers, *remain true to the earth*, and do not believe those who speak to you of superterrestrial hopes!   (Z, 13)

For Bakhtin, the carnival did just this; it remained true to the earth, and denied "superterrestrial" (or as he put it, "non-earthly") hopes which were, of course, related to abstract Christian doctrines of good and evil.

The intensity of Zarathustra's sermons about establishing an affinity with the earth came from the fact that Western society had lost that affinity. For Nietzsche in *The Birth of Tragedy*, it was Socrates who dissociated the Apollonian and the Dionysian by asking such abstract questions as, "What is the Good?" and "What is the Beautiful?" Throughout the first third of the twentieth century, intellectuals all over Europe found in this historical scheme a way to analyze the malaise of their own times. *The Birth of Tragedy* served as a major source for T. S. Eliot, for example, who found that what he called a "dissociation of sensibility" had occurred in the seventeenth century after the death of John Donne, the last poet who could fuse thinking and feeling.[25]

I mention Eliot here because Bakhtin's interpretation of Rabelais sounds a lot like Eliot's interpretation of Donne. Just as Eliot praised Donne's poetry as a high point of creativity, so Bakhtin praised Rabelais's prose. "The sixteenth century is a summit in the history of laughter; the peak

---

[24] Ibid., p. 103.

[25] See F. N. Lees, "T. S. Eliot and Nietzsche," *Notes and Queries*, October, 1964, pp. 386–87.

of this summit is Rabelais' novel"[26] After the peak, the decline began. For Eliot, the dissociation of sensibility began after Donne; more socially minded, and more given to jargon, than Eliot, Bakhtin refers to "the *stabilization* of the new order of absolute monarchy."[27] As a result, "the ambivalence of the grotesque becomes unacceptable."[28] By "ambivalence" here he means what he earlier called "the Janus face" of carnival, and what Nietzsche called *Duplizität*, the interaction of two opposed entities. In short, he means what Nietzsche means by *Duplizität*. In the seventeenth century (he is surely thinking here of Louis XIV and his court) all culture becomes official culture, "and therefore laughter and the grotesque change their nature and are degraded."[29] That is to say, the Apollonian had triumphed, although in various guises: as autocracy in politics, and as monism in philosophy.

Nietzsche related the dissociation of the Apollonian and the Dionysian to philosophical idealism, both in its Platonic and Christian forms. In *The Gay Science*, he said, "In sum: all philosophical idealism to date was something like a disease" (GS, 333). For Nietzsche, idealism was "something like a disease" because it meant roughly the same as monism, which denied *Duplizität*, and thereby weakened Western culture. For Bakhtin, idealism and monism produced a scholarly weakness, the biographical criticism of literature. Bakhtin could not say it this simply, though; what he said was, "The monistic principle, that is, the affirmation of the unity of *being* in idealism, is turned into the principle of the unity of *consciousness*."[30] If critics believe, even unconsciously, that being is monistic, it follows that they cannot make a distinction between authors and their characters, for such a distinction has no ontological justification. Since characters are "the same as," and thus "speak for," their authors, we can—so goes the implicit argument—infer the beliefs of the authors from the actions of their characters. As we all know, many critics—Marxists and non-Marxists alike—find it gratifying to reason in this way. No one but Bakhtin, however, has so trenchantly clarified the presuppositions of this critical methodology. (Incidentally, the same monistic presuppositions hold for the belief, much loved by historians and political scientists, that political figures act as they do because of consciously held ideologies.)

[26] *Rable*, p. 112.
[27] Ibid.
[28] Ibid., p. 113.
[29] Ibid.
[30] Bakhtin, *Problemy*, p. 76.

Clearly, more than Rabelais's work is at stake here; it is the historical relationships among criticism, art, and philosophy that Bakhtin wishes to articulate. After all, biographical criticism was itself a response to a new kind of novel, which most critics called "realistic," and which Bakhtin called "monological." For Bakhtin, the monological novel corresponds to the monistic philosophy of idealism. Bakhtin classifies such illustrious contemporaries of Dostoevsky as Tolstoi and Goncharov as practitioners of the monological novel. Reading between the lines, one can easily sense that Bakhtin considers it an inferior form. Bakhtin says, in effect, that Dostoevsky avoided the dissociation of sensibility which monistic idealism expresses, and that his task was to "build a polyphonic world and to destroy the established form of the European, basically *monological* (homophonic) novel."[31] For whatever reason, Bakhtin never attempted to give a socio-historical explanation for Dostoevsky's uniqueness among his contemporaries, or for Tolstoi's monism.

Bakhtin's distinction between the polyphonic novel (Dostoevsky) and the monological novel (Tolstoi) seems to derive ultimately[32] from the following passage in *The Gay Science*.

> I do not know of any more profound difference in the whole orientation of an artist than this, whether he looks at his work in progress (at "himself") from the point of view of the witness, or whether he "has forgotten the world," which is the essential feature of all monological art; it is based on forgetting, it is the music of forgetting.
>
> (GS, 324)

Artists who can look at their own work with the eye of a witness are not thinking of it as pure self-expression, as an extension of their psyches; they are not people who have forgotten the world by cutting themselves off from it. People who have forgotten the world deliver monologues, for such people have no interlocutor. In effect, people who have forgotten the world constitute isolated, and thus monistic, systems.

Dostoevsky, then, has the "eye of a witness," for Bakhtin denies that we can associate any of his characters with him. Given the way Nietzsche

---

[31] Ibid.

[32] I say "ultimately" here because we have some evidence that at least one member of the Bakhtin circle used an opposition between polyphonic and monological art. One of the most fascinating men of the era, Georgy Chicherin, wrote a book on Mozart in 1930, in which he mentions the use of this opposition in Richard Litterscheid-Essen's "Über polyphone Musik" (*Die Musik* [Music], 10 July 1928, pp. 726–31); see Georgy Chicherin, *Motsart* (Leningrad, 1970), pp. 256–57.

hailed Dostoevsky as "the only psychologist from whom I had anything to learn,"[33] it is not surprising to find that Bakhtin hails him as a superman, a man of will: "The artistic will to polyphony is the will to the combination of many wills, the will to an event."[34]

We thus find a most satisfying consistency among Dostoevsky, Nietzsche, and Bakhtin, in their uses of pluralism. Dostoevsky reacted to the monism of Chernyshevsky and the other radicals of his time by creating novels with pluralistic structures; Nietzsche responded strongly to Dostoevsky because he sensed in his work an analogy with his own reaction to the philosophical monism of Kant. In turn, Bakhtin—during whose lifetime monism triumphed in Russia—read Nietzsche, and drew on him in interpreting Dostoevsky's pluralism.

In the larger context of the history of Russian criticism, Bakhtin has unusual interests. He tended to ask such questions as, "To what genre does work X belong? What is the history of this genre? How can we connect the history of this genre with specific features of work X? What are the philosophical and social implications of this genre?" Hardly any other Russian critic has ever considered these issues, and their presence in Bakhtin's work bespeaks his training in classical studies with Tadeusz Zieliński at St. Petersburg University.

Tadeusz Zieliński was one of the outstanding classical scholars of the twentieth century. Born in the Ukraine of Polish parents, he studied at Leipzig University, and then taught at St. Petersburg University from 1885 to 1921. He emigrated to Warsaw in 1921, where he taught until his retirement. A man of great erudition, he published books and articles in several languages on a wide variety of topics for over sixty years from 1880 to 1941.[35]

Zieliński was unique among the classicists of his time in that he heartily endorsed Nietzsche's work. At a time when virtually all the other classicists in Europe either ignored Nietzsche or attacked him, Zieliński took up his cause as a way of justifying classical studies to the general public. In 1900 he published his first article on Nietzsche, "Nietzsche

---

[33] Quoted in Walter Kaufmann, *Nietzsche: Philosopher, Psychologist, Antichrist*, 3rd ed. (Princeton, 1968), p. 340.

[34] Bakhtin, *Problemy*, p. 33.

[35] See Gabriela Pianko's bibliography of Zieliński's works in *Menander* 8–9 (1959):437–61. There are a number of omissions, but even so it runs to 383 items.

and the World of Antiquity," a revised version of which appeared as the preface to Volume 1 of a translation of Nietzsche's collected works in 1912. In this essay, Zieliński states what was to become the leitmotif of his comments on Nietzsche: "Friedrich Nietzsche is the last child in time of Faust and Helen, the last avatar of the classical Dionysus; his philosophy is the last major contribution of antiquity to contemporary thought."[36]

In "The Ancient World and We" ("Drevnyi mir i my"), a series of eight lectures delivered to the 1903 graduates of the St. Petersburg secondary schools, and translated into English in 1909 as *Our Debt to Antiquity*, Zieliński offered a full-scale interpretation of antiquity in Nietzschean terms—the first such in Europe. He says that in the age of Locke and Voltaire "the significance of the autonomous morality of the school of Socrates was discovered," but that now a "pre-Socratic instinctive morality" has appeared, and that "its resurrector" has chosen as its symbol "the classical god of spring and rising forces—Dionysus."[37] He is talking about Nietzsche, of course, but he was too learned and too thoughtful to let Nietzsche sweep him away. He cleverly interpreted Nietzsche's work itself as another instance of the eternal recurrence: "Of course, every infatuation passes—Voltaireanism passed; Nietzscheanism will pass, too. Only the struggle will not pass, this sole and necessary means of perfecting ourselves."[38] Zieliński does not seem to have left us a complete statement of his own personal credo, but apparently he worked out a synthesis of Darwin, Nietzsche, and Christianity. He may not have believed in the evolution of species, but he certainly believed in the evolution of society in Nietzschean terms. He welcomed the resurgence of Dionysus in his own time as a much-needed counterbalance to what he decried as the highly moralistic influence of Judaism in Christianity. At times, he sounds very much like his remarkable contemporary, Vasily Rozanov, in *The Dark Face*.

Zieliński played a significant role in the intellectual life of pre-Revolutionary St. Petersburg. For example, in addition to his own work, he edited the translations of Euripides into Russian by his colleague, the poet Innokenty Annensky. Such a major figure surely had a lasting impact on Bakhtin—all the more so, since his twin brother Nicholas (1895–

[36] F. Zieliński, "Nitsshe i antichnost'," in *Iz zhizni idei*, 2nd ed. rev. (St. Petersburg, 1908), p. 342.

[37] F. Zieliński, "Drevnii mir i my," *Zhurnal ministerstva narodnogo obrazovaniia* 348 (July–August 1903):74.

[38] Ibid.

1950) also studied with Zieliński. (Nicholas Bakhtin emigrated to Paris, and participated in the émigre circle The Green Lamp, (Zelenaia lampa) where his knowledge of philosophy and philology made him a welcome speaker. He died in England.)

We have only two references to Zieliński in Bakhtin's published work, and they provide our only direct clues to the intellectual relationship between teacher and student. Both of them appear in Bakhtin's notes for an unfinished article from the Twenties, and both of them deal with the classical, that is, the Dionysian element in the development of Christianity. The first goes as follows: "Zieliński. The sexual element did not predominate, since it was antithetical to sculpture. Only with the appearance of the Bacchantes does another, essentially Eastern, stream begin to break through. In Dionysionism there predominates an internal, *but not isolated* transcendence of the body."[39] Although the reference to sculpture remains unclear, Bakhtin seems to be thinking here of Zieliński's article from 1915, "Dionysus in Religion and Poetry." Here Zieliński makes the point that the Bacchantes of Delphi originally came from Thrace, and "were not the people itself, but representatives of the people."[40] And as a result they brought about "an Apollonian reform of religion." They thus represented what Nietzsche would have called an individuating principle. Bakhtin was mulling over the sexual implications of this change.

Bakhtin takes up a related topic two pages later. He lists as the second of his projected topics on the heterogeneous elements in Christianity, "The purely classical idea of the humanization of God (Zieliński) and the deification of man (Harnack)."[41] Here Bakhtin was thinking of a synthesis of the work of Adolph Harnack and Zieliński, as his editor indicates.[42]

Clearly, the young Bakhtin shared Zieliński's breadth of interests. One further quotation from Zieliński will show how Bakhtin took over from him an essential attitude. In an early article, "Cicero in the History of European Culture" (1898), Zieliński states his understanding of a scholar's duty, which resounds with high seriousness in the best sense. "It seems to me that representatives of the historical sciences are called on to sustain in a society a consciousness of the unity of European culture

---

[39] Bakhtin, *Est*, p. 49.
[40] F. Zieliński, "Dionis v religii i poezii," *Russkaia mysl'* 36 (June 1915):3.
[41] Bakhtin, *Est*, p. 51.
[42] See ibid., pp. 388–89.

and respect for those personalities to whom it is obliged in a greater or lesser degree for its high level."[43] "The Unity of European Culture" could serve as a title for an anthology of Zieliński's collected essays. A true cosmopolitan, he dealt with figures from virtually every European literature, and wrote on each one with equal enthusiasm. The fact that we think of Bakhtin in connection with his work on Dostoevsky and Rabelais, writers from two different countries and centuries, may serve as some indication of the extent to which he followed Zieliński's ideal.

A crucial passage from his major theoretical articles of the Twenties, "The Problem of Content" shows how Bakhtin continued Zieliński's concern with the problem of unity and multiplicity. Thus, Bakhtin criticizes the formalists' wish—and I translate literally here—"to build a science about a separate art independently of the knowledge and systematic definition of the uniqueness of the esthetic in the unity of human culture."[44] Bakhtin is denying, as vehemently as his Teutonic syntax will allow, that the formalists, or anybody else, can isolate literature from culture as a whole, and is insisting that literary criticism is a brach of esthetics. To isolate literature from culture as a whole is to deny the unity in multiplicity which—like Zieliński—he considered essential to what we would nowadays call the humanities. One must, he says, work from the general to the specific, not the other way around. "One cannot extract a concept of the esthetic by an intuitive or empirical method: it will be naive, subjective, and impermanent; *for a confident and precise self-definition it requires a mutual definition with other areas in the unity of human culture.*"[45] After reading his book on Dostoevsky, we can understand that he was saying that the study of literature in isolation from any other cultural activity is monologic.

Since Bakhtin, like Zieliński, thought of unity as manifesting itself in multiplicity, neither man thought in static terms. We know that Zieliński believed that humanity perfected itself in struggle. Bakhtin was more interested in literature than in social evolution, and applied the concept of struggle to it. For him, the writer ". . . Must struggle with old or with not so old literary forms, use them and combine them, overcome their resistance or find in them support, but at the basis of this movement lies

[43] F. Zieliński, "Tsitseron v istorii evropeiskoi kultury," in *Iz zhizni idei*, vol. 4 (Petrograd, 1922), p. 20.
[44] Bakhtin, *Vle*, p. 9.
[45] Ibid.

the most essential, definitive *primal artistic struggle* with the gnostic ethical inclination of life and its semiotic life force."[46]

Finally, it is pleasing to note that Zieliński himself made a connection between the world of classical antiquity and Dostoevsky. In one of the lectures from "The Ancient World and We," he suggests that

> . . . We might compare the evolution of the world's literature to a ballistic curve which returns to the place whence it started. Its beginning is the most primitive literature in which man's actions are explained by the supposition that he is possessed by good or evil spirits. . . . Classicism was challenged by the Romantic movement and its descendants, which, though they might bear different names, still bore one hallmark of identity—the supremacy of Will over Reason. The furthest advances in this direction have been made in modern Russian literature, especially by Dostoevsky. His writings form the farthest point as yet reached; the curve has returned to its starting point.[47]

Thus, it would seem, Bakhtin had both Nietzsche's and Zieliński's word for it that Dostoevsky was a man of will, and that his work had a visceral primitivism. No wonder Bakhtin's first book was *Problems of Dostoevsky's Art*.

No one has yet written the intellectual history of the two most fascinating decades of Russian culture, the years from 1897 to 1917, but we know that many thoughtful, learned people were dealing with the same questions as Zieliński in those years. As an incentive to further work on the intellectual climate of pre-Revolutionary Russian thought, of which Nietzscheanism formed such an essential part, I wish to adduce here a few quotations from three such people: Gustave Spaeth (1879–1937); Simon Frank (1877–1937); and Lev Lopatin (1855–1920).

When we do reach a consensus about the intellectual history of pre-Revolutionary Russia, we may well decide that Gustave Spaeth was its most original thinker. A phenomenologist, he studied with Husserl, but had a more accessible style than the master without sacrificing any rigor.

---

[46] Bakhtin, *Est*, p. 171. Obviously, Marx emphasized the concept of struggle, too, but Bakhtin's phrase "primal artistic struggle" distinguishes his use of the term from Marx's.

[47] Professor Zielinski [*sic*], *Our Debt to Antiquity* (London, 1909), p. 97.

(If Bakhtin wrote more like Husserl than Nietzsche, Spaeth wrote more like Nietzsche than Husserl. He published, among other things, a book of *Esthetic Fragments* [*Esteticheskie fragmenty*, 1922].)[48] He interests us here because in his provocative book *History as a Problem of Logic (Istoriia kak problema logiki*, 1916), he made a comment that has a Bakhtinesque ring, which suggests the relevance of the intellectual climate of the time to his work. "Philosophy as a whole and any 'passage' from it is a dialogue, is a certain 'yes' and 'no,' like light and shadow, like waking and sleep—not only side by side with each other, but always together and penetrating each other."[49] If philosophy itself is a dialogue, then it must have readily occurred to a young graduate student that it made sense to interpret in philosophical terms a novelist in whose works dialogue abounds. Whether or not Bakhtin read *History as a Problem of Logic*, Spaeth's comment shows us that other people were pondering the meaning of dialogue at the time.

In a general sense, any investigation of dialogue represents a human instantiation of the subject/object relationships which so concerned Hegel. Two major thinkers of pre-Revolutionary Russia, Simon Frank and Lev Lopatin, dealt with this problem in similar ways. With some help from Vladimir Soloviev's idea of "All-Unity" (*vseedinstvo*), both of them found a higher unity in the world, just as Bakhtin found a higher unity in Dostoevsky. As Bakhtin later did, both of them firmly rejected the idea that a belief in unity implied a belief in monism. For them, rather, the only possible unity was a unity in multiplicity.

In *The Object of Knowledge (Predmet znaniia*, 1915), one of the most important books in the history of Russian philosophy, Frank anticipates the set of theorems that we now know as Gödel's Proof, which state that any coherent system of propositions is inherently and irrevocably incomplete. Thus, Frank attacks the belief in abstract propositions as "adequate" in Husserl's sense of providing a sufficiently complete model. (The subtitle of the book is "On the Foundations and Limits of Abstract Knowledge.")

Frank was greatly influenced by Nicholas of Cusa and by Bergson; referring to an intuition of multiplicity in the spirit of their thought, he says, "Only such a representation of an object which attempts to re-create this intuition as such can give a truly adequate knowledge. The task of

---

[48] Gustave Spaeth, *Esteticheskie fragmenty* (Petrograd, 1922).

[49] Gustave Spaeth, *Istoriia kak problema logiki: Kriticheskie i metodologicheskie issledovaniia, I: Materialy* (Moscow, 1916), p. 9.

such a representation is the task of *art*."[50] While Bakhtin implies that a Dostoevsky novel as a whole may be adequate to its milieu, no one character ever is. Thus, he says of Stavrogin's "Confession" in *The Possessed*, that it does not have a "documentary quality in the usual sense, for such a realistic documentary quality is directed at its object and—for all the dryness of the style—strives to be adequate to all its sides."[51] Since no one voice alone can ever create polyphony, no statements by that voice alone can ever be "adequate" to all the sides of an issue.

Frank states that any individual entity belongs to a larger whole in this important passage:

> However, in any object there is included a fullness of definitions inexhaustible by any one side; and to the judgment "Malice is a vice" can be juxtaposed, for example, the judgments that malice is an expression of a certain energy of life, or that it is only a distorted form of noble impulses and the like. . . . The true meaning of any particular definition is revealed precisely in that fullness of *other* definitions with which it is connected and which consequently are understood in it but remained unexpressed at the moment.[52]

Bakhtin's statement on self-consciousness as the "dominant" of Dostoevsky's characters seems like nothing more than an especially perceptive application of Frank's principle to literature: "Together with the self-consciousness of the character, which takes into itself the whole object world, in the same plane there can be only another consciousness; together with its outlook—another outlook; together with its point of view on the world— another point of view on the world."[53]

Frank called the intuition of unity in multiplicity "All-Unity": "All-Unity is, as has been several times pointed out, the unity of unity and *multiplicity*; this definition of it brings us here to the affirmation that is the unity of itself and its *other*, that is, of a system of determinations."[54] Lev Lopatin had said essentially the same thing two years before in his essay "Monism and Pluralism" (1913). He did not use the term "All-Unity" but he defended the idea vigorously:

[50] S. L. Frank, *Predmet znaniia* (Petrograd, 1915), p. 317.

[51] Bakhtin, *Problemy*, p. 203.

[52] Frank, *Predmet znaniia*, p. 313.

[53] Bakhtin, *Problemy*, p. 57.

[54] Frank, *Predmet znaniia*, p. 320.

Indeed, the concept of unity in *multiplicity* and *multiplicity* in unity not only does not involve a logical contradiction, as has been shown, but one must also say of it: This is the only concept of immediate being which logically does not lead to its own negation and does not fall apart in irresolvable contradictions.[55]

Clearly, then, the concepts of monism and pluralism, and their resolution in unity in multiplicity, which form the philosophical subtext of all of Bakhtin's criticism, were issues that concerned some major Russian thinkers during his university years. One can thus consider Bakhtin's *Problems of Dostoevsky's Work* as the last stage of the discussions of the problem of unity and multiplicity which had concerned a number of Russian pre-Revolutionary thinkers.

After the Marxist Nietzscheans, the mystical anarchists, and the writers, all of whom used Nietzsche briefly and for limited purposes, came Zieliński and Bakhtin, whom we may describe as academic Nietzscheans. They had the openness to understand the power of Nietzsche's thought without feeling threatened by it, as many academics did—and do. Because they were professional academics, they had a context in which they could interpret Nietzsche, and they were not swept away by him. Then, too, other scholars at the time were working on related problems; after all, the relationship between monism and pluralism was not exactly a new problem in the history of philosophy.

Any intellectual movement, even one as diverse as Russian Nietzscheanism, acquires adherents at least in part because it addresses enduring issues which often remain implicit. To understand how the implicit issues in Russian Nietzscheanism remained meaningful after the Revolution, we may conclude by using the context of pre-Revolutionary thought to interpret Bakhtin's differences with his well-known contemporaries, the formalists.

Bakhtin read the same books and articles that Shklovsky, Tynianov,

[55] Lev Lopatin, "Monizm i pliuralizm," *Voprosy filosofii i psikhologii* 113 (January–February 1913):83. Lopatin makes another comment which strikingly anticipates Bakhtin: "There is another question about whose exceptional importance I have already had occasion to speak so much. I have in mind the question of a foreign consciousness or a foreign animatedness. Why does a foreign consciousness exist for me and how am I connected with it?" (*Ibid.*, p. 71). Another essay that has relevance here is Nikolai Berdiaev's blistering attack on monism, "Religiia monizma," in ibid. 118 (January–February 1914):329–43.

and Eichenbaum read; all four of them attended St. Petersburg University during World War I, and may well have taken some classes together. All four were sophisticated critics, all four had done some reading in philosophy, and all four were interested in (among other things) nineteenth-century Russian literature. How did it happen, then, that Bakhtin devoted a good deal of energy to attacking them in the Twenties? It was a contentious period, of course, but so theoretically minded a critic as Bakhtin must have sensed a difference in paradigms, or he would not have bothered.

Some of the formalists' key principles compound the paradox. If Bakhtin, following Zieliński, believed in struggle as the organizing principle of literary history, so did Tynianov. In his famous article on Dostoevsky and Gogol, Tynianov says that in literary history, "There is no continuation of a straight line; there is rather a departure, a pushing away from a certain point, a struggle."[56] If Bakhtin believed in unity in multiplicity, a principle that manifested itself in the interaction of two entities, so did Tynianov: "But if the feeling of *interaction* of two factors (which presupposes the obligatory presence of *two* elements: a subordinating one and a subordinated one) disappears, the fact of art is erased; it is automated."[57] But it was Eichenbaum, the most philosophically minded of the formalists, who stated most clearly the essential agreement on principles that united them with Bakhtin. Speaking for the formalists in 1922, he stated their grievance with previous criticism, which also happened to be their grievance with the Soviet government, in philosophical terms: "No, we have had enough monism! We are pluralists. Life is multiformed—it cannot be reduced to one factor."[58] For Eichenbaum and the formalists, life "cannot be reduced to one factor" just as for Bakhtin, Dostoevsky's polyphonic structure cannot be reduced to Tolstoi's monophonic structures. Given this agreement on principles, what caused Bakhtin to disagree with formalism?

This is not the place to analyze the relevant material in detail, but one might say very generally that Bakhtin disliked the formalists because they were not Germanic enough to be interested in *Geistesgeschichte*. Although they were anything but provincial, the formalists applied general esthetic principles to individual works. That is to say, they concerned

[56] Iury Tynianov, "Dostoevsky i Gogol': K teorii parodii," in *Arkhaisty i novatory* (1929; reprint, Munich, 1967), p. 412.

[57] Iury Tynianov, *Problema stikhotvornogo iazyka* (1923; reprint, Moscow, 1965), p. 29.

[58] Boris Eichenbaum, "$4 \times 5 = 100$," *Knizhnyi ugol*, no. 8 (1922):40.

themselves with the microcosm of the individual work rather than the macrocosm of the history of the genre to which it belonged. To put it even more generally, the formalists did not share the explicit concern with the unity of human culture that Bakhtin had taken over from Zieliński. Ultimately, though, Bakhtin's dislike of the formalists involves a matter of intellectual orientation.

The choice between France and Germany has had a decisive effect in the development of many Russian intellectuals, and it may serve here to distinguish between the formalists and Bakhtin. As I have shown elsewhere,[59] the formalists drew heavily on the work of Bergson. Shklovsky's famous concept of (ostranennie), for example, clearly derives from some principles of perception which Bergson sets forth in Laughter, a book that Bakhtin criticized. This French orientation of the formalists, to simplify greatly, matters here because Bergson, very much in the tradition of Descartes and Rousseau, is concerned with the perceptions of an isolated individual. Thus, estrangement emphasizes the effect of a work, or of a device within the work, on individual perception, and ignores any possible social and philosophical implications. By contrast, Bakhtin, who read Nietzsche and Husserl, and whose mentor Zieliński was trained in Germany, tended to write and think in the German tradition of Geistesgeschichte. Naturally, then, Bakhtin could not understand why the formalists were not concerned with these issues, which seemed essential to him.

Yet, since Bakhtin and the formalists were, after all, at the same place at the same time, and probably knew each other, the question naturally arises: How can we understand their relationship to their culture?

I have noted that the struggle between monism and pluralism was not exactly a new problem in the history of philosophy, but it was an especially vexed one in Russia. Autocracy, whether tsarist or Marxist, is the only political tradition Russia has ever known, and vesting total authority in a single man is tantamount to believing in a monistic ontology, as Bakhtin suggested in his discussions of seventeenth-century French culture. To proclaim one's adherence to pluralism in any form is thus to threaten the pre-suppositions on which the legitimacy of the Russian government has always depended, and to make oneself an outcast. As time passed, Bakhtin and the formalists experienced increasing difficulties when their implicit pluralism conflicted more and more with the monism of the Soviet government. This situation affected their careers in different

[59] See James M. Curtis, "Bergson and Russian Formalism," Comparative Literature 27 (Spring 1976):109–21.

ways. Bakhtin did not publish anything for a long time, Shklovsky and Tynianov worked on novels and screenplays, and Eichenbaum turned to editing. Only in the Sixties did their work, with its echoes of a long-dead philosophical sophistication, seem safe enough to publish.

Considered in this way, the careers of these four great critics resemble those of Russian poets, and we may think of each of them as a critic engaged in a lifelong dialogue with another, with a poet. For the formalists, such interrelationships come readily to mind. We think of Shklovsky in relation to Mayakovsky, of course, not merely because they were friends but because their writing styles express the futurist need to *épater la bourgeoisie*. Eichenbaum seems to present more difficulties, but his simpler, more personal style is associated with acmeism, so it is not surprising that he championed Akhmatova as an innovator at a time when it was unfashionable to do so. As for Tynianov, he wrote both critical essays on Pushkin and a biographical novel about him; he looked like Pushkin, and could even imitate his handwriting.

That leaves Bakhtin. Unlike the formalists, he had a classical education, and was exiled by the authorities because of his work. As soon as we say this, we realize that pairing Bakhtin and Mandelstam can prove very fruitful. For both these great men, the "voice" meant suprapersonal expression that found fulfillment only in dialogue, with a friend or with the past. If, toward the end of his book on Dostoevsky, Bakhtin spoke of the "various-voicedness" (*raznogolosost'*),[60] Mandelstam used almost exactly the same word (*raznogolositsa*)[61] in a lovely synesthetic image for the effect of the churches in the Kremlin. Indeed, Mandelstam's poetry of the Twenties and Thirties lends itself very readily to an analysis in the terms Bakhtin used. But that would be the subject of another essay. For now, I wish to conclude by expressing the hope that sometime during those giddy, pre-Revolutionary years at St. Petersburg University when Russia still was part of Europe, and when everyone was talking about Nietzsche, Bakhtin and Mandelstam met, and that during their dialogue each felt the shock of recognition at finding himself in the other.

[60] Bakhtin, *Problemy*, p. 238.

[61] Osip Mandelstam, *Sobranie sochinenii v trekh tomakh*, ed. G. P. Struve and B. A. Filippov (Washington, D.C., 1967), 1:57.

16.

Nietzsche in Russia, 1892–1919:
A Chronological Checklist

Richard D. Davies

THIS IS A REVISED and abridged version of my "Nietzsche in Russia, 1892–1917: A Preliminary Bibliography," *Germano-Slavica* 2 (Fall 1976) and (Spring 1977). The numeration of the original has been retained in order to facilitate reference to the supplementary biographical and bibliographical annotations omitted from this checklist. A number of errors and omissions have been corrected, most notably where Nietzschean materials in *Novyi Put'* and *Voprosy Zhizni* are concerned, and I am most grateful to Philip M. Oldfield for pointing these out to me. Many gaps and uncertainties remain, however, as a consequence of the bibliography's origin in a compilation of information from a variety of sources, rather than a systematic literature search *de visu*. Both for this reason and because the "submerged" mass of Nietzsche-inspired writing in Russia is not directly reflected in it, this is still very much a preliminary bibliography. The excellent work of Ann M. Lane and Edith Clowes in their doctoral dissertations, "Nietzsche in Russian Thought, 1890–1917" (University of Wisconsin, 1976) and "A Philosophy 'For All and None': The Early Reception of Friedrich Nietzsche's Thought in Russian Literature, 1892–1912" (Yale University, 1981) respectively, has opened the way for the inclusion of much fresh material in a future comprehensive bibliography of Russian Nietzscheanism. The attention paid to the role of the censorship by Edith Clowes and Marianna Choldin ("A Fence around the Empire: Nineteenth-Century Russian Censorship of Foreign Books," Ph.D. diss., University of Chicago, 1979; see also articles by both authors in *Germano-Slavica* 4 [Spring 1983]) has greatly increased awareness of the obstacles faced by Nietzsche's Russian devotees and suggests the need for a detailed study of the quality of Russian translations of Nietzsche's works.

The editor of *Germano-Slavica* has kindly given permission for the publication of this checklist.

1892

CRITICAL LITERATURE

1. Preobrazhensky, V. P. "FN: Kritika morali al'truizma," *Voprosy Filosofii i Psikhologii* [henceforth VFP]15(November 1892):115–60.

1893

CRITICAL LITERATURE

2. Astaf'ev, P. E. "Genezis nravstvennogo ideala dekadenta," *VFP* 16(January 1893):Spetsial'nyi otdel, 56–75.
3. Bichalets, Ivan [A. Ia. Antonovich]. "Chelovek-lopukh i chelovek-zver'," *Kievskoe Slovo*, no.1873, (3 April 1893): 1.
4. Bulgakov, F. I. "Uchenie N o zhelanii vlasti i t.d.," *Vestnik Inostrannoi Literatury* [henceforth VIL] 5(1893):206–216.
5. Grot, N. Ia. "Nravstvennye idealy nashego vremeni: FN i Lev Tolstoi," *VFP* 16(January 1893):129–54.
6. Grot, N. Ia. *Nravstvennye idealy nashego vremeni: FN i Lev Tolstoi* (Moscow: I. N. Kushnerev, 1893).
7. Lopatin, L. M. "Bol'naia iskrennost': Zametki po povodu stat'i V. Preobrazhenskogo 'FN'," *VFP* 16(January 1893):109–114.
8. M. "Filosof budushchego," *Sever* 45(1893):2381–82.
9. Nordau, M. *Vyrozhdenie* (St. Petersburg, 1893 and Kiev, 1893). Translation of *Entartung*, vol.2 (Berlin, 1893). Reviewed in *Russkoe Bogatstvo* 2(1894):66–69.
10. Skriba, P. [E. A. Solov'ev]. "Sovremennye literaturnye motivy: Simvolisty, dekadenty," *Russkaia Zhizn'* 27(1893):2.
11. Chuiko, V. V. "Obshchestvennye idealy FN," *Nabliudatel'* 2(1893):231–47.

1894

TRANSLATIONS

12. "Vagnerianskii vopros: Muzykal'naia problema," trans. O.O.R.
    [Princess A. D. Tenisheva?], *Artist* 40(1894):61–75.
13. "Pis'ma N," *Severnyi Vestnik* 2(1894):sec. 2, 93–95. Translations
    of letters taken from Georg Brandes, *Menschen und Werke:
    Essays* (Frankfurt/M., 1894).

CRITICAL LITERATURE

14. Mikhailovsky, N. K. "O Makse Shtirnere i FN," *Russkoe Bo-
    gatstvo* 8(1894):sec. 2, 151–72.
15. Mikhailovsky, N. K. "'Eshche o FN," *Russkoe Bogatstvo*
    11(1894):sec.2,111–31.
16. Mikhailovsky, N. K. "I eshche o FN," *Russkoe Bogatstvo*
    12(1894):sec.2,84–110.
17i. Preobrazhensky, V. P. *FN: Kritika morali al'truizma*, 2nd ed.
  ii. Grot, N. Ia. *Nravstvennye idealy nashego vremeni: FN i Lev Tol-
    stoi*, 3rd ed. (Moscow,1894). 28pp. 1,200 copies.
17a. Solov'ev, V. S. "Pervyi shag k polozhitel'noi estetike," *Vestnik
    Evropy* 1(1894):297-98.

1895

TRANSLATIONS

18. " 'Vse spit glubokim snom': Na motiv iz FN," trans. N. N. Poli-
    lov, *VIL* 10(1895):134.
19. " 'Chem glubzhe padaet moi dukh': Na motiv iz FN," trans. N.
    N. Polilov, *VIL* 8(1895):54.

CRITICAL LITERATURE

20. "Idei FN," *VIL* 2(1895):193–206.
21. "Novaia rabota o 'filosofii' FN: Po povodu stat'i Shiure o N,"
    Nauchnoe Obozrenie 36(1895):1144–47. [Edouard Schuré,

"L'Individualisme et l'anarchie en littérature: FN et sa philosophie," *Revue des deux mondes* 130(1985):775–805.]

1896

TRANSLATIONS

22. " 'Po tikhomu moriu': Na motivy iz FN," trans. N. N. Polilov, *VIL* 7(1896):208.
23. " 'Ia berega tvoi pokinul odinoko': Na motivy iz FN," trans. N. N. Polilov, *VIL* 4(1896):154.

CRITICAL LITERATURE

24. Andreas-Salome, L. "FN v svoikh proizvedeniiakh: Ocherk," trans. Z. V[engerova], *Severnyi Vestnik* 3(1896):273–95; 4(1896): 253-72; 5(1896):225–39. Partial translation of Lou Andreas-Salomé, *FN in seinen Werken* (Vienna, 1894).
25. Volynsky, A. [A. L. Flekser]. "Literaturnye zametki: Apollon i Dionis," *Severnyi Vestnik* 11(1896):232–55.
26. Nordau, M. *Vyrozhdenie: Psikhopaticheskie iavleniia v oblasti sovremennoi literatury i iskusstva* (St. Petersburg: P. P. Soikin, 1896).

1897

TRANSLATIONS

[27. "Stikhotvoreniia N," *Obrazovanie* 2(1897):42–44. Inaccurate reference in Lenin Library catalogue. Correct version not established.]

CRITICAL LITERATURE

27a. V[engerova], Z. "Nitsshe (Fridrikh Vil'gel'm Nietzsche)," in *Entsiklopedicheskii slovar'*, vol. 41 (St. Petersburg: Brokgaus i Efron, 1897), pp. 204–206.
27b. Kareev, N. "N o 'chrezmernosti istorii'," in *Sbornik v pol'zu ne-*

dostatochnykh studentov Moskovskogo universiteta, ed. V. A. Gol'tsev (Moscow, 1897), pp. 14–39.

[28. Novus [P. B. Struve]. "FN," *Novoe Slovo* 3(1897):198–99. Uncertain reference.]

[28a. Novus [P. B. Struve]. "Na raznye temy," *Novoe Slovo* 12 (1897). Issue destroyed by the censors. Original of no. 153a.i?]

29. Tsertelev, D. N. "Kritika vyrozhdeniia i vyrozhdenie kritiki," *Russkii Vestnik* 3(1897):56–82; 4(1897):79–102; 11(1897):1–22; 12(1897):1–28.

30. Tsukerman, S. "Poseshchenie zhilishcha FN," *Nauchnoe Obozrenie* 9(1897):116–19.

31. Shcheglov, V. G. "Graf Lev Nikolaevich Tolstoi i FN: Ocherk filosofsko-nravstvennogo ikh mirovozzreniia,' *Vremennik Demidovskogo Iuridicheskogo Litseia* 74–78 (1898–1900 [issued 1897]).

32. Shcheglov, V. G. *Graf Lev Nikolaevich Tolstoi i FN: Ocherk filosofsko-nravstvennogo ikh mirovozzreniia* (Iaroslavl': Sovet Demidovskogo Iuridicheskogo Litseia, 1897 [on cover 1898]). Reviewed (with no. 38) *Russkaia Mysl'* 5(1898): sec.2,189–91.

1898

TRANSLATIONS

33. "Tak govoril Zaratustra: Kniga dlia vsekh i ni dlia kogo: Simvolicheskaia poema FN," trans. Iu. M. Antonovsky, *Novyi Zhurnal Inostrannoi Literatury* [Henceforth *NZhIL]* 5–6, 8–10,12(1898).

34. *Tak govoril Zaratustra: Kniga dlia vsekh i ni dlia kogo: Simvolicheskaia poema FN*, 10th German ed., trans Iu. M. Antonovsky (St. Petersburg: NZhIL, 1898). Reviewed (with no. 48) by N. Minsky, [N. M. Vilenkin]. *Novosti*, 31 December 1898.

CRITICAL LITERATURE

35. Gast, P. "Predislovie k sochineniiu FN *Tak govoril Zaratustra*," trans. N. Z. V-[asil'e]v, *Zhizn'* 35(1898):237–52; 36(1898):312-

26. Translation of Peter Gast, Introduction, *Also sprach Zarathustra*, *Ns Werke, Erste Abteilung*, vol. 6, 3rd ed. (Leipzig, 1894).

[36. See no. 54a]

37. Mikhailovsky, N. K. "Darvinizm i nitssheanstvo," *Russkoe Bogatstvo* 2(1898):132–62.

38i. Ril', A. *FN kak khudozhnik i myslitel'*;

ii. Zimmel', G. *FN: Etiko-filosofskii siluet*, trans. N. Iuzhin (Odessa: E. I. Fesenko, 1898) 2,400 copies.

Translation of Alois Riehl, *FN der Künstler und der Denker* (Stuttgart, 1897); Georg Simmel, "FN: Eine moral-philosophische Silhouette," *Zeitschrift für Philosophie und philosophische Kritik* 107(1896):202–215.

Reviewed by Iu. I. Aikhenval'd, *VFP* 39(September-October 1897):697–701 (of Riehl original); *Russkaia Mysl'* 5(1898), sec. 2, 189–91; *Severnyi Vestnik* 5(1898):49.

39. Ril', A. *FN kak khudozhnik i myslitel'*, trans. Z. A. Vengerova (St. Petersburg: Obrazovanie, 1898).

Translation of Alois Riehl, *FN der Künstler und der Denker* (Stuttgart, 1897).

40. Tiurk, G. *Filosofiia egoizma: N, Ibsen i Shtirner*, 2nd German ed., trans. and introd. A.Ch. (St. Petersburg: D. V. Chichinadze, 1898). 16 pp. 2,000 copies. Translation of Hermann Türck, *Der geniale Mensch* (Jena, 1897) (10th chapter). Reviewed by *Severnyi Vestnik* 5(1898):49–50.

41. Shtein, L. "FN i ego filosofiia: Kritiko-biograficheskii ocherk," trans. N. Berdiaev, *Mir Bozhii* 9(1898):61–79; 10(1898):51–69; 11(1898):63–79. Translation of Ludwig Stein, *FNs Weltanschauung und ihre Gefahren: Ein kritischer Essay* (Berlin, 1893).

1899

TRANSLATIONS

41a. "Aforizmy FN," *Zhizn'* 7(June 1899):89–96. From *Jenseits von Gut und Böse*.

42. *Vagnerianskii vopros*, trans. O.O.R. [Princess A. D. Tenisheva?] (Kiev: V. A. Prosianichenko, 1899).

43. "Iz FN (s nemetskogo): 'To v polnoch' veter ostorozhnyi . . . ',"
trans. M. Slavinsky, *Zhizn'* 1(January 1899):12. [Translation
of "Der geheimnisvolle Nachen" from "Lieder des Prinzen
Vogelfrei" in *Die fröhliche Wissenschaft?*]

44. "O predrassudkakh filosofov," trans. N. N. Polilov, *Zhizn'*
11(November 1899):205–221. Translation of "Von den Vorurteilen der Philosophen" from *Jenseits von Gut und Böse.*

45. "Predislovie k *Chelovecheskomu, slishkom chelovecheskomu* FN,"
trans. D. Zhukovsky, *Zhizn'* 2(January 1899):11–16. Translation of introduction to *Menschliches, Allzumenschliches.*

46. *Proiskhozhdenie tragedii: Metafizika iskusstva,* trans. [and introd.]
N. N. Polilov (St. Petersburg: Akademiia Nauk, 1899). 288
pp. 1,200 copies. Reviewed by D. Z[elenin], *Zhizn'*
4(1899):314–49.

47. "Svobodnyi um: Aforizmy," trans. N. N. Polilov, *NZhIL* 11
(1899):143–48; 12(1899):230–35. Translation of "Der freie
Geist" from *Jenseits von Gut und Böse.*

48. *Tak govoril Zaratustra: Kniga dlia vsekh i nikogo: Deviat' otryvkov,*
trans. [and introd.] S. P. Nani (St. Petersburg: M. M. Stasiulevich, 1899). xiv + 103 pp. 1,250 copies. Nine extracts from
Also sprach Zarathustra with parallel translations. Reviewed
by T., *Vestnik Evropy* 1(1899):409–411; *Russkaia Mysl'*
2(1899), Bibliograficheskii otdel, 29–31; V. P. Preobrazhensky, *VFP* 46(1899), Obzor knig, 41–48 (see no. 58); N. Minsky [N. M. Vilenkin], *Novosti,* 31 December 1898 (with no.
34).

49. "Tak govoril Zaratustra: Simvolicheskaia poema," *Chitatel'* 16–
35(1899).

50. *Tak govoril Zaratustra: Simvolicheskaia poema* (Moscow, 1899).
236 pp. 1,200 copies.

51. "FN o zhenshchinakh," trans. N. N. Polilov, *NZhIL* 7(1899):23–
26. From *Jenseits von Gut und Böse.*

CRITICAL LITERATURE

52. "O bezumii N," *NZhIL* 9(1899):169–71.

53. Baratov, L. S. "Istoricheskii metod i teoriia poznaniia: Kriticheskie zamechaniia k stat'iam Rilia i N; Darvinisticheskaia gno-
seologiia FN," in *Darvinizm i teoriia poznaniia Georga Zim-*

melia, FN i Aloiza Rilia, Darvinisticheskaia Biblioteka, 1 (St. Petersburg, 1899), pp. 59–78, 79–86. Includes "Von den Vorurteilen der Philosophen" from *Jenseits von Gut und Böse*.

54. Grot, N. Ia. *Nravstvennye idealy nashego vremeni: FN i Lev Tolstoi* (Moscow: A. P. Mamontov, 1899).

54a. Kozlovsky, V. "FN," *Nauchnoe Obozrenie* 1(1899):22–44.

55. Likhtenberzhe, A. "FN: Etiud," *Obrazovanie* 10(1899):17–34. Translation of introd. to Henri Lichtenberger, *Aphorismes et fragments choisis de N* (Paris, 1899).

56. Pogodin, A. "Filosof-dekadent: FN," *VIL* 3(1899):3–28; 4(1899):3–16.

57. Polianin, S. "Khudozhnik-myslitel' FN: Ocherk," *Literaturnye vechera "Novogo Mira"* 3(1899):140–47.

58. Solov'ev, V. S. "Ideia sverkhcheloveka" (1899). Response to V. P. Preobrazhensky's review of no. 48 in *VFP* 46(1899). First published in posthumous collected works?

59. Stoliarov[-Sukhanov], M. *Etiudy o dekadentstve* (Khar'kov, 1899). Reviewed by T., *Vestnik Evropy* 10(1899):842–45.

60. Shteinberg, S. "FN," *Zhizn'* 9(September 1899):85–111.

61. Cherny, M. N. "Dekadentstvo v filosofii," in *Filosofiia dekadentstva: Kriticheskii ocherk* (St. Petersburg, 1899), pp. 48–69.

1900

TRANSLATIONS

62. "K estestvennoi istorii morali: Aforizmy, "trans. N. N. Polilov, *NZhIL* 2(1900):186–91; 4(1900):71–76. Translation of "Zur Naturgeschichte der Moral" from *Jenseits von Gut und Böse*.

63. "Mysli i aforizmy N," *Sever* 43(1900):1369–72; 48(1900):1531–32.

64. "Otryvki iz N," *Ezhemesiachnye Sochineniia* 5–6(1900):115–20.

65. *Pomrachenie kumirov: Sbornik proizvedenii: S prilozheniem kritiko-biograficheskogo ocherka i portreta* (Moscow: V. V. Chicherin, 1900), 330 pp. 2,400 copies.

   i. "Genii 'budushchego' " [*Der Fall Wagner*],

  ii. "Ocherki 'nesvoevremennogo' " ["Streifzüge eines Unzeitgemässen" from *Götzen-Dämmerung*],

iii. "Chem ia obiazan drevnym" ["Was ich den Alten verdanke" from *Götzen-Dämmerung*], trans. E. K. G[ertsyk];

iv. "Stikhotvoreniia," trans. A. N. E-[mel'iano]v[-Kokhanovsky];

v. *Nitsshe protiv Vagnera*, trans. E. K. G[ertsyk];

vi. *Pomrachenie kumirov*, trans. O.I.S.;

vii. A. N. E-[mel'iano]v[-Kokhanovsky], "Kritiko-biograficheskii o-cherk o FN."

66i. *Po tu storonu dobra i zla*, trans. and ed. A. N. E-[mel'iano]v [-Kokhanovsky];

ii. "Neskol'ko slov o *Chelovecheskom, sovershenno chelovecheskom*," trans. A. N. E-[mel'iano]v[-Kokhanovsky] (Moscow: D. P. Efimov, 1900). 334 pp. 2,400 copies. N's introduction to *Menschliches, Allzumenschliches*.

67. *Po tu storonu dobra i zla*, trans. and ed. N. N. Alekseev, in *Sobranie sochinenii*, vol. 2 (Moscow: M. V. Kliukin, 1900). 319 pp. 2,400 copies.

68i. *Proiskhozhdenie tragedii*,

ii. "Otryvki iz knigi *Ob Antikhriste*,"

iii. "Rechi, allegorii i kartiny" (Moscow: V. V. Chicherin, 1900).

ii. Excerpts from *Der Antichrist*.

69. "Rikhard Vagner v Bareite," trans. A. Koptiaev, *Mir Iskusstva* 3–4 (1900):59–63; 5–6(1900):99–102; 17–18(1900):95–99. Incomplete trans. of "Richard Wagner in Bayreuth" from *Unzeitgemässe Betrachtungen*.

70. *Tak govoril Zorastr: Kniga dlia vsekh i nikogo: Dvenadtsat' pritch iz misticheskoi poemy*, trans. and introd. G. P. Erastov (St. Petersburg, 1900). 80 pp. 1,000 copies.

71. *Tak govoril Zaratustra:Simvolicheskaia poema*, trans. D. Borzakovsky, ed. Arsenii I. Vvedensky and Vasil'ev, *Sobranie sochinenii*, vol. 1 (Moscow: M. V. Kliukin, 1900). 359 pp. 2,400 copies.

72. *Tak govoril Zaratustra*, trans. A. V. Perelygina, *Sobranie sochinenii*, vol. 1 (Moscow: V. V. Chicherin, 1900). 322 pp. 300 copies.

73. *Tak govoril Zaratustra*, trans. A. V. Perelygina, *Sobranie sochinenii*, vol 1, 2nd ed. (Moscow: V. V. Chicherin, 1900). 339 pp. 3,600 copies. Including "Proiskhozhdenie knigi *Tak govoril Zaratustra*," translation of Elisabeth Förster-Nietzsche, "Wie der Zarathustra entstand," *Zukunft* 6(1897):11–24.

74. *Tak govoril Zaratustra: Kniga dlia vsekh i ni dlia kogo,* trans. Iu.
    M. Antonovsky (St. Petersburg: B. M. Vol'f, 1900). 635 pp.
    2,000 copies. Reviewed in *NZhIL* 6(1901):624–26; *Russkaia
    Mysl'* 5(1901):Bibliograficheskii otdel, 139; *Ezhemesiachnye
    Sochineniia* 1(1901):94; S. Shteinberg, *Obrazovanie* 2(1901):
    sec. 2, 78–80.

75. *Chelovecheskoe, slishkom chelovecheskoe,* trans. L. I. Sokolova
    (Moscow: V. V. Chicherin, 1900). 367 pp. 3,600 copies.

CRITICAL LITERATURE

76. "N v Rossii," *NZhIL* 1(1900):100–103.

77. "Mertvyi filosof i bol'naia filosofiia," *VIL* 9(1900):366–71.

77a. "[Nekrolog],"*Mir Iskusstva* 17–18(1900):1.

78. "Smert' N," *Istoricheskii Vestnik* 9(1900):1127–30.

79. "N i zhenshchiny," *VIL* 11(1900):373–76.

79a. Boborykin, P. D. "O nitssheanstve: Pamiati V. P. Preobrazhen-
    skogo," *VFP* 54(September–October 1900):539–47.

80. Brandes, G. "FN: Aristokraticheskii radikalizm," trans. from the
    Danish by V. S-[passk]aia, *Russkaia Mysl'* 11(1900):sec. 2,
    130–53; 12(1900):sec. 2, 143–61. Translation of Georg
    Brandes, *En Afhandling om aristokratisk radikalisme* (Copen-
    hagen, 1889).

80a. Ger'e, V. I. "Pamyati V. P. Preobrazhenskogo," *VFP* 54 (Sep-
    tember–October 1900):731–40.

81. Karutov, N. "Dve smerti: Vladimir Solov'ev i FN," *Novyi Vek*
    10(1900):507–10.

82. Koptiaev, A. P. "Muzykal'noe mirovozzrenie N," *Ezhemesiach-
    nye Sochineniia* 2–3(1900):165–93.

82a. Kotliarevsky, N. "Vospominaniia o Vasilii Petroviche Preobra-
    zhenskom," *VFP* 54 (September–October 1900):501–38.

83. Minsky, N. [N. M. Vilenkin]. "FN," *Mir Iskusstva* 19–20
    (1900):139–47.

84. Mikhailovsky, N. K. "*Dobro v uchenii gr. Tolstogo i FN g. L.
    Shestova,*" *Russkoe Bogatstvo,* 2(1900):sec. 2, 155–67. Re-
    view of no. 96.

85. Mikhailovsky, N. K. "O N," in *Literaturnye vospominaniia i so-
    vremennaia smuta,* vol. 2, chaps. 13–16. (St. Petersburg,
    1900).

86. P. B. "Bolezn' FN," *Zhizn'* 2(January 1900):340–42. Summary of Elisabeth Förster-Nietzsche, "Die Krankheit FNs," *Zukunft* 14(1900):9–27.

87. Rachinsky, G. A. "Tragediia N: Opyt psikhologii lichnosti: Chast' I: Dionis i Apollon," *VFP* 55 (November–December 1900):963–1010.

88. Rachinsky, G. A. *Tragediia N: Opyt psikhologii lichnosti* (Moscow: I. N. Kushnerev, 1900).

89. Reingol'd, A. "Bol'noi filosof," *Ezhemesiachnye Sochineniia* 8(1900):253–58.

90. Sibiriak, N. K. [N. K. Mel'nikov]. "V Veimare v gostiakh u N," *Novoe Vremia*, illustrated supplement, 26 April 1900, pp. 7–8.

91. Skif. "Kriticheskie zametki [on die Fernsten-Liebe]," *Sever* 9(1900):283–86.

92. Struve, G. E. *Sovremennaia anarkhiia dukha i ee filosof FN* (Khar'kov, 1900). 55 pp. (Originally in *Vera i Razum* for 1900).

92a. Trubetskoi, E. N. "Pamiati Vasiliia Petrovicha Preobrazhenskogo," *VFP* 54(September–October 1900):481–500.

93. Ferster-Nitsshe, E. "Bolezn' FN," trans. E. G[ertsyk], *Russkaia Mysl'* 4(1900): sec. 2, 183–93. Extract from Elisabeth Förster-Nietzsche, "Die Krankheit FNs," *Zukunft* 14(1900):9–27.

94. U[manov]-K[aplunov]-sky, V. [V. V. Kaplunovsky]. "Kriticheskie zametki [on *Götzen-Dämmerung*]," *Sever* 47(1900):1491–94, 1497–1500.

95. Tsigler, T. *Umstvennye i obshchestvennye techeniia XIX v.* trans. and annotated G. Genkel' (St. Petersburg: B. Zvonarev, 1900), pp. 478–92. Translation of Theobald Ziegler, *Die geistigen und sozialen Strömungen des 19. Jahrhunderts* (Berlin, 1899).

96. Shestov, L. [L. I. Shvartsman]. *Dobro v uchenii gr. Tolstogo i FN: Filosofiia i propoved'* (St. Petersburg: M. M. Stasiulevich, 1900). xiv + 209 pp. Reviewed by P. Pertsov, *Mir Iskusstva* 5–6 (1900); Andreevich [E. A. Solov'ev], *Zhizn'* 2(1900); no. 84.

97. Shuliatikov, V. M. "Novoe iskusstvo: Mechty o sverkhcheloveke," *Kur'er*, 29 December 1900, p. 3.

98. E[ngel'gardt], A. "Druzhba i razryv N s Vagnerom," *NZhIL* 9(1900):294–300.

1901

TRANSLATIONS

99. *Veselaia nauka*, trans. A. Nikolaev from 2nd German ed., *Sobranie sochinenii*, vol. 7 (Moscow: M. V. Kliukin, 1901).

100i. *Veselaia nauka*, trans. A. N. Achkasov;
   ii. "Pamiati N," trans. E. G.[ertsyk] (Moscow: D. P. Efimov, 1901) 4,000 copies.

101. *Veselaia nauka*, trans. A. N. Achkasov, *Sobranie sochinenii*, vol. 9 (Moscow: V. V. Chicherin, 1901).

101a. *Nesvoevremennye razmyshleniia*, trans. A. and E. Gertsyk (Moscow: Borisenko i Breslin, 1901).

102. " 'Novyi Kolumb,' " trans. V. Savad, *Russkii Vestnik* 2(1901):356. [From "Lieder des Prinzen Vogelfrei" in *Die fröhliche Wissenschaft?*]

103. *Pereotsenka vsego tsennogo: Chelovecheskoe, slishkom chelovecheskoe*, trans. and ed. L. P. Nikiforov, *Sobranie sochinenii*, vol. 5 (Moscow: M. V. Kliukin, 1901). 359 pp. 2,400 copies.

104. "[Pis'ma k Gersdorful]," *Nauchnoe Obozrenie* 7(1901):177–87; 8(1901):204–24. Ten letters (1865–1867) to Carl von Gersdorf.

105. *Po tu storonu dobra i zla*, trans. A. N. E-[mel'iano]v[-Kokhanovsky], 2nd ed. (Moscow: Borisenko i Breslin, 1901). 335 pp. 2,400 copies.

106i. "Strannik i ego ten'," trans. A. A. Zablotskaia;
   ii. "Stikhotvoreniia 1871–88 godov," trans. A. N. E[mel'iano]v[-Kokhanovsky], *Sobranie sochinenii*, vol. 7 (Moscow: V. V. Chicherin, 1901). 331 pp. 3,600 copies. Translation of "Der Wanderer und sein Schatten" from *Menschliches, Allzumenschliches* and poems of 1871–1888.

107. *Sumerki kumirov, ili kak filosofstvovat' molotom*, trans. and ed. L. P. Nikiforov, *Sobranie sochinenii*, vol. 6 (Moscow: M. V. Kliukin, 1901). 340 pp. 2,400 copies.

108. *Utrenniaia zaria: Mysli o moral'nykh predrassudkakh*, trans. I.I.S., *Sobranie sochinenii*, vol. 3 (Moscow: M. V. Kliukin, 1901). 352 pp. 2,400 copies.

109. *Utrenniaia zaria: Razmyshleniia o nravstvennykh poniatiiakh*, trans.

E. G[ertsyk] (Moscow: D. P. Efimov, 1901). 383 pp. 200 copies.

110. *Utrenniaia zaria,* [trans. L. I. Sokolova?], *Sobranie sochinenii,* vol. 8 (Moscow: V. V. Chicherin, 1901).

111i. "Tsennost' evropeiskoi kul'tury,"
  ii. "Posmertnye aforizmy: Iz vremeni Zaratustry,"
  iii. *Proiskhozhdenie morali,*
  iv. "O pol'ze i vrede istorii dlia zhizni," trans. Friuling and Rinsky, *Sobranie sochinenii,* vol. 9 (Moscow: M. V. Kliukin, 1901). 325 pp.
    iv. "Vom Nutzen and Nachteil der Historie für das Leben" from *Unzeitgemässe Betrachtungen.*

112. *Chelovek, kak on est',* trans. L. I. Sokolova, *Sobranie sochinenii,* vol. 6 (Moscow: V. V. Chicherin, 1901). 454 pp. 3,600 copies. Translation of *Menschliches, Allzumenschliches.*

113. *Chelovecheskoe, slishkom chelovecheskoe: Kniga dlia svobodnykh dukhov, Sobranie sochinenii,* vol. 4 (Moscow: M. V. Kliukin, 1901). 401 pp. 2,400 copies.

CRITICAL LITERATURE

114. "FN," *NZhIL* (1901)—1:1–28; 2:162–68; 3:257–66; 4:351–60; 5:472–78; 6:590–96; 7:72–81; 8:160–97; 9:220–25; 10:299–308; 11:366–73. A biography (see nos. 142, 167, 185 for continuation).

115. "Kul't N," *Mir Bozhii* 5(1901):25–27.

116. "N kak moralist," *Russkii Vestnik* 275 (October 1901):562–66. Review of Alfred Fouillée, "La morale aristocratique du surhomme," *La Revue des deux mondes* 9(1901).

117. A-ch, E.[E. A. Solov'ev]. "Ocherki tekushchei russkoi literatury: O N," *Zhizn'* 4(1901):286–321.

118. Vagner, V. A. "Renan i N: O zvere v cheloveke," *VFP* 57(March–April 1901):199–217.

119. Vol'tmann, L. "Sistema moral'nogo soznaniia v sviazi s otnosheniem kriticheskoi filosofii k darvinizmu i sotsializmu: Uchenie N o sverkhcheloveke," in *Teoriia Darvina i sotsializm: Opyt estestvennoi istorii obshchestva,* trans. M. Engel'gardt, pp. 225–28 (St. Petersburg: F. F. Pavlenkov, [1901]).

Translation of Ludwig Woltmann, *Die Darwinische Theorie und der Sozialismus* . . . (Düsseldorf, 1899).

120. Gerasimov, N. I. *Nitssheanstvo* (Moscow: I. N. Kushnerev, 1901). 207 pp. 700 copies. Reviewed in *Zhizn'* 4(1901):355–56.

121. G[ornfel'd], A. "Perepiska N," *Russkoe Bogatstvo* 3(1901): sec. 2, 76–108. Review of and extracts from *Gesammelte Briefe*, ed. Peter Gast and Arthur Seidl, vol. 1 (Berlin and Leipzig, 1900).

122. G[ornfel'd], A. "[Review of Julius Zeitler, *Ns Ästhetik* (Leipzig, 1900); Paul Deussen, *Erinnerungen an FN* (Leipzig, 1901)]," *Russkii Vestnik* 9(1901):252–61.

123. L[ebedeva], E. A. "Filosofskie vozzreniia N," *Strannik* 11(1901):432–61; 12(1901):569–89.

124. Levitsky, S. "Sverkhchelovek (Übermensch) N i chelovek Khrista," *Bogoslovskii Vestnik* 7–8, 9(1901).

125. Levitsky, S. *Sverkhchelovek (Übermensch) N i chelovek Khrista* (Moscow: 1901).

126. Likhtenberzhe, A. *Filosofiia N*, trans., ed., and introd. M. Nevedomsky [M. P. Miklashevsky], (St. Petersburg: O. N. Popova, 1901). cxliv + 244 pp. Translation of Henri Lichtenberger, *La Philosophie de N* (Paris, 1898). Reviewed in *Russkaia Mysl'* 6(1901):174–75; *Niva* 6(1901):360; Mikhail Likharev, *Obrazovanie* 1(1902): sec. 2, 81–83; no. 131a.

[127. See no. 131a.]

128. Ril', A. *FN kak khudozhnik i myslitel'*, trans. Z. Vengerova, 2nd corrected ed. (St. Petersburg: 1901). 3,000 copies.

129. Ril', A. *FN kak khudozhnik i myslitel'* (Moscow: M. V. Kliukin, 1901). 2,400 copies.

130. Savodnik, V. F. "Nitssheanets 40-kh godov: Maks Shtirner i ego filosofiia egoizma," *VFP* 59(September–October 1901):560–614; 60 (November–December 1901):748–82.

131. Struve, P. B. "Na raznye temy [On Hauptmann and N]," *Mir Bozhii* 1(1901), sec. 2, 13–19.

131a. P. I. [P. B. Struve]. "K voprosu o morali [Review of no. 126]," *Mir Bozhii* 10(1901):sec. 1, 186–97.

132. Tarle, E. V. "Nitssheanstvo i ego otnoshenie k politicheskim i sotsial'nym teoriiam evropeiskogo obshchestva," *Vestnik Evropy* 8(1901):704–50.

133. Ferster-Nitsshe, E. "Kak voznik *Zaratustra*," trans. M. Antonovskaia, *Zhizn'* 3(1901):85–96. Translation of Elisabeth Förs-

ter-Nietzsche, "Wie der Zarathustra entstand," *Zukunft* 6(1897):11–24.

134. Filippov, M. M. "Pis'ma o sovremennoi literature: Velikii dekadent: N i ego pis'ma o sverkhcheloveke," *Nauchnoe Obozrenie* 1(1901):206–26.

1902

TRANSLATIONS

135. *Izbrannye aforizmy i mysli*, ed. Anri Likhtenberzhe, trans. M. S. Model' (St. Petersburg: 1902). 239 pp. 4,000 copies. Translation of Henri Lichtenberger, *Aphorismes et fragments choisis de N* (Paris, 1899).

136. " 'Noch' pod Novyi god: Iz zapisnoi knizhki, Bonn, Sochel'nik 1864 g.'," *NZhIL* 1(1902):57. Translation of "Ein Silvestertraum" from *Autobiographisches aus den Jahren 1856–1869*.

137. "Predislovie: K nenapisannoi vtoroi chasti *Menschliches, Allzumenschliches*," *Kur'er*, 6 May 1902, p. 3.

138. *Proiskhozhdenie tragedii, ili Ellinizm i pessimizm*, trans. Iu. M. Antonovsky (Moscow: M. V. Kliukin, 1902).

139. *Sumerki kumirov (Pomrachenie kumirov)*, trans. E. K. Gertsyk, 2nd ed. (Moscow: D. P. Efimov, 1902).
   i. *Vagnerianskii vopros*,
   ii. *Sumerki kumirov*,
   iii. *N protiv Vagnera*,
   iv. "Stikhotvoreniia."

140i. *Tak govoril Zaratustra*,
   ii. "David Shtraus," *Sobranie sochinenii*, vol. 1, 2nd ed. (Moscow: M. V. Kliukin, 1902). 559 pp. 2,400 copies.
   ii. is translation of "David Strauss, der Bekenner und der Schriftsteller" from *Unzeitgemässe Betrachtungen*.

CRITICAL LITERATURE

141. "Nravstvennost' i beznravstvennost'," *Ezhemesiachnye Sochineniia* 2(1902):151–60.

142. "FN," *NZhIL* (1902)—8:148–58; 9:238–42; 10:37–46; 12:202–313.

143i. A-ch, E. [E. A. Solov'ev]. *N*;

   ii. Deissen, P. *Vospominaniia o N* (St. Petersburg: B. Zvonarev, 1902). 204 pp. 2,450 copies.

   ii. is translation of Paul Deussen, *Erinnerungen an FN* (Leipzig, 1901) (reviewed in *Kur'er*, 18 July 1901, p. 3).

144. Bobrishchev-Pushkin, A. M. "Poet mysli," *NZhIL* (1902—1:34–46; 2:143–48; 3:286–98; 4:60–64; 5:181–97; 6:273–84; 7:39–56.

145. Gautama. *Koe-chto o Nitssheantsakh* (St. Petersburg: N. N. Klobukov, 1902). 182 pp.

146. Ivanov, I. M. "Zhurnal'noe obozrenie: N i Giugo," *Vsemirnyi Vestnik* 2(1902): 184–98.

147. Lunacharsky, A. V. "Russkii Faust," *VFP* 63(1902):783–95.

148. Nalimov, A. P. "Lermontov i N: 1841–1901," *Literaturnoe Obozrenie* 1(1902):43–45.

149. Nordau, M. *Vyrozhdenie,* 3rd ed. (Kiev, St. Petersburg, and Khar'kov, 1902), pp. 232–48.

150. Rode, A. *Gauptmann i N: K ob"iasneniiu "Potonuvshego kolokola",* trans. V. Meierkhol'd and A. Remizov (Moscow: V. M. Sablin, 1902). 32 pp. Translation of Albert Rode, *Hauptmann und N: Ein Beitrag zum Verständnis der "Versunkenen Glocke"* (Hamburg, 1897).

151. Rukavishnikov, G. "Tvorchestvo N: Kriticheskii etiud," *Novyi Mir* 78(1902):87–88.

152. Rukavishnikov, G. "Sverkhchelovek: Ocherk," *Novyi Mir* 80(1902):113–17.

153. Savodnik, V. F. *Nitssheanets 40-kh godov: Maks Shtirner i ego filosofiia egoizma* (Moscow: I. N. Kushnerev, 1902). Reviewed in no. 170a.

153a. Struve, P. B. *Na raznye temy, 1893–1901 gg.: Sbornik statei* (St. Petersburg: A. E. Kolpinsky, 1902), pp. 170–86, 279–90, 508–21.

   i.[no. 28a], ii. no. 131, iii. no. 131a.

154. Tikhomirov, N. D. "N i Dostoevskii: Cherty iz nravstvennogo mirovozzreniia togo i drugogo," *Bogoslovskii Vestnik* 7–8(1902).

155. Tikhomirov, N. D. *N i Dostoevskii: Cherty iz nravstvennogo mirovozzreniia togo i drugogo* (Moscow, 1902).

156. Faiginger, G. *N—kak filosof,* trans. A. A. Malinin from 2nd Ger.

ed. (Moscow: A. V. Vasil'ev, 1902). viii + 85 pp. Translation of Hans Vaihinger, *N als Philosoph* (Berlin, 1902).

157. Shvarts, M. N. "Kul'turno-eticheskie idealy Giuio i N," *VFP* 65 (November–December 1902): sec. 2, 977–1015.

158. Shestov, L. [L. I. Shvartsman] "Dostoevskii i N: Filosofiia trage-dii," *Mir Iskusstva* (1902)—2:69–88; 4:230–46; 5/6:321–51; 7:7–44; 8:97–113; 9/10:219–39.

1903

TRANSLATIONS

159. *Aforizmy, izrecheniia i allegorii*, trans. [and introd.] V. A. Popov (Moscow, 1903).

159a. "Vechnoe vozvrashchenie," trans. V. Peremilovsky, *Novyi Put'* 5(1903):34–51. Translation of "Darstellung und Begründung der Lehre" and "Wirkung der Lehre auf die Menschenheit" as in *Gesammelte Werke*, vol. 11 (Munich, 1924), pp. 172–88.

159b. "Dopolneniia k okonchennym chastiam Zaratustry," trans. V. Peremilovsky, *Novyi Put'* 3(1903):123–32. Partial translation of "Entwürfe und Gedanken zu den ausgeführten Theilen des Zarathustra" as in *Gesammelte Werke*, vol. 14 (Munich, 1924), pp. 133–70.

160. *O filosofakh*, trans. and ed. L. P. Nikiforov, *Sobranie sochinenii*, vol. 10 (Moscow: M. V. Kliukin, [1903]).

161i. "Pis'mo k tovarishcham ot 28 iiulia 1862 g.,"
    ii. "Chudovishchnaia rukopis': Evforion,"
    iii. " 'Vozvrashchenie domoi'," *VIL* 1(1903):313–17.

162. *Po tu storonu dobra i zla*, trans. A.N.E.-[mel'iano]v[-Kokhanov-sky], ed. V. N. Lind, 3rd ed. (Moscow: D. P. Efimov, 1903).

163i. *Po tu storonu dobra i zla*,
    ii. *Rikhard Vagner*, trans. A. Nikolaev and E. Vorontsova, *Sobranie sochinenii*, vol. 2, 2nd ed. (Moscow: M. V. Kliukin, 1903).

164. *Proiskhozhdenie tragedii*, trans. [and introd.] N. N. Polilov, 2nd ed. (St. Petersburg: 1903). 242 pp. 593 copies.

165. *Tak govoril Zaratustra: Kniga dlia vsekh i ni dlia kogo*, trans. Iu. M. Antonovsky, 2nd corrected ed. (St. Petersburg: Al'tschuler, 1903). 440 pp. 5,000 copies.
166. *Tak govoril Zaratustra*, trans. A. V. Perelygina, ed. V. N. Lind, 3rd ed. (Moscow: D. P. Efimov, 1903).

CRITICAL LITERATURE

167. "FN," *NZhIL* (1903)—1:67–72; 2:159–67; 4:48–54; 5:149–59.
168. "Novoe o FN," *VIL* 1(1903):312–13.
168a. Verner, I. "Tip Kirillova u Dostoevskogo," *Novyi Put'* 10(1903):48–80; 11(1903):52–80; 12(1903):128–82.
169. Geilikman, T. "N i evreistvo," *Knizhki "Voskhoda"* 8(1903):29–38.
170. Gel'rot, M. "N i Gor'kii: Element nitssheanstva v tvorchestve g. Gor'kogo," *Russkoe Bogatstvo* 5(1903):24–68.
170a. L[undberg?], E. "V. Sadovnik, *Nitssheanets 40-kh godov: Maks Shtirner i ego filosofiia egoizma*," *Novyi Put'* 5(1903):172–78. Review of no. 153.
171. Markelov, G. "Filosofiia N, kak kul'turnaia problema," *Mir Bozhii* 10(1903):197–213; 11(1903):145–60.
172. Roberti, E. de. "N, ego filosofiia i sotsiologiia: Opyt obshchestvennoi kharakteristiki," *Nauchnoe Obozrenie* 2(1903):13–31; 3(1903):121–41.
172a. Smirnov, A. V. "Dostoevskii i N: Publichnaia lektsiia," *Uchenye zapiski Kazanskogo universiteta* 4(1903):49–96.
173. Smirnov, A. V. *Dostoevskii i N: Publichnaia lektsiia* (Kazan': A. A. Dubrovin, 1903). 51 pp.
174. Solov'ev, V. S. "Ideia sverkhcheloveka (1899)," *Sobranie sochinenii* (St. Petersburg: 1903), 8:310–19.
175. Trubetskoi, E. N. "Filosofiia N: Kriticheskii ocherk," *VFP* (1903)—66:1–36; 67:190–230; 68:256–90; 69:329–78.
176. Faiginger, G. *N, kak filosof*, trans. P. O. Shutiakov (Moscow: S. Skirmunt, 1903). 59 pp. Translation of Hans Vaihinger, *N als Philosoph* (Berlin, 1902).
176a. Filosofov, D. "Prof. Evg. Trubetskoi o N," *Novyi Put'* 2(1903):167–70.
176b. Filosofov, D. "Propoved' idealizma: Sbornik *Problemy idealizma*," *Novyi Put'* 10(1903):177–84.

177. Frank, S. L. "FN i etika "liubvi k dal'nemu"," *Problemy idea-lizma: Sbornik statei,* ed. P. I. Novgorodtsev, pp. 137–95 (Moscow: Moskovskoe Psikhologicheskoe Obshchestvo, [November 1902] 1903). Reviewed by A. V. Lunacharsky, *Obrazovanie* 2(1903); *Kur'er,* 11 April 1903, p. 3; Volzhsky [A. S. Glinka], *Zhurnal dlia Vsekh* 4(1904); no. 180a.

178. Ful'e, A. "N o Giuio: Po neizdannym dokumentam," *Russkoe Bogatstvo* 1(1903):125–54. Translation of Alfred Fouillée, "Les judgements de N sur Guyau d'après des documents inédits," *Revue des deux mondes* 1(1901):563–94.

179. Kheisin, M. L. "Dostoevskii i N," *Mir Bozhii* 6(1903):119–41.

180. Shestov, L. [L. I. Shvartsman]. *Dostoevskii i N: Filosofiia tragedii* (St. Petersburg: M. M. Stasiulevich, 1903). Reviewed by M. Kh[eisin?], *Obrazovanie* 7(1903); M.G-an [M. Ia. Gol'tsev], *Vestnik Evropy* 9(1903); T. Sozhin, *Kur'er,* 24 March 1903.

180a. Sh-sky. "S. Frank, 'FN i etika liubvi k dal'nemu' (Sbornik *Problemy idealizma*)," *Novyi Put'* 3(1903):206–12. Review of no. 177.

1904

TRANSLATIONS

181i. "David Shtraus v roli ispovednika i pisatelia,"
  ii. "Rikhard Vagner v Baireite," (Moscow: M. V. Kliukin, 1904).

181a. "Kritika vysshikh tsennostei," *Novyi Put'* 9(1904):240–55. Translation of "Kritik der bisherigen höchsten Werthe . . ." from *Der Wille zur Macht.*

182. "N o stile: Iz *Chelovecheskogo, slishkom chelovecheskogo,*" trans. Manchin, *Zhurnal dlia Vsekh* 3(1904):159.

183. "Novye aforizmy FN,' *VIL* 12(1904):332–34.

184i. "Sil'-Mariia,"
  ii. "Vdali gremiat raskaty groma,"
  iii. "Skuchnyi den' otzvuchal,"
  iv. "*Veselaia nauka,*"
  v. "K novym moriam,"
  vi. "Novyi Kolumb,"

vii. "Sredi vragov,"
viii. "K gletcheru," trans. Ellis [L. L. Kobylinsky], *Immorteli* 2(1904): 121–36.

CRITICAL LITERATURE

185. "FN," *NZhIL* (1904)—6:279–88; 7:36–43; 8:127–35.
186. "N i ego bolezn'," *Mir Bozhii* 4(1904):99–101.
187. Bitner, V. V. *FN i ego proizvedeniia* (St. Petersburg: V. V. Bitner, 1904). 64 pp. (Free supplement to *Vestnik Znaniia* 6[1904]).
188. Dubinsky, M. I. "Filosofiia kulaka: N," in *Za druzheskoi besedoiu: Kriticheskie stat'i* (St. Petersburg: Tsepov, 1904), pp. 248–70.
189. Ivanov, V. I. "N i Dionis," *Vesy* 5(1904):17–30.
189a. Ivanov, V. I. "Ellinskaia religiia stradaiushchego boga," *Novyi Put'* (1904)—1:110–34; 2:48–78; 3:38–61; 5:28–40; 8:17–26; 9:47–70. Continued in no. 206a.
189b. Ioel, K. "N i romantizm," trans. Dvorchikov, *Novyi Put'* 6(1904):107–46; 7(1904):30–66. Translation of Carl Joël, "N und die Romantik," *Neue deutsche Rundschau* 14(1903):458–501. (Reviewed in no. 211a.)
190. Mandel'shtam, M. "Eticheskie idealy N," in *K pravde* (Moscow: 1904), pp. 82–107.
191. N-r, E. "Filosofiia N," *Strannik* 4(1904):621–30.
192. Trubetskoi, E. N. *Filosofiia N: Kriticheskii ocherk* (Moscow: I. N. Kushnerev, 1904). iv + 159 pp. 1,600 copies.
193. Fisher, L. *FN: "Antikhrist" v noveishei filosofii*, trans. M. Voskresensky (Moscow: I. N. Kushnerev, 1904). 171 pp. Translation of Engelbert Lorenz Fischer, *FN: Der "Antichrist" in der neuesten Philosophie* (Regensburg, 1901). Reviewed by S. S[olov'ev], *Vesy* 4(1905):61–62 (with no. 199).
194. Ful'e, A. "Religiia N v kriticheskom izlozhenii Al'freda Ful'e," trans. A. Vvedensky, *Vera i Razum* 1(1904):36–48; 4(1904):148–70. Translation of Alfred Fouillée, "La religion de N," *Revue des deux mondes* 1(1904):563–94.
195. Khmelevsky, I. K. *Patologicheskii element v lichnosti i tvorchestve FN: Rech', 22 fevralia 1903 g.* (Kiev: I. N. Kushnerev, 1904).

1905

TRANSLATIONS

195a. "Difiramby Dionisa," *Voprosy Zhizni* 7(1905):84–99.
196. *Nesvoevremennye razmyshleniia*, trans. A. and E. Gertsyk (Moscow: D. P. Efimov, 1905).
196a. "N o iudaizme," in *Iudaizm: Karl Fokht* . . . ; *Karl Marks* . . . ; *N* . . . ; *Genrikh Ibsen* . . . (Odessa, Novaia Zaria, 1905).
197i. *Po tu storonu dobra i zla: Predliudie k filosofii budushchego*,
  ii. *Dionisovy difiramby*, trans. N. N. Polilov (St. Petersburg: D. E. Zhukovsky, 1905).
198. *Po tu storonu dobra i zla*, trans. M.N.T. and L. I. Sokolova, ed. V. V. Bitner (St. Petersburg, 1905).

CRITICAL LITERATURE

199. Berg, L. *Sverkhchelovek v. sovremennoi literature: Glava k istorii umstvennogo razvitiia XIX veka*, trans. L. Gorbunova (Moscow: I. N. Kushnerev, 1905). 258 pp. 2,400 copies. Translation of Leo Berg, *Der Übermensch in der modernen Literatur* . . . (Paris, Leipzig, Munich, 1897). Reviewed by S. S[olov'ev], *Vesy* 4(1905):61–62 (with no. 193).
200. Bronzov, A. A. "FN," *Russkii Palomnik* 13(1905):189–91; 14(1905):203–207.
201. Geilikman, T. "Teoriia poznaniia N," *Pravda* 6(1905):154–74.
202. G[ornfel'd], A. "N i Brandes," *Russkoe Bogatstvo* 4(1905):sec. 2, 1–25.
202a. Davydov, I. "Amoralizm N i ideia dolga," *Voprosy Zhizni* 2(1905):223–46.
203. Efimenko, A. Ia. "N i ego Zaratustra," *Vestnik i Biblioteka Samoobrazovaniia* 7(1905):199–204.
204. Efimenko, A. Ia. " 'Sverkh-chelovek' i 'Poslednii chelovek' v uchenii N," *Vestnik i Biblioteka Samoobrazovaniia* 8(1905):231–36.
205. Efimenko, A. Ia. " 'Pereotsenka tsennostei' u N," *Vestnik i Biblioteka Samoobrazovaniia* 10(1905):297–300.
206. Zarubin, N. "Nitssheanskie romany tolpy: Ocherk," *Vestnik Literatury* 14(1905):310–15; 15(1905):336–39.
206a. Ivanov, V. I. "Religiia Dionisa: Ee proiskhozhdenie i vliianie,"

Voprosy Zhizni 6(1905):185–220; 7(1905):122–48. Continuation of no. 189a.

207. Mirtov, D. P. "Nravstvennaia avtonomiia po Kantu i N," *Khristianskoe Chtenie* (1905).

208. Mirtov, D. P. *Nravstvennaia avtonomiia po Kantu i N* (St. Petersburg, [1905?]). 66 pp.

209. Mikhailovsky, N. K. "O N," in *Literaturnye vospominaniia i sovremennaia smuta*, 2nd ed. (St. Petersburg, 1905), vol. 2, chaps. 13–16.

210. Nalimov, A. P. "Nitssheanstvo u nashikh belletristov," in *Interesnye romany, povesti i rasskazy luchshikh pisatelei* (St. Petersburg, [1905]), pp. 94–99.

211. Slobodskoi, I. *FN pri svete khristianskogo mirovozzreniia, Khristianstvo, nauka i neverie na zare XX veka*, vol. 4 (St. Petersburg, 1905). 120 pp.

211a. F[rank], S. "Karl Ioel, 'N und die Romantik'," *Voprosy Zhizni* 9(1905):277–79.

212. Ful'e, A. *N i immoralizm* (St. Petersburg: 1905). 323 pp. 1,200 copies. Translation of Alfred Fouillée, *N et l'immoralisme* (Paris, 1902).

213. Ful'e, A. "Sotsial'nye idei N," *Vera i Razum* 14(1905):60–64; 15(1905):84–120. Translation of Alfred Fouillée, "Les idées sociales de N," *Revue des deux mondes* 9(1902):400–431.

214. Khvostov, V. M. "Etika N," *Russkaia Mysl'* 7(1905) sec. 2, 46–79; 12(1905): sec. 2, 11–41.

1906

TRANSLATIONS

215. *Pesni i rechi Zaratustry, 1882–1883*, trans. P. Dunaevsky (Khar'kov: Tsederbaum, 1906).

216. *Tak govoril Zaratustra*, trans. A. N. Achkasov (Moscow: D. P. Efimov, 1906). 448 pp. 4,000 copies.

CRITICAL LITERATURE

217. "N i Kant," *VIL* 3(1906):311–13.

218. "N vo vtoroi polovine svoei zhizni," *VIL* 6(1906):272–75.

219. Abramovich, N. Ia. *Chelovek budushchego: Ocherk filosofskoi uto-pii FN* (St. Petersburg: Prometei, 1906). 99 pp.

220. Avksent'ev, N. D. *Sverkhchelovek: Kul'turno-eticheskii ideal N* (St. Petersburg: Sever, 1906). 267 pp. 4,000 copies. Originally Nicolaus Awxentieff, *Kultur-ethisches Ideal Ns: Darstellung und Kritik* (Halle, 1905). 153 pp. (dissertation). Reviewed by [A. P. Kudriavtsev], *Russkoe Bogatstvo* 9(1907): sec. 2, 156–58.

221. Znamensky, S. P. "Sverkhchelovek N," *Vera i Razum* (1906)—1:1–19; 2:33–50; 3–4:67–79.

222. Znamensky, S. P. *Sverkhchelovek N* (Khar'kov, 1906).

223. Znamensky, S. P. "Sovremennyi individualizm v eticheskom ot-noshenii," *Bogoslovskii Vestnik* 12(1906).

224. Znamensky, S. P. *Sovremennyi individualizm v eticheskom ot-noshenii* (Sergiev Posad, 1906).

225. Likhtenberzhe, A. *Filosofiia N*, trans. from 9th ed. supervised by A. G. Genkel', Populiarno-nauchnaia Biblioteka, 13 (St. Petersburg: Slovo, 1906). Translation of Henri Lichtenberger, *La philosophie de N*.

226. Nalimov, A. P. "Obshchee u Geine i N," *Priroda i Liudi* 30(1906):474–76.

227. Fal'kenfel'd, M. *Marks i N*, trans. and introd. Ia. V. Perovich (Odessa, 1906). 24 pp. Translation of Max Falkenfeld, *Marx und N* (Leipzig, 1899).

1907

TRANSLATIONS

228. *Antikhrist*, trans. N. N. Polilov (St. Petersburg: Prometei, 1907). Reviewed by P. Iu[shkevich], *Sovremennyi Mir* 5(1907):107–108.

229. *Antikhristianin: Opyt kritiki khristianstva*, trans. V. A. Flerova, ed. A. Ia. Efimenko (St. Petersburg: M. V. Pirozhkov, 1907).

230. " 'Nevedomomu bogu'," trans. A. P. Dobrokhotov, *VIL* 9(1907):26.

231. *N o Vagnere: 1, Vagner kak iavlenie; 2, N protiv Vagnera*, trans. and introd. N. N. Polilov (St. Petersburg: [A. S. Suvorin], 1907).

232. *Po tu storonu dobra i zla,* trans. M.N.T. and L. I. Sokolova, *Biblioteka dlia Samorazvitiia* 11–12(1907).

233. *Po tu storonu dobra i zla,* trans. M.N.T. and L. I. Sokolova, ed. V. V. Bitner (St. Petersburg: Vestnik Znaniia, 1907).

234. *Sumerki idolov ili kak filosofstvuiut molotom,* trans. N. N. Polilov (St. Petersburg: [A. S. Suvorin], 1907). Reviewed by P. Iu[shkevich], *Sovremennyi Mir* 4(1907):94–96; *NZhIL* 9(1907).

235. *Tak govoril Zaratustra: Kniga dlia vsekh i ni dlia kogo,* trans. Iu. M. Antonovskii, 3rd ed. (St. Petersburg: F. Vaisberg i P. Gershunin, 1907).

CRITICAL LITERATURE

236. "Detstvo N," *VIL* 7(1907):272.

237. Bauler, A. [A. V. Gol'shtein]. "Otzvuki parizhskoi zhizni: N vo frantsuzkom romane," *Russkaia Mysl'* 7(1907): sec. 2, 137–45.

238. Geffding, G. *Sovremennye filosofy,* trans. A. Smirnov, ed. A. A. Pogodin (St. Petersburg: O. N. Popova, 1907), pp. 141–74. 210 pp. 5,200 copies. Translation of Harald Høffding, *Moderne Filosoffer* (Copenhagen, 1904).

239. Zimmel', G. *Modernizirovannaia nravstvennost': Filosofiia FN,* trans. M. and E. Markov, Politko-istoricheskaia i populiarno-nauchnaia biblioteka, 12 (St. Petersburg, 1907). 63 pp. (Free supplement to *Birzhevye Vedomosti*). Translation of Georg Simmel, "FN: Eine moral-philosophische Silhouette" (see no. 38ii.?)

240. Ivanov, M. M. "N i Vagner," *Novoe Vremia* 19 and 26 March, 2 April 1907.

241. Iezinggaus, V. *FN o zhenshchine, liubvi i brake,* trans. A. G-n (Moscow: A. P. Mamontov, 1907). 63 pp. Translation of Walter Jesinghaus, *Ns Stellung zu Weib, Liebe und Ehe* (Leipzig, 1907).

242. Tasteven, G. E. "N i sovremennyi krizis: Filosofskii etiud," *Zolotoe Runo* 7–9(1907):110–15.

243. Fomin, otets P. I. "Za prava zhizni i lichnosti: Uchenie FN i moral'naia otsenka etogo ucheniia," *Vera i Razum* (1907)—6:775–85; 7:71–80; 8:216–24.

244. Shestov, L. [L. I. Shvartsman]. *Dobro v uchenii gr. Tolstogo i FN:*

Filosofiia i propoved', 2nd ed. (St. Petersburg: M. V. Pirozh-kov, 1907). x + 133 pp. Reviewed by L. Ortodoks [L. I. Girsh], *Sovremennyi Mir* 3(1908):112–15.

1908

TRANSLATIONS

245. *Genealogiia morali: Pamflet*, trans. V. A. Veinshtok, ed. V. V. Bitner (St. Petersburg, 1908) (Free supplement to *Vestnik Znaniia* 12[1908]).

246i. "Pis'mo k baronesse Mete fon Salis-Marshlins ot 7-go sentiabria 1888 g.,"

ii. "Pis'mo k sestre ot 20-go oktiabria 1888 g.," *Baian* 2(1908):119–20.

247. "Ecce homo," trans. V. Ia. Briusov, *Vesy* 12(1908):43–48. Introduction to *Ecce homo*. Continued in no. 257.

CRITICAL LITERATURE

248. Abramovich, N. Ia. *Chelovek budushchego: Ocherk filosofskoi uto-pii FN* (St. Petersburg, 1908).

248a. Arsky [N. Ia. Abramovich]. "Motivy solntsa i tela v sovremennoi belletristike: O nitssheanstve v *Sanine*," *Voprosy Pola* 2(1908):28–30; 3(1908):27–31.

249. Bely, A. [B. N. Bugaev]. "FN," *Vesy* (1908)—7:45–50; 8:55–65; 9:30–39.

250. Kogan, P. S. "Nashi literaturnye kumiry: N," *Russkoe Slovo*, no. 206, 5 September 1908, pp. 2–3.

251. Likhtenberzhe, A. "FN," in *Etiudy moral'noi filosofii XIX veka* (Moscow, 1908), pp. 174–98. Translation of Henri Lichten-berger, *Etudes sur la philosophie morale au XIXe siècle* (Paris, 1904).

252. Khvostov, V. M. "Etika N," in *Etiudy po sovremennoi etike* (Moscow, 1908), pp. 3–105. 2,500 copies.

253. Chizh, V. F. "N, kak moralist," *VFP* 94(September–October 1908):335–76; 95(November–December 1908):480–512.

1909

TRANSLATIONS

254i. "Iz zakliuchitel'noi pesni,"
  ii. "O chtenii pisem,"
 iii. "Pesn' nochi,"
  iv. "Pifiia i molniia," trans. A. V. P[erelygina], *Antologiia sovremen-
      noi poezii* (1909), vol. 4, 209–15.
254a. *Nesvoevremennye razmyshleniia,* trans. A. and E. Gertsyk, ed. V.
      N. Lind (Moscow: D. P. Efimov, 1909).
255i. *Nesvoevremennye razmyshleniia,*
  ii. "Iz posmertnykh proizvedenii, 1873–1875: My filologi," trans. and
      ed. S. Frank and G. Rachinsky, commentary E. Metner, in
      Polnoe sobranie sochinenii . . . , vol. 2 (Moscow: Moskov-
      skoe knigoizdatel'stvo, 1909).
256. "Pis'ma N," *Istoricheskii Vestnik* 1(1909):365–72. From *La Re-
      vue,* 15 September 1908.
257. "Ecce homo," trans. V. Ia. Briusov, *Vesy* 2(1909):44–48.

CRITICAL LITERATURE

258. Abramovich, N. Ia. "FN," in *Literaturno-kriticheskie ocherki* (St.
      Petersburg: Tvorchestvo i Zhizn', 1909), vol. 1, 122–43.
259. Brandes, G. "N," trans. M. V. Luchitskaia, *Sobranie sochinenii,*
      vol. 14 (St. Petersburg: Prosveshchenie, 1909).
260. Ivanov, V. I. "N i Dionis," in *Po zvezdam: Stat'i i aforizmy* (St.
      Petersburg: Ory, 1909), pp. 1–20.
261. Koptiaev, A. P. "N i Gast: Stranitsa pereotsenki sovremennoi opery,"
      Ezhegodnik Imperatorskikh Teatrov 2(1909):57–70.
262. Mikhailovsky, N. K. "Literaturnye vospominaniia," in *Polnoe so-
      branie sochinenii* (St. Petersburg, 1909), vol. 7, cols. 859–
      86, 923–46, 945–76.
263. Plekhanov, G. V. "O knige Ivanova-Razumnika *O smysle zhizni:
      Fedor Sologub, Leonid Andreev, Lev Shestov,*" *Sovremennyi
      Mir* 3(1909).
264. Plekhanov, G. V. "O tak nazyvaemykh religioznykh iskaniiakh v
      Rossii: Stat'ia tret'ia: Evangelie ot dekadansa," *Sovremennyi
      Mir* 12(1909).

265. Polovtsova, V. N. "Po povodu avtobiografii FN," *VFP* 98(1909):501–20.

266. Ril', A. *FN, kak khudozhnik i myslitel'*, trans. I. V. Postman from 5th Ger. ed., introd. G. Ia. Polonsky, Biblioteka "Iasnoi Poliany", 3 (St. Petersburg: K. A. Chetverikov, 1909). Translation of Alois Riehl, *FN der Künstler und der Denker*.

267. Ril', A. *FN, kak khudozhnik i myslitel'*, trans. I. V. Postman from 5th Ger. ed., introd. G. Ia. Polonsky, Biblioteka Znaniia (St. Petersburg: Iasnaia Poliana, 1909). Translation of Alois Riehl, *FN der Künstler und der Denker*.

268. Rogachev, B. *FN: Skhematizirovannaia interpretatsiia ego filosofii* (Paris, 1909). xvi + 548 pp.

269. Slonimsky, L. Z. "N o samom sebe," *Vestnik Evropy* 11(1909):395–402.

270. Shel'vin, R. *Maks Shtirner i FN: Iavleniia sovremennogo dukha i sushchnost' cheloveka*, trans. N. N. Vokach and I. A. Il'in, introd. S. L. Frank, "Shtirner i N v russkoi zhizni" (Moscow: N. N. Klochkov, 1909). 167 pp. Translation of Robert Schellwien, *Max Stirner und FN: Erscheinungen des modernen Geistes und das Wesen des Menschen* (Leipzig, 1892).

271. Shestov, L. [L. I. Shvartsman]. *Dostoevskii i N: Filosofiia tragedii* (St. Petersburg: M. M. Stasiulevich, 1909). 245 pp.

1910

TRANSLATIONS

272i. "Venetsiia,"

ii. "K novym moriam," trans. A. Dobrokhotov, *VIL* 2(1910):174. From "Lieder des Prinzen Vogelfrei" in *Die fröhliche Wissenschaft*.

273. *Volia k vlasti: Opyt pereotsenki vsekh tsennostei* (1884–1888), ed. G. Rachinsky and Ia. Berman [A. B. Derman?], *Polnoe sobranie sochinenii . . .* , vol. 9 (Moscow: Moskovskoe knigoizdatel'stvo, 1910). Translation of *Der Wille zur Macht: Versuch einer Umwerthung aller Werthe*. Reviewed by G. F[lorovsky], *Izvestiia Odesskogo Bibliograficheskogo Obshchestva* 1, no. 6(1912):227–28.

274i. "Nevedomomu bogu,"
  ii. "K mysliam,"
  iii. "Venetsiia," trans. K. M. Antipov, in *Novye nemetskie poety* (Belaia Tserkov', 1910), pp. 10–43.

CRITICAL LITERATURE

275. "Desiatiletie so dnia smerti FN," *VIL* 10(1910):22–28.
276. Abramovich, N. Ia. *FN*, Kriticheskaia Biblioteka, vol. 4 (Moscow: Zaria, 1910). 79 pp.
277. Abramovich, N. Ia. "FN," in *Literaturnye portrety* (Moscow, 1910), pp. 176–249.
278. Gornfel'd, A. G. *Na zapade: Literaturnye besedy: N, Giugo, Geine, Ten, Pol'-Lui Kur'e* (St. Petersburg: Mir, 1910), pp. 1–45, 46–79.
279. Kaufman, A. E. " 'Vsechelovek' i 'sverkhchelovek': V. S. Solov'ev† 31 iiulia 1900 g. i FN† 12 avgusta 1900 g.," *Vsemirnaia Panorama* 67(1910):11–12.
280. Plekhanov, G. V. "O knige V. Vindel'banda *Filosofiia v nemetskoi dukhovnoi zhizni XIX stoletiia* . . . ," *Sovremennyi Mir* 1(1910).
280a. Felitsyn, S. "Komnatnyi Zaratustra," *Izvestiia Knizhnykh Magazinov Tovarishchestva M. O. Vol'f* 1(1910):17–18.
281. Frank, S. L. i. "N i etika 'liubvi k dal'nemu,' "
  ii. "Shtirner i N v russkoi zhizni," in *Filosofiia i zhizn': Etiudy i nabroski po filosofii kul'tury* (St. Petersburg: D. E. Zhukovsky, 1910), pp. 1–72, 367–74.
281a. Ellis [L. L. Kobylinsky]. *Russkie Simvolisty* (Moscow: Musaget, 1910), pp. 24–26, 30–31, 46–48.

1911

TRANSLATIONS

282i. *Avtobiografiia*, trans. and ed. Iu. M. Antonovsky;
  ii. " 'Slava i vechnost' '," trans. I. Sherman (St. Petersburg: Prometei, [1911]). Translation of *Ecce homo* and "Ruhm und Ewigkeit" from *Dionysos-Dithyramben*. Reviewed by I. D., *Sovre-*

mennyi Mir 9(1912):321–22; Iu., *Priroda i Liudi* 21(1912):336;
N. Lerner, *Novaia Zhizn'* 1(1912):274–76.

283. *Tak govoril Zaratustra: Kniga dlia vsekh i ni dlia kogo*, trans. Iu.
    M. Antonovsky, 4th ed. (St. Petersburg: Prometei, 1911).

284. *Tak govoril Zaratustra* (Free supplement to *Probuzhdenie* [1911]).

285i. *Chelovecheskoe, slishkom chelovecheskoe*,

  ii. "Iz posmertnykh proizvedenii, 1874–1877: Otdel'nye zamecha-
    niia o kul'ture, gosudarstve i vospitanii," ed. and introd. S.
    Frank, in *Polnoe sobranie sochinenii . . .* , vol. 3 (Moscow:
    Moskovskoe knigoizdatel'stvo, 1911).

286. *Ecce homo*, trans. from French ed. Ia Danilin (Moscow, 1911).

CRITICAL LITERATURE

287. "Pis'ma N," *Za 7 dnei* 31(1911):14.

288. "Koe-chto o N," *Istoricheskii Vestnik* 9(1911):1173–76.

289. Bely, A. [B. N. Bugaev]. "FN," in *Arabeski* (Moscow, 1911), pp.
    60–90.

290. Galevi, D. *Zhizn' FN*, trans. A. N. Il'insky, ed. and introd. V.
    N. Speransky (St. Petersburg: M. O. Vol'f, 1911). 317 pp.
    Translation of Daniel Halévi, *La vie de N* (Paris, 1909). Re-
    viewed by I. Gurevich, *Istoricheskii Vestnik*, 2(1912), 764–
    65.

291. Zelinsky, F. F., "FN i antichnost'," *Vseobshchii Ezhemesiachnik*
    12(1911):13–27.

292. Rogovich, M. *Neskol'ko slov ob uchenii N* (Free supplement to
    Zhenskii Vestnik 10[1911]).

293. Rogovich, M. *Neskol'ko slov. ob uchenii N* (St. Petersburg: P. P.
    Soikin, [1911]). 39 pp.

294. Faiginger, G., *N: Filosof otritsaniia*, trans. N. M. Gubsky (St.
    Petersburg, 1911). 61 pp. Translation of Hans Vaihinger, *N
    als Philosoph* (Berlin, 1902).

295. Shestov, L. [L. I. Shvartsman]. i. *Dobro v uchenii gr. Tolstogo i
    FN: Filosofiia i propoved'*, in *Sobranie sochinenii*, vol. 2 (St.
    Petersburg: Shipovnik, [1911]); ii. *Dostoevskii i N: Filosofiia
    tragedii*, in *Sobranie sochinenii*, vol. 3 (St. Petersburg: Shi-
    povnik, [1911]).

296. Iushkevich, P. S. "FN i filosofiia illiuzii," *Novaia Zhizn'*
    13(1911):113–38.

1912

TRANSLATIONS

297i. *Rozhdenie tragedii,*
  ii. "Iz posmertnykh proizvedenii, 1869–1873," ed. F. F. Zelinsky
      [includes no. 291], *Polnoe sobranie sochinenii*, vol. 1 (Mos-
      cow: Moskovskoe knigoizdatel'stvo, 1912).

CRITICAL LITERATURE

298. Anichkov, E. V. "Doloi N," *Novaia Zhizn'* 9(1912):114–39.
299. Plekhanov, G. V. "Iskusstvo i obshchestvennaia zhizn'," *Sovre-
     mennik* 11(1912); 12(1912); 1(1913).

1913

TRANSLATIONS

300. *Tak govoril Zaratustra: Kniga dlia vsekh i ni dlia kogo*, trans. Iu.
     M. Antonovsky, 5th ed. (St. Petersburg: Zhizn' dlia Vsekh,
     1913).
301. *Tak govoril Zaratustra: Kniga dlia vsekh i ni dlia kogo*, trans. V.
     Izraztsov, introd. E. Ferster-Nitsshe (St. Petersburg: 1913).
     Introd. translation of Elisabeth Förster-Nietzsche, "Wie der
     Zarathustra entstand," *Zukunft* 6(1897):11–24.

CRITICAL LITERATURE

301a. "Nitsshe—Fridrikh . . . ,' *Entsiklopedicheskii slovar'* F. *Pavlen-
      kova*, 5th ed. (St. Petersburg: Trud, 1913), col. 1582.
302. Veresaev, V. V. [V. V. Smidovich]. "Apollon: Bog zhivoi zhizni,"
     Slovo 1(1913):5–35.
303. Solov'ev, V. S. "Ideia sverkhcheloveka (1899)," *Sobranie sochi-
     nenii*, 2nd ed. (St. Petersburg: 1913), vol. 9, 265–74.
304. Uspensky, I. D. *Vnutrennii krug: O "poslednei cherte" i sverkhche-
     loveke: Lektsiia* (St. Petersburg, 1913). 149 pp.

305. Faiginger, G. *N kak filosof* (St. Petersburg, 1913). Translation of Hans Vaihinger, *N als Philosoph* (Berlin, 1902).
306. Shvarts, M. N. "N i Shopengauer," *Russkaia Mysl'* 12(1913):sec. 2, 33–39.

1914

CRITICAL LITERATURE

307. "N o germanskoi kul'ture," *Priroda i Liudi* 45 (1914):732.
308. Veresaev, V. V. [V. V. Smidovich]. "Apollon i Dionis: O N," *Sovremennyi Mir* (1914)—2:1–29; 3:42–64; 4:76–100; 5:1–25; 11:25–41.

1915

CRITICAL LITERATURE

309. Veresaev, V. V. [V. V. Smidovich]. *Apollon i Dionis: O N, Zhivaia zhizn'*, pt. 2 (Moscow: A. A. Levenson, 1915). 145 pp. 3,000 copies.
310. Krivinskaia, A. L. "Zhenshchiny v zhizni N," *Russkaia Mysl'* 8(1915): sec. 2, 50–71.

1916

CRITICAL LITERATURE

311. Satrapinsky, I. I. "Filosofiia N v ee otnoshenii k khristianstvu," *Pravoslavnyi Sobesednik* (1916)—1:25–40; 2/4:127–43; 5/6:501–41; 7/8:22–39; 9/10:188–209; 11/12:319–43.
312. Satrapinsky, I. I. *Filosofiia N v ee otnoshenii k khristianstvu* (Kazan', 1916).
313. Speransky, V. N. "Nitsshe Fridrikh Vil'gel'm," *Novyi Entsiklopedicheskii Slovar'* (Petrograd: Brokgauz i Efron, 1916), vol. 28, pp. 650–57.

1917

CRITICAL LITERATURE

314. Iaugert, Anna. *Chto takoe liubov': Nauchno-psikhologicheskoe is-sledovanie: Po N* (Vladivostok: Dalekaia Okraina, 1917). 40 pp.

1919

CRITICAL LITERATURE

314a. Speransky, V. N. "Nitsshe, Fridrikh . . . ," *Entsiklopedicheskii slovar' Granat*, 7th ed. (Moscow, 1919), vol. 30, cols. 254–62.

314b. Friche, V. "Nitssheanstvo," *Entsiklopedicheskii slovar' Granat*, 7th ed. (Moscow, 1919), vol. 30, cols. 262–63.

INDEX OF TRANSLATIONS
OF NIETZSCHE'S MAJOR WORKS

INDEX OF TRANSLATORS, AUTHORS, AND EDITORS

(Selected publishers have also been included to facilitate tracing successive volumes of the various collected works.)

Afterword: Nietzsche's View of Russia and the Russians

Susan Ray

THE CHAPTERS THAT precede this one all deal with the way various individual Russians were influenced by or used the philosophy of Friedrich Nietzsche to further their own ends. This chapter represents the converse, for it concentrates on the way Nietzsche viewed Russia and the Russians and examines a related, although by no means tangential question: If this is what Nietzsche thought about Russia and its people, what does that say about Nietzsche himself?

Much has been written about the philosopher's encounter with Russian literature, particularly with the works of Tolstoi and Dostoevsky. But what preceded his enthusiasm, what prepared the ground, as it were, for the reaction he experienced, especially from his contact with a French translation of Dostoevsky's *Memoirs from the House of the Dead*, is essential for an understanding and appreciation of the very few references he ever made to the topic of Russia and the Russians. Nietzsche selected for the target of his praise Dostoevsky, "a great poet, but an abominable person, utterly Christian in his emotional life and at the same time utterly sadistic," as Georg Brandes described him in a letter to Nietzsche.[1] Interestingly enough, this is an exact parallel to the way various Russians approached and interpreted Nietzsche's own ideas, taking what they could use, manipulating it when necessary, and abandoning or ignoring the rest. Perhaps most revealing in this context is the fact that, when compared with the views of his contemporaries, the convictions that Nietzsche held concerning Russia and its people did not go much beyond the traditional and, by his time, already commonplace attitudes toward that gigantic and mysterious enigma in the East.

[1] Peter Fuss and Henry Shapiro, *Nietzsche: A Self-Portrait from His Letters* (Cambridge, Mass., 1971), p. 132. The letter was dated 16 November 1887.

The broad outlines of these traditional attitudes can be described in almost ideal-type terms, and they hold true whether the bearer is positively or negatively inclined toward the subject.[2] The bearers in this case are the many influential "Gebildeten"—members of the generally well-informed, university-educated class in nineteenth-century Germany. Their views of the Russian spanned three distinct categories, albeit with many overlappings: the uncultured "natural" man, or barbarian; the man inclined to use sophisticated political power or unmitigated brute force to gain his ends; and the religious man of a specifically Russian, that is, non-European if not virtually Eastern, variety.

Common to all three of these views was the belief that the Russian, both singly and collectively, was a phenomenon caught up in the process of *becoming*. As such, the Russian possessed an enormous but as yet untapped potential, one that lacked the essential initiative to realize itself and to create something of lasting (cultural, political, metaphysical, or moral) value. It was this ambiguity or uncertainty in the minds of the Germans, and not the least of them Nietzsche himself, that led either to a fear of the Slavs from the East or to a hope for progress and an auspicious promise for something like salvation that would somehow emanate from them. This resulted in a rather widespread Russophobia that emerged during the days of the Holy Alliance and had not yet disappeared by the end of the century,[3] although certain inroads had been made by that time.

The most significant of these developments for Nietzsche was the gradual dissemination and popularization of Russian literature in Western Europe and the concomitant intellectual open-mindedness and receptivity it fostered on the part of the German intelligentsia as a whole toward things Russian, be they social structures, political institutions, or moral/metaphysical values.

Of course, there were other forces at play as well in Nietzsche's case: his thoroughly documented saturation and disgust at the state of civilization in Germany; his hunger and drive for the unspoiled, the original, the strong, the Dionysian "overman"; his general knowledge of Russian events and his specific acquaintances and friendships with Russians and those interested in them, including the Wagner circle, Malwida von

---

[2] The following description of these traditional views is based upon the very informative article by Heinrich Stammler entitled "Wandlungen des deutschen Bildes vom russischen Menschen," in *Jahrbücher für Geschichte Osteuropas*, new ser., vol. 5, (Munich, 1957), p. 274.

[3] Ibid., p. 284.

Meysenbug, Olga Herzen, Lou Andreas-Salomé, and Franz Overbeck, as well as the contacts he had with Count Urusov and Countess Anna Dmitrievna Tenicheva;[4] and finally his serendipitous discovery of Dostoevsky in a bookshop in Nice. To the weary philosopher living in a decadent Europe, Russia, with her people, her poets, and her potential, took on the aura of hope and prophetic investment, and Nietzsche lent this aura expression in terms of his vision of "grosse Politik" ("great politics," sometimes translated in this context as "international politics" and sometimes even as "power politics").

Nietzsche's ideas on politics do not diverge from the main tenet of his whole philosophy, which is, simply stated, man's freedom in a moral sense and the ultimate attainment of man's highest potential as far as culture and civilization are concerned. Of course, for Nietzsche, moral systems and politics were inextricably intertwined and mutually determinative—one need only refer to the first essay of *The Genealogy of Morals* to see how closely related political systems were to the development of the master and slave moralities. Since, according to Nietzsche, all moral categories grew out of the attempts by the possessors (of whatever, be it property, creativity, honor, nobility, intelligence, ethics) and by the non-possessors (those defined by the possessors as the "have-nots") to gain power over each other, all morality is in the end a form of politics, and power politics at that. As is well known, Nietzsche maintained that all aspects of Western culture as he knew it were coming to an end. Contemporary culture had reached a stage of decadence, an in-between state where the old traditional values, although withered and impotent, had not yet been relinquished and the new not yet conceived. This is a world devoid of all meaning, in other words, a state of nihilism. Instead of seeing in this state of nihilism the incipient realization of his vision of a fundamental revaluation of all values, Nietzsche recognized it for what it was, namely, absolutely nothing, and tried to overcome it. His efforts led to his philosophy of the will to power, his vision of great politics, and his concept of eternal recurrence as a countermovement against his nihilism.[5]

[4]Cf. Nietzsche's letters to Peter Gast of 14 October and 9 December 1888, to Georg Brandes of 20 October 1888, to Franz Overbeck of 13 November 1888 and the one to his mother dated 21 December 1888. Christopher Middleton, *Selected Letters of Friedrich Nietzsche* (Chicago, 1969), pp. 312, 333, 317, 322, and 337 respectively.

[5]Cf. Karl Jaspers, *Nietzsche: An Introduction to the Understanding of His Philosophical Activity*, trans. Charles F. Wallraff and Frederick J. Schmitz (Tucson, 1965), p. 247. This book is particularly informative for an understanding of Nietzsche's concept of "grosse Politik."

Nietzsche's conviction that the foundations of the structures that continued to hold society together—the depleted and hollow moral, epistemological, and political value systems of his day—had to be expunged
and replaced by more appropriate attitudes, namely by the revaluation of
all values, is indeed a call to political engagement, for "by means of
volition and domination it seeks to replace one form of existence by another".[6] It must be said, however, that Nietzsche's ultimate goal was not
political in a narrow sense, but rather moral in a broad, all-encompassing
sense, for he believed that the fundamental mission of the civilization he
envisioned should be "non-political and cultic, indeed mythopoeic".[7]

The contemporary political situation in Germany and in Europe as a
whole—the master/slave syndrome and its interrelatedness with Nietzsche's
scathing criticism of Christianity, the advent of nihilism and its concomitant phenomena of progressing democratization, hence (in Nietzsche's
eyes) diminution and leveling of all men, and ultimately of socialism—
was a hopeless and, paradoxically, a promising state of affairs in the mind
of the philosopher. Hopeless because it could never lead anywhere beyond nihilism; promising because it gave those individuals who had eyes
to see and ears to hear what Zarathustra had preached the opportunity to
throw off the shackles of *ressentiment*[8] and to realize the potential inherent in every "higher man." The only way out of this dreadful impasse
was embodied in Nietzsche's vision of "great politics," for he felt this was
the only course that might lead to conditions conducive to a cultural
renaissance based upon the revaluation of all values. And yet, great politics was only a means to an end; the end was the creation of a new
culture, a new civilization, a new state, such as the world had never
known before.

What Nietzsche foresaw for the twentieth and twenty-first centuries
were wars of ideologies, the consequences of which were as yet incon-
ceivable to the modern European:

> For when truth enters into a fight with the lies of millennia, we
> shall have upheavals, a convulsion of earthquakes, a moving of
> mountains and valleys, the like of which has never been dreamed

---

[6] Tracy B. Strong, *Friedrich Nietzsche and the Politics of Transfiguration* (Berkeley, 1975),
p. 187.

[7] J. P. Stern, *A Study of Nietzsche* (Cambridge, 1979), p. 47; see also the existentialist
criticism by Karl Jaspers.

[8] The term refers to the process of allocating responsibility and blame to others for the
pain and privation one suffers.

of. The concept of politics will have merged entirely with a war of spirits; all power structures of the old society will have been exploded—all of them are based on lies: these will be wars the like of which have never yet been seen on earth. It is only beginning with me that the earth knows *great politics*.   (*EH*, 327)

And these wars will more than likely involve Russia and Germany and all of Europe before they have spent their energies. One of the short notes Nietzsche left behind in the *Nachlass* shows the direction of his thought: "Signs of the next century: entrance of Russia into culture. A grandiose goal. Proximity of barbarism. Awakening of the arts, magnanimity of youth, and fantastic madness."[9]

Since achieved culture was such an integral part of Nietzsche's philosophy and of his vision of the future, it is perhaps disconcerting at first to note that he here speaks very positively of a nation that is supposed to inaugurate his ideas in terms of its *entrance* into culture. This ambivalence is not all that surprising, however, if one weighs it against the uncertainty and widespread consternation expressed in the traditional views of the Russians held by contemporary Western thinkers. The ambivalence that Nietzsche expressed in his views about Russia and the Russians was due on the one hand to the fact that they represented a compilation of many of the clichéd beliefs of the times and, on the other hand, to the fact that he saw this emerging giant as a double threat. He sometimes expressed the potential that Russia represented for him as a warning in terms of the threat it posed for Europe, and at other times as the great hope that it embodied for the ultimate realization of his philosophy and political visions. The threat was that the peoples of Russia, being relatively untouched by the process of democratization, still possessed a noble sense of barbarism despite the cultural heights they had already achieved, and if they ever managed to throw off the shackles of their present state and were to respond to their own and Russia's (i.e., their collective) will to power, that nation would pose an extraordinary threat to the decadent nihilistic civilization of contemporary Europe.

If this will is present, there is established something such as the *Imperium Romanum*: or such as Russia, the *only* power today which has durability in it, which can wait, which can still promise some-

---

[9]As quoted in Jaspers, *Nietzsche*, p. 265; cf. also Stammler, "Wandlungen," p. 288, note 62 (where he gives the reference to the Kröner edition of Nietzsche's works, vol. 82, p. 365).

thing—Russia, the antithesis of that pitiable European petty-state politics and nervousness which with the foundation of the German Reich has entered a critical phase.   (*TI*, 13)

As the source of hope, on the other hand, Russia represented for Nietzsche the force that might finally bring about the realization of one of his most tenaciously held dreams, that of the economic and political unification of Europe. If this were to happen, Europe would develop into a strong and unified state resting on social structures and institutions that would provide a vent for its own political will to power while at the same time channeling all remaining energies into the formation of a new culture and civilization based upon the completed revaluation of all values and upon the rule of the so-called "masters of the earth" or "higher men." It was only in the bosom of such a state that the ultimate development of creative "overmen" could and would be fostered. However, this was to remain little more than a vision for Nietzsche, for he freely admitted that "I write for a species of man that does not yet exist, for the 'masters of the earth' . . . Englishmen, Americans, and Russians" (*WP*, 503, 504). He was thus in no doubt as to precisely whom he was addressing with his remarks about great politics, and he was also perfectly aware of the distance yet to be traveled before this vision would be realized. After all,

> The strength to will, and to will something for a long time, is a little greater in Germany, and more so in the German north than in the center of Germany; but much stronger yet in England, Spain, and Corsica, here in association with indolence, there with hard heads— not to speak of Italy, which is too young to know what it wants and still has to prove whether it is able to will—but it is strongest and most amazing by far in that enormous empire in between, where Europe, as it were, flows back into Asia, in Russia. There the strength to will has long been accumulated and stored up, there the will— uncertain whether as a will to negate or a will to affirm—is waiting menacingly to be discharged, to borrow a pet phrase of our physicists today. It may well take more than Indian wars and complications in Asia to rid Europe of its greatest danger: internal upheavals would be needed, too, the shattering of the empire into small units, and above all the introduction of the parliamentary nonsense, including the obligation for everybody to read his newspaper with his breakfast.
> I do not say this because I want it to happen: the opposite would

be rather more after my heart—I mean such an increase in the menace of Russia that Europe would have to resolve to become menacing, too, namely, *to acquire one will* by means of a new caste that would rule Europe, a long, terrible will of its own that would be able to cast its goals millennia hence—so the long-drawn-out comedy of its many splinter states as well as its dynastic and democratic splinter wills would come to an end. The time for petty politics is over: the very next century will bring the fight for the dominion of the earth—the *compulsion* to large-scale politics.   (*BGE*, 131)

If the potential of Russia did indeed give Nietzsche pause in contemplating the future, the actuality of certain Russian characteristics and individuals, most notably Dostoevsky, provided a certain degree of comfort to the lonely man on the brink of a complete mental breakdown. In a letter to Malwide von Meysenbug dated 12 May 1887, Nietzsche once again expressed a typical disdain for his fellow Germans, but couched it in terms very telling of his appraisal of what he took to be Russian traits. "To come to Versailles—Oh if it were only possible! For I greatly admire the group you associate with there (a strange confession for a German; but in present-day Europe I feel kinship only with French and Russian intellectuals, and not at all with my cultured compatriots who judge everything by the principle 'Deutschland, Deutschland über alles')".[10]

Toward the end of his productive years Nietzsche often associated himself with other, in his eyes equally elevated, Slavic personality traits. He even went so far as to claim Polish ancestry based upon a rather questionable etymology of his name. He claimed that his forefathers were Polish aristocracy, and, more specifically, that his paternal great-grandmother was a Pole.[11]

Another Slavic characteristic Nietzsche also claimed to share had to do with what he called "Russian fatalism." In the section entitled "Why I Am So Wise" in *Ecce Homo*, Nietzsche explains that

Sickness itself is a kind of *ressentiment*.

Against all this the sick person has only one great remedy: I call it *Russian fatalism*, that fatalism without revolt which is exemplified by a Russian soldier who, finding a campaign too strenuous, finally lies down in the snow. No longer to accept anything at all, no longer

[10] Fuss and Shapiro, *Letters*, p. 99.

[11] Letter to Heinrich von Stein, early December 1882, in Middleton, ed. *Selected Letters of Friedrich Nietzsche*, p. 197.

to take anything, no longer to absorb anything—to cease reacting altogether.

    This fatalism is not always merely the courage to die; it can also preserve life under the most perilous conditions by reducing the metabolism, slowing it down, as a kind of will to hibernate. (*EH*, 230)

Nietzsche claims that he had been forced repeatedly to rely upon this "Russian fatalism" in his efforts to endure many unbearable individuals, accommodations, situations, and places throughout his lifetime (*EH*, 231).

    However, for all the positive characteristics Nietzsche associated with the Russians, there were also a few negative ones. He felt particularly strongly about one "decadent" characteristic he considered overly represented by Tolstoi in his novels, namely, pity. He gave strong expression to his thoughts on this trait in the *Antichrist*, where he attacked not only pity, but "(unfortunately also [our] entire literary and artistic decadence from St. Petersburg to Paris, from Tolstoi to Wagner). . . . Nothing in our unhealthy modernity is more unhealthy than Christian pity" (*A*, 119).

    In an overall cultural context Nietzsche considered Tolstoi neither the only and certainly not the best representative of Russian authors—that position was reserved for Dostoevsky. In a letter to Franz Overbeck dated 23 February 1887, Nietzsche mentions the sudden kinship he sensed when first becoming acquainted with Dostoevsky's works: "I also knew nothing about Dostoevsky until a few weeks ago—uncultivated person that I am, reading no 'periodicals'! In a bookshop my hand just happened to come to rest on *L'Esprit souterrain*, a recent French translation. . . . The instinct of affinity (or what shall I call it?) spoke to me instantaneously—my joy was beyond bounds; not since my first encounter with Stendhal's *Rouge et Noir* have I known such joy."[12] And to Peter Gast, on March 7th of the same year, Nietzsche exclaimed: "Dostoevsky happened to me just as Stendhal did earlier, by sheer accident: a book casually flipped open in a shop, a name I'd never even heard before—and the sudden awareness that one has met with a brother."[13]

    Finally, in a letter to Georg Brandes, an eminent Scandinavian critic and the professor of literature at the University of Copenhagen who was the first formally to introduce Nietzsche's philosophy to a foreign audience, Nietzsche replied in superlatives to Brandes's disparaging remarks

[12] Middleton, *Selected Letters*, pp. 260, 261.
[13] Fuss and Shapiro, *Letters*, pp. 97, 98.

about Dostoevsky quoted at the beginning of this chapter: "I believe every word you say about Dostoevsky, and yet he has given me my most precious psychological material. I'm grateful to him in a very special way, much as he constantly offends my most basic instincts."[14] And in the *Twilight of the Idols*:

> In regard to the problem before us [the criminal], the testimony of Dostoevsky is of importance—Dostoevsky, the only psychologist, by the way, from whom I had anything to learn; he is one of the happiest accidents of my life, even more so than my discovery of Stendhal. This *profound* human being, who was ten times justified in despising the superficial Germans, found the Siberian convicts in whose midst he lived for a long time, nothing but the worst criminals for whom no return to society was possible, different from what he himself had expected—he found them to be carved out of about the best, hardest, and most valuable timber growing anywhere on Russian soil. (*TI*, 99)

From such statements as these it is obvious that at the end of his productive life Nietzsche was still fascinated by the question that initiated his philosophical studies, the question of esthetics and moral values, of the relation of art to civilization and culture. His whole life's work revolves around this problem and it is therefore not surprising that the same question should arise in connection with his thoughts on the Russians. In the *Twilight of the Idols* Nietzsche quotes a popular saying: "Evil men have no songs," and then stops short with a query that at one and the same time expresses the ambiguity he felt and the hope he invested in the enigma that was Russia: "How is it, then, that the Russians have songs?"[15]

[14] Ibid., p. 132.
[15] Friedrich Nietzsche, *Twilight of the Idols*, in *The Portable Nietzsche*, ed. and trans. Walter Kaufmann (New York, 1984), p. 469. Readers familiar with Nietzsche and his style have had many opportunities to realize and appreciate his lighthearted approach to clichés and popular adages of his day. His intent was to shake the reader out of his long-established complacency by means of puns and plays on words which were meant to put the point in a different light. Although, as Hollingdale states, "böse Menschen" comes from a popular saying of the time, and thus he translates it as "bad men" (*Z*, 25), it can safely be surmised that Nietzsche has here presented his readers with another of his characteristic word plays. I therefore agree with and prefer Walter Kaufmann's translation of "evil" instead of "bad" here, especially in light of the fact that Nietzsche devoted fully one-third of his *Genealogy of Morals* to explicating his distinction between "bad" and "evil." This distinction underlies his attitude toward the Russians.

CONTRIBUTORS

VIRGINIA H. BENNETT is Assistant Professor of Russian Language and Literature at the University of California, Davis. The author of "Echoes of Friedrich Nietzsche's *The Birth of Tragedy* in Andrej Belyj's *Petersburg*" (1980) and of other articles on Russian literature, she is currently preparing a monograph on Bely's *Petersburg* and an analysis and translation of Bely's *Reminiscences of A. A. Blok*.

EVELYN BRISTOL is Associate Professor of Russian Language and Literature at the University of Illinois at Urbana-Champaign. She is editor of *Russian Literature and Criticism: Selected Papers from the Second World Congress of Soviet and East European Studies* (1982) and author of *Russian Poetry: A History*, Oxford University Press, forthcoming.

EDITH W. CLOWES is Assistant Professor of Russian Language and Literature at Purdue University. She is the author of "A Philosophy 'For All and None': The Early Reception of Friedrich Nietzsche in Russian Literature, 1892–1912" (Ph.D. diss., 1981), "The Integration of Nietzschean Ideas of Time, History, and Higher Nature in the Early Historical Novels of Dmitry Merezhkovsky" (1981), "The Nietzschean Image of the Poet in the Early Works of Konstantin Bal'mont and Valery Briusov" (1983), "Friedrich Nietzsche and the Russian Censor" (1983), and *Maxim Gorky: A Research Bibliography*, G. K. Hall, forthcoming. She is working on a study of Nietzsche and Russian literature.

ANNA LISA CRONE is Associate Professor of Slavic Languages and Literatures at the University of Chicago. She is the author of *Rozanov and the End of Literature* (1978) and of numerous articles on Russian literature. Her current projects are *City of the Buried Sun: The Petersburg of the Word in Twentieth-Century Russian Letters* and a volume of annotated translations of selected literary critical articles by Vyacheslav Ivanov.

JAMES M. CURTIS is Professor of Russian at the University of Missouri, Columbia. He is the author of *Culture as Polyphony* (1978) and

Solzhenitsyn's Traditional Imagination (1984) and has a longstanding interest in the relationship between literary criticism and philosophy. He has written on Nietzsche's influence on Shestov and on Bergson's influence on the Russian Formalists.

RICHARD D. DAVIES is 'New Blood' lecturer at the University of Leeds (England) and archivist of the Leeds Russian Archive. He is the editor of *Leonid Andreyev, Pered zadachami vremeni: Politicheskie stat'i 1917–1919* (1975) and author of "Nietzsche in Russia, 1892–1917: A Preliminary Bibliography" (1976, 1977) and of articles on Andreev and other topics in Russian literature.

ALINE ISDEBSKY-PRITCHARD is Art Curator of the Leo Baeck Institute, New York City, and Consultant to the U.S. Holocaust Memorial Council. She is the author of *The Art of Mikhail Vrubel* (1982).

GEORGE KALBOUSS is Professor of Russian Language and Literature at Ohio State University. He is the author of *The Plays of the Russian Symbolists* (1982) and of numerous articles on Russian literature. He is currently preparing a book on Sologub's mythology.

GEORGE L. KLINE is Milton C. Nahm Professor of Philosophy at Bryn Mawr College. Among his books are *Spinoza in Soviet Philosophy* (1952, rpt. 1981), *Religious and Anti-Religious Thought in Russia* (1968), and translations of V. V. Zenkovsky's *A History of Russian Philosophy* (2 vols., 1953), *Boris Pasternak: Seven Poems* (1969, 2nd ed. 1972), and *Joseph Brodsky: Selected Poems* (1973, 1974). Among his seventy-five articles are " 'Nietzschean Marxism' in Russia" (1969) and "The Nietzschean Marxism of Stanislav Volsky" (1979).

ANN M. LANE is an economist with the U.S. government and the author of "Nietzsche in Russian Thought" (Ph.D. diss., 1975).

MARY LOUISE LOE is Professor of History at James Madison University in Virginia. She is the author of "Mak'sim Gor'kii and the Sreda Circle, 1899–1905" (1985) and is currently preparing a book-length study of Maxim Gorky.

MIHAJLO MIHAJLOV, author and human rights activist, is Special Analyst for Soviet and East European Intellectual and Ideological Affairs,

Research Division, Radio Free Europe. He has given courses in Russian Literature and Philosophy at leading western universities. His major works, *Moscow Summer* (1965), *Russian Themes* (1968), and *Unscientific Thoughts* (1979) have been translated into many languages.

SUSAN RAY is Associate Professor of German at Fordham University. She is the author of *Gottfried Benn: Geschichtspessimismus und Moral-vorstellung* (1982) and of critical articles on Franz Kafka and Friedrich Nietzsche. Her most recent article is "Teaching Zarathustra" (1986).

BERNICE GLATZER ROSENTHAL is Professor of Russian History at Fordham University. Her publications include *D. S. Merezhkovsky and the Silver Age* (1975), *A Revolution of the Spirit: Crisis of Values in Russia, 1890–1917* (with Martha Bohachevsky-Chomiak (1982), and numerous articles on Russian intellectual and cultural history, the most recent of which is "Wagner and Wagnerian Ideas in Russia" (1984). She is currently preparing a book-length study of Russian culture from 1890 to 1917.

ZENOVIA SOCHOR is Assistant Professor of Government at Clark University, and is also a Research Fellow at the Russian Research Center, Harvard University. She is the author of *Revolution and Culture: Alternative Theories of Lenin and Bogdanov*, forthcoming, and of numerous articles on A. A. Bogdanov and related topics.

A. L. TAIT lectures in the Department of Russian Language and Literature, University of Birmingham and is Secretary of the British Universities Association of Slavists. He is the author of *Lunacharsky: Poet of the Revolution* (1984) and has published numerous articles on Soviet cultural history.

TARAS D. ZAKYDALSKY is with the Canadian Institute of Ukrainian Studies, University of Toronto, and has translated Russian and Ukrainian materials. He is the author of "N. F. Fyodorov's Philosophy of Physical Resurrection" (Ph.D. diss., 1976) and is editor and translator of the *Encyclopedia of the Ukraine* project.

INDEX

Library of Congress Cataloging-in-Publication Data

Nietzsche in Russia.

Includes index.
1. Nietzsche, Friedrich Wilhelm, 1844–1900—Influence.   2. Philosophy, Rus-
sian.   I. Rosenthal, Bernice Glatzer.
B 3317.N4945   1986   001.3'0947   86-12290
ISBN 0-691-06695-7 (alk. paper)
ISBN 0-691-10209-0 (pbk.)

B E R N I C E G L A T Z E R R O S E N T H A L is Professor of History at Fordham University. She is the author of *D. S. Merezhkovsky and the Silver Age: The Development of a Revolutionary Mentality* (Martinus Nijhoff).